UNPACKING
SILVER
CITY

UNPACKING SILVER CITY

REVEALING THE RICH TAPESTRY OF A HISTORIC TOWN

Edited by Bart A. Roselli

— CONTRIBUTORS —

Susan Berry, Tom Hester, Javier Marrufo, Karen J. Leong,
Andy Hernandez, Stephen Fox, Scott Fritz,
James L. Smith, Douglas M. Dinwiddie, Heather Moorland

MIMBRES PRESS
of Western New Mexico University

MIMBRES PRESS
of Western New Mexico University

Mimbres Press of Western New Mexico University
www.mimbrespress.wnmu.edu

Media and Publisher Inquiries:
Mimbres Press of WNMU
1000 West College Ave.
Silver City, NM 88062

Cover and interior design GKS CREATIVE
Editing by Shelley Chung and Cindy Doty
Portrait images by Jay Hemphill

978-1-958870-26-6 (hardcover)
978-1-958870-27-3 (IS paperback)
978-1-958870-28-0 (KDP paperback)

FIRST EDITION

First printed in the United States

Library of Congress Case # 1-14532506781

TABLE OF CONTENTS

INTRODUCTION

Welcome to the Stories of Silver City and Grant County

This volume is the first comprehensive work on the region's past since the groundbreaking "Built to Last" was published more than thirty years ago. Thanks to a generous grant from the New Mexico Humanities Council, the Silver City Museum was able to host a series of explorations led by skilled historians and writers. Public talks were presented, and essays written to create this collection exploring the of depth and color Grant County and Silver City, New Mexico's past.

The origin of this project came out of a series of gatherings of local historians planning the New Mexico Historical Society's annual conference. The conference was fully designed but interrupted due to the COVID pandemic. Regardless of the cancellation of the conference, the energy generated by this roundtable of historians thrust the group forward to examine the many facets of the human experience in the southwest corner of New Mexico.

Many captivating topics and interesting themes arose from the collective brainstorming. Hundreds of topics arose spanning the experience of the Apache; mysteries of the so-called Mimbrenos; the hook that the myth of Billy the Kid has held; battles among ranchers, conservationists, and the federal government; migrations and community building of the first Mexican miners to this area; the gamut of institutions that arose to create a unique culture; an expansion of education and health care institutions; undeniable impact of big mining companies; many wars, fights for

1

independences, struggles for human rights, enduring plagues, surviving gunfights, battles for union expansions, onslaught of automobiles, undeniable discrimination; generations of ranch families, skilled saddle makers, rodeo stars; an astonishing diversity of European and Asian settlers to what would become known as Grant County and Silver City. Thousands of people and their stories, life events, tragedies, and triumphs are represented and populate this volume.

The range of topics generated combined with a survey of museum goers, research by museum staff, input from trustees, volunteers and other scholars helped decide what stories to embrace first. The project coalesced around distinct lenses through which to make some sense of all this "history."

No single lens is the *perfect* lens, and all are intertwined providing some new light upon this place. The themes make room for and even encourage more topics to explore and other ways of seeing, experiencing, understanding, and using the stories of the past. This volume, the first of many perhaps encapsulates these themes:

The Love and Use of Environment ... Fundamentally, we are all connected to this land, whether rancher, environmentalist, farmer, miner, landowner, or outdoor enthusiast. Exploring the challenges of sharing the land is this theme's focus.

The Enduring Myth of the Wild West ... There is no doubt that the violence and independence experienced at the turn of the 19th century has continued to grab the attention and imagination of Grant County residents and tourists for more than a century. The media, tourist traps, novelists, movie producers, and wannabe cowboys and gunslingers have kept the myths growing and changing.

Governing and Government ... Exploring the Mexican roots of governance here in Grant County and the coming independence efforts during Territorial Days and into the present understanding of local governance sheds light on all the other topics and challenges regarding land and natural resources utilization, who gets to vote, how the community is taxed and spends resources.

Medicine and Healing ... addressing a still problematic part of our modern community with evolving technologies and treatments, work of clinicians, medical and environmental challenges, and the economics of and access to health care.

Building Community ... this theme explores the civilizing efforts across time of our community-creating efforts, whether building religious institutions, unions, women's groups, cultural organizations, business associations, fraternal societies, and social networks. These are the institutions that build and sustain unifying efforts within the larger community.

Expressing Culture and Identity ... from the beginning of recorded history and thousands of years before that this region was a diverse collection of peoples populated this land. Defined by ethnicity, nationality, language, religious beliefs, artistic interests, and values, the expression of self and group are rich and varied. This diversity provides color, texture, and quality to the community to this day.

The Evolving Economy ... economy drives the growth or recession affecting the region. Grant County's economy is dynamic, with transitions over time determining what work employs citizens, which companies control the economic base and the effects of a rising and shrinking community wealth.

Finding an alliance in Mimbres Press of Western New Mexico University was a critical step in bringing these stories and history to life. As one of the newest university presses in the country, the folks at Mimbres Press are dedicated to shed light on our regional history. The partnership of the Silver City Museum and Mimbres Press proudly present these glimpses into the past. Enjoy!

Bart A. Roselli
Silver City Museum Director

Bart A. Roselli brings expertise in management, educational programs, exhibit and collections development, fundraising, community building and other aspects of museum work. He is honored to have been the Director of the Silver City Museum since 2018. He began his career more than 30 years ago in a recreated 19th Century village museum in his hometown of Middletown located in the Hudson Valley of New York State. He studied museum education and management at Bank Street College of Education in New York City and at the Getty Institute of Museum Management in Berkeley, California. He has plied his trade in museums of history, art, natural history, science and even a zoo. He has served on state, regional, and national museum associations and on boards of other community non-profits and business associations. Roselli serves as Vice President of the Grant County Prospectors and the Grant County Silver City Chamber of Commerce. He has served as the president of the Silver City Rotary Club, Secretary for the Grant County Silver City Chamber of Commerce, Executive Committee of the Southwest Word Fiesta. He also serves as a member of the Silver City Historic District Review Commission, Steering Committee member of the Grant County Give Grandly Coalition, and plays banjo in the local band the Big Ditch Crickets. He and his wife Gail make their home in an historic adobe on Chihuahua Hill in Silver City, New Mexico.

4

CHAPTER 1:

Built to Last: The Ongoing Evolution of Silver City

By Susan Berry

Many early mining camps in southwest New Mexico—places like Gold Hill, Paschal, Leopold, Gold Gulch, Ivanhoe, Park City, Azure, Rattlesnake City, Alumina, Ruby Camp, Brockman, Carbonate City, Fleming, Ricolite, Sylvanite, Steeplerock, Villines, Pyramid City, Victorio—have disappeared, blown away, sunk back into the earth, their names all but forgotten. Why and how has Silver City managed not only to survive, but thrive for over 150 years?

Multiple elements worked to the town's advantage in its early years, especially its location. The marshy spring-fed valley known as the San Vicente *cienega*,[1] home to ancient peoples[2] and long a favorite camping ground of the Apaches, had a valuable year-round water source. Permanent settlement would almost certainly have been made at this site under Spanish or Mexican governance if not for the formidable Apache presence in the region. Timing of the silver discovery in 1870 was also auspicious.

---

1 San Vicente is among area names mentioned in accounts of a 1780 expedition in southwest New Mexico by Spanish New Mexico governor Don Juan Bautista de Anza. Alfred Barnaby Thomas, *Forgotten Frontiers: A Study of the Spanish Indian Policy of Don Juan Bautista de Anza Governor of New Mexico 1777-1787,* (Norman: University of Oklahoma Press, 1969)

2 Archaeologist Adolph Bandelier documented traces of two pueblos at the north end of the valley in 1884. *The Southwestern Journals of Adolph F. Bandelier 1883-1884,* Charles H. Lange and Carroll L. Riley (Eds.) (Albuquerque: University of New Mexico Press, 1970)

Though still relatively isolated, Grant County was two years old and home to some 1,500 residents in scattered settlements. Four years earlier Pinos Altos, nine miles to the north, had seen a resurgence of gold mining activity and Fort Bayard established a military presence in the region.

Significantly, most early Silver City residents were accustomed to the rigors of life in the Southwest and many had a practical knowledge of mining. They used the American legislative framework to secure permanence for the community through the early pursuit of a townsite patent, a town charter, and a public school system. A commitment to solid construction helped establish Silver City as the well-built nucleus for surrounding settlements. Geographic isolation and the challenges of frontier living instilled a kind of resourcefulness and resilience that helped the community weather economic crashes and natural disasters and allowed multiple reinventions over time.

This high-speed review traces the broad arc of Silver City's first 150 years, focusing on periods and circumstances that helped shape the unique personality of this place. As it chiefly examines Silver City history, only brief mention will be made of the surrounding region when needed for context.

The Settlement Period
1869-1875

On the first day of 1869, the future site of Silver City is taken up by four daring—some would say foolhardy—Pinos Altos miners. William Milby and John Bullard lay out and begin improvements on a 320-acre "ranch" just above the *cienega* springs, while Andrew Hurlburt and James McGee stake out an equal-sized property below it. Their pre-emption claims are held by possessory title, as the San Vicente area has not yet been surveyed. The men clear the *tules* growing in the rich bottom land, build log cabins, and prepare to grow crops for market in Pinos Altos (approximate population 250). Milby's cabin is constructed in two sections to accommodate details of Fort Bayard soldiers assigned in pairs to guard the farmers and their crops. This is only the latest in a series of sporadic agricultural efforts at the *cienega* during the nineteenth century.

Milby soon leaves the venture and leases his cabin to Hurlburt, who occupies it with his wife and child.[3] Bullard is joined in the farming effort by his brother James and others. With good reason, the Apaches consider the *cienega* a resource worth fighting for and await a chance to drive out the interlopers. It comes one morning in late August 1869, when Andrew Hurlburt is working alone in the fields. His partners head off to Pinos Altos for supplies and the soldiers start for Fort Bayard before their relief is due to arrive. Too late, Hurlburt hears screams from his cabin and realizes he has left his rifle behind. His wife and child are killed, and he barely escapes with his life.[4] Farming at the *cienega* resumes a few weeks later, but Hurlburt soon sells his share. His home has been baptized in blood.

Early the following May several Grant County men ride through the Burro Mountains to examine a reported silver discovery at Ralston, near the Arizona line. On seeing the mineral John Bullard exclaims, "If that's silver ore, I know where there's plenty of it!"[5] He and his companions quickly return to the *cienega*. Within two weeks ore has been sampled and assayed, and claims—including the famous Legal Tender mine—are located. A group of miners gather at the former Hurlburt cabin on May 30, 1870, to organize the Silver Flat mining district and select a name for their future town.[6] San Vicente, the traditional name, is considered but is set aside in favor of something a bit shinier. Silver Flat and Silver Cliff are put forward, but Silver City wins out in the end.

---

3   Hurlburt's marriage was likely a common-law arrangement; he lists himself as a single man on deeds to the *cienega* properties. The child's age and gender vary in different accounts.

4   A letter from Grant County signed "Observer," and dated September 7, 1869, reports the killing of a woman and child at the San Vicente Cienega "within the past ten days." (*Santa Fe New Mexican*, September 21, 1869)

5   Many variations of Bullard's exclamation appear in recollections of old-timers.

6   The *Silver City Independent* of June 18, 1907, reports the rediscovery of minutes from this meeting, at which the Silver Flat mining district was established. Silver City's naming is detailed in Enos Culver's account of what was almost certainly the same meeting. He locates the gathering at the Hurlburt cabin; other versions place it at the Legal Tender Corral, which immediately adjoined the cabin.

R. C. McLeod is hired to survey a one-square-mile townsite, starting work at midnight and setting his instruments by the North Star. He plats Silver City in a tidy grid, with scant consideration for prevailing drainage patterns. Later town surveys will retain and build upon this original layout of blocks and lots. Some streets are named for early residents (a "McLeod Street" briefly exists) while others are numbered, oddly starting with Sixth. Broadway, a major thoroughfare, is extra wide to allow teams and wagons to turn around. Unlike the older Hispanic towns in New Mexico, Silver City is laid out without a central plaza. Its first shanties are fashioned from any available material, with log cabins scattered throughout the townsite. The Bullard brothers and fellow farmers give up their pre-emption claims in exchange for a few choice lots.

The 1870 U. S. census, taken when Silver City is less than two months old, lists 80 residents. The Anglo population consists of 65 men, nearly a quarter of them foreign-born, along with two women and one child. There are eleven Hispanic residents: six men, three women and two children. One Black man completes the roster. Silver City's founder, John Bullard, will not live long enough to see the new town develop. He is killed in February 1871 at the age of 29, engaged in battle with Apaches nine months after leading his companions to the bonanza. Bullard is the first resident to be buried in the Silver City cemetery, located on open ground above the town limits on Ninth Street (the future College Avenue).

Juan Nepomuceno Carrasco, the first experienced silver miner to arrive in camp, uncovers an enormous deposit of silver-bearing quartz just west of town in September 1870. His discovery, La Providencia Ledge, is soon proclaimed the richest yet found in New Mexico.[7] The Chloride Mining District is immediately organized on what will henceforth be called Chloride Flat. A frenzy of mining proceeds as well as possible through the coming months with available equipment; there are only three sets of miner's tools in camp.[8]

---

7   Letter to the Editors of the Santa Fe New Mexico, written from Las Cruces and dated September 21, 1870, by a correspondent signing himself "Verdad" publication date is September 26, 1870.

8   Reported in the Las Cruces *Borderer*, March 16, 1871.

8

Carrasco quickly recruits a labor force in the mining regions of his native Chihuahua, Mexico. He directs workers to set up a compound of structures at the south end of Bullard Street, including residences, *arastras* (primitive mule-powered mills for pulverizing ore) and adobe furnaces. Using centuries-old technology, Carrasco's smelter turns out Silver City's first silver bullion in April 1871, eleven months after the original silver discovery.[9]

For others, the quest for Industrial Age ore-processing methods—stamp mills, reverberatory furnaces, reduction works—is a major preoccupation. A cluster of mills and smelters appear in the lower part of the valley below Carrasco's compound. Smokestacks rise, steam engines blast, metal stamps rise and fall with thunderous force. Mechanical breakdowns are frequent, and tall smokestacks prove no match for New Mexico's spring winds. A mining company organized in Chicago arrives in 1873 with a colony of 50 men, women, and children and constructs the Pioneer Smelting Works. Their venture fails within a year, though some colonists stay on. Other milling and smelting enterprises are merged, sold, or abandoned as their owners find the road to riches strewn with obstacles.

Well-established Mesilla Valley and El Paso merchants[10] soon open stores in the nascent town, and when brick clay is located nearby they waste no time in erecting handsome brick establishments (their merchandise is delivered over dangerous routes by mule trains). Smaller frame and adobe shops, saloons, restaurants, hotels, and corrals are scattered among cabins in a loosely defined downtown area. Silver City becomes the Grant County seat in 1872.[11] That December a visitor reports, "On my arrival here I was astonished to find a large town with many good houses, four large two story brick stores, streets wide and regular, numerous families, women and children plenty, together with

---

9   In less than two years its reported output is $200,000 (2024 value roughly $4.7 million).

10   These include Reynolds & Griggs, Bennett Bros., Martin Amador and Jose Macias, Isaac N. Cohen, David Abraham, and Max and Aaron Schutz. Henry B. Porter soon arrived from Cimmaron.

11   Central City (now Santa Clara) was the first seat of Grant County in 1870; followed by Pinos Altos in 1871.

all the other comforts of life—places of amusement not excepted; and yet the first shanty here is not three years old!"[12]

The earliest known image of Silver City, taken December 1872, shows extensive development less than two years after the town's founding. *University of Arizona Library, Cornelius Bennett Collection*

Despite social, cultural, and language differences, the "American" and "Mexican" residents, as they refer to themselves and each other, are all in it together in the early 1870s. Survival depends on collaboration and constant vigilance against Apache attack, though the well-armed populace does not deter theft of livestock in nighttime raids. Many veterans of the California Column, who protected the Pinos Altos gold mines during the Civil War, have remained in southern New Mexico and married Hispanic women. A number of these men and their families will form a core of early Silver City residents, and many more cross-cultural

---

12   Letter to the Editor of the Santa Fe *New Mexican*, written from Silver City and dated December 14, 1872, by a correspondent signing himself "Summit"; publication date is December 23, 1872.

marriages take place as the town grows. The mixed Anglo-Hispano participation in social events, especially the *bailes* (dances) that virtually everyone attends, occasionally results in fights over eligible women. At least one ends fatally.[13]

The Mining Life, Silver City's first newspaper, is launched in 1873. Its pages recount doings of the Social and Literary Club, Bachelor's Festive Club, and a Lyceum with weekly lectures. A Masonic Lodge is dedicated. Horse races, baseball, and shooting matches figure in holiday celebrations, along with gambling on the results of competitions. Sporadic terms of free public school are funded by public subscription, keeping youngsters occupied and enabling Spanish-speaking children to learn English (some of their English-speaking classmates—including a future famous outlaw—pick up Spanish). Public halls attached to saloons host *bailes*, church services, traveling entertainers, district court sessions, and the first school classes. The town's largest adobe structure, the St. Vincent de Paul Catholic church, gradually takes shape in the hands of its parishioner-builders.

Silver City is eager to establish local government and begins lobbying the Territorial legislature for a charter in 1872; a long wait lies ahead. Meanwhile, determined to avoid future title disputes, residents raise funds for a survey and succeed in obtaining a federal patent to a one-square-mile townsite in 1874. Its southern edge soon expands with the addition of 31 blocks below Spring Street to incorporate the traditionally Hispanic neighborhood known as Chihuahua. The portion lying north of Sonora Street occupies relatively level ground, and many houses here are built of adobe. Just below Sonora the terrain abruptly rises into a steep, rocky hillside where small dwellings for laborers and their families crop up. Many early homes on this rougher ground are fashioned with rock from the hill

---

13   Gambler David "Hog" Davis shot Peter Hildreth, his rival for the affections of Librada Valencia, in front of numerous witnesses (Las Cruces *Borderer*, September 7, 1872); Hildreth died about two weeks later (*Santa Fe New Mexican*, September 27, 1872); Davis is acquitted of murder (*Mining Life*, November 8, 1873). Librada Valencia's identity as the object of this shooting is mentioned in *Los Angeles Herald*, March 22, 1906.

itself, laid up in adobe mortar; others are *jacales*, made up of vertical posts or branches chinked with mud. Level building sites are created with stone terraces, and larger adobe structures will be constructed there.

With the town patent in hand, the Probate Judge begins to issue deeds for town lots, officially starting chains of title. Silver City's first public building is the diminutive county jail on Hudson Street. Praised as "the neatest and strongest jail in the Territory,"[14] the stone structure is deemed "absolutely insecure" by a grand jury[15] five months after its completion in 1874. A sturdier lockup is built the following year and will be increasingly full as a growing population and new rich discoveries attract a lawless element. Harvey Whitehill's stalwart presence as Grant County sheriff from 1875 through 1882 maintains relative order in a time of rapid change, but vigilantism is not unknown. The local press does its part in calling out "bad actors."

While awaiting a municipal government, residents take civic duties upon themselves. Cottonwood trees are planted along the downtown streets, giving the town a metropolitan air. A volunteer fire department organizes after fire guts the leading carpentry shop, and funds are gathered through public subscription to buy a fire engine. Collections are taken up to help the destitute and contribute toward the costs of various desired improvements. Citizens pitch in to help with street repairs and cleanup after serious floods arrive in 1874 and '75, destroying several buildings. In those early years, few can foresee the impact that flooding will have on the literal face of Silver City.

The Mining Booms and Busts Era
1876-1899

The opening of a rich new silver deposit in Martin Bremen's '76 Mine on Chloride Flat launches a new avalanche of fortune-hunters and hangers-on. In 1878 Silver City at last receives its charter from the Territorial Legislature, granting the town autonomous government. The charter provides for election of a mayor and town council, who appoint a clerk

14   Silver City *Mining Life*, January 24, 1874
15   Silver City *Mining Life*, July 18, 1874

12

and marshal. It also places responsibility on the shoulders of local citizens: all able-bodied men are required to contribute up to three days of labor on the streets annually or pay a fine. Local taxes can at last be collected, and New Mexico's first publicly funded school system becomes reality (an actual schoolhouse is still a few years off).

The 1880 U. S. census for Silver City sets the population at 1,800, about one-third of them women. Hispanic and Anglo residents are distributed fairly evenly throughout the town, along with a handful of Chinese and Black residents. With the closure of the Amador, Macias & Co. store in 1878, downtown is almost entirely in the hands of Anglo businessmen. A handful of Chinese laundries and restaurants, enchilada parlors run by Hispanas, and a few businesses operated by Anglo women are exceptions. The social dynamic gradually shifts with the presence of more Anglo women, who take a lead in developing the school, a reading room, churches, and local entertainments. Much is made of Silver City's character as an "American" town (the unspoken implication: "not Mexican").

Outside capital is actively sought as the mining boom roars on. Variety theaters and an opera house appear in the early 1880s, sparking an increase in local musical and theatrical productions as well as performances by traveling troupes. The more elegant saloons feature female vocalists. A skating rink and soda fountains offer diversions, and townspeople are entertained by Mexican circuses, tightrope walkers, and balloon ascensions. The Fort Bayard band often performs at local events.

Silver City's North Addition ("the flat above town") was appended to the original townsite in the 1870s but sees little development. By the 1880s the two generously sized blocks constituting the town cemetery begin to look like prime real estate. Several stately houses are built in the North Addition after the graves are opened and their occupants reinterred three miles east of town in 1882. At the south end of town, the early homes in Chihuahua are gradually enlarged and improved. In keeping with Mexican building tradition, the houses sit at the street edge with more protected space at the back of the lots. Silver City's footprint continues to expand to the west and northwest.

A local newspaper proclaims Silver City "the future Denver of New Mexico"[16] in April 1883, a year that will be one of the most eventful in Silver City history. A rich silver deposit is found near Bear Mountain and Camp Fleming springs up almost literally overnight. The Silver City, Deming, and Pacific Railroad arrives from Deming, greatly easing travel and opening access to distant markets. Electric streetlights and telephones are introduced. Women's influence is increasingly felt in various aspects of Silver City life: sewing circle members see the need for a local hospital and organize the Grant County Charity Hospital Society; the three-story convent school of the Sisters of Mercy nears completion on Kelly Street; and Kate Stewart's elegant new bordello anchors an unofficial red-light district taking shape near the corner of Texas and Spring streets.

Unprecedented building activity takes place in 1883, even as a fire prevention ordinance requires all new construction to be of masonry (brick or adobe). Settlement-era structures gain new life through expansion, remodeling, or changes of purpose, and two-story brick stores replace smaller commercial buildings. The new Broadway Hotel supersedes an earlier version of itself, the Tremont House is expanded, and a three-story addition transforms the old Exchange Hotel into the fabulous Timmer House with 105 rooms, elevator, and steam heat. The long-awaited schoolhouse is completed and a handsome new courthouse is taking shape at the head of Broadway. A former county office on Hudson Street is enlarged to become the new hospital, run by its female founders and known as the Ladies Hospital. Two banks are under construction, one whose vault is said to cost considerably more than the new courthouse. Many fine brick houses also result from the boom of 1883, along with large numbers of more modest dwellings.

The year-long party ends abruptly in December with the failure of both new banks and the bankruptcy of a leading contractor. The electric plant and telephone exchange are shut down and a cascade of business failures ensues. Still, important development takes place as the 1880s proceed. La Capilla, a small adobe chapel, is added to the Chihuahua sky-

---

16   *Silver City Enterprise*, April 27, 1883

line by the wealthy Manquero sisters in 1885. The railroad is converted to standard gauge and extended to the north end of Silver City. A depot is built in the Pope street right-of-way. A stonemason completes the Silver City Waterworks above town in 1886, pumping from a deep well to a reservoir on the nearby hilltop. The Waterworks, a private business with a Town franchise, feeds downtown fire hydrants and pipes fresh water to business and residential customers. Meanwhile, a new generation of smelters and reduction works is appearing in the south end of town.

This undated image shows an easy interaction among locals, visitors, and hotel staff in front of the Timmer House on Broadway. *Silver City Museum, Image #00275*

After two decades of booms and busts, the 1890s bring a sharp contraction to Silver City. A nationwide crash in the price of silver in 1893 shuts down silver mining virtually overnight. The community returns to survival mode, and very little new construction takes place. It is also a time of environmental reckoning. Extensive timber harvesting, woodcutting, and open-range grazing carried on for the past twenty years have stripped the surrounding hills of vegetation. Summer flooding is now so predictable that annual monsoons are known as the "flood season." An epic deluge in July 1895 fills the entire downtown with three feet of rushing water, after which the lower end of Main Street is no longer a viable thoroughfare. Flood-damaged structures are torn down and not replaced.

15

Despite major setbacks, the solidly built town remains the legal, business, and educational hub for the county. Children of the frontier era are reaching adulthood and starting new endeavors. Many original owners of boom-era houses have lost their homes along with their fortunes but remain as valued citizens. In 1893 the New Mexico Territorial Normal School is established in Silver City after years of tireless lobbying by local leaders. Old Main, its first structure, is an instant landmark on a hilltop in the northwest part of town. Two key events take place at a federal level in 1899. Fort Bayard is no longer needed as a military post, but the stellar health records of those stationed there have not gone unnoticed; the former fort becomes the Army's first hospital for tubercular patients. And that same year President McKinley signs a bill creating the Gila River Forest Reserve, now the Gila National Forest.

The Health Era

1900-1929

Tuberculosis is a deadly and incurable plague, but the "climate cure" offers a modest ray of hope to consumptives with mild cases and the means to travel West. They began arriving long before Silver City's first formal promotion of its health-giving climate in 1887, and their presence grows exponentially in the early 1900s. The presence of health-seekers, often accompanied by family members, significantly boosts the post-silver economy. St. Joseph's Sanatorium, Silver City's first medical facility for treatment of tuberculosis, opens in 1902. The boom-era Timmer House becomes Hotel San Vicente, offering elegant lodgings and medical oversight for well-heeled consumptives. Patients occupy small cottages at New Mexico Cottage Sanatorium ("Cottage San") north of town, started in 1905 with generous support from Eastern benefactors. Many similar institutions are started in and around Silver City over the next few years. Several wealthy health-seekers build homes for themselves that are mansions by local standards.

The health era brings authors, composers, baseball magnates, politicians, captains of industry, heiresses, musicians, and everyday folk to

16

Silver City. Former President Theodore Roosevelt and sons come to visit friends who are seeking the climate cure. Health-seekers serve as newspaper editors, ministers, photographers, and shopkeepers, and account for a surprising number of doctors. Cottage San's business manager organizes the Silver City Strollers and produces musical shows to entertain local audiences. Lasting friendships and more than a few marriages come from interactions with area residents. A Chamber of Commerce, organized in 1907, promotes "Silver City with the Golden Clime" via pamphlets, articles and advertisements in national publications. It even offers lectures at the 1915 Panama-Pacific Exposition in San Diego.

Nurse Lulu Kirkpatrick and Matron Anna Howell are pictured on the Hudson Street porch of the Grant County Charity Hospital, ca. 1902. *Silver City Museum, Image #00165*

As sophisticated health-seekers pour in, locals become conscious of their town's rundown appearance. Silver City sees its first major upgrades in two decades. Insurance agent Elizabeth Warren and former school principal Matilda Koehler go into business building concrete sidewalks. Strong demand for housing sparks a construction boom, with modest-sized homes cropping up north and west of town. A modern school on Sixth Street, equipped with electric lights, plumbing, and heating, replaces the frontier-era schoolhouse in 1910. Large plate-glass

This 1914 view shows a group of health-seekers setting forth from Cottage San on an outing. *Silver City Museum, Image #02829*

display windows are installed in older downtown storefronts and automotive garages appear. Dependable electrical and telephone service is put in place. A sewer system is installed, and many residents install indoor plumbing. A teacher training school, gymnasium, and dormitories are added to the Normal School campus.

On August 24, 1902, a flood of Biblical proportions turns Main Street into a yawning chasm overnight, creating the Big Ditch as we know it. Timely stabilization saves Elizabeth Warren's house, which will ultimately be the last original Main Street building to survive. The gulch grows deeper and wider with every storm; ever-sturdier bridges and dams are built and swept away. The old Timmer House is undermined by floodwaters in 1904 and demolished; salvaged building materials go into new projects. Main Street's loss is Broadway's gain in prominence, with an imposing new armory anchoring its east end and blocks of storefronts clad in decorative metal facades. Denizens of the red-light district are discretely relocated to Hudson Street, now isolated and requiring access by bridge. The ditch itself provides a valuable outlet for storm runoff, and the severity of flooding slowly abates as new plantings on the forest reserve start to heal the watershed.

By the early 1900s the descriptive term "Spanish-American" is taking the place of "Mexican" in reference to Hispanic residents. A local chapter of the Alianza Hispano-Americana is chartered in 1904. The Alianza, a mutual-aid society, promotes civic virtues and reinforces cultural identity in the face of discrimination. In 1915 Silver City's board of education announces plans to build a new school at the western edge of Chihuahua Hill, explaining that the site was "thought to be most convenient for the greater number of children to be accommodated."[17] The new Lincoln School is an attractive modern building, but its siting on Chihuahua Hill is viewed as thinly disguised segregation. It soon becomes official: Lincoln School is made "wholly Spanish-American,"[18] purportedly to allow pupils more time to complete their work. Another Hispanic neighborhood, variously referred to as Perros Bravos or Sonora Hill, grows on the eastern side of town in the early 1900s. By the 1940s it is known as Brewer Hill after its best-known resident, Rebecca Brewer.[19]

A handsome new Mission-style railroad depot is built at the southern end of downtown in 1915. Bullard Street and Broadway are paved, with overhead wires buried and ornamental streetlights installed. The Ladies Hospital moves from Hudson Street into the old convent building, just in time for the 1918 flu epidemic. Saint Mary's Academy opens on Alabama Street. After long negotiations, the Town acquires the Waterworks property. The Normal School becomes the New Mexico State Teachers College in 1923, and in 1926 the gymnasium built a decade earlier is named

---

17 "School Board Makes Statement on New Ward School Building," *Silver City Enterprise*, June 25, 1915.

18 Helen M. Calkins, *History of the Public Schools of Silver City (New Mexico): A History of the School from 1874 to 1928* (Privately published, ca. 1928).

19 Rebecca Brewer, locally known as "Madam Brewer," was an African-American *curandera* who came to Silver City around 1910 and owned much property in the neighborhood that bears her name. She died in 1969 at the reported age of 100 years (*Silver City Enterprise*, June 12, 1969).

Fleming Hall to honor longtime civic leader John W. Fleming. Light Hall and Bowden Hall are added to campus in 1928. Ninth Street—originally the town's north boundary—is renamed College Avenue in 1929. By this time Silver City has expanded over a mile northward. Its newest neighborhood, Silver Heights, has just been platted.

World War I, a subsequent shutdown of area mines, and the failure of four local banks in the early 1920s take a heavy psychic and economic toll on the community and are factors in the decline of Silver City's health era. After a quarter-century as a boarding house that sheltered many health-seekers, the former H. B. Ailman house on Broadway becomes city hall in 1926. Even Cottage San, Silver City's leading sanatorium, can no longer compete with better-funded institutions elsewhere in the Southwest. Its property is sold in 1930. Albuquerque has not only attracted nationally sponsored sanatoria; it also lured off quite a few Silver City doctors. No one can the deprive the Silver City area of its salubrious year-round climate, however, and many health-seekers and their families stay on.

The Great Depression and Wartime Era

1930-1945

By the time the Great Depression arrives, Silver City is well accustomed to thrift and a focus on local needs. Chapters of the Rotary and Lions clubs and the League of United Latin American Citizens (LULAC) are established, along with the Grant County Archaeological Society. Local rodeos, first seen in the early 1900s, become a Fourth of July staple in the 1930s when celebrated rodeo director Johnny Mullens takes charge of the annual event. The newly chartered Women's Division of the Chamber of Commerce cleans up local cemeteries, organizes a Cub Scout troop, and launches a tree-planting campaign (the drought-resistant Siberian elms and Trees of Heaven will unfortunately survive all too well). A Spring Street house is donated for use as a community center and serves as headquarters for the National Youth Administration and other New Deal social service programs. The *Silver City Daily Press* debuts in 1935.

A new courthouse, with third-floor jail, replaces its Victorian counterpart at the head of Broadway in 1930. A year later the Town of Silver City acquires a former bank on Bullard for use as city hall and the newly vacated Ailman house becomes the fire station. The Town builds a ten-mile water line across the Continental Divide from Allen Springs to supply the local Waterworks. A natural gas pipeline reaches Silver City in 1937. Downtown buildings are modernized; fluorescent lighting and neon appear. Construction of the five-story Murray Hotel in 1938 represents a huge private investment in the community's future. An east extension of Pope Street is named Silver Heights Boulevard, and the pueblo-style Clark Court is the first tourist court built there. Even as new houses go up in Silver Heights, the venerable Elephant Corral still operates on Hudson Street. Many large homes from the mining boom era are converted into apartments.

New Deal funding enables many important local projects. Silver City's first public artworks—murals painted for the courthouse lobby—are completed in 1934.[20] The new postoffice on Broadway in 1935 and the modern hospital completed in 1937 are Silver City's first such facilities designed specifically for those purposes. Graham Gym, James Stadium, and a new high school building are added to the campus of what has become New Mexico State Teachers College. Silver City's first junior high (today's Sixth Street School building) is placed on the site of the old convent school. Public works projects include miles of new sidewalks, Big Ditch stabilization and planting, and paving on Cooper, Market, and Yankie Streets. Little Walnut picnic grounds are among the many Civilian Conservation Corps (CCC) projects completed in the area.

A flagpole is set in the middle of the Bullard-Broadway intersection in 1942, reflecting community concern for local members of the 200th Coast Artillery captured in the Philippines at the start of World War II. The father of a POW raises the flag each morning. As the world conflict proceeds, a Roll of Honor listing area servicemen is set in front of the fire

---

20 The murals, depicting Grant County mining and ranching scenes, were created by Santa Fe artist Theodore van Soelen.

21

station; the fire chief's wife is tasked with painting color-coded stars by the names of those missing, wounded, or killed. At war's end, the news is grim: roughly half the local men in the 200th Coast Artillery, who endured the Bataan Death March and transportation on "hell ships" to Japanese prison camps, did not survive their prolonged ordeal. Some Hispanic men returning from European duty recall having more respectful treatment by foreign allies than they had previously received in Grant County.

The Postwar and Baby Boom Era
1946-1982
Silver City's postwar building boom takes off as soon as materials become available. Lots in the San Vicente subdivision are offered at pre-war prices. In 1947 the Elgin Block Company gears up to manufacture cinderblocks, using volcanic cinders found near Bear Mountain. Elgin blocks go into the Gila Theater, North Silver Elementary, the Cox Mortuary on College Avenue, an addition doubling the size of the Murray Hotel, and numerous owner-built homes. Radio station KSIL goes on the air and Silver City's first municipal swimming pool opens. The Public Library is launched in 1953, moving to newly completed quarters on College Avenue in 1959. A modern junior high school is built above Silver Heights to accommodate adolescent Baby Boomers. The Town acquires the old homestead of the Scotts, a pioneer African American family, to build a golf course and ballfields for use by Little Leaguers and adult players. Sports of all kinds become increasingly popular for residents of all ages.

WWII surplus buildings find new life on the college campus, where many veterans apply their GI Bill benefits. In 1949 the State Teachers College becomes New Mexico Western College, adopting purple-and-gold school colors and Mustangs team name. A fieldhouse is added to Graham Gym, a new training school replaces the 1900 version, and other college buildings are expanded or renovated. An Air Force battalion moves onto campus for training as clerk-typists in the early 1950s. Miller Library takes the place of Old Main in 1957, and the new administration building, science building, men's dorm, married student housing and a quirky student union (the "Cooler") soon follow, all clad in white brick. Older campus buildings are painted white to match. The college becomes Western New Mexico University in 1963.

A large group of area residents and soldiers gathered on October 5,1942 in front of the Silver City Fire Station to dedicate the Grant County Roll of Honor. *Silver City Museum, Image #21003*

The automotive age is in high gear. Rail passenger and express service to Silver City ends in 1955, and the depot is shuttered for the next 20 years. All goods will now arrive by truck. A steel and concrete bridge on Broadway replaces its rickety one-lane predecessor, and parking meters and highway-scale streetlights are installed downtown. Small shopping centers, filling stations, drive-ins, and car dealerships appear along Pope Street and Silver Heights Boulevard; the hospital's entrance is moved around back for vehicular access and parking. Some 200 residential blocks are paved in 1959 and '60 and a new four-lane highway connects Bayard and Silver City, ending abruptly at College Avenue. The old Southern Hotel is razed; the modern Drifter Motel is the first with a swimming pool.

The year 1967 proves as dense with major developments as 1883 had been. Phelps-Dodge announces it will resume mining at Tyrone after a 40-year hiatus. Silver High school, overrun with Baby Boomers, runs classes in split shifts while a larger building takes shape in the upper part of town. New subdivisions and trailer parks extend residential areas in every direction. Santa Rita is demolished for mine expansion, and many houses are moved into Silver City. The million-dollar Fine Arts complex nears completion on the WNMU campus, its large auditorium equipped to handle major performances. A Holiday Inn opens at the start of '67 and a country club at year's end. The Silver City Museum debuts in the Ailman House on July 1 with little fanfare. It will share space with the fire department for three more years, pending completion of the Public Safety Building.

By the early 1960s roughly a quarter of the WNMU student body is Hispanic, many of whom become teachers and principals in the region. Hispanos are increasingly elected to public office and bilingual education is incorporated into the Silver Schools curriculum, but the status quo is slow to change. Activism heats up. In 1969 the locally organized El Grito, Inc., takes over the Silver City Head Start. A group of area families organizes to support residents with physical and developmental disabilities; the Special School for Special Children opens at Fort Bayard. Silver City celebrates its centennial in 1970, with businesspeople dressing in old-timey garb every Friday. The three historic houses constituting the recently closed red-light district are demolished; elsewhere the first handful of early homes are lovingly restored. Silver City's first master plan is completed, sparking controversy over zoning.

Native son Harrison Schmitt visits the moon in 1972 and becomes a U. S. Senator four years later (Jeff Bingaman, another hometown boy, will fill his Senate seat in 1983 and remain for 30 years). The Grant County Humane Society, Border Area Mental Health Services, and Gila Native Plant Society are established. Indian Hills subdivision grows north of town and a new detached jail is built behind the courthouse. Lobbying for paving and sewer service on Chihuahua and Brewer Hills grows more confrontational in the 1970s; the term "Chicano" gains currency. Silver City's poorest neighborhoods finally gain the basic amenities and services long enjoyed in other parts of town. The timing of Paving Project 11, including downtown handicap ramps as well as extensive street paving on Brewer Hill, unfortunately coincides with the national energy crisis when oil costs are at their highest.

La Plata Middle School and Harrison Schmitt Elementary are built at opposite ends of town, and North Silver Elementary is renamed in 1974 in memory of former Assistant Chief of Police Jose Barrios. It is the first public building named for a local Hispano. The WNMU Museum opens its doors and the Silver City Food Co-op is founded. Demolition of the long-shuttered railroad depot in 1975 sparks local preservation efforts, and the Silver City Historic District is listed on the National Register of Historic Places. K-Mart's arrival ignites concern for the survival of downtown. The Gough Park gazebo, built as a U. S. Bicentennial project in 1976, finally gives Silver City with a plaza or "commons" for public events. The Big Ditch Park project is the Town's first major citizen-launched initiative.

Into the 21st Century
The seeds of each new era quietly germinate while the previous one is still in progress, often requiring a decade or more to become evident and take hold. Throughout the 1960s and '70s a wide range of individuals—back-to-the-landers, artists, adventurers, "snowbirds"—find their way to Silver City. Over time many of these self-styled discoverers are joined by friends and family or raise families of their own. Newcomers in this cohort, like the health-seekers of old, bring a wide range of interests and life experience to their new hometown. They quietly help to lay the groundwork for the Silver City of today.

Completion of Gila Regional Medical Center in 1983, a century after the hospital's founding, is a major community milestone. A year earlier, however, massive layoffs at area copper mines sent Grant County's unemployment rate to 40%. It is a major wake-up call: local leaders recognize the importance of diversifying the economic base. Many possibilities, including a racetrack, are discussed and much energy goes toward bringing a large employer to the area. More modest initiatives prove effective in the long run. Early efforts focus on attracting residents whose income does not depend on local jobs: retirees, part-time residents, and people able to "work from anywhere," a category that greatly expands with the rise of the Internet.

Appreciation for area history and heritage grows during the 1980s, and tourist materials feature sites and stories from the early years. Additional historic districts are listed on the state and national registers. Several larger historic properties undergo rehabilitation. Silver City becomes one of New Mexico's first Main Street communities in 1985, at which point downtown has seen little attention since the Great Depression. Over the next 36 years Silver City MainStreet will leverage over $6.4 million in major infrastructure projects. An energized downtown draws a new generation of shops, restaurants, galleries, and events. The Silver City Museum undergoes a multi-phase historic rehabilitation and a full-scale replica of La Capilla appears on the crest of Chihuahua Hill through neighborhood initiative. Long vacant, the Murray Hotel regains its former glory after a years-long rehabilitation.

Arts and culture, always a lively element of Silver City life, becomes a viable economic asset in the late twentieth century as the homegrown artist community expands organically. The Mimbres Region Arts Council launches the Silver City Blues Festival in the late 1990s. New theater groups and a women's fiber arts collective are formed; children design play structures for Penny Park; the Youth Mural Program unleashes creative energy throughout the region. The Silver City Art Association offers collaborative tours, exhibits, and promotional materials. WNMU adds Fiesta Latina to its already robust year-round schedule of cultural events, and the university museum completes a million-dollar transformation. KURU community radio goes on-air. The Western Institute for Lifelong Learning (WILL), founded in 2005, offers courses to older adults led by their knowledgeable peers. Cultural festivals become major visitor attractions.

Outdoor recreation and the Gila natural area are increasingly important assets for residents and visitors. The Tour of the Gila cycling stage race, started in 1987, draws worldwide attention to the region and spawns an avid cycling community. Boston Hill receives protection as the town's first open space, linked into a growing system of local trails. The Gila River Festival celebrates the natural and cultural history of the Gila region through the arts, humanities, and natural sciences. Learning from and in nature is a guiding principle for the Aldo Leopold Charter School, started in 2003. The Gila Resources Information Council (GRIP), formed in 1998 to hold area mines accountable for groundwater pollution, expands its role to encompass healthy rivers, water resources protection, and community resilience. Silver City is named a gateway community for the Continental Divide Trail in 2014, and a decade later the historic Silver City Waterworks property prepares to become the official gateway headquarters.

A community is a living organism, bolstered by tradition but refreshed with infusions of new blood from time to time. After long reliance on an extractive economy, Silver City is creating value around its area history, character, and environment. The Red Paint Pow Wow reinforces and celebrates the region's Native heritage, and Apache voices increasingly contribute to public discourse. Degraded landscapes, as well as historic houses, are being restored. Many important initiatives involve collaboration between local governments, organizations, and community members, to the benefit to all. An educational thread runs throughout the efforts detailed above, with youth involvement and mentorship built into many programs. Volunteerism remains a core community value.

In 2024 Silver City is the only New Mexico town operating under a Territorial charter, a fact that is the basis for an annual celebration. The *Silver City Daily Press*, established in 1935, can trace its origins back through multiple mergers and name changes to the town's first newspaper in1873. A continuing voice for independent journalism, the *Daily Press* buys the *Deming Headlight* from a corporate chain in 2022. Gila Regional Medical Center, directly descended from the Ladies Hospital, is New Mexico's last county-owned hospital. Grant County takes care of its own, on many levels; multiple groups work to fill the basic needs of our most vulnerable residents and to ensure future sustainability. Twenty-first century challenges are serious and plentiful, but the community's well-developed spirit of resilience is a valuable and time-tested asset.

An ever-changing cast of characters has shaped a unique collective personality over fifteen decades. Silver City has gained insight from past mistakes and let go of some unproductive attitudes while becoming a more resourceful, imaginative, determined, creative, forward-looking place, sometimes ornery but almost always fun-loving. Ultimately the town's greatest wealth lies in its human capital, the people who call it home.

Additional Reading

Berry, Susan and Sharman Apt Russell. *Built to Last: An Architectural History of Silver City, New Mexico*. Silver City, NM: Silver City Museum Society, (second ed.) 1995.

Lundwall, Helen J., ed. *Pioneering in Territorial New Mexico: The Memoirs of H. B. Ailman*. Silver City, NM: Silver City Museum Society, 2008. (Originally published in 1983 with the title *Pioneering in Territorial Silver City* by the University of New Mexico Press in conjunction with the Historical Society of New Mexico)

Lewis, Nancy Owen. *Chasing the Cure in New Mexico: Tuberculosis and the Quest for Health*. Santa Fe: Museum of New Mexico Press, 2016.

Miller, Darlis A. *The California Column in New Mexico*. Albuquerque: University of New Mexico in cooperation with the Historical Society of New Mexico, 1982.

Naegle, Conrad Keeler. "The History of Silver City, New Mexico: 1870-1886." Thesis, University of New Mexico, 1943.

Poole, Joy and Mike Olsen. "Enos and Jennie Culver Memoir, Travel Diary and Correspondence while Traveling the Santa Fe Trail and El Camino Real 1869-1871." https://www.nps.gov/safe/learn/historyculture/trailwide-research.htm. (Santa Fe: National Park Service, nd)

SUSAN BERRY co-authored *Built to Last: An Architectural History of Silver City, New Mexico* and has published many articles, and made presentations on regional history at numerous conferences. She served as director of the Silver City Museum for 36 years and serves on the board of the Historical Society of New Mexico.

CHAPTER 2:

Somebody in Nowhere: The World Comes to Silver City

By Tom Hester

Miss Nobody of Nowhere was America's first novel set partly in Silver City, a town of about 2,000 lodged in the wilderness of southwestern New Mexico Territory. The year was 1888.

Miss Nobody's author, Archibald Clavering Gunter, was a bi-coastal creature. English by sentiment and heritage, he was reared in California and after attending university there, moved to America's cultural capital, New York City. A playwright for Broadway and a publisher as well as a novelist, Gunter specialized in florid romances peopled with stereotypes.

We discover the title character to be a member of English nobility and "nowhere" dissolves into Boston, London, and New York. In the novel's closing pages, Silver City lawman, Brick Garvey, based on Harvey Whitehill, travels to New York to bring to justice Miss Nobody's evil uncle. Possibly the most fanciful notion in *Miss Nobody of Nowhere* is that Grant County would pay per diem and travel to its sheriff to arrest a murderer in New York.

We ought not criticize Gunter too severely for his mythmaking and inaccuracies. Ideals of a pluralistic society promoting the dignity of persons from every cultural background were—before the civil rights movement of the last half of the 20th century—largely confined to utopian societies, radical reformers, and high-flown thinkers.

That's the guiding idea in today's exploration of Silver City. Mexicans; Mexican Americans; African Americans; Jews from Eastern Europe,

29

Russia, and the Near East; Chinese and Chinese Americans; first-generation Germans and Irish and French comprised almost two-thirds of Silver City's population in the late nineteenth and early twentieth century.

Bicycle race on Yankie Street Source: Silver City Museum

Nevertheless, the imposed cultural norms came from St. Louis, New York, and Boston. Silver City's styles—the fads, the values, and ideals—copied American urban models. Silver City's elite were determined from the beginning to speak English with the slang of a sophisticate, to bring in the best that the Eastern seaboard had to offer, to look modern and be fashionable.

The best single source revealing our town's past, Susan Berry's and Sharman Russell's *Built to Last* presents the idea that Silver City deliberately avoided being a sleepy, dusty southwestern village (Berry and Russell, p. 17). Those early faded photographs of the mining town recorded the reality against which the founders apparently struggled. Berry elaborated just that thesis in her presentation in this series.

Berry and Russell quote a visitor from Santa Fe's *Daily New Mexican:* "Silver City looks like a New England town picked up bodily and set down here between the hills to serve as a model for the rest of the 'great growing country' , , , People may come here expecting to enjoy more of the luxuries of city life than they would in the eastern towns

30

of the same size, and they will not be disappointed." (quoted by the *Enterprise,* July 23, 1886)

Hear Joan Mooman, wife of a Silver City physician, writing for the Woman's Club 28 years after the Santa Fe visitor: "Silver City is a conservative town, nestled among the hills of Grant County. It is an American town recruited from the pick of the East and the West, made up in considerable part of successful businessmen and their families. . . ." *(Council Fires,* 1913, p. 24)

Then, 29 years after Mrs. Mooman, history student Conrad Naegle described Silver City in his master's thesis about the town: "Picturesquely set amid mountains of precious metals, the base of the gem was composed of the very finest type of Anglo-American pioneers, who, oblivious to the fact that they were in the land of 'Poco Tiempo,' rolled up their sleeves and went to work with such energy that they exemplified a type of American genius, enterprise, and intelligence which amazed the whole Southwest." (Conrad Keeler Naegle, p. 4)

What this presentation is about is not to erase those soaring words that would make a Chamber of Commerce publicist glow. This paper aims to reassign some of the credit and widen our collective vision. We can keep in our minds one of the best novels of the last century, *Invisible Man.* Ralph Ellison's character speaks for a majority of Silver City residents, if you include women, during its span of 150 years, "I am an invisible man . . . I am a man of substance, of flesh and bone, fiber and liquids—and I might even be said to possess a mind. I am invisible, understand, simply because people refuse to see me." (Ralph Ellison, p. 3)

To capture the basic nature of Silver City, an observer must acknowledge that the town, like much of the West, was made up as it grew. Every adult resident in its early years had rejected a previous place to live in order to live in a remote village. Yet, part of the reason Silver City differed from other towns in the West can be explained by its divergence from some of the "eleven laws of migration," laid down by Ernst Georg Ravenstein. Ravenstein was an English geographer who had immigrated from Prussia and who published his "laws" in 1885, close to the time of Gunter's novel.

These are Ravenstein's Laws of Migration:

- Every migration flow generates a return or counter-migration.
- The majority of migrants move a short distance.
- Migrants who move longer distances tend to choose big-city destinations.
- Urban residents are often less migratory than inhabitants of rural areas. Most people move from agricultural areas to urban areas.
- Females are more migratory than males within the areas of their birth, but males more frequently venture beyond.
- Most migrants are young adults; families rarely migrate out of their country of birth.
- Large towns grow more by migration than by natural increase.
- Families are reluctant to cross an international border.
- Migration has positive economic development.
- Most people move for economic reasons.
- Technology and transportation improve migration. (Ravenstein, passim)

We will learn that while most people migrated to Silver City from a short distance, an appreciable number had traveled half the world. They settled not in a teeming city, but in a small town scattered over a terrain that marked the northern edge of an expansive grassy desert. Whole families had migrated, primarily from Chihuahua.

The element stoking the migration to Silver City was snared in its name. E.S. Culver, a Wisconsin attorney, described to a relative his experiences as a young man hanging out with former Union soldiers.

"[We] camped under a large cedar tree near a large spring. Here we remained two- or three-weeks prospecting and locating claims. This was the very first beginning of a settlement on the ground where Silver City now stands. We each located several claims. There had been a little hut there, but the Mexican woman and her little boy were murdered by the Indians while the husband escaped by flight. We elected a recorder whose business was to record our claims and description of the same, and when we became satisfied by different assays made that our mines were rich in silver, we concluded to lay out a town. The Bullard boys, John and James, and Joe Yankie claimed the prior right to the largest share of the town site. As some thought it worthwhile to dispute about it, they hired a surveyor to lay out the new town. I remember we met at midnight so that the surveyor could adjust his instrument by the North Star, and now as we were to have a city, we must have a name. Accordingly, notices were tacked on trees or bushes that a meeting would be held in a cabin which had been erected in the meantime, naming the evening.

The cabin was crowded with would-be citizens. One of the Bullard boys made a motion that the town should be named Silver Flat as the location was in a nice level valley. Another amended the motion by naming Silver City. I think this was Judge Richard Hudson who now lives in Deming (Luna County). I opposed the name of Silver City on the ground that there were in Colorado and in other mining states towns by that name, and further that it was a very inappropriate name in as much as we occupied at that meeting the only cabin in the city. I therefore proposed Silver Cliff to be the name as the surrounding cliffs or hills were supposed to contain silver enough to make us all rich, and that the prosperity of the city depended entirely upon the cliffs surrounding it. Upon a vote being taken, it was found that the name Silver City had the majority of the votes, and so Silver City was christened without further argument. Then building commenced in earnest. (*Enterprise,* January 15, 1904)

It's noteworthy that Culver wrote as a retired attorney in Wisconsin, not as a retired mine owner in Silver City. It's also important that Culver in his letter failed to mention Jennie, his wife, and his two year-old son, both of whom he had lodged in Ft. Bayard while he made worthless mining claims. In letters home, she described her fears of the Indians who wounded or killed men brought every day to the fort. She expressed hope to return home in the spring of 1872 but died of tuberculosis in the fall of 1871. Jennie Culver was the fourth person buried in the fresh Silver City cemetery north of town. (Davis and Humble, p. 37)

Culver's account also failed to mention the Mexican village on Chihuahua Hill that the Rev. Stanley, priest at Saint Vincent de Paul Church, described in his history of the parish. Father Stanley wrote: "This was really a summer adobe settlement for woodcutters, sheep herders, and Indian traders. They built a chapel mostly for the use of the Hermanos de la Morada de Nuestro Padre J. Nazareno." (F. Stanley, mimeographed history)

In 1870, Anglo men dazzled by the prospects of instant wealth crowded into a cabin. Woodcutters and sheep herders and chapels interested them not a whit. They took a vote to name where they wanted to live and the name they chose emphasized the key to its *present silver*—and the conceit of its future—*city*. Almost as quickly as that cabinful of Anglo seekers of silver set out to make a city, the place filled up with Mexican and Eastern European immigrants. The whole enterprise at first depended on Chihuahuan miners who could apply the brutal methods of separating silver from its quartz matrix.

Silver City profile, 1880

The 1880 Census of Silver City counted 1,798 individuals with an average age of 26.3 years. Of that total, persons born in Mexico (646) or persons with Mexican heritage and born in New Mexico, Texas, California, or Arizona (298) comprised 53 percent of the total. Other foreign-born persons accounted for 9 percent.

The handwritten census pages make clear that there existed little residential segregation for ethnic populations. Chinese residents often lived near the store or restaurant or laundry where they worked. There was no equivalent to San Francisco's Grant Street.

Thirty-eight percent of Silver City residents with a heritage other than Mexican were born in the United States or one of its territories. The 285 Anglo natives of New Mexico Territory formed the largest component of the 38 percent. The five states providing most of the birthplaces other than New Mexico were New York, Ohio, Texas, Missouri, and Pennsylvania. Those who came from the former Confederacy (162) accounted for about a third of the Silver Citians born in the United States, excluding persons born in the New Mexico Territory.

The five countries, other than Mexico, which provided the largest number of Silver City residents, were Canada (29), Germany (29), England (27), China (24), and Ireland (19). The other foreign-born persons hailed from 13 other nations.

All but four of the Mexicans who specified the state where they were born were from northern Mexico. Six hundred and one of the 646 total were Chihuahuans. If Silver City ever decides to erect a statue honoring our forebearers, a Chihuahuan should furnish the model.

The U.S. Census has long recorded the race of the American populace, and it depended on its enumerators to decide whether a respondent or household member was "Black" or "Mulatto." In Silver City 1,742 persons were considered white; 16, black; 18, mulatto; 27, Chinese; and 2, American Indian. The number of male versus female residents was lopsided: 62 percent male and 38 percent female.

Of Silver Citians age 15 or older, 6.5 percent were widowed, 35 percent were married, and 58.5 percent were single. Four persons reported that they were divorced.

James L. Smith drew such a clear portrait of Billy the Kid's society, concluded that our communities were violent. A summary of Silver City's population in 1880—predominately unmarried, poorly schooled men in their teens and twenties, a majority away from their families of origin, with a saloon on nearly every commercial block—helps to explain the source of that violence.

Let's now try to enliven the numbers with names and details of individuals. I want to introduce you to extraordinary Silver Citians from

Mexico, China, Germany, Poland, and Syria. Be forewarned, most are male. And in a country where a workingman earned an average $1 for 12 hours of work, many of the immigrants I am about to describe were a good deal better off.

Economic historians point out that considering the whole of U.S. history, the post–Civil War period, which Mark Twain coined as the Gilded Age, had the greatest division of wealth between magnates and the average worker. It was even more pronounced than today's chasm separating Jeff Bezos from you and me. (Josephson, p. 179; Kolko, p. 288.)

It's illustrative that Henry Flagler, a Rockefeller lookalike who helped found Standard Oil, visited Silver City to inspect his property, the Silver City reduction works. Imagine now a Mexican charcoal burner standing on the works' railroad siding. He makes out Flagler, severe in a black suit, walking from his private rail car. Amid a clutch of sycophants, Flagler limps with a cane toward the mill, smoking and heaving as it pounds rock to dust. Let's keep such a scene with that charcoal burner in our minds as we consider some of Silver City's primary citizens.

Regard three unique, seldom considered families. The census listings only, with no photographs, marked their presence here.

This is the only source we will have to know of the Beltran family in 1880. Jose, age 48, and Simona, age 30, were living with Jose's older brother Tomas and with their two sons, Lucas, 12, and Martin, 11. Jose was a miner, and Simona, a homemaker, while their sons were roustabouts and Tomas, a farmworker.

This is the only source we will have to know Jose Maria Jordan, 40, Clara Hermosilla Jordan, 32, and Refugia, 15. Jose Maria, a native of Zacatecas, was an overseer of a coal mine. Clara, a housekeeper, was born in Chihuahua. Their daughter was born in New Mexico Territory.

This is the only source we will have to know Pascual and Epimena Taria, brother and sister, ages 26 and 20. Both were born in Texas of Mexican parents. Pascual did day labor. Epimena kept house and cared for Miguel Taria, age 7. We don't know Miguel's relationship to Pascual and Epimena.

We do know quite a lot about Las Cruces merchant Jose Martin Amador. Born in 1836 in the town that would become Ciudad Juárez, Amador moved north as a child. The border soon shifted as well, and Amador became an American. The family moved to the village of Las Cruces where Amador's mother owned a small store. As an adult, Amador formed a freight company to haul cargo between Chihuahua and Santa Fe, later established the Amador Hotel, and opened two grocery or mercantile stores, one in Las Cruces and one in Silver City. Meanwhile, Amador invented a plow, served as Dofia Ana County treasurer and deputy U.S. marshal. Early Las Cruces public schools were built on land he had contributed to.

The Amador grocery, built in 1873 in Silver City, stood on South Bullard. Four years later, Amador created a partnership with Jose Macias and J.S. Garcia to operate a mercantile. Garcia, who had come from Colorado, was the designated manager. The store's notice in the newspaper bragged on 25,000 pounds of merchandise that was being freighted from the nearest railroad terminal, wherever that was. *(Grant County Herald,* March 31, 1877) Within less than a year, however, the partnership was dissolved, and Amador concentrated on his businesses in Las Cruces, although he continued to have mining and real estate investments in Grant County. *(Grant County Herald,* January 19, 1878; Berry and Russell)

Juan Nepomecano and Lorenzo Carrasco
For Juan Nepomecano Carrasco, father, and Lorenzo Carrasco, son, I'm offering you a sort of mystery, derived in part from my shortcomings as a researcher and in part from an uncharacteristic silence about the Carrascos in the local newspapers.

I need to detour here to describe 19th Century journalism in small towns. Most flourishing towns had at least two newspapers, one a Democratic sheet and the other, a Republican organ. That arrangement permitted county and court officials to post public notices in the correct newspaper—the one they agreed with.

Editors of small-town weeklies were as adept with their scissors as with their pens, for a large fraction of a paper's space was filled with clippings from so-called "exchanges." Although reporters supplied longer articles and news from outlying towns, W.A. Leonard, editor of the *Silver City Enterprise* during the early 1880s, collected news items from visitors to his office or from fellow diners at his lunch table. Hence, a hundred and forty years later, we're reading in part from Leonard's social journal.

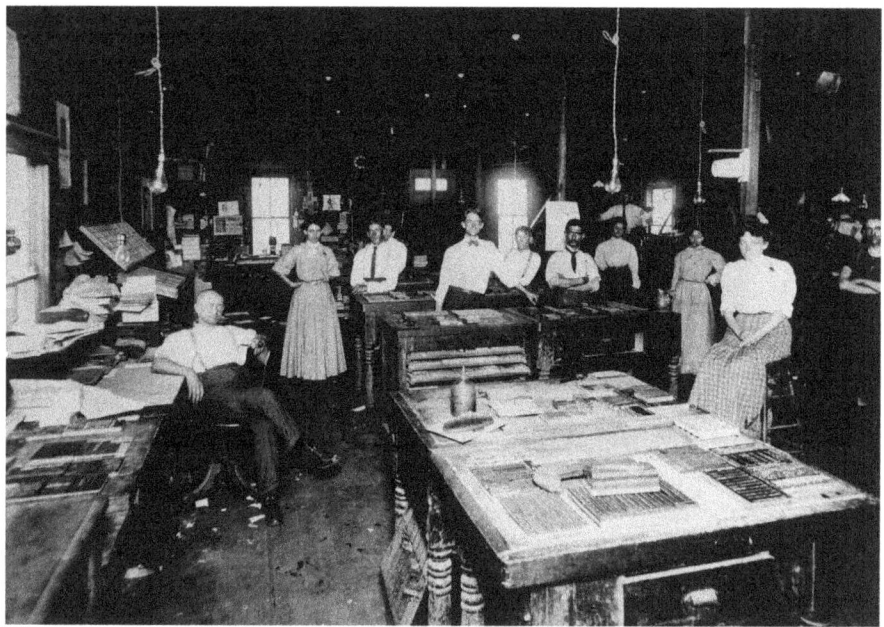

An interior view of the press room, probably of the *Silver City Enterprise*; c. 1910
Source: Silver City Museum

To my knowledge, although Silver City had several Canadian editors, all the newspapers reflected the social concerns and affiliations of English speakers. Whether a reader regularly scanned the *Enterprise* or the *Watch Dog* or the *New Southwest* or *Mining Life* or the *Grant County Herald* or the *Mining Gazette* or the *Telegram* or the *Eagle* or the *Independent,* that reader was informed by Anglo men who socialized with the town's elite men.

That said, let us now pay attention to the mystery and our important subject: the Carrascos.

Juan Nepomecano was a Chihuahua silver man from the Sierra Madre or the Sierra Tarahumara. He arrived shortly after Silver City's boom exploded. On August 17, 1870, Carrasco, J.R. Johnson, Aaron H. Hackney, Edwin J. Orr, and James Corbin joined in a claim on the hill behind the current county courthouse. The next month, Carrasco, who an outstanding local historian, Helen Lundwall, described as the only experienced silver miner in the camp, filed another claim. He, J.R. Johnson, James Atkinson, Jesus Armijo, and Manuel Moreno filed the first claim in the Chloride Flat district, a mile west of Silver City. Their silver mine was to be the rich La Providencia.

Carrasco built his hacienda at the southern end of Bullard Street, on the west side of what was more· trail than street, though I've read accounts of the hacienda being perched over San Vincente Creek. The compound enclosed a house, a store, a corral, adobe brick furnaces, and arrastras for pulverizing ore. In the spring of 1871, the Carrasco smelters made the first silver bullion in Silver City. The smelting relied on century-old techniques of Spanish and Mexican miners. They burned oak and later hitched a horse to a fan to stoke the flames. Both mining and smelting must have prospered, for in 1873 O.L. Scott of *Mining Life* reported that son Lorenzo was bringing workers from Mexico. *(Mining Life,* May 17, 1873)

Editor Scott later reported that Lorenzo, over two years, had refined $200,000 worth of silver, which translates to $4.7 million in 2021. Lorenzo's father seemed to have settled in as an influencer in local politics, for someone had claimed to the *Mining Life* that Juan Nepomecano was supporting a candidate for probate judge. That claim he denied. Soon after, someone nominated both father and son as Republican candidates for local positions, but the convention did not support them.

So, what's the mystery? Less than five years after *Mining Life's* reporting about La Providencia's wealth, the *Grant County Herald* ran a single sentence: "The families of the late Jose Macias and Nepomecano Carrasco have returned to Mexico." (*Grant County Herald*, August 21, 1878) The hacienda had been sold.

While Juan Nepomecano had left, there were 1880 census records for several Lorenzo Carrascos. One lived in Silver City. Both *Lorenzo* and *Carrasco* are fairly common names, belonging to men of the right age in Georgetown and San Lorenzo. There can be no certainty that the Silver City Lorenzo is Juan's son. And the census reports Lorenzo's occupation as "grain merchant," not as smelter manager.

If asked to guess about the identification of the 1880 Lorenzos, I would choose the simplest explanation. Lorenzo had left the mining business and was living with family members who had not wanted to return to Las Cruces or Chihuahua. Modern technology had supplanted the family's antique smelting processes. In 1883, the *Enterprise* published a long, front-page article on the replacement of adobe furnaces with more efficient "water jacket blast furnaces." The article reported:

> "A few years ago, Silver City contained several of these [adobe] furnaces which were kept more or less employed by their owners. They have gradually fallen into disuse until now there are but two that make any pretensions to running at all. One of the latter is located just off Bullard Street, to the west, opposite Bremen's corral . . . (*Silver City Enterprise,* July 13, 1883)

It is likely that Juan Nepomecano, seeing the technological handwriting on the wall, had sold his holdings, gathered up the family who agreed to leave, and retired to the mountains of Chihuahua. He was almost 60 years of age. He, like Amador, may have been attracted to other places. Nevertheless, it is puzzling to see Hispanos who had enjoyed some success in Silver City abandoning the town.

Juan Nepomecano had been absent about six years when Cipriano Baca's name appeared on the first page of the Grant County Corporation Record Book: January 3, 1884. Baca, scion of an old New Mexico family, was born in California, where his father had gone to take advantage of a Spanish land grant. At about age 20, Cipriano sought to cure a lung ailment in Arizona. Cousins had established a ranch in Chihuahua, south of Palomas, and that possibly led to Cipriano's incorporation of the Mimbres River Cattle Company, with an estimated and very ambitious evaluation of $500,000.

It was the worst possible time to go into cattle ranching on the east side of Cooke's Peak. A drought scorched the Southwest in 1886 and 1887. The blizzard of 1887 froze most of Baca's herd. That year Baca became a Grant County deputy sheriff, and for the rest of his life, except when he was a butcher or the tax assessor for Socorro County, Baca was a law enforcement officer. His deeds and exploits I don't have time to relate, for they were many. Nor can I explain the details of his trial for murdering a man in Mogollon.

Baca participated, however, in an insignificant episode that deserves mention. In 1893, a tumultuous year when Congress repealed the Sherman Silver Purchase Act, a distinguished company of 65 Silver Citians formed what they called the Silver Convention. Two Hispanos, Baca and J.A. Ancheta, were part of the reception committee. Ancheta had a long history in the area, beginning in Pinos Altos. In 1893, he ranched in the Mimbres Valley. He had been a justice of the peace and a Republican activist. His son, a Notre Dame graduate, had served as Grant County's first district attorney and as a representative to the territorial legislature.

That Silver City power brokers could name four in-town German Americans but only one in-town Hispano, a deputy sheriff, points to their criteria of wealth and connections.

The pattern in the chronology of relationships between the two dominate ethnicities—Hispanos and Anglos—shows that the era of respect that had begun and continued in a time of war, permitting election of Apolonio Barela to a term on the town council, had sputtered to a halt by the mid-eighties. In the nineties, a fatal Pinos Altos fight between two miners, an Hispano and an Anglo, had the sheriff and the *Independent* using words like "race-labor riot," pitting Mexicans against "Europeans."

Dr. Stephen Fox, one of our presenters, has described in an article the period between 1890 and 1950 as that of *Los Reyes de Jaime Cuervo*, Jim Crow laws or customs, when Southern segregationist-style measures restricted public institutions serving, or not serving, Mexican Americans. Some Hispanos responded to this hostility in Anglo-only associations by forming their own societies.

The Alianza Hispano-Americana was founded in 1894, in Tucson, as a fraternal benefit society, *una sociedad mutualista,* primarily providing a venue for social activities and insurance for burial expenses. The Alianza spread rapidly across the Southwest, including multiple chapters in Grant County. The society sought to preserve Hispanos' cultural heritage and to engage members in learning and applying American political ideals. (Handbook of Texas website, "Allianza Hispano-Americana")

The Silver City lodge, chartered in 1904, was, according to the *Enterprise* "in a highly flourishing condition and new initiates are being added to it at every regular meeting." (*Enterprise*, February 5, 1904) Two years later, the Silver City lodge was one of the largest in the jurisdiction. The first lodge building was on the corner of Pinos Altos and San Vicente Streets on Chihuahua Hill; in the 1920s, the Allianza moved to Texas Street, south of Broadway. In 1930, it celebrated its twenty-fifth anniversary with a big dance at the National Guard Armory. And in 1944, when Silver City had two lodges, Jose Morales, president of Lodge 17, chaired the regional convention in Silver City. After the war, however, the organization lost its fervor. Its membership drifted away during the 1950s.

In the late 1940s when the Hispano community wanted to celebrate the Sixteenth of September, Mexico's Independence Day, they turned to the Knights of Silence, who were not silent at all, for they exploded dynamite on La Capilla Hill before the *Grito,* the start of the parade and a dance at the Armory.

St. Vincent de Paul Catholic Church was perhaps the only institution in Silver City that knitted together Spanish speakers and English speakers. The church celebrated the *doce de diciembre* observance of the Virgen de Guadalupe. When the capilla still stood, the church processed to the little chapel. The community lit bonfires or luminarias to guide the way of the men carrying a statue of the Virgen.

La Capilla about 1900 Source: Silver City Museum

In more recent times, two councils of the League of United Latin American Citizens or LULAC provided a voice for some Hispanos. A LULAC council now occupies a former church building in the Chihuahua Hill neighborhood. Its commitment to education has raised hundreds of thousands of dollars that it has granted in college scholarships to local students.

Although Grant County Hispanos volunteered and sacrificed in military service during World War I, the changes introduced by the Second World War were longer lasting. Women had been hired during the war to operate heavy equipment at the Chino mine, and throughout the region women filled positions left vacant by servicemen. Mexican American servicemen and medical personnel returned from the war with both new skills and a keener awareness of justice. Those changes in perspectives and ambitions, so deftly treated by Rodolfo Anaya in *Bless Me, Ultima*, were focused by Grant County's labor union, Local 890 of the International Union of Mine, Mill and Smelter Workers. The local thrived despite the

Taft-Hartley Act, because it found strength among mine workers. Those workers faced harsh working conditions and, in some contracts, had to fight a dual pay system in which Hispanos received lower pay and no chance for promotion.

What follows are just a few of the names of community and labor leaders during the 1940s and the 1950"s, every one a Mining District or Mimbres Valley resident: Joe T. Morales, Darfa Chavez, Brijido Provencio, Albert Muñoz, Anita Torrez, Art Flores, Juan Chacon, Virginia Chacon, Lorenzo Torrez, Cipriano Montoya, Joe Ramirez.

In the 1950s, the men and women of Local 890 lived out the truth of J. Webster, the teacher of all Silver City children in 1874. Webster reported to the local board: "I am sure when this people [that is, the Hispanos] become better known, their detractors will become more cautious . . . [about ignoring] the truth in regard to this people, for it is highly probable that from the rising generation of this people, that some will take a prominent part in the halls of Congress." (Helen Calkins, p. 14)

African American residents
If the historical record of the majority population, the Hispanos, was thin, public attention to the smaller African American population was almost non-existent. There was one reported individual, John Gaskin, at the beginning of the 20th Century. Gaskin, an owner of a vacuum cleaner shop, received a gubernatorial appointment to a Denver conference on African American issues. He was also the secretary of a Grant County organization to organize Black voters in 1912. After the formation of the group, however, there was no other news.

From 1890 to 1926, Anita Scott Coleman, daughter of a retired buffalo soldier, graduate of New Mexico Teachers College, lived in or just outside Silver City before moving with her husband, a printer and photographer, to Los Angeles. From 1919 to 1925 Coleman published short stories in national magazines like *The Crisis* and *The Messenger.* Those periodicals served as the outlets for the Harlem Renaissance, a major flowering of African American literature and art. Coleman's stories consistently and eloquently conveyed the views and lives of persons, especially women, oppressed by poverty and bigotry. To the Silver City of her day, however, Anita Scott Coleman was invisible.

Chinese residents

In 1874, at the age of 24, Charley Sun came to Silver City and established a laundry. He was the first Chinese resident. By 1877, Sun owned a restaurant on the corner of Bullard and Broadway. Sun's wife was Rafaela. In 1882, Sun returned to China for 18 months. We know all these facts because the newspapers reported them. I suggest that the newspapers reported on the Chinese residents and their celebrations, while scarcely ever taking note of Mexican *quincenarias* and *tomaladas, posadas* and *bailes,* because the Chinese customs were more exotic and because *every* week Chinese owners of restaurants and laundries dropped by the newspaper office to pay for their advertisements.

The nature of the reporting was mixed. Editors shuffled through their thesauruses to find synonyms: Celestials, Mongolians, opium smokers, heathen Chinese, China Boy. Stories about Chinese residents often mangled admiration for an ancient civilization with juvenile insults. Other times, a news item gave an unadorned report: "The Chinese are flying kites which attracted much attention." *(Enterprise,* April 5, 1895)

The most dreadful feature of the Chinese in Silver City was their victimization by vicious personal crimes. The editor or reporter often expressed horror at the gruesome violence. In one account, a Gold Hill miner, a Cornishman, attacked a Chinese man who had loaned him money and had asked for repayment. The offender beat or kicked an eye of the victim out of its socket. He told the judge that he didn't consider such treatment of "Chinamen" to be a crime.

Reporters maintained respect when describing the Chinese procession to their graveyard that was next to the city corral overlooking San Vincente arroyo. Similarly, when the Chinese Masonic Lodge buried members, a newspaper gave dignified comment on the funeral and its attendees.

But more typical was *Southwest Sentinel's* blurb about Chinese truck farmers who rented fields adjacent to the town: "The heathen Chinese are crowding the market in Silver City with vegetables." (*Southwest Sentinel*, May 26, 1883)

Uhli Block, completed in 1897 on the southwest corner of Broadway and Texas. Steven Uhli standing in front of his Cave Saloon and two men stand in front of McMillen Meat Market. Man identfied as Mr. Brent stands to the far left. Source: Silver City Museum

Or consider the report by *The Eagle* on Lew Sam, whom the paper decided was Len Sam. After praising Sam as a naturalized citizen, the editor appended his racial theorizing "Two or three years ago . . . he took unto himself a wife from among the dark-eyed maidens of the native race, and last week he reached the acme of American citizenship when his spouse presented him with a daughter, whose features are of the highest type of beauty of the Andalusian and Mongolian races." *(The Eagle,* January 8, 1896)

Susan Berry has already commented on the Methodists' outreach to Silver City's Chinese residents. The son of a Methodist minister in the early 1890s recalled his mother giving English classes to the young men who worked in Silver City restaurants. They expressed their gratitude by preparing a Chinese meal for her. The dinner featured a whole trout baked with almonds substituting for the fish scales. (Benjamin Elmer Pierce, *Memories of Pierces in Parsonages*) There may be reasons to call our Silver City predecessors foolish, but surely one of the best reasons was their insistence that Chinese-owned restaurants serve only 'good ol' American food.

The list of Chinese-owned businesses is long. Many persons who lived in Silver City from the 1950s recall with great fondness buying their groceries from Lee Do Toy, who gave personalized service.

One of the most remarkable business histories belonged to a remarkable couple—Sue and Mah Foon Lime. Mah Foon, known as Lem, and Sue Lime operated the Manhattan Grill on Bullard and then the Chef Grill on Texas for well over a half century.

Sue's father was one of three brothers who homesteaded in the Mimbres Valley. They moved to Deming to raise vegetables in the Chinese garden. Sue was born in Deming in 1910 and after graduating from New Mexico Teachers' College she married Lem in 1934. They had six children. Lem had started his career in 1918 at the French Kitchen, which he later owned. In 1929, as a precursor to current restaurateurs raising their own produce and meats, Lem was operating Silver City's Chinese gardens. (*Independent*, October 15, 1929) When her father returned to China because he wanted to die where he had been born, Sue assumed responsibility for her siblings. The Lime children recall working in the restaurants when they were growing up. Successful in their careers, they left Silver City but remained in the American West. Lem died in 1977 and Sue in 1995.

Several Western graduates have told me that hungry, impoverished students knew that they could go to Sue's restaurant for a free meal. It was her private scholarship program.

In its history, Silver City has experienced two major events centering on separate ethnic groups. First the Chinese faced the Committee of Ten's effort to remove them from Silver City in 1885 and then the Hispanos demanded equal pay among other demands in the Mine-Mill workers' strike against Empire Zinc in 1950-52. Both events involved labor unions and both, at least indirectly, resulted from political ideologies and business notions circulating in the larger U.S. society.

In 1882, Congress passed the Chinese Exclusion Act, forbidding the immigration of Chinese into the country. Then, in a period of increasing labor turmoil, the Friends of Labor, a populist and largely ineffectual movement, demanded that Chinese and Mexicans be removed from their jobs. In November, 1885, a mass meeting that involved both local judges and doctors but not men on Silver City lists of the most influential or wealthy, resolved the following: "It will be necessary to notify the people of Chinese nationality who had not declared citizenship or who were not owners of real property within a period of 24 hours to leave the city." *(Enterprise,* November 27, 1885) Judge Ginn argued against this vigilantism, but he was shouted down. Except for some random incidents of vandalism, the meeting's demands produced no action.

The 1890s did bring efforts to enforce strict exclusion laws. William Burns, a federal agent, spent several days in town collecting about 100 photographs of Chinese townspeople for "Uncle Sam's portrait gallery," to use the *Enterprise's* attempt at humor. *(Enterprise,* March 23, 1894) *The Independent* in 1902 reported, "Charles Mehan, the Chinese inspector, was in the city yesterday in connection with the Fong Jay case. Mr. Mehan has recently made a big roundup of Chinese along the Mexican border . . ." *(Independent,* February 18, 1902)

The Salt of the Earth Strike, named for the movie about the strike, had longer lasting effects than the xenophobic mass meeting of 1885. The strike widened the splits in Grant County society: Anglo versus Mexicano, anti-Communism versus union solidarity, urban versus rural, ruthless industrialism versus individual workers and their families. The best interpreter of the strike and the movie, Ellen Baker, described an ultimatum that echoed the demands from 67 years earlier: "Events surrounding the film shooting may have occasionally looked like those surrounding the Empire Zinc strike, but vigilantes

48

soon carried the tensions to an even higher pitch. About 70 small businessmen delivered an ultimatum to Jencks and the film crew on March 4: leave town in twelve hours or leave in black boxes." (Ellen R. Baker, p. 228)

Europeans and Syrians

Occasionally, there exist together a place and the people in that place and a time, all perfectly arranged to be a movie. The characters are straight out of John Ford. It could be a buddy movie, Butch and Sundance on steroids. Can you hear a haunting Aaron Copeland tune as the theme? And the place is beyond comparison, spread over a valley beneath hills so situated that no matter from what direction you enter you receive a sensation of sudden beauty, rightness, and an excitement that curiosity creates. Do you see it now, the opening shot as the aerial camera swoops from on high?

The place, of course, is Silver City. The time? 1872 to 1920. And the people, who seem to be just eight deceptively proper businessmen, are all immigrants. The Awesome Eight. They transformed a town in the wilderness.

Here they are: John Brockman. Isaac Cohen. Henry Lesinsky. Stefan Uhli, David Abraham and his two sons Abe and Hyman. Presumably because the valley was empty and a town to be a town needs buildings, all of them were associated with building something. Only Brockman built somewhere else, in Southern California. And Hyman just had a house on Cooper Street if you don't count the number of renovations of his barbershop. But the rest? What a set of accomplishments in Silver City—hotels, theaters, office and store blocks, houses, and rental units.

Thinking about the overwhelming masculine cast, one is tempted to slip in Nellie Montoya Lesinsky Shutz, who was Lesinsky's child by a woman not his wife but who was taken into Lesinsky's family, educated for a time in New York, and then wed to haberdasher and hotelier Max Shutz, about 15 years her senior. Silver City newspapers were almost delirious in describing the Lesinsky-Shutz wedding at the Lesinsky home, followed by a dinner dance at the Exchange Hotel until four thirty in the morning.

Where did the eight come from? To say Las Cruces or El Paso might be correct in the strictest sense, but their lands of origin sometimes registered an emotional importance. Isaac Cohen, for example, was born in Jerusalem and took his young son to visit his birthplace. Lesinsky, Brockman, and Uhli all came from Germany. The Abraham sons were born in England, where their parents had stayed after leaving Poland.

Lesinsky's father died when Lesinsky was in his early teens so that his family sent him to England to learn stone carving. Instead, he persuaded an Anglican charity to pay his way to Australia, for he wanted to explore for gold. All the gold was claimed, forcing Lesinsky to go to California, only to discover that their gold, too, had been spoken for. An uncle invited him to New Mexico. Lesinsky entered into the trading business with his uncle, with whom he constantly disagreed. By getting a government supply contract, Lesinsky made enough money to finance his dream—buying a mine. The mine he bought, however, was a copper mine at Morenci, Arizona. Throughout this entire period, Lesinsky owned a store and other investments in Silver City. His brother Charles was recruited to manage those investments.

Brockman came to Grant County at age 17 and established a cattle ranch on the Mimbres, more or less where the Nan Ranch is today. Brockman planted an orchard, imported the first Angus cattle into New Mexico, and established a store at Mimbres. His nickname was Polled Angus. In the 1880s, Brockman entered the banking business, while keeping both ranch and store. When Ailman's bank went to ruin, Brockman picked up the pieces for pennies on the dollar. He invested his gains in Arizona mining ventures and made millions.

Uhli also came to Silver City as a teen and apprenticed in a butcher shop. He saw that the most profitable concerns in Silver City were saloons, and he soon entered that business. Always competitive, bar ownership had a rapid turnover. Uhli was soon planning to construct his own handsome building on Broadway for permanent quarters of his bar. A civic leader and an active member of the Silver City town council, Uhli died

50

of an aneurysm at age 39. His widow, a Canadian, and their small child remained in Silver City.

David Abraham (1824-94), whose Polish name was Dobrzinsky, arrived in Silver City to build the first major brick building on Bullard and Spring, to enter the hotel business with the Southern Hotel, to concoct ventures like selling ice, and to insist that Silver City had to plant street trees. He had five sons and three daughters. He was survived by his second wife.

Hyman Abraham, perhaps the least venturous of the Abrahams, was a barber, often offering cowboys coming off the range the best hot bath and close shave in Silver City. Later in life, he became a probate judge.

Abe Abraham, perhaps the most dramatic of the Abrahams, led the symphonic society, sang opera, and played a major role in "The Pirates of Penzance." At times, Abe was in the confectionery business. He had a go at the Centennial Bar. He opened the Princess Theatre, arranging for a house band to accompany the silent films. He reconstituted hotels.

The Abrahams were the only members of the eight to remain in Silver City, although the hotel business in Clifton, Arizona, tempted Abe away. Lesinsky retreated to an executive position and a Park Avenue address. Cohen announced that his children needed a better education, so he, too, assumed a company post in New York. Brockman bought many city blocks in what would become downtown Los Angeles, where he retired.

We have come to the end of this account but not of our subject. Maybe a book rather than a paper would permit an approach to completion, that ever-receding goal. This presentation has attempted to expand the definition of who it was who made this place, this City of Silver. Somebodies *were* in nowhere, though like that charcoal burner, their names and contributions often remain unknown, while a Florida millionaire, in Silver City for a day or two, receives all the attention.

We learned along the way that while Mexican immigrants comprised the overwhelming proportion of the town's populace, so much so that Spanish surely must have been the lingua franca in 1880, the Hispano left a relatively dim mark on the traditional historical record. With some energy and attention and cooperation, that dimness may be made boldly luminescent. Persons who have a deep interest in that story, persons like Patricia Cano, who revived the Grant County Hispano music scene of the last century, and Alicia Edwards, who photographed the women of the Salt of the Earth Strike, can give life and faces to a complete story for our slice of nowhere.

BIBLIOGRAPHY

Anaya, Rudolfo A. *Bless Me, Ultima.* Berkeley, CA: Quinto Sol Publications, 1972.

Baker, Ellen R. *On Strike and on Film: Mexican American Families and Blacklisted Filmmakers in Cold War America.* Chapel Hill, NC: The University of North Carolina Press, 2007.

Berry, Susan and Russell, Sharman Apt. *Built to Last: An Architectural History of Silver City, New Mexico (Revised Second Edition).* Silver City, New Mexico: Silver City Museum Society, 1995.

Calkins, Helen M., compiler. *History of the Public Schools of Silver City (New Mexico).* Silver City, New Mexico: unknown publisher, 1929[?].

Calvin, Ross, editor. *Lieutenant Emory Reports: Notes of a Military Reconnaissance.* Albuquerque: The University of New Mexico Press, 1951

River of the Sun: Stories of the Storied Gila. Albuquerque: The University of New Mexico Press, 1946

Sky Determines: An Interpretation of the Southwest. Albuquerque: The University of New Mexico Press, 1965.

Chavez, John R. *The Lost Land: The Chicano Image of the Southwest.* Albuquerque: The University of New Mexico Press, 1984.

Davis, Carolyn O'Bagy and Humble, Terrence M. *Silver City: Image of America.* Charleston, South Carolina: Arcadia Publishing, 2013.

Fox, Stephen. "Jaime Crow in New Mexico: Mexicans and Whites in Grant County since 1870," *New Mexico Historical Review,* 94:2, Spring 2019, pp. 123-43.

Hornung, Chuck. *Cipriano Baca, Frontier Lawman of New Mexico.* Jefferson, North Carolina: McFarland and Company, Inc., 2013.

Huggard, Christopher J. and Humble, Terrence M. *Santa Rita del Cobre:*

A Copper Mining Community in New Mexico. Boulder, CO: University Press of Colorado, 2012.

Josephson, Matthew. *The Robber Barons.* New York: Harcourt-Brace Jovanovich, 1962.

Kolko, Gabriel. *The Triumph of Conservatism: A Reinterpretation of American History, 1900-1916.* Chicago: Quadrangle Books, 1963.

Naegle, Conrad Keeler. "The History of Silver City, New Mexico, 1870-1886," University of New Mexico: a master of the arts thesis, 1943.

Pierce, Benjamin Elmer. *Memories of Pierces in Parsonages.* Privately printed, n.d.

Ravenstein, Ernst Georg. "The Laws of Migration," *Journal of the Statistical Society of London,* Vol. 48, No. 2, June 1885, pp. 167-235.

Russell, Sharman Apt. *Songs of the Fluteplayer: Seasons of Life in the Southwest.* New York: Addison Wesley Publishing Company, 1991.

Sanchez, George I. *Forgotten People: A Study of New Mexicans.* Albuquerque: The University of New Mexico Press, 1949.

Tobias, Henry J. *A History of the Jews in New Mexico.* Albuquerque: The University of New Mexico Press, 1990.

Unknown. *First United Methodist Church Centennial, 1873-1973.* Silver City: privately printed, 1973.

Woman's Club of Silver City. *Council Fires,* 1913.

Newspapers
The Eagle
The Grant County Herald
Mining Life
The Silver City Enterprise
The Southwest Sentinel
The Independent

Additional Reading

Berry, Susan and Sharman Apt Russell. *Built to Last: An Architectural History of Silver City, New Mexico.* Silver City, NM: Silver City Museum Society, (second ed.) 1995.

Lundwall, Helen J., ed. *Pioneering in Territorial New Mexico: The Memoirs of H. B. Ailman.* Silver City, NM: Silver City Museum Society, 2008. (Originally published in 1983 with the title *Pioneering in Territorial Silver City* by the University of New Mexico Press in conjunction with the Historical Society of New Mexico)

Lewis, Nancy Owen. *Chasing the Cure in New Mexico: Tuberculosis and the Quest for Health.* Santa Fe: Museum of New Mexico Press, 2016.

Miller, Darlis A. *The California Column in New Mexico.* Albuquerque: University of New Mexico in cooperation with the Historical Society of New Mexico, 1982.

Naegle, Conrad Keeler. "The History of Silver City, New Mexico: 1870-1886." Thesis, University of New Mexico, 1943.

Poole, Joy and Mike Olsen. "Enos and Jennie Culver Memoir, Travel Diary and Correspondence while Traveling the Santa Fe Trail and El Camino Real, 1869-1871." https://www.nps.gov/safe/learn/historyculture/trailwide-research.htm. (Santa Fe: National Park Service, nd)

Tom Hester trained as a sociologist and historian. He followed a career as a social statistician and editor. He has been a volunteer researcher in the history of Silver City and southwestern New Mexico, serving both the Silver City Museum and the Silver City Public Library.

CHAPTER 3:

Chihuahua Hill: Silver City's First Neighborhood

By Javier Marrufo

Since the beginning, the history of Chihuahua Hill acted as a backdrop for the town of Silver City. The neighborhood sits at the southern end of the town, creating a natural barrier between the gentle hills of Silver City and a vast expanse of Chihuahuan Desert. La Capilla, a small chapel overlooking the neighborhood, is visible from nearly every part of Silver City, creating a literal backdrop for the town. Chihuahua Hill's history spans the entire 154 years of Silver City, and possibly longer. Many identify the neighborhood as an extension of the community of San Vicente, a spiritual predecessor of Silver City settled by Spanish or Mexican herders, miners, and farmers in the decades prior to the town's American founding. In this sense, Chihuahua Hill serves as a through line connecting an American mining community to earlier periods of Hispanic settlement in New Mexico.

Following the official founding of Silver City, Chihuahua Hill was known as the Mexican neighborhood of the booming mining community. Nearly all its residents were of Mexican descent, either being from the area prior to the discovery of silver in the nearby hills or arriving after in the flood of immigrants converging on the mineral rich region. Throughout the 19th century, the neighborhood remained physically, culturally, and economically separate from the rest of Silver City. Over the next 100 years, the residents of Chihuahua Hill contended with the realities of a Mexican American holdout in an Anglo-American power structure. In the first half of the 20th century, racism, discrimination, and the push for cultural assimilation reached their highest peaks before giving way to waves of activism urging for equality, representation, and higher standards of living, education, and occupations.

In its time, the Chihuahua Hill has evolved from scattered collections of stone and adobe homes built on a desolate rocky hill, to the dense and lush modern neighborhood it is today. It is no longer the Mexican quarter of town. The stables, bars, shops, and restaurants that once operated on the rocky hill have all closed, leaving the neighborhood almost strictly residential. Although Chihuahua Hill has evolved over the past century and a half, it retains much of its original character. Unfortunately, written history usually minimizes the importance of the neighborhood, instead focusing on Silver City as the so called "first Anglo settlement" in New Mexico. This sentiment has historical roots, as primary documents from the era of Silver City's founding were mostly written by the droves of Anglo immigrants arriving to the mining camp. Most failed to document the history of the town's Mexican American population, people whose expertise and labor contributed to the development and success of Silver City for the past 150 years. The exclusion of this community has persisted for much of the neighborhood's history and, as a result, the story of Chihuahua Hill has remained largely untold. The Chihuahua Hill History Project, started in 2021, serves to address this issue, and to uncover those stories that would otherwise be lost to time.

San Vicente de la Cienega

Many oral histories identify Chihuahua Hill as an extension of the earlier community of San Vicente. "The beginnings of Silver City was at La Cienega de San Vicente. It was very sparce back then, and what happened is when they were working the copper . . . Eventually, when they found silver there was even more white people that moved to Silver City, and that's when they changed it from San Vicente to Silver City."[21] According to folk history, the

---

21   Marrufo, Javier, and David Duarte. scm_ch20210803_Duarte Family Oral History. Other. Silver City Museum, n.d.

community originates before the foundation of the American settlement of Silver City in 1870. To this day, not much is known about La Cienega de San Vicente other than what exists in a few written documents, and a handful of oral histories hint at the scope of that community.

The area that became Silver City was first designated San Vicente in the Spanish period of New Mexico when in 1805 it was named on a hand-drawn map made by Ensign Juan Pedro Walker from the Presidio at Janos, Mexico. Made at the command of Comandante General Nemesio Salcedo y Salcedo, the map shows the region surrounding the copper mines at Santa Rita, Nuevo Mexico.[22] The map shows a trail passing through San Vicente to nearby Santa Lucia, present day Mangas Valley, meaning the area must have held some importance to the Spanish since 1805. At that time, the entire surrounding region remained the territory of the semi-nomadic Apache, who used the San Vicente area as a seasonal campsite.[23] In the 1790s, the Spanish entered a tenuous peace with local Apache groups after adopting a policy of pacification rather than outright extermination.[24] From that point onward, Spanish, and later Mexican miners, ranchers, and farmers, remained in the vicinity, utilizing the surrounding country to water and feed the livestock that supported the growing Santa Rita Mines, which operated until 1837. While San Vicente was most likely utilized in this way during this period, it is unlikely it existed as a built community. This serves as the first outside use of the area known as San Vicente.

The area drops out of the historical records until the 1850s when sources detail use and possible settling of La Cienega de San Vicente. Hank Smith, who passed through the area in the 1860s with his father, commented, "La Cienega de San Vicente was a favorite camping place for

---

22   Walker, Juan Pedro. Map. *"Mapa Geografico, Que comprehende los Terrenos de las P de I, Coahuala, Nueva Biscaya y NM, que de orden del Sor comte Gral de Todas las ynternas de N España, Don N. Salcedo y Salcedo, ha reconocido el Alferez de la Co. Presidial de Janos, 1805."* Map Collection, University of Texas El Paso

23   Marrufo, Javier, and Bill Bradford. scm_ch20220603_Bradford_Bill. Other, 2022.

24   Griffen, William B. "The Compas: A Chiricahua Apache Family of the Late 18th and Early 19th Centuries." American Indian Quarterly 7, no. 2 (1983): 21. https://doi.org/10.2307/1184685.

both Mexicans and Indians, before the 'white man' dreamed of such a valley at the foot of the slope from Pinos Altos"[25] Smith describes Mexican herders running about 4,000 sheep and goats to supply food to nearby Pinos Altos which was settled by Americans in 1860, demonstrating that the area known as San Vicente was used by Mexican settlers in the decade leading up to the founding of Silver City.

In 1924, Catholic historian Reverend F. Stanley described San Vicente as, "a summer adobe settlement for wood cutters, sheep herders and Indian traders."[26] With "a chapel mostly for the use of the Hermanos de la morada de Nuestro Padre J. Nazareno"[27] Stanley gives names of the families he credits with originally settling San Vicente. He lists Juan Antonio Garcia with 14 servants; Jose Barrios and two brothers; Patricio Lucero; Miguel de Herrera and two friends; Simone Talamonte; Don Ramon Garcia and two brothers; Antonio Provencio; Mateo Telles; Vincente Quaron; Matias Valencia; Jose Garcia and one servant who settled the Doña Ana country. From this colony principally came the people who were to settle San Vicente."[28] Stanley ends by directly stating that San Vicente became the neighborhood of Chihuahua Hill. While this source seems like a golden documentation of the community of San Vicente, the document the author sourced information from pertains to a small strip of land in what became Doña Ana County called El Bracito, so it remains unclear how it relates to San Vicente.[29] However, oral histories conducted in 2022 contain multiple mentions of a Jose Barrios, an old man living in Silver City in the 1930s, who claimed to be a founding father of San Vicente in the 19th century.[30]

---

25   Alexander, Bob. *Six-Guns and Single-Jacks: A History of Silver City and Southwest New Mexico*. Silver City, NM: Gila Books, 2005. 44

26   Stanley, F. "Historian Outlines Local History At Centennial." Essay. In *The Centennial Anniversary of the Foundation of the Parish of St. Vincent de Paul 1874-1974*, n.d. 2

27   Ibid.

28   Ibid.

29   "New Mexico, U.S., Land Records of New Spain, 1692-1916." Reports 4-6, n.d.

30   Gomez, Greg, and Javier Marrufo. Chihuahua Hill History Project: Greg Gomez Oral History. Personal, 2022

Two oral histories from the Civilian Conservation Corps WPA oral history project in 1937 provide further information, fleshing out the extents of settlement in San Vicente. Informant Jose Morales stated, "San Vicente was settled in 1858 by the Ne Poseno family, and followers. Their purpose was to build a place of worship. They built La Capilla which was burned in 1910. Mother Abel Acerio was the leader of the church . . . The church was finished in 1890, but Father Lamy, the bishop from Santa Fe, would not bless the church . . . Arthur Joseph Ancheta, early native district attorney for the Territory of New Mexico, worshipped in this church."[31] Ne Ponseno is most likely a corruption of the first name Nepomuceno. A likely candidate for this unknown settler could be Nepomuceno Ancheta, who helped develop early Pinos Altos and San Lorenzo. According to census records, Ancheta came to the United States in 1858, most likely fleeing the violence during the War of the Reform in Mexico.[32] In further corroboration, Ancheta's son, Jose Arturo Ancheta, served as a district attorney for the Territory of New Mexico and died in Silver City. Details about Jean-Baptiste Lamy muddy the details as his last year serving as bishop was 1885 before dying in 1888.[33] This does not necessarily disprove the informant, who gives no indication when construction began, or when the bishop refused its consecration. Although, folk history of the Capilla suggests it was a local priest who refused to consecrate the chapel rather than a bishop.

The idea of San Vicente being a place of worship is once again repeated in the recollections of Richard Clark who came to Grant County with the United States Army in 1870. Arriving in Fort Bayard on November 19, 1870, Clark recalls, "There wasn't a Silver City at this time, only San Vicente . . . John Bullard, Tom Bullard, Joe Yankee, John Switcelm [*sic*], and Dick

---

31   Morales, Jose, and W. C. Totty. Place Name: San Vicente. Other. *Fray Angélico Chávez History Library's WPA New Mexico Collection*, October 20, 1937.

32   US Census Bureau, 1900 US Census, San Lorenzo§ (n.d.). https://www.ancestry.com/imageviewer/collections/7602/images/4120504_00671?pId=21414279.

33   February 13, 1888 - Roman Catholic Diocese of Dodge City. Accessed November 21, 2023. https://www.dcdiocese.org/images/necrology/LamyJeanBaptiste2-13-1888.pdf.

Amos lived at Ralston, now Shakespeare."[34] This sentence in and of itself does not help identify if San Vicente existed as a settlement or placename. Luckily, Clark clarifies in his closing statement of the interview. "I am 69 years old and have seen Silver City from San Vicente a place to worship to its present city."[35] Once again, San Vicente is identified first as a place of worship before turning into the mining hub of Silver City. Unfortunately, the interviewer did not follow up on this piece of information.

A final piece of corroborating evidence in this vein comes from the first official survey of the town of Silver City, conducted in 1873. According to the field notes of surveyor Robert M. Kidder, the survey started on Boston hill, moved eastward and up Chihuahua Hill, known then to the locals as *El Cerro de la Cruz*, The Hill of the Cross.[36] This adds further credence to the idea that San Vicente existed before Silver City not only as a placename for the area, but as some sort of semi-settled/religious site.

While the extents of La Cienega de San Vicente remain unclear, oral traditions help corroborate sources throughout history. Families, living on Chihuahua Hill, tell stories of ancestors settling San Vicente. "Urbano Bermudez and his brother Bruno came to San Vicente, Mexican Territory (Silver City, New Mexico) with Spanish explorers in the early 1800s. . . . At the time, all that was present in the area around San Vicente were mines and a few ranches. There were not to be any Yankee's in this area for another 40 years . . . Urbano proceeded to homestead a large area of land on Chihuahua Hill in what was then southwest San Vicente."[37] Evidence found in Silver City during the 1870s gives credence to this story. In 1872, an old mining shaft and tunnel were discovered in the Chloride District of Silver City containing silver ore. The shaft and tunnel reportedly extends

---

34   Clark, Richard, and Frances Totty. Silver City from 1870. Other. *Fray Angélico Chávez History Library's WPA New Mexico Collection*, October 9, 1937.

35   Ibid.

36   Kidder, Robert M. "Townsite Survey, Silver City, New Mexico." General Land Office Records. Accessed 2024. https://glorecords.blm.gov/details/survey/default. aspx?dm_id=119577&sid=yy5pdhsc.nxi.

37   Marrufo de Melendres, Cecilia. "The Marrufo y Melendres Family History." Silver City, New Mexico, 1

Chihuahua Hill c. 1890s. looking southwest. A freighting wagon sits beside a newer adobe home behind the wooden structure. Stone Jacales can be seen in the background. Source: Silver City Museum

downward to an unknown depth.[38] In 1902, a small Spanish adobe smelter was uncovered in main street Silver City just north of the Timmer House. "The general opinion seems to be that it really is the remains of an ancient Spanish smelter, used to treat the Santa Rita copper ores. Evidence of the ancient smelter at Fierro and the fort at Santa Rita are still plainly visible, and Mr. Brent's discovery is probably contemporaneous with them . . ."[39] The timeframe for being contemporary to Spanish operations in Santa Rita is 1800-1821, and 1821-1837 for the Mexican period of the mine. A second smelter was found six years later, the local newspaper detailed, "The parish addition in the western portion of the city is the site of an old smelter . . . a lot of slag was found and besides this evidence the existence of a smelter, upward of 50 or 100 pounds of copper and lead silver bullion was noted. Diligent inquiry among the old settlers has failed to elicit any

---

38   "Discovery of an Old Shaft and Tunnel at Silver City." Borderer. September 21, 1872.

39   "Walls of Furnace." *Silver City Enterprise*, September 19, 1902.

61

information regarding the smelter and the conclusion arrived at from the information at hand is that the find is pre-historic, and evidence that long before the Cienega El San Vicente was settled, this immediate neighborhood was the scene of active mining and smelting operations."[40]

The history of La Cienega de San Vicente is important because it addresses the viewpoint that negates the events and the people who lived prior to the foundation of Silver City. Regardless of the veracity of previous settlement in La Cienega de San Vicente, a Hispanic origin cannot be denied. In the typical founding story of Silver City, Andrew Hurlbert was the first to build a cabin at San Vicente with his "Spanish-American wife" and nine-year-old daughter. They were followed by the Bullard brothers, James McGee, William Milby, John Swisshelm, and Joseph Yankie.[41] In March of 1869, Hurlbert's Hispanic wife was killed by Apache while he escaped to Pinos Altos, nine miles north. Hurlbert's wife, a Mexican woman who remains unnamed to history, deserves just as much credit as her husband who is now remembered as the first to settle San Vicente while she remains little more than a mutilated illustration of the realities of frontier life. Her story is a perfect encapsulation of the role that Hispanic people would come to fill in the succeeding era. They are the people around, extras to populate the stage, but rarely at the center.

Chihuahua Hill in the 19th Century.
Whatever the extents of San Vicente, silver was discovered in the nearby hills in 1870, leading to the foundation of the American town of Silver City. Here, the hill to the south formerly known as El Cerro de la Cruz became Chihuahua Hill. There are few sources that mention Chihuahua Hill in the initial years of Silver City. By the mid-1870s, the neighborhood had solidified itself as the Mexican neighborhood of a booming town. While the 1870 census counts only 80 residents of Silver City, just three

---

40   "Ruins of Old Spanish Smelter Discovered." *Silver City Independent*, March 3, 1908.

41   Naegle, Conrad Keeler. "The History of Silver City, New Mexico 1870-1886," 1943.

62

years later, a local newspaper detailed a population of 350 American inhabitants and 700 Mexicans.[42] These numbers are merely estimates, and it was known at the time that the population of Mexican neighborhoods was probably greater than reported. "It is impossible to give the number of people resident in the territory. The census of 1870 is reliable as far as it goes, but it was necessarily imperfect. In many parts, the canvassers were supposed to be unfriendly conspirators against the inhabitants, Indian and Mexican, and were avoided or purposefully misinformed."[43] Many Mexicans arriving with this flood of immigrants settled around Chihuahua Hill.

The densely packed neighborhood swelled throughout the 1870s and '80s. Some of the earliest pictures of Silver City clearly display the growing differences between Chihuahua Hill and the rest of Silver City. Houses of Silver City were brick or wood framed. Painted picket fences outlined family yards, and sidewalks lined well-defined streets. In contrast, Chihuahua Hill's houses sprawled about the rocky hillside, built upward wherever the ground allowed with whatever materials were available. Many were built in the style of a Jacal, an Indigenous Mexican style hut with rock walls, dirt floor, and wooden vigas holding a roof. Extended or multiple families often lived in a single home. Although many were involved in mining operations around Silver City, more worked as freighters, servants, general laborers. Others filled roles including adobe maker, silversmiths, or gamblers. Photos of the era display the reality of two separate Silver Cities, one built by those who became the authorities of the place hailed as the "first Anglo town in New Mexico," and another built by those whose unrecognized labor and expertise contributed to the success of the town.[44]

Little information about this population of Chihuahua Hill made its way into historical record. Throughout the 19th century, some of the only

42 "Grant County, Its Resources and Future Prospects." *Mining Life.* June 15, 1873.
43 Wallace, Lew, University of Oklahoma College of Law Digital Commons § (n.d.). https://digitalcommons.law.ou.edu/cgi/viewcontent.cgi?article=6693&context=indianserialset. 452
44 *Silver City Enterprise*, November 16, 1882.

people of Mexican descent from Chihuahua Hill named in local sources were the Carrascos, hailing from an important mining family. "Juan N. Carrasco's smelter was near the creek at the lower end of Bullard Street. He operated several small adobe furnaces with blast supplied by blacksmith bellows. Up to May 1873, it was estimated that Carrasco had treated some three hundred tons of ore and produced about $200,000 in bullion."[45] The family is now remembered as smelting the first silver bullion to come out of the mining camp of Silver City. The Carrasco family, like many others who settled in Chihuahua Hill, came from Chihuahua during the mass immigration of the 1870s. The family's patriarch, Lorenzo Carrasco, was admired by his contemporaries and one of the few Mexican people to make an impact on area politics. "Mr. Carrasco, who had the right kind of ore and understood the business, having been successful in Chihuahua, Mexico. His success at smelting was largely responsible for giving this section of the country a favorable reputation."[46] Although the Carrasco family remains an important factor in the development of early Silver City, their experience was the exception rather than the rule.

By 1880, Silver City's population ballooned to 1,768 with 1,030 being of Mexican descent. Of that number, 351 were born in New Mexico, with the remainder immigrating from Mexico, mostly from the state of Chihuahua.[47] This is most likely where the neighborhood gained its name. With the exception of those few citizens such as Lorenzo Carrasco, the residents of Chihuahua Hill were largely invisible to 19th century mainstream sources. The first use of the name Chihuahua applied to the neighborhood came in an 1875 newspaper article, saying, "We learn of another case of smallpox in "Chihuahua." Our citizens should be careful in their peregrinations of that burg."[48] Although limited, this is prime example of the extent that Chihuahua Hill entered the historical record in that period. Any

---

45   "Locals." *Mining Life*. March 17, 1873.

46   Ailman, H. B. *Pioneering In Territorial Silver City. H.B. Ailman's Recollections of Silver City and the Southwest, 1871-1892*. Edited by Helen J. Lundwall. Albuquerque, New Mexico: University of New Mexico Press, 1983.

47   1880 Census, Territory of New Mexico, Silver City § (n.d.).

48   *Grant County Herald*. December 5, 1875.

documentation was terse, and usually relegated to a few sentences in the margins. Since the population of Chihuahua Hill was overlooked during this time and coupled with the largely illiterate population arriving from Porfirian era Mexico, little documentation regarding the social history of the people living in Chihuahua Hill was created. While census records can tell names, ages, and occupations, they tell nothing of the social interactions, individual experiences, or relationships among Chihuahua Hill residents. The Chihuahua Hill History Project has uncovered stories of those living in those times, filling the empty streets and houses of historic photos with life and stories, and giving us a glimpse of the work, culture, and lives of the neighborhood's earliest residents. Instead of providing a history devoid of human perspective, the project allows us to demonstrate how history affects people and how they affect history.

Perception, Discrimination, and Social Circumstance.
To understand the history of Chihuahua Hill, it is imperative to understand the historical outlooks surrounding people of Mexican descent in Grant County. An important theme that emerged early in Anglo-produced sources is the insistence to view Silver City's population as binary, either Mexican or American, meaning white. Although census records record the race of every Mexican as white, they were still singled out in local sources such as newspapers or personal correspondence. Meanwhile, nationality did not matter when applied to white citizens who were simply addressed as American rather than the multitude of countries they originated from. This conflicting documentation introduces a principal concept of the history of Chihuahua Hill. People of Mexican descent were legally white, but socially "other." Legally, they were subject and eligible to the same laws and rights as all other Americans. In reality, barriers were constructed around them based on origins, ethnicity, language, or willingness to conform to American values.

One of the greatest sources of primary information from Silver City in the late 19th century are the many newspapers of the era. These sources were invariably created by new coming Americans eager to promote

Anglo hegemony over the mineral rich region. One of the most pervasive trends in 19th century sources is a negative representation of the Mexican population, as first evidenced by a series of articles detailing Grant County to prospective American immigrants. The author, F. Sturenburg, reassures the audience of the intentions of the article by saying, "we do not flatter ourselves of being able to produce a very elaborate and interesting narrative, but our readers may rely upon being told the truth, and nothing but the truth, unbiassed by individual considerations."[49] From Sturenburg's articles emerge the first documented appearances of anti-Mexican rhetoric which helped solidify a perception that lingered into the 20th century. Strictly regarding the Mexican population of Grant County, Sturenburg writes, "Our southern sister republic unfortunately is far behind as regards progress and civilization. Lawless strife and still more the powerful labors of the priesthood, supposed to the diffusion of knowledge and enlightenment, have retarded, heretofore, the advancement of the moral condition of the area and of her citizens. Furthermore, the injurious institution of peonage, almost synonymous with slavery, keeps the lower classes of the people in servitude and dependence and renders impossible moral amelioration. Thus barilly [*sic*] any of the Christian virtues are known to them; superstition and bigotry keep sway over their conscience."[50] The Mexico Sturenburg describes existed in the tumultuous era of the Second French Intervention of Mexico, the War of Reform, and the outset of the authoritarian rule of dictator Porfirio Diaz. The author applies a generalized view of moral inferiority, ignorance, and general backwardness to not only the Mexicans of Grant County, but upon the entire nation of Mexico. He continues by consigning the population to its perceived place in Grant County's social structure.

... being treated in their native country scarcely better than

---

49   Sturenburg, F. "Grant County, N.M. Its Resources and Future Prospects." *Silver City Mining Life*, June 7, 1873.

50   Ibid.

66

beasts and depriving most miserable remuneration from their hard labor, *they at once give to that great desideration in mining communities cheap labor and enable us to develop our mineral resources at comparatively little cost.* This actual advantage, however, does not meet with general appreciation as the American laborer finds it difficult to compete with this cheap labor, but no matter, whether personal interest is opposed to or not, is certainly a well-established principle of political economy, and California has proved beyond a doubt the great benefit resulting to the community at large from the introduction of *cheap labor.*[51]

This sentiment, especially when taken with the previous point of moral inferiority, reveals the true intention of his words. Mexicans are useful in that they were cheap, ignorant, labor. For economic reasons, they were viewed as more valuable to emerging settlements than American labor, and so necessary to the development of the region. The statement about California indicates that this was a prevailing sentiment throughout the West, and one that painted most interactions and experiences between Anglo and Mexican people in Grant County. Dispelling any doubt or vagueness in his words, the author published a redaction a week later, most likely after public outcry for the articles which labeled people of Mexican descent a "degraded race."[52] "We have resided for some time in the Mexican Republic, and can assure our readers, that there is just as much education and high learning to be found in that country as anywhere else . . . *But heretofore, only the lowest element of that people have come into general contact with our population,* and from that reason the generally incorrect ideas in regard to these people have found their way to the public. *An increase of immigration of Mexican families belonging to the better class would*

---

51   Ibid.

52   Ibid.

Closeup of a Chihuahua Hill family in front of their home c.1890s. Few pictures of Chihuahua Hill residents exist from this time. None in the picture are identified. Source: Silver City Museum

be very desirable to our community . . ."[53] The author confirms that there exists a negative view of Mexicans, but only because those in Grant County constituted the lowest of the low, demonstrating that from the beginning, Mexican families, many of whom settled on Chihuahua Hill, were decried as inferior to the incoming American masses. The comments made by the journalist were simply the opening salvo in the creation of a mythology of the Mexican population of Silver City that was continuously reinforced through representation, policies, and actions. Local newspapers throughout the remainder of the 19th century and early 20th century either represent people of Mexican descent through negative depictions, or simply exclude them. Imposed social perceptions bled into the experiences of the residents of Chihuahua Hill, within all aspects of their

---

53   "Grant County, N.M. Its Resources and Future Prospects." *Silver City Mining Life*, June 12, 1873.

68

history. In turn, those realities were used as justification for the actions made at the expense of the Chihuahua Hills Mexican American population. From this point onward, the community of Chihuahua Hill contended with overarching systems of poverty, discrimination, and assimilation. They confronted these issues by relying on a strong sense of community, a continual emphasis on education, and organized mutual aid.

Poverty, Standards of Living, and Opportunity
Echoing the sentiments described by the series of articles written in 1873, the term "Mexican" quickly became synonymous with laborer.[54] Evidence of this is found in era newspapers where businesses regularly advertised the need for Mexican workers specifically. "Wanted, a number of Mexicans to work in the Pinos Altos gold mines, contracts given or work. -J.S. Johnson"[55] The 1880 Silver City census shows people with Spanish surnames working in a labor market with half as much opportunity as their Anglo counterparts.[56] From the 101 different job titles listed on the census, only 50 were occupied by people of Mexican descent. The majority of these 50 jobs were unskilled labor such as carbon making, day laborer, freighting, mining, wood cutting, or servants. Conversely, Anglo citizens occupied the total breadth of jobs available, unskilled or skilled positions. They did, however, occupy unskilled labor positions in lower numbers than their Mexican counterparts. Meanwhile, highly lucrative positions such as assayers, attorneys, engineers, law enforcement, physicians, or teachers were solely occupied by Anglos. Divisions are intensified with the fact that people of Mexican descent provided just over half of the labor needs for Silver City, and overall worked at both younger and older ages than their Anglo counterparts. Every child working in Silver City under the age of 15 was of Mexican descent. The youngest, Monica de la Cruz, was only five years old. In a poignant detail gleaned from the data, both

---

54 Sturenburg, F. "Grant County, N.M. Its Resources and Future Prospects." *Silver City Mining Life*, June 7, 1873.

55 "Locals." *Mining Life*. October 31, 1874.

56 1880 Census, Territory of New Mexico, Silver City § (n.d.).

69

youngest and oldest workers included in the census, 5-year-old Monica de la Cruz and 75-year-old Rosa Lopez, worked as servants. The occupations that employed the most in Chihuahua Hill were freighting with 72, mining with 64, servants with 45, and day laborers with 37. [57]

The general trend of residents of Chihuahua Hill working in lower job positions, and thus having lower standards of living, remained long enough to be remembered by the eldest participants of the Chihuahua Hill History Project. The single greatest through line between separate experiences on Chihuahua Hill in the 20th century is poverty. This theme was relayed by the very first participant of the project, within the first minute of the first interview. "I was born and raised on south Bayard Street. It was the poor area of the town . . . Everybody was poor."[58] Throughout the first half of the 20th century, standards of living in Chihuahua Hill remained similar to the 19th century. While Mexican Americans slowly integrated into more occupations, a vast majority remained confined to lesser unskilled positions. "After high school, I got a summer job with Kennecott . . . I first worked in the track, spiking rails in the track, which is where Hispanics always worked . . . while the white people were placed in helpful jobs, helping electricians, helping carpenters. Other occupations which were not as menial as the railroad."[59]

In a parallel experience to the job market, the physical environment of Chihuahua Hill in the 20th century, especially in its differences with the rest of Silver City, echoed the preceding century. As Silver City grew and advanced with modern buildings, electric lights, paved roads, and sewers, Chihuahua Hill lagged behind with rough dirt roads free of streetlights and outhouses instead of indoor plumbing. "At the time I was there, it was poor housing, poor everything. That's what it was . . . very poorly. No water inside. Faucets outside. Dirt floors. We did have wood, *carbon* that

---

57   Ibid.

58   Marrufo, Javier, and Maria Arellano. scm_ch20210711_Maria Arellano. Silver City Museum, 2021.

59   Marrufo, Javier, and Rudy Dominguez. Rudy Dominguez of Mimbres, New Mexico Oral History. Silver City Museum, 2021.

we used to have to go down and scrounge, down at the depot."[60] By the mid-20th century, new houses on Chihuahua Hill were built in modern styles but remained modest, indicative of the working-class neighborhood. Others became extensions of the original adobe structures of the 19th century. Homes often grew with the family; all the work being done by hand. "My dad decided to build a house there, close to grandma's. He started digging out a basement. And from that basement, he made the adobes . . . Finally, he built a two-bedroom house . . . But my dad worked on it until it was about 11 rooms."[61]

The inequality of improvements to the neighborhood compared to the rest of Silver City was one of the greatest issues for Chihuahua Hill in the 20th century. The neighborhood remained without paved roads or a sewer system well into the 1960s and '70s. Through nearly a century of neglect, many cited the historic discrimination faced by the neighborhood as the root cause of these inequalities. "Silver City never cared very much for Chihuahua Hill anyway . . . w had to fight about everything . . . I don't guess Hispanics never mattered much to them. That's the difference."[62]

The fight for basic standards of living was long. Throughout the 1960s and '70s, Greg Mesa, Chihuahua Hill resident, radio broadcaster, and funder of Spanish language newspaper *El Reportero* regularly appeared before the town council to advocate for "Chicano districts" of Silver City, meaning Chihuahua Hill and Perros Bravos, or Brewer Hill. In 1975, Greg Mesa leveled charges of discrimination against the town of Silver City in an open letter to State Senator Joseph Montoya. Mesa wrote that the town "refused to install sewer services to Chicano areas that have been in the city limits for over a hundred years" before concluding to the local press "I refuse to accept it that the city can't make improvements, I accept only that they won't. These kids here deserve a chance. They are now condemned

---

60   Marrufo, Javier, and Steve Aguirre. scm_ch20211008_Aguirre_Steve. Silver City Museum, 2021.

61   Marrufo, Javier, and Billy Maldonado. scm_ch20220421_Arroyo_Reynaldo_Maldonado_Billy. Silver City Museum, 2022.

62   Marrufo, Javier, and Margarita Asevedo. scm_ch20220329_Asevedo_Margarita. *Silver City Museum*, 2022.

not to poverty but to being second class citizens."[63] Another resident, Consuelo Muñoz, remembers meeting with the mayor of Silver City in the 1960s to ask that actions be taken to bring both paved roads and a sewer system to the neighborhood. "There was a mayor named Lowell Cane . . . I went to a meeting with him and he said we cannot dig for your plumbing where you live. And I said, 'You can't dig? Tell me where you're going to put it and I'll dig it myself.' He said, 'No, sorry.' And this and that. But when they decided to do it, we were getting these giant bills. They left a big [mess] there and they didn't fix it or nothing. My husband had to fix it."[64] The work of community advocates brought incremental change. Modern amenities of paved streets, plumbing, and streetlights were installed from the mid-1960s to the early 1980s, not only in Chihuahua Hill, but in Perros Bravos as well. "[Tom Powers] and Librado [Maldonado] really worked on getting a grant for the sewers and water on Brewer Hill, or Perros Bravos, because, you know, the city fathers weren't going to put effort into that. They just said there wasn't any money."[65]

While poverty was an overarching theme in the history of Chihuahua Hill, residents often found solutions to mitigate it. This was especially true of the women of Chihuahua Hill who faced even more restrictive occupational opportunities than their male counterparts. No stories exemplify this more than the family restaurants, stores, and bootlegging operations in Chihuahua Hill in the mid-20th century. Bootlegging was common in Grant County throughout the early 20th century as Blue Laws prohibited the sale of alcohol on Sundays, frustrating citizens and alcohol-serving establishments alike.[66] Multiple participants of the Chihuahua Hill History Project identify one bootlegger in particular, Josefa Salazar, as a person who made ends meet while extending care to her community. In

---

63 "Resident Blasts Town of Silver City." *Silver City Daily Press*, January 25, 1975.

64 Castillo, Katina, Marrufo, Javier, and Consuelo Muñoz. scm_ch20210806_Consuelo Munoz. Silver City Museum. 2021.

65 Marrufo, Javier. scm_ch20220607_Maldonado_Buckley_Bonnie. Silver City Museum, 2022.

66 Castillo, Katina, Javier Marrufo, and Jose Ray. scm_ch20211001_Jose Ray. Silver City Museum, 2021.

the 1940s, Josefa struck a deal with the owners of La Alianza bar at the foot of Chihuahua Hill to secure a supply of alcohol to sell on prohibited days.[67] The reciprocal relationship allowed La Alianza to offset a loss of Sunday sales, while providing Josefa an opportunity to make her own. She dedicated a room of her house as a recreation area for her clientele where a beer could be enjoyed with a game of cards or a bowl of menudo. Josefa's bootlegging business slowly expanded, and she began paying neighborhood residents to deliver the weekend's sales. Three quarts of beer only cost $2, so profits were humble yet lucrative for the time. Josefa's grandchildren, who helped her bootlegging operation, spoke on how she spent her earnings. "A lot of people claimed that she was rich. I don't know how rich she was, but I can tell you one thing. She had a lot of property."[68] Josefa rented most of her properties, multi-room apartments and old adobe houses. Her renters often consisted of elders, widows, and divorcées. She would take them in, feed them from time to time, and provide affordable living. Other properties were reserved for her family, some of whom retain ownership to this day.

Josefa's story was not entirely uncommon. Although strictly residential today, Chihuahua Hill of the '30s, '40s, and '50s was full of small family-run businesses, with many owned and operated by women. Restaurants and grocery stores were often part of family homes, in converted front rooms or freshly built additions. One of the most remembered establishments was the South Side Groceries, also called Pic and Pak, owned by the Jaurequi family.[69] Doña Avelina and Gavino Jaurequi originally bought a block on San Vicente Street where they started out grinding corn and selling masa before transitioning to a full-blown store and restaurant. Avelina's grandchildren remember that she would let people buy groceries on credit or give food away for free to those in need. "There were several little family markets in the neighborhood. It was one of several . . .

---

67   Marrufo, Javier, and Mary Madrid. scm_ch20210831_Mary Madrid. 2021.

68   Marrufo, Javier. scm_ch20220113_Fernandez_Fred. Silver City Museum, 2022.

69   Castillo, Katina. and Amy Jaurequi. scm_ch20211108_Amy Jaurequi. 2021.

They would always have beans, bologna, cheese, and chile for anyone that needed a plate of food. Avelina would save the produce that was bruised or ripened for a couple of women who lived alone."[70] The Southside Groceries eventually transitioned to one of the Jaurequi's sons, Greg "Goyo" Jaurequi who maintained the store until it closed.

Chihuahua Hill in the early 20th century. Modern homes replaced the earlier stone jacals. The baren hillside now has several trees, most likely planted by earlier residents. A strong sense of community was formed through family and religious bonds of the densely populated community. Source: Silver City Museum

Restaurateurs, grocers, and bootleggers were often one and the same. Many look favorably on their bootlegging ancestors with a sense of pride that they did all they could with what they were given. "I'm not ashamed, she was a bootlegger," recalls Fred Fernandez, grandson of Josefa Salazar. "She made her living. She had to. They *had* to. They had to do what they had to do to make a living, because there was only the mines ... She had to make a living. One way or another."[71] Bootlegging lasted only as long as the Blue Laws. Stores and restaurants typically lasted until the deaths of their

---

70   Ibid.

71   Marrufo, Javier. scm_ch20220113_Fernandez_Fred. Silver City Museum, 2022.

74

owners. The arrival of brand stores like J.C. Penny or Kmart provided the final nail in the coffin for most family-owned businesses on Chihuahua Hill.

Community and Religion

One greatly positive outcome from the poverty of Chihuahua Hill was the strong sense of community forged in the neighborhood. Most of the participants of the Chihuahua Hill History Project cite this as a way they contended with both the discrimination and poverty nearly everyone faced. Close physical proximity to other families in the dense neighborhood meant nearly everybody knew each other. The social institution of *compadrazgo*, or godparenthood, formally solidified ties among families across Chihuahua Hill. The sentiment of community care was apparent in nearly every oral history, and perfectly summarized as, "Hispanics in Grant County, we're always related by blood, by love, or by religion."[72] Neighbors looked after each other's children, provided food to those who didn't have any, or pooled money whenever someone was in need. The sense of community forged throughout the neighborhood insulated the lives of Chihuahua Hill residents, so much so that the concept of poverty never crossed many people's minds until they began associating with more people outside of their tight-knit community. "Everybody was so poor, but we didn't know it. We did not know that everybody around there was so poor. And if anybody bought a big side of beef or whatever, a part for this neighbor and a part for that neighbor. Everybody shared. That's one thing that my mom always taught me, and my grandmother. They always taught us that we had to share whatever we had. We were very poor, but we didn't know we were poor. Because everybody around us was, you know, the same."[73]

One of the greatest expressions of communal unity was the religion that most of the people shared. As a Mexican American neighborhood for most of its history, most of the residents of Chihuahua Hill during the 20th

---

72   Marrufo, Javier, and Patsy Madrid. scm_ch20220301_Madrid_Patsy. Silver City Museum, 2022.

73   Marrufo, Javier. scm_ch20220203_Margaret Ogas. Silver City Museum, 2022.

century had roots in Catholicism. To most, religion was an integral part of everyday life, a social glue that connected families, provided places to gather, and a common identity. Many cite their faith as the prime pathway for overcoming discrimination or poverty. "It was a hard time. But when they think back, you know, it was a time of being together, even though it was hard. [They] never called that *sufrir*. [They] never said anything about suffering. You know, it was just work hard and keep your faith and everything will be okay."[74]

Chihuahua Hill has had a close connection with religion since the days of San Vicente, who many refer to as a place of worship. The hill that the neighborhood was built on was originally known as El Cerro de la Cruz, the hill of the cross, and many oral histories tell of a chapel, altar, or meeting place near the hill prior to the foundation of Silver City. The religious sentiment carried over into the American era where the residents of Chihuahua Hill patronized the St. Vincent de Paul Parrish before there was a dedicated church building. The first recorded death service of the church was of Antonio Benavidez on February 3, 1874, and the first recorded baptism for the Catholic parish that became St. Vincent's was Maria Dolores Holguin on March 27, 1874. The first recorded marriage was between Jose Anselmo Rojas and Encarnacion Gomez on April 2, 1874.[75] In that same month, the local press detailed "the religious exercises by Father Ruelas on Good Friday were largely attended by our Mexican citizens," and informed of Father Ruelas's intention of erecting a church building.[76] After the building of the church commenced, Silver City newspapers lamented that the monetary contributions to the construction were not as liberal as they'd hoped.[77] As Chihuahua Hill was an economically impoverished neighborhood, residents and members of the Church contributed in any way they could. In lieu of

---

74   Marrufo, Javier, and Patsy Madrid. scm_ch20220301_Madrid_Patsy. Silver City Museum, 2022.

75   Stanley, F. "Historian Outlines Local History At Centennial." Essay. In *The Centennial Anniversary of the Foundation of the Parish of St. Vincent de Paul 1874-1974*, n.d.

76   *Mining Life.* April 4, 1874.

77   *Grant County Herald.* June 6, 1875.

76

money, many volunteered time and labor, making adobe bricks or building walls and ceilings. Jose Trujillo and his adopted son Felicitio Esquiviel oversaw construction of the 40'x 60' building complete with bell tower and shingled roof. The gross work was finished by early 1876 and the church was consecrated that same year.[78]

Similar to the community connection to St. Vincent de Paul Church, La Capilla, a small chapel overlooking Chihuahua Hill was built by community members in the mid-1880s. The folk history of La Capilla has since engrained itself into the cultural fabric of the neighborhood. According to the oral tradition, two sisters from Chihuahua, Mexico, Beatrix and Hipolita Manquero, funded the building of the original Capilla. There are different versions of why they built the chapel. In one, the sisters were refused the rights to worship at St. Vincent's Catholic Church a short distance away from Chihuahua Hill. Devout and undeterred, they built their own chapel, La Capilla, where all people were free to worship. In another, one or both sisters were prostitutes from Chihuahua, Mexico, a profession they left once they came to Silver City. Wanting to atone for their former lives, they erected the chapel dedicated to La Virgen de Guadalupe. In yet another, the sisters built it simply so the neighborhood of Chihuahua Hill would have a closer place to worship. In this version, the local priest, or bishop, refused to consecrate the building as Hipolita had no rights to the land the chapel was built on, and she wanted to keep the keys for herself. Regardless of the true history of La Capilla, the story of the Manquero sisters' devotion has become emblematic of the neighborhood's cultural and religious history, and the chapel itself a physical expression of the neighborhood's religious roots. The first adobe bricks of the chapel were reportedly laid by Perfecto Rodrigues, who later served as justice of the peace, and that the building was finished by Jose Alvillar with woodwork by Ramon Cordova.[79]

78   Heitz, Henry. *Historical Notes on St. Vincent de Paul's Parish*. Silver City, NM, 1924.

79   Stanley, F. "Historian Outlines Local History At Centennial." Essay. In *The Centennial Anniversary of the Foundation of the Parish of St. Vincent de Paul 1874-1974*, n.d.

77

Both La Capilla and St. Vincent de Paul's church remained important features in the lives of many people living on Chihuahua Hill in the 20th century. A 1906 photo of the first church choir is composed of children from the neighborhood. Nearly every family has stories about their relationship with the church. "My father would take care of Saint Vincent's. It was still a wooden building . . . My sister and I, my mother, and my father, and the two boys would go and clean the church."[80] Although the original Capilla was the site of many religious rituals, it fell into disrepair in the early 20th century and was demolished in 1915. The Capilla hill remained important to neighborhood residents who continued to utilize the space during the yearly posadas, processions mimicking the Catholic nativity story in the days leading up to Christmas.

In 1944, the church's community center was converted into a parochial, private, and church-run school. Here children received both religious and regular education. "Most of us came to school at St. Vincent's, which was a Catholic school that was adjacent to the church, so most of us received our primary education there, from first grade through eighth"[81] The St. Vincent's School had its own baseball and basketball teams, branded the Catholic Youth Organization teams. The school was closed on May 31, 1966, by order of Father McDonald, the superintendent of schools. In its place, St. Mary's was made as an inter-parochial school for high school-age children. Many women from Chihuahua Hill organized The Society of Our Lady of Guadalupe in April 1967.[82] The society formed to instill honor, love, dedication, devotion, and reverence for Nuestra Senora de Guadalupe, just as the Manquero sisters did 80 years earlier. The group is historically Mexican American and remains to this day one of the longest standing religious societies in Silver City.

---

80   Marrufo, Javier, and Juanita Escobedo. scm_ch20210811_Juanita Escobedo. Silver City Museum, 2021.

81   Marrufo, Javier, and Rosemary Peru. scm_ch20220413_Peru_Rosemary. Silver City Museum, 2022.

82   Stanley, F. "Historian Outlines Local History At Centennial." Essay. In *The Centennial Anniversary of the Foundation of the Parish of St. Vincent de Paul 1874-1974*, n.d.

The importance of both St. Vincent de Paul Catholic Church and La Capilla are apparent in the modern day. In 1975, a booklet celebrating the centennial of St. Vincent was written with the help of the community. The book contains history that specifically mentions San Vicente de La Cienega, Chihuahua Hill, the families of the earliest parishioners, and features many families from Chihuahua Hill. Although the original Capilla was torn down in 1915, the name Capilla remains interchangeably used with Chihuahua Hill to describe the neighborhood. In July of 2001, a group of community members created La Capilla Project which sought to recreate the Capilla. The project was spearheaded by Senovia Ray, a resident of Chihuahua Hill who stated, "We respected where the main Capilla used to be many years ago."[83] In 2004, after three years of planning, fundraising, and historical research, the team built a replica of La Capilla. It now stands as a landmark and symbol like the original a century earlier. In much the same vein, a project began to produce a second St. Vincent de Paul Catholic Church book celebrating the 150-year anniversary of the church, once again with the help of parishioners who have roots in Chihuahua Hill.

Education of Chihuahua Hill

An emergent theme in Chihuahua Hill history is the view of education to confront social issues faced by the community. Just three years after the founding of Silver City, the newspaper, *Grant County Mining Life,* debated the issue of teaching Mexican children in their native Spanish or English. Arguing that instruction in English would ultimately bring children more success, Silver City schools determined to only teach Spanish-speaking children in English.[84] Initially, there was no separation of students in schools, and children of all ethnic backgrounds were allowed to attend the Silver Public School for "free." However, due to the lack of a bilingual education, the need to work younger to support the family, or the inability to afford books needed for school, most Mexican children did not attend school throughout the 1870s-1880s.

83　Marrufo, Javier, and Senovia Ray. scm_ch20210723 Senovia Ray. 2021.

84　"Our Public School." *Mining Life*. January 24, 1874.

79

On January 17, 1874, an article was published in *Grant County Mining Life*, addressing this issue. "Why should an impediment be erected to deter the rising Mexican generation from receiving the elements so essential to their future, prospective fits of a common school education ... we assert that such impediments have been raised by the actions of the commissioners in their appointment of an incompetent teacher ... [the commissioners] have made the private selection of a teacher who is as little qualified to teach Mexican children as the commissioners, themselves, are to decipher the hieroglyphics of the tombs of the catacombs"[85] The article was signed only with the word, Justice.

School became compulsory in the 1890s yet remained a luxury unavailable to most living on Chihuahua Hill. Spanish-speaking children still contended with a language barrier in their learning experience. Throughout the late 19th and early 20th centuries, the question of bilingual education never made its way into historical documentation.

By the early 20th century, overcrowding in schools compelled the building of a new school building at the corners of Cooper and San Vicente Street in Chihuahua Hill, with the school board announcing, "... the town will be divided into school wards by the proper authorities and all children residing in these wards so established and belonging in the grades taught in said wards will be required to attend the school located in the ward in which they reside ... Special work in both buildings will be in charge of special teachers. It is hoped that the patrons of the school and the citizens in general will do all that they can to make the new school a decided success."[86] While the main rationale for the creation of a ward school was the overpopulation of the public-school building, contending with issues stemming from Spanish-speaking students was a prime ulterior motive. The location of the Lincoln School in the newly established ward, the south side of town, guaranteed that its students were primarily Spanish-speaking children of Mexican descent. Rather than address the need for bilingual and culturally inclusive education, the

---

85   "Justice." *Mining Life*. January 17, 1874.
86   *Silver City Enterprise*, June 1915.

school board instead began a campaign of eradication against the Spanish language, a policy that lasted into the 1940s. By 1919, it was apparent that only teaching native Spanish speakers in English was still not conducive to learning, with children needing more work time than their Anglo counterparts. "With a view of giving the Spanish-American children a longer time in which to do the work, the Lincoln School was made wholly Spanish American."[87] From that point onward, the segregated Lincoln School largely served to prepare Spanish-speaking children for the English-only public schools. The Lincoln School is a traumatic point of history for many people who went there. The overall sentiment being that the school was ruled by discriminatory actors and did not have the education of its students at the forefront of its mission. "One of the things that impacted my life was the discrimination that was in place at that particular time . . . as a child, we were forced to bathe in single file, and naked . . . I would hear the teachers, who were all white, say to each other, 'those dirty little Mexicans' . . . I identified with being Mexican, but I was hurt because every time I'd walk down to those stalls, the bathing showers, it was dark down there and damp, and we were supervised by a male maintenance man. Little girls . . . I was ashamed."[88] She finishes her recollections, now, in the present, acknowledging the pain and the wounds caused by this history. "I'll never forget that I was forced to bathe. How dare they. I can say that now. How dare they."[89]

There was a smaller portion of children from Chihuahua Hill who never attended the Lincoln School. Most of these were instead enrolled in the Saint Vincent de Paul Parochial School. The dividing factor for these students was the small monthly tuition needed to attend the church school. Nevertheless, Spanish-speaking children attending the church school fell into many of the same experiences as their public-school counterparts. "The nuns from Kansas were there . . . They were kind of

---

87   Calkins, Helen M. *The Public Schools of Silver City (New Mexico): A history of the school from 1874 to 1928*. Helen M. Calkins, 1928. 63

88   Marrufo, Javier, and Manuelita Ordonez. scm_ch20220301_Ordonez_Manuelita. Silver City Museum. 2022.

89   Ibid.

81

prejudiced. They favored the whites, you know, but there wasn't that many white people, so it was hard for them to work with Mexicans ... And then, of course, they insisted that we speak English. I got slapped. The teacher slapped me in the playground for speaking Spanish. Oh yeah, she knocked the heck out of me."[90]

Children left the Lincoln and St. Vincent schools when they reached middle school where they transitioned to the Silver City Public School. Even here, Mexican American children remained separated from their white counterparts. By the mid-20th century, a tiered grade system, where each grade was broken down into 4-5 different levels, continued to segregate Mexican American children. "At lunchtime, we didn't have a cafeteria where to take our own lunch. If you ate, good. If you didn't, they didn't care ... they had three classes. They had blue birds, yellow birds, and red birds. The yellow birds were the dumb ones. So, the Chicanos, we were in that section. Then the blue birds were smart Chicanos and whites, and then the white were the smart ones [red birds]."[91] It is important to note that the segregation of the schools did not necessarily inform social interactions outside of school. "They weren't allowed to play with the Anglo kids. There wasn't actually a line across the playground, but there was an imaginary one ... If a ball from the Mexican side went over to the other side, they couldn't go get it. And yet, after school, they were all together in the streets playing ball ... So they were breaking away in their own way."[92]

Educational discrimination affected generations of Chihuahua Hill residents throughout their entire school careers, and similar stories are told from nearly every stage of school.

"High school wasn't any better. There was a lot of teachers, they were disciplinarians, and some of them didn't care ... One occasion I was taking algebra. And I liked it. So I thought I'm going to take

---

90   Marrufo, Javier, and Arthur Sanchez. scm_ch20210722_Arthur Sanchez. Silver City Museum, 2021.

91   Marrufo, Javier, and Victor Peña. scm_ch20220601_Pena_Victor. 2022.

92   Marrufo, Javier. scm_ch20220607_Maldonado_Buckley_Bonnie. Silver City Museum, 2022.

Algebra 2. The counselor refused it, and he told me, 'You're never going to make it.' I said, 'Well, how do you know? I passed Algebra 1, why can't I pass Algebra 2?' He said, 'No, you're not going to make it.' So he took me to the principal, and the principal said, 'Well, why don't we give him a chance?' I went into Algebra 2 and no problems at all. And how many Hispanic kids were in the Algebra 2 class? Two. And this counselor at the time, he would try to minimize the Hispanics getting into some of those classes to where it was basically white. And it would be, you know, it was obvious."

On the level of higher education, the Normal School, later called New Mexico Teacher's College, and eventually Western New Mexico University, followed the same trajectory with Spanish-speaking students as the public schools of Silver City. The university was founded in 1894 as the Normal School. The mission of this school was to train teachers, producing a new generation of New Mexico educators. In its first 19 years, the institution produced no Mexican American graduates. The first, Fortuna Guererro, graduated in 1913 and hailed from San Lorenzo, the only community in Grant County to include bilingual education in their curriculum.[93] For the first 30 years of the university's history, 579 students graduated from the institution. Of that number, only 10, or 1.7 percent were Mexican American. Change came slowly, and throughout the 1920s and '30s, Spanish surnamed graduates slowly increased.[94] Military service in the 20th century galvanized change in regard to higher education. Chihuahua Hill is no exception to this. "The Hispanic kids were basically told, 'well join the service, and the Army will pay for your education.' They didn't try to find scholarships for them as much as they did the Anglo kids. So, you know, these bright kids had to make

---

93   *New Mexico State Normal School Yearbook*. Silver City, NM: New Mexico State Normal School, 1916.

94   *New Mexico State Normal School Yearbook*. Silver City, NM: New Mexico State Normal School, 1925.

it on their own."[95] Serving across the United States or overseas showed many young residents a world outside of Silver City. It also provided a way to get an education with the GI Bill, which provided benefits for veterans to pay for college or vocational training programs. Through the GI Bill, many Chihuahua Hill residents were able to gain access to new opportunities in education and occupations.

By the 1950s and '60s, people who attended the Lincoln School as children became the next generation of educators throughout Grant County Schools. Mexican American educators with roots in Chihuahua Hill such as Librado Maldonado and Henry Marrufo became the first Mexican American teachers in Silver City.[96] The first bilingual programs in Silver City schools began in the 1960s with Maria Spencer's Spanish program, which in time transformed into bilingual and cultural education programs. Maldonado and Delfina Warnack championed the cause of bilingual education from the 1960s and throughout their entire careers, with Maldonado going as far as to make education his prime focus during his stint in state politics.[97] The needs of a largely Spanish-speaking Chihuahua Hill began to be addressed thanks to the work of those people who lived through discriminatory practices, and whose ancestors were denied education due to the circumstances of their birth. By 1975, there was a Parents' Advisory Council of the Bilingual Program of the Sixth Street School and Western New Mexico University made bilingual education a prime concern.[98] Education afforded many who grew up in a system of oppression the tools to combat their experiences. Those who struggled for equality went on to teach new generations of children from Chihuahua Hill, usually attended places like the Lincoln School, worked their way through college, and sought to better their communities. "It kind of works

---

95 Marrufo, Javier. scm_ch20220607_Maldonado_Buckley_Bonnie. Silver City Museum, 2022.

96 Marrufo, Javier. scm_ch20220607_Maldonado_Buckley_Bonnie. Silver City Museum, 2022.

97 Lanning, Laura. "Maldonado Targets Education." *Deming Headlight*, September 1, 1998.

98 "School Happenings." *Silver City Daily Press*, January 23, 1975.

on your psyche. I think that's one of the reasons that I loved working here. Because I knew I could help those kids, especially from my barrio. I could really relate to them. So, it was easy."[99]

For nearly 100 years, language was the point of contention between the community and non-Spanish-speaking educators. The language was kept alive only through the oral tradition, as it was not taught, and even outright discouraged, in local schools. Although the bilingual education of the mid-20th century seemed to promise a future for the native tongue of many Chihuahua Hill residents, there has been a slow loss of language in a clearly defined pattern. The oldest generations almost invariably grew up speaking Spanish, the next generation understands the language but does not speak it, while the youngest know little if any. As of 2023, there are no bilingual programs in local schools, and Western New Mexico University no longer offers degrees in Spanish. However, many local institutions founded through the help of Chihuahua Hill residents continue to impart the importance of education to the younger generation.

Community-Based Social Organizations

On the back of the ongoing struggles for educational equality were organized social movements born from the community of Chihuahua Hill. The neighborhood has a long legacy of resistance to racial, economic, and educational oppression dating as far back as the first decade following the official founding of Silver City. In 1877, a group of citizens petitioned the board of county commissioners to create a new precinct in the vicinity of Chihuahua Hill, with the northern boundary being at Broadway Street.[100] "The desire for this precinct seems to arise principally among our Mexican residents and is caused by some real or fancied grievance which they allege exists in the trial of cases in the justice's court. They, it seems, wish a Mexican justice of the peace . . . we know naught of anything in the management of the causes that come before Justice Rilea, our American

---

99   Marrufo, Javier, and Rosemary Peru. scm_ch20220413_Peru_Rosemary. Silver City Museum, 2022.

100   *Grant County Herald*. February 3, 1877.

justice, that can justify any complaint whatever."[101] The dismissive tone to the allegations from the Chihuahua Hill residents would become the common response to the communities voicing of issues. Regardless of the success of the petition, it displays the neighborhood actively campaigning for their own betterment from the earliest days of Silver City.

Civil rights movements from Chihuahua Hill became more organized in the 20th century. The first officially formed Hispanic institution in Chihuahua Hill was La Alianza Hispano-Americana in 1905. La Allianza Hispano-Americana was a national organization originally founded on January 14, 1894, in Tucson, Arizona. It served as a sociedad mutualista, or a mutual benefit society, that offered life insurance and social activities for Mexican Americans in response to hostile attitudes against Mexican Americans in the Southwest. The organization transitioned into a fraternal insurance organization by 1896.[102] Allianza Lodge 17, the first in Silver City, was founded on Chihuahua Hill in 1905 on the corner of Pinos Altos and San Vicente Streets.[103] By 1944, it had 52 members, making it the second largest of the seven Alianza lodges in Grant County. Another chapter, Alianza Lodge 67, opened in Silver City with another 43 members in 1915. Lodge 67 was a woman's organization, with the words *Circulo de Señoras*, Women's Circle, written in bold print on their banner.

In addition to providing mutual aid, La Allianza sought to preserve Mexican American culture and taught its members democratic traditions, ensuring that ethnically Mexican communities retained cultural values as they transitioned into American society. La Alianza's motto, *Protección, Moralidad, Instrucción* [Translated] Protection, Morality, Instruction, was embroidered onto the banner hanging from the lodge on Chihuahua Hill.

Correspondence from the local chapters of La Alianza showed that its members strove to live up to the creed that appeared in official letters. *"El hombre fraternalista ... esta siempre dispuesto a sacrifarse por su projimo.*

101 Ibid.

102 Texas State Historical Association. "Alianza Hispano-Americana." Texas State Historical Association. Accessed February 14, 2024. https://tshaonline.org/handbook/online/articles/vna02. 8

103 *Silver City Daily Press*, May 20, 1965.

86

Es el que imparte el bien a los demas, sin detenerse en detalles, ni examinar a las personas, a las que protege o ayuda. [Translated] The fraternal man ... is always willing to sacrifice himself for his neighbor. He is one who imparts good to others, without dwelling on details or examining the people he protects or helps."[104]

The Alianza lodge on Chihuahua Hill was older than most of the residents who participated in the Chihuahua Hill History Project, although some remember their parents participating in the Silver City Lodge or one of the many others around Grant County. "The Allianza was the La Allianza Hispano-Americano. It was an organization that was organized for La Raza to better themselves, to fight discrimination and all that. They had chapters in Santa Rita and Hanover. Matter of fact, my mother belonged to that."[105] Many records from La Allianza 17 and 67 still exist at the University of Arizona. All the records were written in Spanish and give informa-

One of the two Alianza banners that were hung outside of the Alianza Building on San Vicente and Pinos Altos. Both banners were rescued by first Silver City Museum director, Harry Benjamin, after the building was torn down in the 1960s. They are now part of the Silver City Museum's Collection. Source: Silver City Museum Collection

104   Ibid.

105   Marrufo, Javier, and Thomas Ryan. scm_ch20210902_Thomas Ryan. 2021.

87

tion about membership, dues, insurance, and relationships with the larger institution. From these records, we have glimpses of those from Chihuahua Hill who were a part of the organization.[106] Some of those involved with La Alianza were active in other advocacy groups around Silver City. Alianza secretary Carlos Melendez was an active member of Western New Mexico University's Catholic Youth Recreational Organization (CYRO). CYRO was founded in 1939 for the purpose of recreation, social intercourse, general culture, civic improvement, and the welfare of others.[107] As was often the case, advocacy in Chihuahua Hill usually spread beyond the scope of the neighborhood.

Chihuahua Hill's Alianza lodge was active. Delegates from the Chihuahua Hill Logia 17 regularly attended regional and national Alianza meetings, no doubt connecting the neighborhood to the bigger ideas surrounding civil rights and community organizing. In the 1940s, President of Logia 17, Jose Morales, opened the Alianza bar and dance hall on South Texas Street. More than just a place of community activism, La Alianza also acted as a social hub, a gathering point for recreation, drinking, and dances. The members of Logia 17 worked toward the betterment of Chihuahua Hill in fulfillment of their motto: Protección, Moralidad, Instrucción, Protection, Morality, Instruction.

La Alianza was not the only social organization aimed at helping residents of Chihuahua Hill. By the second half of the 20th century, three organizations were founded with the intent of helping the underrepresented youth of the neighborhood, particularly in the area of education. These were the El Grito Headstart, El Chicano Youth Center, and LULAC (the League of United Latin American Citizens) Council 8003.

---

106 "University of Arizona Alianza Hispanoamericana Récords." Courtesy of University of Arizona Libraries, Special Collections: MS 663, Convention Files, Complete Listing of delegates, 1941, n.d.
This source shows 1,941 officers, expresidente Francisco R. Gonzales, presidente José V. Morales, Vicepresidente Refugio Ortiz, Secretario Carlos P. Melendrez, Tesorero Antonio Jaquez, 1er Sindico Manuel Duarte, 2ndo Sindico Manuel Z. Holguin, 3er Sindico Jose Benavidez, Conserge J.D. Zapata, Ujier Ygancio Ortiz, Portero Pedro Ramierez.

107 *El Corral.* Silver City, NM: Western New Mexico College, 1942.

The mid-20th century was a time of change for Chihuahua Hill. The neighborhood itself was becoming more modern. On the heels of physical changes were waves of activism transforming the social standing of the neighborhood. The Chicano Movement didn t impact rural Grant County as much as large urban centers like Los Angeles, California, or Denver, Colorado. Dr. Luis Quiñones remembers some of us have always felt that the Chicano Movement kind of bypassed Grant County, in a way . . ."[108] Although the movement was not widespread in Southwest New Mexico, there were some advocates who learned from the Chicano Movement and advocated for the Hispanic population of Grant County. Patsy Madrid remembers, ". . . there was a group of us that went to Abiquiu, to Ghost Ranch, for a week . . . we had a lot of the top Chicano activists there . . . it was really enlightening . . . We all came up with the same consensus that we needed to encourage our people to get an education."[109] The group consisted of local Silver City residents Rosa Ortiz Aguilar, Consuelo "Chelo" Aguilar, Lydia Chacon, Patsy Madrid. This same group, along with lawyers from Long Island, New York: Jeff Levine, Jeff Gordon, and Larry Brahm, founded El Chicano Youth Center in 1970.

Standing at the foot of Chihuahua Hill, on the Northwest corner of San Vicente and Bayard streets, El Chicano Youth Center was founded to give neighborhood youth an experiential learning hub and social gathering place. The youth center was run completely by volunteers. In the 1970s, it partnered with Western University of New Mexico, creating a program called Upward Bound aimed at preparing local Chicano kids for college. ". . . they would get students and house them and show them classes and all that at the university. And that way, when they did enroll and come, they would feel comfortable. Because being Hispanic, there's a fear. It's unknown. Nobody in your family has done it, so they can't tell you . . . So that was a really good program that they were able to put together with the university." El Chicano Youth Center's history is brief but impactful.

108   Marrufo, Javier, and Luis Quiñones. Luis Quiñones El Reportero Interview. 2023.
109   Marrufo, Javier, and Patsy Madrid. scm_ch20220301_Madrid_Patsy. Silver City Museum 2022.

Chicano Youth Center in the early 1970s. The building still exists, but is part of a private residence. The photo was donated to the Silver City Museum by Yolanda Martinez during the Chihuahua Hill History Project. Source: Silver City Museum

The organization closed in the mid-1970s and is remembered fondly by those who utilized it.

El Grito Headstart is yet another social service founded in part by residents of Chihuahua Hill and former students at the segregated Lincoln School. The Headstart program started in Silver City in 1969, first operating out of a spare classroom in the Western High School and old St. Vincent de Paul school building before moving to the former Lincoln School building.[110] The organization was started to provide crucial early education for impoverished children. Greg Jaurequi, business owner, activist, and Chihuahua

---

110   Castillo, Katina, Javier Marrufo, Frances Jacquez, and Carmen Muñoz. scm_ch20211102_Frances Jaquez and Carmen Munoz. 2021

Hill resident was an instrumental figure in the development of El Grito Headstart. As a person who attended segregated Lincoln School as a child, where children were punished for speaking Spanish, Greg understood the need for early childhood education that catered to the needs of the community. His family relayed his influence in the continued education of the neighborhood, pointing out a meeting announcing the closing of the St. Vincent de Paul School. "They had this open forum meeting that allowed the parents to come to let them know that they were going to have to close it down . . . my dad stands up in the meeting and said, 'Well, then we got to start our own. We got to do something about this. If this is going to happen, let's just do our own thing.'"[111] A few years later, Greg Jaurequi served on the first board of El Grito Headstart, which served primarily low-income, and usually Hispanic, children. El Grito Headstart provided some of the first bilingual and cultural education programs in Silver City. The outset of El Grito, especially with its bilingual focus, reveals the social conditioning created through a century of discrimination, educational segregation, and anti-Spanish curriculums. "There was a lot of controversy getting teachers who spoke Spanish, because most of the kids attending, you know, were Hispanic and Spanish was their first language. But again, some of that discrimination was in the culture. Even some of the Hispanics, there was pushback that, well, no, we want white teachers to teach our children."[112]

El Grito Headstart continues to remain an important neighborhood institution that continuously contributes to the betterment of not only Chihuahua Hill but Grant County. In the 21st century, they began providing summer enrichment programs for local youth. ". . . we would take them to Albuquerque and give them the zoo, the museum, the science center experience . . . So that would be an experience those kids never would never have. Many of them."[113]

111   Castillo, Katina, and Joseph Jaurequi. scm_ch20211118_Joseph Jaurequi. Silver City Museum, 2021.

112   Castillo, Katina, and Amy Jaurequi. scm_ch20211108_Amy Jaurequi. Silver City Museum, 2021.

113   Castillo, Katina, Javier Marrufo, Frances Jacquez, and Carmen Muñoz. scm_ch20211102_Frances Jaquez and Carmen Munoz, 2021

The work of El Grito Headstart has helped to rehabilitate the Lincoln School building, which contributed to so much historical trauma for the neighborhood. "It's just amazing to me, the generations of kids and families and parents that have been supported through that institution, after having talked to all these elders, that recall their fairly traumatizing experience of going to it as the Lincoln School. What a transformation."[114]

El Grito Headstart has helped heal some of the generational trauma faced by Chihuahua Hill and continues to help families all over Grant County. It still serves as a reminder of the legacy of hardships faced by the community that persist to this day. Enrollment in the Headstart program still operates under a low-income criterion, and so becomes reflective of the issues that continue to plague the community. "I can tell you that when I started, as far as picking up and recruiting and enrolling the children, I think we had 99.9 percent Hispanic. Okay, now I can say that we have probably maybe 94 percent-95 percent Hispanic and 5 percent Anglo."[115]

At the other end of the educational spectrum, higher education, sits LULAC 8003, a Chihuahua Hill institution since 1981. LULAC is the nation's largest and oldest Hispanic civil rights organization. LULAC first appeared in Grant County in the early 1970s. Spiritual successors of the earlier Alianza lodges of Silver City, LULAC became staunch supporters of Latino rights, particularly educational rights. Throughout the 1970s, LULAC repeatedly urged the Silver School System to adhere to the 1973 Affirmative Action plan. In 1975, New Mexico State LULAC president Sam Garcia accused Silver City schools of discriminatory hiring practices, citing teachers with Spanish surnames being wildly underrepresented in the school district. Chihuahua Hill native and New Mexico State Senator, Ben Altamirano, urged the Grant County board of education that the problem should be nipped in the bud and LULAC member be assigned to the committee investigating the charges.[116] The next year, the local

114   Castillo, Katina. scm_ch20211118_Joseph Jaurequi. Silver City Museum, 2021.

115   Castillo, Katina, Javier Marrufo, Frances Jacquez, and Carmen Muñoz. scm_ch20211102_Frances Jaquez and Carmen Munoz. n.d.

116   *Silver City Daily Press*, April 16, 1975.

LULAC, under President Rudy Jacquez, filed official charges of discrimination with the Dallas HEW against the school district for continuing to fail to address the representational needs of the affirmative action plan. Jacquez informed local newspapers, "We, the LULAC officials, believe the Silver Consolidated School District practices a deplorable policy of neglect and discrimination toward Mexican American citizens, both in their hiring and educational practices."[117] David Lee, the superintendent of Silver Schools at the time, refuted all charges with the same dismissive tone of the justice of the peace issue nearly 99 years before. "It is very unfortunate that communities and schools have to be continually torn up by a small group of individuals who for some reason decide the world is against them."[118] LULAC was instrumental in that it forced local institutions to acknowledge issues that plagued the community of Chihuahua Hill for nearly a century. In later iterations of the organization, LULAC sought to directly better those of the community through a readjusted emphasis effort.

LULAC Council 8003 was established in 1981 from Council 8005 when Apolonio "Polo" and Donna Sierra decided a shift was needed to move the council in a new direction. Both understood the importance of continued education and the limited means of many Grant County residents. They envisioned the newly formed LULAC 8003 as a scholarship-producing institution. The first meetings of the council were held in various locations around Silver City before a building—formerly La Primera Iglesia Hispana Baptist Church on the south side of Chihuahua Hill—was purchased in the early 1980s.[119] Polo Sierra used his own money as down payment for what would become LULAC Council 8003's current hall. Determined to give back to the community and contribute to the continued education of Grant County's Mexican American youth, the council developed partnerships with Silver and Cobre school districts, as well as Western New

---

117   *Silver City Daily Press*, January 5, 1976.

118   Ibid.

119   Marrufo, Javier, and Fred Baca. Interview with LULAC 8003 President, Fred Baca. Personal, 2023

Mexico University. The small organization received little outside funding, instead relying on fundraising efforts, sometimes from as little as six members. The council's scholarship program had a rough start before finally becoming a staple of the community. "The first scholarship was $250. We couldn't find anyone to take it, so we had to go hunting door-to-door to give it away."[120] The scholarship program has since found its stride, with as much as $20,000 awarded in some years. Since its inception, Council 8003 has awarded more than $200,000 in scholarships to local youth, many of whom have gone on to become community leaders, doctors, business owners, government officials, and contributing members of their community.

Change

Chihuahua Hill has undergone great change in the 21st century. The activism from the community in the 20th century ensured that the neighborhood developed much more steadily than it did a century prior. The neighborhood now bears little resemblance to that original Mexican community built over a rocky landscape with homes that looked as if they just emerged from the earth. There has also been a demographic shift in the residents of Chihuahua Hill. No longer a strictly Mexican American neighborhood, every year brings new people, with different cultures and experiences. Today, you can find families who have lived in Chihuahua Hill for generations, living side by side with those who came this year.

While the overall look of Chihuahua Hill has changed in the past 150 years, many aspects of the neighborhood remain the same. Homes, buildings, and landscapes have been altered over time, but many remain recognizable. Most homes, by nature of the terrain, are built close together. Many former residents say that driving through Chihuahua Hill is like being in a time machine. One of the greatest changes noted by past residents is the overwhelming sense of community.

---

120   Ibid.

94

A birds eye view of the modern neighborhood of Chihuahua Hill c. 2023. El Grito Headstart can be seen on the far right. La Capilla near the center. The once barren hill is now lush with trees. Source: J. Marrufo

Chihuahua Hill became far less insulated in the second half of the 20th century. Increased activism led to greater educational opportunities, which in turn saw residents of Chihuahua Hill more integrated into the workforce than ever before. Symptomatic of this change was the Silver City police force where multiple Chihuahua Hill residents such as Steve Aguirre, Jose Barrios, Bodi Chavez, Rudy Jacquez, or Tommy Ryan served as policemen or chiefs of police, a position that was strictly off limits in the 19th century. In 1965, Chihuahua Hill resident Steve Aguirre was elected as Grant County's first Hispanic sheriff, nearly 100 years after the town was founded. The neighborhood produced local and state politicians such as Librado Maldonado, and Benny Altamirano, who advocated for the fair treatment of Mexican Americans not only in Silver City but throughout New Mexico. El Grito Headstart, spearheaded by Greg Jaurequi, provided an avenue for the poorest families to have equitable education. LULAC Council 8003 provided means for Hispanic children across the county to

95

attend higher education. Notably, Howie Morales, who received a LULAC scholarship as a youth, now serves as New Mexico's Lieutenant Governor.

The integration of other Mexican Americans into public offices happened slowly over the course of decades. Former Chief of Police Tommy Ryan proudly relayed a story of how his mixed ancestry began the integration of cultures on Chihuahua Hill. "We were looking for a place to live. I went down to see Mrs. Flores and when I first started talking to her about renting the apartment, she was kind of hesitant and kept looking at me and talking to me in English. She didn't know whether she should rent the apartment to me or not. So then I started talking to her in Spanish. And she said, *Oh, ¿hablas mexicano? Hablas bien español'...[I responded]* *'Yeah, si, pues soy mexicano.'* With that she said, *'tenía miedo para rentarte el apartamento porque si eres gabacho, no se como hacerte con la Raza.'* So she rented me the apartment."[121] Ryan's experiences is indicative of the historic distrust that formed between different cultures in Silver City, although that distrust was usually quickly dispelled after people spent time with their new neighbors. "One thing I might add is when we moved to the neighborhood, I was the only Anglo in the neighborhood. Willie Flower's mother lived one block south of here. She was a Black lady, and I was the only Anglo. Everybody else was Hispanic... Didn't matter to me, we've always had good neighbors."[122]

As standards of living increased, and many Chihuahua Hill residents became more established in the workforce, families sought to move out of the historically "poor" neighborhood. In the second half of the 20th century, more people left the neighborhood than ever before, destined for new additions in Silver City, or new cities and states. Most past residents of Chihuahua Hill agree that the neighborhood began to change as the elders of the late 20th century began to die. "It seems like when the grandparents died, when their great grandparents die off, it's kind of like the glue that holds the family together. And everybody kind of goes a different

---

121   Marrufo, Javier, and Thomas Ryan. scm_ch20210902_Thomas Ryan. 2021.
122   Marrufo, Javier, Charles Deming, and Clara Deming. scm_ch20220414_Deming_Clara_and_Charles. *Silver City Museum*, 2022.

way . . . And that holds true for a lot of families, you know, offspring find a decent job, they have to go somewhere else."[123] Family homes were largely abandoned, sold off, or fell into disrepair. From the 1990s and onward, many dilapidated homes were bought for cheap prices by newcomers to Silver City. At present, a wave of new residents of Chihuahua Hill continue to renovate old neighborhood homes. Many take great care to retain as much of the original spirit of these houses as they are gradually brought back to life. Thanks to the dedication of people like this, Chihuahua Hill continues to evolve and become the home of new people with new stories.

The cultural shift of Chihuahua Hill is an important question for the generational families of the neighborhood. Opinions are varied, but general sentiment being happy that the neighborhood is gaining new life, while lamenting that the culture and community of their youth is gone. "I remember it used to be full of Chicanos, that whole hill. Kids running up and down. The *chavacano* trees, the plum trees. It's so quiet now. And we've noticed we're probably the only Chicanos on the block . . . It is sad, I do miss hearing all the kids running up and down, the hollering. To me, it was the sound of joy. Now, everyone's just, you know, to themselves. They're not unfriendly, but everyone's to themselves, and I liked it the other way."[124] On the other hand, many new residents of Chihuahua Hill cite the sense of community still alive in many of the older residents as the main reason for choosing the neighborhood. "Ray and Goya Mesa were the first people we really knew . . . she was so welcoming and accepting and so ready to treat me like a neighbor. That's really all you can ask for. You know, it's like I told my husband with this house. The house is a lot of work. You can change a house. You can bulldoze it; you can remodel it. You can make it bigger, smaller, whatever. You cannot change a neighborhood. So, the neighborhood was a big draw."[125] On top of the sense of community, many newer residents, residing in houses built through

---

123   Ibid.

124   Marrufo, Javier, and Mary Madrid, Stella Madrid. scm_ch20210831_Mary Madrid. Silver City Museum, 2021.

125   Marrufo, Javier, and Mikki Jemin. scm_ch20220401_Jemin_Mikki. 2022.

generations, often find appreciation for the previous inhabitants of their homes, often without ever meeting them. "The gardens that used to be on Chihuahua Hill, those people who had gardeners up here were great gardeners. They had talent. Because on ours, we have a few places that will actually grow things . . . Its a challenge . . . I think most people would say, we grow a lot of caliche. Yeah, we get a lot of that. You have to know what you're doing."[126] This appreciation for the past creates a connection based on some aspect of common experience between those inhabiting Chihuahua Hill now and the residents of the past.

A close up of the mural painted by Carlos Callejo depicting Chihuahua Hill in the late 1800s. The mural was painted in 2021. Subject matter for the mural was determined through community input. Many residents from the neighborhood helped in its creation. Source: J. Marrufo

As with most history, there is a sweet middle ground somewhere in the experiences. A poignant statement in this vein was given by Senovia Ray, the oldest participant of the Chihuahua Hill History project, when

126   Marrufo, Javier, Jan Merchant, and Mike Merchant. scm_ch20211103_Jan and Mike Merchant. 2021.

98

asked about the changes she's seen in the neighborhood over the years. "I don't mind. I miss all those people I used to know. You know? But like I tell you, I like to make friends. I like to meet people. I've learned a lot in my life that we don't have to be *Catolico o Americano* or whatever. They're part of what we make out of Silver City. Ok, get together. Like I tell you, it's the first time that I'm alive. I try my best. Because we're nothing in this world. We all go to the same place. I think they should preach more about it."[127]

In the past few years, much more attention has been paid to the community of Chihuahua Hill. In 2020, a new park was built by the town of Silver City, along with a mural painted by Los Angeles-based artist, Carlos Callejo. The same year also saw the beginning of the Chihuahua Hill History Project.

"Normally, when you're dealing with that type of conditions . . . the artist has to do the overall composition, according to the dimensions of the wall, all in paper, in order for it to be approved . . . And this particular one, it was a little different, because we sort of got the central area of the wall, and they approved it, and then and then they said, the rest of it is going to be more spontaneous. As community engagement comes in, as the stories come in, then we're going to be reflecting on those stories. So it wasn't like already a predetermined kind of design, it was in the process. So that's that makes it very, very unique. Because really, truly, that really is public art. Because you're engaging the public in the in the decision-making process of your composition . . . The artists only becomes the voice of the particular community where it's being done . . . they just become the tool, the voice for that particular community, speaking about that community struggles, their aspirations, their celebrations, whatever it happens to be, and you just become, you know, and those. That really is truly community public art."[128]

The mural was dedicated in a celebration put on by both LULAC Council 8003 and the Silver City Museum in 2021. The celebration served

---

127   Marrufo, Javier, and Senovia Ray. scm_ch20210723 Senovia Ray. 2021.
128   Marrufo, Javier, and Carlos Callejo. scm_ch20210922_Carlos Callejo. 2021.

as a recognition of the neighborhood, but a starting point for the Silver City Museum's Chihuahua Hill History Project.

The Chihuahua Hill History Project was envisioned by the Silver City Museum to bring the community, as a whole and as individuals, to the forefront of history. It concerns itself less with dates and events and more with the context that surrounds them. Having worked in history museums for so many years, I knew every community had a story. And most often, those stories are not told in the local history museum, for a variety of reasons. But I looked around at the Silver City Museum, what we had done in the past, and we weren't doing a lot of community-based history projects. And living here, I've lived here for a while, I got to know a little bit about Chihuahua Hill, and my neighbor's family who's been here for generations was telling me about what it was like when he was a kid. So, I just knew there were stories to be told that the museum hadn't been telling."[129] Experiences, memories, and perspectives. The project demands that history only becomes important when understood through the lens of human life. With this in mind, the project was built from the ground up around oral history. Themes, or areas of importance, emerge from the stories told by Chihuahua Hill residents. Making personal experience the centerpiece of our research provides a new toolkit for collecting and presenting local history. It reorients our emphasis back to the community we serve, transforming our institution from a place that tells you what history is into a mirror that reflects the communal experience. It is history for and by the community. History isn't composed from one single perspective, but of many. Every perspective is important because every person is important, not just the rich or the powerful, or those whose lives are written about and well documented. History is not just about their voice, or your voice, or mine, but all of ours. *Nuestra Voz*. Our voice, as a collective, is what brings the past to life, and what makes history more than just words in a book, or on a wall.

---

129   Marrufo, Javier, and Bart Roselli. scm_ch20220425_Roselli_Bart. Silver City Museum, 2022.

100

It is important to note that economic, racial or social segregation of Silver City was de facto rather than de jure. There were now official laws relegating Mexican Americans to these positions or this neighborhood, rather social and economic realities dictated that they would most likely perform in certain roles or live in certain parts of town.

Addendum: Chihuahua Hill was admitted into the National Register of Historic Places on January 23, 1984.

JAVIER MARRUFO, Curator Silver City Museum. BA WNMU; master's in history WNMU; Marrufo began his museum career in 2019 joining the staff as curator and chief researcher for the Chihuahua Hill History Project. He went on to complete more than 80 interviews for the project while also providing research and curatorial expertise for the "Life and Times of Arturo Flores" exhibit. As curator he serves as the chief researcher for all the museum's exhibitions and select public programs. He has been accepted to the University of New Mexico's doctorate program in Chicano/a Studies. He continues to lecture publicly about his research into regional history and culture.

CHAPTER 4:

Chinese Settlers in Silver City, New Mexico: An exploratory study

Karen J. Leong, Department of History, University of New Mexico

When Silver City Museum Director Bart Roselli contacted me in in the fall of 2023 about writing a chapter about the Chinese American experience in Silver City, I was a relatively new settler in New Mexico myself, having just arrived in late summer. I wanted to learn more about the Asian American experience in New Mexico, already aware of the ways that the Arizona Asian American experience was distinct from the dominant U.S. western states narrative. I accepted the invitation to produce a chapter, with Susan Berry generously sharing with me her census and newspaper research about Chinese in Silver City and Grant County, a binder of materials compiled by Silver City Museum staff, and Silver City documents and newspapers digitized by the Silver City Public Library. In the process, I have been surprised by how distinct New Mexico is in relation to its neighbors in the Southwest—Arizona and Texas—

and intrigued by the common experiences shared by generations of Chinese immigrants and Chinese American communities across the United States.[130]

This chapter, then, offers an exploratory study of Chinese settlement and the development of the Chinese American community in Silver City from the 1870s. It seeks to provide the broader national and international contexts of Chinese settling in Grant County, New Mexico Territory and the Chinese American community that developed in Silver City, New Mexico, by the mid-twentieth century (only to decline by the century's end as the region and nation have changed). Due to the limitations of time for research, this chapter emphasizes the early history of Chinese settlers in Silver City in relation to the geopolitical context of why Chinese migrated to the United States and specifically to Grant County, New Mexico, how the national debates about Chinese immigration to the U.S. affected Silver City, and the emergence of the Chinese Gardens and Silver City's developing Chinese American community in the early 20th century. It ends with suggestions for future research.

The particularities of Silver City's New Mexico location in the U.S.-Mexican borderlands and the region's already racially and economically diverse composition after the U.S. conquest of Mexico and the U.S. Civil

---

130   My thanks to the Silver City Museum: to Director Bart Roselli for introducing me to Silver City and its rich and diverse history, to Ashley Smith for assistance with collections, Javier Marrufo for collaborating on the oral histories, David Phillips for his research in the local newspapers, and Sarah Zamora for locating valuable information. I am grateful to Silver City Public Library head librarian Ken Dayer for providing me with important resources, and the other librarians for their assistance. I thank Raul Turrieta whose support for my research in the Grant County Assessor archives (and his foresight in saving and preserving historical documents) has been invaluable. My thanks as well to the Grant County Records staff for their assistance, and to Debbie French and Sylvia Ligocky for providing me resources from the Deming Luna Mimbres Museum archives. I thank Susan Berry and Tom Hester for sharing their knowledge and insights about Chinese in Silver City, and Herbert Toy whose family history and knowledge about the Chinese American family markets in Silver City requires a separate chapter and has inspired ideas for future research. Special thanks to Diane for her generous hospitality, museum volunteers and staff, and other residents who welcomed me during my research trips.

War, converged to create unique social landscape in which Chinese immigrants from both the West Coast and Mexico sought their fortunes and built new lives. The majority of the 60,000 Mexicans who became U.S. residents overnight already lived in what was established as New Mexico Territory in 1850 (and expanded in 1852 with the Gadsden Purchase). The Civil War brought more White Americans to the territory. At least 300 Union veterans remained in the territory and the majority of those married Hispanic women, a pattern that seems to have continued with the arrival of more White men after the railroads arrived in 1878.[131] American Indians, Mexicans, Hispanics, Blacks, and Whites were joined by immigrants from Southern and Eastern Europe and China by the late 19th century.[132] During these decades, the United States underwent an industrial transformation after the war with the building of national transportation infrastructure, possibly due to technological advances that allowed the mass production of steel in the late 1850s, and federal subsidies promised by the 1862 Pacific Railway Act. Ironically, Chinese labor that helped to complete the Transcontinental Railroad in 1870 and the Southern Pacific and Atchison and Topeka railroads across the south, also contributed to the economic conditions that would find expression in anti-Chinese violence, recorded first in western states, and then expanding into the rural areas of the interior west.

---

131   Darlis A. Miller, "Cross-Cultural Marriages in the Southwest: The New Mexico Experience, 1846–1900," *New Mexico Historical Review* 57, 4 (1982): 339, 342.

132   A note on the changing and complicated language of race and ethnicity: in this chapter I use "White" to refer to Americans of European descent; if I mention southern and eastern Europeans, this is because they were not always accepted as White during the 19th and early 20th century. I use "Black" to refer to African Americans, and American Indian to refer to members of American Indian nations, also known as Native Americans. When the local newspapers refer to specific American Indian nations, I also differentiate and provide the specific national affiliation. I tend to use "Chinese settlers" to refer to those Chinese immigrants who settled in Silver City or Grant County, and Chinese American to refer to U.S.-born persons of Chinese descent. Other scholars and the local newspapers I quote use the terminology common at the time of publication. In New Mexico, Hispanic and Mexican are not the same ethnic identity; Hispanics trace their lineage to Europe and Mexicans refer to persons of Mexican nationality of Hispanic heritage.

Locating Chinese in New Mexico History

The discovery of silver ore in southern New Mexico must have attracted some Chinese—already facing anti-Chinese violence in California and already venturing east toward new opportunities—to New Mexico. Chinese businesses were reported in Albuquerque as early as 1868.[133] Dorothy Watson, in her study of Pinos Altos in Grant County, describes miners in search of gold even before the Civil War. After the Civil War ended, moreover, more miners arrived. The town had "600 to 700 inhabitants in 1868," and was incorporated that June. She notes the early presence of the Chinese, stating that "Chinese had been among the early settlers, and they lived in ditches along the gulches. They foresaw that cooking for the miners and washing for them would be more profitable than placering, so they discarded their gold pans for dish pans and wash tubs."[134] In California and other western states, the number of Chinese miners dropped beginning in 1870 as other opportunities for other work emerged, including railroads, restaurants, and laundries.[135]

Documentation of Chinese mine holdings and Chinese miners, however, is not easy to find. Some scholars of New Mexico Territory have observed that, while "probably present," Chinese workers and miners likely were overlooked or ignored by census takers.[136] Sue Fawn Chung, a historian of early Chinese rural settlements in the West, cites statistical analyses that demonstrate large inconsistencies of census counts. "All scholars have agreed that the census manuscripts provided an inaccurate snapshot of the Chinese individuals in their communities, yet they

---

133   Victor Westphall, "Albuquerque in the 1870's." *New Mexico Historical Review* 23, 4 (1948): 264.

134   Dorothy Watson, *The Pinos Altos Story* (Silver City, NM: The Silver City *Enterprise*, 1970), 13.

135   Sue Fawn Chung, *In Pursuit of Gold; Chinese American Miners and Merchants in the American West* (Urbana: University of Illinois, 2011), 30.

136   Roberta Key Haldane, "Gold-Mining Boomtown; People of White Oaks, Lincoln County, New Mexico Territory," 2012, 6, cited by Christine Copper-Rompato, "The Earliest Patent by a Woman in New Mexico: Eunice Trim's Combination Comfort Canteen." *New Mexico Historical Review* 92, 3 (2017), 321.

106

have been the only indicators of the residents of communities."[137] Some of the census takers would only count Chinese persons if someone who spoke English (usually a merchant who regularly needed to interact with non-Chinese in English) was available to identify other Chinese present. Even if the census takers were negligent because they could not or would not communicate with non-English speakers to obtain the information requested, Chinese immigrants may have actively avoided being counted either due to previous poor experiences with census takers in China or in the United States. "Because the Chinese sometimes avoided both the tax collectors and the census takers, tracing individual male Chinese has been difficult."[138] Even though there were less women than men among Chinese immigrant communities, Chinese women often were not even reported to the census takers. Chung also notes, "Chinese merchants often were known by their company name rather than their personal name."[139] When the Grant County assessor began listing the names of restaurants like American Kitchen or English Kitchen to assess the value of the property, the value of improvements made to the property, and any total assessed value, the owners of the establishments no longer were listed by personal name unless they owned other property. The erasure of individual names suggests that property can take the place of persons in the records. The owners of businesses may change, but we would not know that unless other records exist such as listings in the local newspapers. Fortunately, new owners often placed newspaper announcements when they purchased new businesses, primarily so that the new owner would not be held liable for past business debts.

The accuracy of Chinese names listed in documents presents another challenge. Chung, who has researched rural towns' records of Chinese residents in Nevada, Oregon, and California, notes that Chinese women often were referred to by the press (and presumably in person) as "China Mary" because it was easy to pronounce, and that married Chinese women often

---

137 Chung, *In Search of Gold*, xx.
138 Chung, *In Search of Gold*, xxi.
139 Chung, *In Search of Gold*, xxx.

added "Shee" to their last name, which would be mistaken as their first name. Chinese traditionally provide their last name first, and census takers often would confuse the correct order of names.[140] Chung adds, "Another common mistake was to assign "Ah," a term of familiarity as a person's first or last name."[141] Some names' spelling may vary depending on each census taker's phonetic instincts. Additional challenges in tracking Chinese in the records relate to inability to accurately identify who is Chinese. While Sam Hing or O.D. Wing might reasonably be expected to be Chinese, the romanization of Lem to Lime is not obvious without corroboration from other source. Bill Young or George Bilinda are even less obviously Chinese. Chung explains that "Nineteenth-century, first-generation Chinese Americans who considered themselves "Americanized Chinese" often took a Euro-American name, like Sam Gibson and Joseph Tape (Chinese name, Zhao Qia or Chew Dip in Cantonese) of the famous *Tape v. Hurley* (1885) fame."[142]

In fact, some of the Chinese in Grant County, New Mexico, appear to have either been born in Mexico or taken Mexican names. Sam Chung, listed in the 1880 census, lived in Georgetown and worked as a huckster. Although he is racially identified as Chinese, his place of birth is listed as Chihuahua, where he also stated his parents were born. This may indeed be the case, but Chung also may have been a migrant who arrived in Mexico in the 1870s and then came with other migrants from Mexico to the United States. Hu-Dehart writes, "Although there is good evidence that some Chinese had arrived in Mexico and set up small businesses as early as the mid-seventeenth century, the result of regular traffic between the Spanish colonies of New Spain (Mexico) and the Philippines during the long Manila Galleon trade, Chinese did not migrate to or settle in Mexico in any significant numbers until the last quarter of the nineteenth century."[143] By the 1880s, some Chinese who entered the United

---

140 Chung, *In Search of Gold*, xxxi.

141 Chung, *In Search of Gold*, xxxi.

142 Chung, *In Search of Gold*, xxxi.

143 Khun Eng Kuah-Pearce, and Evelyn Hu-Dehart, *Voluntary Organizations in the Chinese Diaspora* (Hong Kong University Press, 2006), 141.

States by crossing the Mexican border during the Chinese Restriction and Exclusion periods disguised themselves as Mexican citizens, who were not subject to immigration restrictions until the 20th century. Lim notes, "By 1895, immigration officials had become aware that 'many more Chinamen are slipping across the line into this country than is generally known' by resorting to a variety of schemes, "the method most in favor being to don Mexican garb, thus concealing their nationality, as those who have resided in the sister republic for any length of time speak the language fluently."[144] Whether these individuals had disguised themselves as a Mexican national, identified as a Chinese Mexican, or were born in Mexico, would require painstaking research and cross-referencing document—if they can be found. However, any of these explanations is possible. Notably, Chung lived among a community of people who also were listed as being born in Chihuahua, which suggests he was part of that community.[145]

The other four Chinese enumerated in Georgetown's 1880 census lived together, possibly in the restaurant run by Navito Santo, a twenty-three-year-old man who is listed as having been born in China to parents who both were born in China. His name, however, unlike those of the three Chinese cooks (all listed with the "Ah" before their last names), appears to be Mexican or Hispanic.[146] At what point did Santo acquire this name and how? These records of unexpected names suggest that interethnic interactions took place regularly enough for individuals to adopt names resonant with their newfound communities, as has been evidenced among other Chinese American settlers. Such names speak to the movement of Chinese throughout the borderlands, crossing the U.S.-Mexico border in both directions from the 1870s throughout the era of Chinese Exclusion.

---

144 Julian Lim, *Porous Borders. Multiracial Migrations and the Law in the U.S.-Mexico Borderlands* (Chapel Hill: University of North Carolina Press), 106.

145 U.S. Census Bureau, 1880 Census, Grant, Territory of New Mexico, Population Schedule, Georgetown, p. 4, enumeration district (ED) 86-17, dwelling 78, family 59, Navito Santo: 1880 United States Federal Census, Ancestry.com. DW 77 Sheet.

146 U.S. Census Bureau, 1880 Census, Grant, Territory of New Mexico, Population Schedule, Georgetown, p. 4, enumeration district (ED) 86-17, dwelling 78, family 59, 1880, United States Federal Census, ancestry.com.

Lim explains that Chinese immigrants "took advantage not only of a poorly guarded border but also the multiracial tableau of the borderlands. They and their Mexican, black, and white associates manipulated and played with U.S. immigration officials' racial preconceptions."[147] This human element of adaptation and acculturation, in addition to racial and class prejudice, further complicates the historical record of who is recognized and counted as Chinese.

Arrivals to Silver City

The earliest documented record of a Chinese person's presence in Silver City, New Mexico, is found in the newspaper *Mining Life*. In October 1874, it reported that a Chinese man had arrived from Albuquerque and planned to stay in Silver City. The *New Southwest* describes Sun as the "oldest resident Chinaman of Grant County."[148] Subsequent items in November and December recorded the presence of two Chinese laundry operators, Charley Sun and Sam Chung, respectively. Yet these two reports suggest that the laundries already were in business and not that these businesses had just opened. Sun had a partner in the laundry business by November. Did this partner enter Silver City with him, or did this person join later? What was his name? At what point did Sam Chung arrive and open a different laundry? These questions require further archival research, but they do establish the first documented presence of a Chinese person in the town.

By the time Sun and Chung set up laundries in Silver City, Chinese had established a presence on the West Coast for nearly three decades, beginning in 1848 after the discovery of gold at Sutter's Mill in California inspired the arrivals of hundreds of thousands of persons from around the world to mine for gold. Among these arrivals were hundreds of Chinese seeking their fortune from "Gold Mountain," as the United States came

---

147   Julian Lim, *Porous Borders. Multiracial Migrations and the Law in the U.S.-Mexico Borderlands* (Chapel Hill: University of North Carolina Press), 97.

148   *New Southwest*, Jun 24, 1882. See also Koenig, Terry. "The Chinese of Silver City 1870-1855" Dec 14, 1981. Local History, Dr. Cook. Silver City Public Library Collection, 5.

to be known. The Chinese primarily departed from a southeastern province in China known as Guangdong from the Pearl River Delta region. The Chinese from this area already had a history of immigration along the southern coast of Asia, with some Chinese settling in Southeast Asia as merchants and participating in a vast trade network. Natural disasters and foreign incursions during the 1840s and 1850s had left southern Chinese peasants in dire economic straits. Most rented lands for farming, and the cost of indemnities China owed to the European powers after suffering defeats in the two Opium Wars were passed along to landlords who then raised rents. This caused Chinese peasants to fall into even greater debt because of poor harvests due to a series of famines and floods. Trying to hold onto their way of life, Chinese peasants sought other sources of wealth and were attracted by promises of gold or labor recruiters' promises of wealth from wage-earning work. Many would pledge future earnings in exchange for transport via steamship to their new destination.[149] A mostly male Chinese labor out-migration initially found work on the plantations of the Kingdom of Hawai'i, South America, or the Caribbean. Even if their returns were delayed (as was often the case) they regularly sent funds home to support their families.[150]

The construction of a U.S. national railroad that spanned the continent offered a new source of employment for Chinese workers beginning in 1864 as the Civil War came to an end. Funded by the 1862 Pacific Railway Act, Central Pacific Railroad Company began hiring Chinese away from mining camps. "By late 1865, Chinese workers composed the vast majority of the labor force on the Central Pacific and numbered in the thousands. As Leland Stanford reported in a letter to U.S. President Andrew Johnson that year, "Without them it would be impossible to complete the western portion

---

149 Chung, *In Search of Gold*, 20.

150 Marlon K. Hom, *Songs of Gold Mountain: Cantonese Rhymes from San Francisco Chinatown* (University of California Press, 1987); Judy Yung, *Unbound Feet: A Social History of Chinese Women in San Francisco* (University of California Press, 1995); Erika Lee, *At America's Gates: Chinese Immigration during the Exclusion Era, 1882-1943, new edition 1* (Chapel Hill: The University of North Carolina Press, 2004).

of this great national enterprise, within the time required by the Acts of Congress."[151] Chang estimates that Chinese workers numbered up to 20,000 over the course of completing the transcontinental railroad[152] After they completed the Central Pacific railroad line, most Chinese looked for other work. Chang reports that "Chinese veterans of the Central Pacific, along with additional compatriots newly arrived from China, also helped build scores of other railroads through the United States and Canada during this period, a time in which the rail mileage of the country more than tripled. Their work continued well into the twentieth century."[153]

Chinese workers clearly were in demand as railroad workers yet surprisingly little is known about their contributions to building railroads in New Mexico, particularly in Deming, where the Southern Pacific line from the west connected with the Rio Grande, Mexico, and Pacific Railroad from El Paso on March 8, 1881. Another railroad built in the early 1880s connected Silver City and Deming. There is scant mention of Chinese working on these New Mexico railroads in either newspapers or local archives. O.W. Williams, postmaster of Silver City in 1881, attributed Silver City's increased Chinese population to the railroads:

> When the Southern Pacific Railroad was built through New Mexico by Chinese labor, Silver City caught much of the drift from its labor camps. They especially took over the labor of raising vegetables on the flat below the town, where the springs provided the necessary water. And they were preferred over the Mexicans in most kinds of manual labor.[154]

---

151 Chang et al., Introduction, 2.

152 Gordon H. Chang, Shelley Fisher Fishkin, and Hilton Obernzinger. "Introduction to The Chinese and the Iron Road." *Journal of transnational American studies* 10, no. 2 (2019), 2.

153 Chang et al., Introduction, 18.

154 O.W. Williams, Vertical file "Chinese," Silver City Public Library; probably from O.W. Williams, and Samuel D. Myres. 1966. *Pioneer Surveyor, Frontier Lawyer: The Personal Narrative of O.W. Williams, 1877-1902* (El Paso: Texas Western College Press).

112

Documentation about Chinese railroad workers in New Mexico is conspicuously missing. Susan Robinson, a journalist for the *Deming Headlight*, did some research on the Chinese railroad workers in Deming. She writes, "As near as I've been able to determine—A Chinese workforce of about 250 were working across N. Mexico." It's not clear if she ever finished the remaining research for the full report about Chinese in Luna County and New Mexico.[155] The Chinese Railroad Workers in North America Project at Stanford (2012-2020) undertook a recovery project that spanned disciplines and national borders to recover the experiences of the tens of thousands of Chinese who contributed to railway construction. The project documented Chinese working on the railroads in California, Arizona, and Texas in the 1870s and 1880s. The oral history of Ellen Wong Leung, who was born in Albuquerque when her father worked on the railroads, is the only mention of New Mexico.[156] Archaeologists have found some material traces: University of New Mexico's Maxwell Museum's website, "The Chinese Diaspora in New Mexico," features a photograph of a Chinese coin found by archaeologists along train tracks in Deming as evidence of Chinese railroad workers. The museum website also cites another study "found the remains of a camp made by Chinese railroad workers" along a line northwest from El Paso. Along with other items, two coins found in this camp "were struck between 1862 and 1875."[157] Gordon Chang attributes the lack of documentation to incomplete and poor business records and an inhumane labor system where railroads worked through Chinese labor contractors and never learned the names of the

---

155   Susan Robinson, Untitled notes about Chinese railroad workers in Deming, n.d., p.2 A 88-17, provided by archivist, Deming Luna Mimbres Museum Archive, Deming, New Mexico.

156   Ellen Wong Leung Interview. Ellen Wong Leung, Interviewee and Connie Young Yu, Interviewer, and Barre Fong, Interviewer, Oct 10, 2023. Chinese Railroad Workers Oral History Project, 2013-2018. https://exhibits.stanford.edu/crrw/catalog/fv652ry4242

157   David Phillips, "The Chinese Diaspora and New Mexico," *China Then and Now*, Maxwell Museum of Anthropology, University of New Mexico, Albuquerque, NM. Jan 5, 2018. https://www.unm.edu/~toh/china/chinese-diaspora.html

actual Chinese workers themselves.[158] Noting that "we now believe that many [railroad workers] were literate," and would have communicated when they sent money to family in China, Chang writes,

> Violence and destruction, rather than their lack of schooling, may be better explanations for why we have nothing from them today: the home areas of the workers in China suffered extensive devastation due to social conflict and war in the nineteenth and twentieth centuries, and every Chinese community in America in the mid- to late nineteenth centuries, and every Chinese community in America in the mid- to the late nineteenth century suffered arson, looting, and other forms of obliteration.[159]

A marked increase in the Chinese population of Silver City and Grant County took place in the late 1880s, which may be due to the railroads. Notably, when the Southern Pacific Railroad from Los Angeles to El Paso was completed in the summer of 1881, "about 300 Chinese decided to stay in El Paso. ... [and] formed the basis of the El Paso Chinese colony."[160] The 1885 Territorial Grant County New Mexico census records a little over 300 Chinese in the entire territory, with 76 Chinese residing in Silver City. In 1900, Grant County recorded a total of 195 Chinese, with Silver City accounting for 95 of those residents.[161] Perhaps Chinese did not decide to remain in New Mexico as they did in southwestern Texas because of the violent environment. Newspapers regularly reported attacks against Chinese—sometimes by other Chinese but often by Whites and Mexicans;

---

158   Chang et al., Introduction, 4.

159   Chang et al., Introduction, 4.

160   Jaime Portillo, and Joanna Atilanoc, "Borderlands: Chinese Immigrants Helped Build the Railroad in El Paso." *EPCC Library Research Guides* vol 19, 2000, EPCC, University of Texas, El Paso, Texas. https://epcc.libguides.com/c.php?g=754275&p=5406122 .

161   1885 U.S. Census. Grant Co, New Mexico, pop. Schedule, Jun 1885, 116-117, 121-122, 123, 125-127, 129-134, 137, 139. Enumeration Dist. No. 11. Retrieved from ancestry.com.

it is likely these were underreported (attacks against Mexicans and American Indians rarely were reported). In the 1870s and '80s, newspapers published regular warnings from the military about bands of "hostiles" (American Indians for whom southern New Mexico was home, and who were responding against the violence of U.S. settlement in and seizure of their lands) in the region, and this also may have encouraged Chinese to settle elsewhere.

Chinese already had diversified their economic activities by the 1870s. Many had agricultural talents because they had originally been farmers. Others found opportunities presented by the highly imbalanced gender ratio not just among Chinese but across the communities of male migrants in California and other western states. In mining camps, small towns, and growing cities, Chinese provided needed services such as preparing food, laundering clothes, cultivating, and selling vegetables and fruits, or cleaning homes. Some Chinese started small businesses including restaurants, laundries, and food markets.[162] These ventures employed fellow Chinese who often shared village connections or clan ties. The demand for house servants and day laborers encouraged the continued practice for a small number of Chinese to serve as labor brokers, providing labor as needed for farming, mining, railroad work, ditch digging, and so forth. These activities built upon existing traditions of entrepreneurship that had accompanied Chinese into the diaspora throughout the Americas. The shift to service work was not universal and some Chinese men continued to work their own mines or work as laborers for mining companies; however, the move into towns to develop small businesses resulted in documentation that allows us to locate and identify some of the early Chinese settlers in Grant County and Silver City.

Fragmentary newspaper accounts document the first Chinese arrivals in Silver City. *Mining Life* took note of Charley Sun and his business partner, and Sam Chung opening and operating two laundries in Silver City in late 1874, but it found little else about their lives newsworthy. The presence of two Chinese washhouses apparently did not present an economic

---

162   Chung, *In Search of Gold*, 30-31.

threat and may even have been welcome by those living and working in the surrounding mining camps. The *Weekly New Mexican* lightheartedly reported about competition between Chung's washhouse with Nellie Johnson's establishment. By April 1875, Chung, still in the laundry business, was preparing to sell fresh vegetables in town.[163] Misfortune, on the other hand, befell Sun: both he and Chung saw their businesses robbed, but Sun lost clothing, blankets, and two revolvers worth up to $200 in September 1875, and the following July his wife gave birth to a stillborn daughter. Sun was arrested after the stillborn child was found near the Catholic church; while originally reported as infanticide, Judge Rilea cleared him of any wrongdoing and released him.[164] Sun also expanded his business interests in 1877, opening the Home Restaurant on Bullard south of Broadway.[165]

These later accounts about Chung and Sun indicate that they were recognized Silver City residents, that Chung was entrepreneurial enough to see a need in the town for fresh produce and develop a new venture, and that Sun had a wife. It is not clear whether Sun's wife was from China or not. In 1874 Silver City and Grant County, Chinese women were rare, and it may have been that Sun's wife was not Chinese. The court case, however, also shows that the judge was sympathetic to the loss of their child and accepted their explanation that the child was stillborn. On August 3, 1878, the *Herald* announced that two Chinese men and one Chinese woman had arrived in town, increasing the Chinese population. That same day, the paper reported that "Some fifty Chinamen have arrived at Clifton Arizona and will be put to work on the mines and furnaces."[166]

The absence of newspaper reports about anti-Chinese sentiment toward the Chinese in the 1870s is a marked difference from the charged racial climate of California. The reference by two different Grant County newspapers to the Chinese as "Celestials" between 1874 and 1878, along

163 *Mining Life*, Mar 11, 1875.
164 *Grant County Herald*, Jul 22, 1876, and Jul 29, 1876.
165 *Grant County Herald*, Nov 24, 1887.
166 *Grant County Herald*, Aug 3, 1878.

with the lack of the term "Chinaman," also suggests that Silver City residents did not harbor strong sentiments toward the Chinese other than a curiosity about their foreign culture. Sun and Hung are referred to by name and the exoticness of their foreign culture is remarked upon with interest as opposed to negativity. Even the competition between Johnson and Chung is reported without any comments about Chinese men doing the laundry or taking business away from washer women (the newspaper made a comment about creating a "new breed," but a census search for Johnson was unsuccessful; could she have been Black?). This was a stark contrast with commentary in papers of California, Washington, and other western states about Chinese men doing what at the time was assumed to be feminine work. Chinese men providing services traditionally occupied by wives and women raised questions for some about Chinese culture and values. The apparent lack of regard for "natural" masculine and feminine activities inspired questions about whether the Chinese were too foreign to fit in with American values and society. No newspaper addressed that Chinese men were willing to do whatever work needed to support their families in China, including work that many White American men did not have to do because they were not excluded from certain jobs and better-paying positions.

The lack of Chinese women reflected Chinese culture, however. The family was the primary social unit in Chinese society, and a wife's primary duty was to their husband's family. Stem family households, where two generations shared the same home, were the norm in Chinese villages. Split households, where members of a family unit live in separate spaces was the result of the global labor market, where wage-earning jobs in the late 19th century were found in industries feeding into infrastructure like railroads or large-scale mining, or on large-scale agricultural plantations relying on low-paid, intensive labor. Judy Yung explains, "… Chinese women (following the Confucian teaching, 'A women's duty is to care for the household, and she should have no desire to go abroad') remained at home, attended to their children and in-laws, and awaited the return of their husbands. This was not an easy task, considering that the separation could extend anywhere from ten years to a lifetime, depending on when finances would allow the husband a visit home or a final return."[167] Due to economic hardship, it was not unusual for Chinese men to leave their villages to seek wage labor. The development of steam engines that could propel ships across the Pacific Ocean only extended their journeys further into the Americas.

This apparent lack of wives and nuclear family structure contributed to some White Americans' erroneous assumptions that Chinese did not value families. In addition, many Chinese women who accompanied the early migrant stream of Chinese male workers to the United States were brought in as sex workers. Most newspapers on the West Coast also reported about the presence of Chinese women prostitutes. The ratio of sex workers to wives fueled misinterpretations that Chinese culture did not value women. These impressions also supported by the reports of American missionaries who would raise support for their China missions by focusing on the need for the civilizing influence of Christianity.[168] The large numbers of Chinese males living together without wives or families, in addition to the hypervisibility of Chinese prostitutes, fed the idea that Chinese were immoral and could never fit into White American society, which defined itself as civilized in comparison to American Indians, African Americans, and Mexicans. These perspectives of Chinese were shared by middle-class and working-class Americans, and the employers whose fortunes relied on the hard labor of the Chinese alike.[169] While Grant County newspapers occasionally commented about sex workers or a random "shady lady," none were identified as Chinese.

By 1878, four years after the first reports of Sun and Chung's washhouses, the *Herald* announced that the Chinese population in Silver City was "just twenty." These new arrivals were not announced in the newspapers, but apparently were operating restaurants, boarding houses,

---

167   Judy Yung, *Unbound Feet*, 20.

168   Stuart Creighton Miller, *The Unwelcome Immigrant; the American Image of the Chinese, 1785-1882*, Berkeley: (University of California Press, 1969).

169   Chang et al., Introduction; Miller, *The Unwelcome Immigrant*.

118

and purchasing property. Sam Lee was identified as another "Chinese Laundryman."[170] Wing Chong bought out Charley Sun's portion of Home Restaurant and was providing rooms for let at $5 a week on Bullard Street.[171] At least one group of Chinese made bricks for sale, and others were reportedly "becoming owners of Real Estate, with a vengeance," and "Nearly every coach from Clifton brings additions to our Chinese population."[172] (New Mexico did not pass an Alien Land Law in 1921, so Asians were able to purchase land at this time.) Perhaps these new arrivals were leaving the copper mines to establish their own small businesses in the fast-growing Silver City, or possibly they were coming directly from California to avoid the ongoing hostility and violence led by the state's Workingmen's Party.

Emergence of Anti-Chinese Agitation on the West Coast

Negative views of Chinese immigrants on the West Coast intensified further with the completion of the Transcontinental Railroad, which brought more internal migrants westward in search of jobs. The increased population in western states resulted in greater competition for work, even as the industrialists sought to keep wages down. In 1871, a mob of angry working men in Los Angeles burned down Chinese encampments and chased the Chinese out of town—some of whom moved eastward in search of safety. The 1873 economic depression fueled greater unrest among workingmen, who blamed low rates of employment and financial duress on the Chinese. White working-class men and women alike blamed the Chinese for bringing down wages because they did not have families to support and taking domestic jobs from White women and driving families into ruin.[173] Denis Kearney founded the Workingmen's

---

170   *Grant County Herald*, Aug 27, 1879.

171   *Daily Southwest*, Mar 1, 1880.

172   *Daily Southwest*, Jul 14, 1880.

173   Karen J. Leong, "A distinct and antagonistic race" Constructions of Chinese Manhood in the Exclusionist Debates, 1869-1878," Matthew L. Basso, Dee Garceau, Laura McCall, eds. Across the Great Divide: Cultures of Manhood in the United States West (NY: Routledge Press, 2001) 131-148.

Party of California, which attracted recent White European immigrants and rapidly grew into a political force.[174]

The unrest of White laborers, economic uncertainty as the railroad contributed to rapid population growth in western states, and growing antipathy toward Chinese who were seen as taking jobs from White men and women, constituting a foreign threat to civilized society, and overrunning the West Coast crystallized into the anti-Chinese movement. Labor tracts declaring, "The Chinese Must Go!" or urging patrons to boycott Chinese laundries due to their uncleanliness, were no longer localized to western municipalities but grew into a national condemnation of the unnatural and foreign Chinese. Where in the 1860s California and other western state politicians' claims of being overrun by foreign hordes were dismissed, a shift in attitudes took place nationally. California representative Horace Page introduced legislation in the U.S. Congress to limit undesirable immigration of those who might be public charges, unfree contract labor, or women from China brought in for "immoral purposes" or prostitution. The Page Act became law in 1875, constituting the first time a group of persons was restricted based on nationality.[175]

The 1875 Page Law gave U.S. authorities at ports in China great discretion in determining which women were not truly wives seeking reunification with their husbands. In practice, George Anthony Peffer has demonstrated that the majority of Chinese women seeking to enter the United States, even as more and more legal wives came to join their husbands, were perceived to be prostitutes and thus denied entry. This exclusion contributed to the lack of community growth (and limited the numbers of U.S.-born Chinese children who would rightfully be U.S. citizens).[176] It also laid the foundation for the U.S. to restrict the entry of Chinese laborers as an undesirable class of persons based on distorted

---

174   Alexander Saxton, *The Indispensable Enemy; Labor and the Anti-Chinese Movement in California*. Berkeley: University of California Press, 1971.

175   Leong, "A distinct and antagonistic race."

176   George Anthony Peffer, *If They Don't Bring Their Women Here: Chinese Female Immigration before Exclusion*. Urbana: University of Illinois Press, 1999.

120

notions of being too foreign to belong in the United States.[177] Within seven years, U.S. diplomats revised existing treaties with China to allow continued imports of goods to the Chinese markets, and unrestricted travel of Americans to China, and to allow exclusion on which Chinese were permitted to enter the U.S. The 1882 Chinese Restriction Act barred Chinese laborers from entering the United States for ten years. Only those who could prove their residency in the United States would be allowed to return if they left for China. The 1882 law also explicitly stated that Chinese could not become naturalized citizens of the United States, something that already was implicit in existing citizenship law.[178]

While this 1882 law long has been described as the beginning of Chinese Exclusion that drastically lessened Chinese entry into the United States, Beth Lew-Williams's careful reading of the series of restrictive immigration laws limiting Chinese entry into the United States demonstrates that the 1882 law actually did not accomplish its goal. This law was a first attempt at lessening the numbers of Chinese immigrants and instituting paperwork (return certificates) to document those who were in the country legally or illegally. Concessions to the Chinese government in order to maintain positive diplomatic relations allowed those Chinese workers already in the United States prior to 1882 to depart and reenter. Thus, thousands of Chinese continued to enter the United States in the late 1880s (some newcomers falsely claiming they had been in the U.S. prior to 1882.) In fact, more than the average number of entries prior to 1882.[179] Challenging the misreading of the 1882 law by past historians, Lew-Williams persuasively argues that the tightening of restrictions on Chinese immigrants took place in two phases—Chinese Restriction in 1882, with Chinese Exclusion enacted in

---

177 Karen J. Leong, *The China Mystique Pearl S. Buck, Anna May Wong, Mayling Soong, and the Transformation of American Orientalism*. (University of California Press, 2005) 10.

178 Beth Lew-Williams, "Before Restriction Became Exclusion: America's Experiment in Diplomatic Immigration Control," *Pacific Historical Review* 83, no. 1 (2014): 24–56, 33.

179 Lew-Williams, "Before Restriction Became Exclusion," 25.

1888, strengthened in 1904, and lasting until repeal of Chinese Exclusion in 1943.[180]

The height of anti-Chinese violence took place in the 1880s, with 91 recorded events, a rate three times the number of events in the 1870s. Lew-Williams's analysis of patterns of anti-Chinese violence reveals that antagonisms against Chinese surged in California in the late 1870s, but a rash of anti-Chinese violence exploded across the interior west *after* 1882 and shifted to the Pacific Northwest. She argues that the visible ineffectiveness of the 1882 law at slowing the arrival of Chinese led to some of the most egregious violent attacks on Chinese in the 19th century. Additionally, the 1882 Chinese Restrictive Law added official weight to popular perceptions of Chinese as undesirable. Lew-Williams observes that "the law now cast Chinese as illegal aliens (or suspected illegal aliens), setting them apart from all other nationalities and further degrading their status in the United States.[181] Li and Wunder compiled 153 events of anti-Chinese violence in the U.S. West from 1852 to 1903 that dislocated 10,500 Chinese from their places of residence and business. They included New Mexico which had not been included in earlier analyses of anti-Chinese violence in the U.S. West.[182] New Mexico accounted for four violent outbreaks: one in Raton in 1885, two in Silver City in 1885 and 1886, and one in Deming in 1888. These combined events dislocated 200 Chinese, a significant number in proportion to the Chinese population in the state at the time.[183] The timing of this violence in New Mexico reflects the increased numbers of new arrivals—internal migrants from other states, as well as Chinese

---

180   Lew-Williams, "Before Restriction Became Exclusion," 26.

181   Lew-Williams, "Before Restriction Became Exclusion," 34.

182   John R Wunder and Liping Zhu, *Gold Mountain Turned to Dust, Essays on the Legal History of the Chinese in the Nineteenth-Century American West* (University of New Mexico Press, 2018). The states include the West Coast states of California, Oregon, and Washington; the interior west states of Arizona, Colorado, Idaho, Montana, Nevada, New Mexico, South Dakota, Utah, Wyoming; and the territories of Alaska and Hawaii.

183   Wunder and Zhu, *Gold Mountain Turned to Dust,* 7.

122

and European immigrants—to the territory as well as the influence of national discussions about Chinese workers and the incompatibility of Chinese with American values.

The Anti-Chinese Movement and Silver City

Chinese settlers began arriving in New Mexico by the late 1870s and through the 1880s in the hopes of creating lives absent the heightened scrutiny of Chinese businesses and workers in other western states. By 1881, Chinese businesses in Silver City had enough capital to buy ad space in local newspapers. Sing Kee advertised his laundry services, noting "I do all the washing for the Tremont House. Guests and others leaving their orders at the hotel office will have them promptly attended to." And Ben Hun Lun, owner of the Restaurant and Chop House located above Sam Hop's laundry on Broadway, promised "HOT COFFEE at all hours, DAY or NIGHT." Sue Le, owner of the "HOME" Restaurant on the East side of North Bullard Street, and nearly opposite C.F. Bottom's City Meat Market gave notice that he had purchased Charley Sun's interest in the "well-known and justly popular restaurant" and was offering rooms for let.[184] By the end of 1881, however, Chinese hopes to escape the anti-Chinese laws that proliferated other western states were disappointed. On December 1, 1881, the *Mining Herald* reported that, "The city council last night levied a tax of $25 per quarter on the Chinese laundry establishments in town." This extra tax on Chinese laundries was like the foreign miner's taxes that western states earlier had levied on Chinese, Native Hawaiian, and Mexican miners. In the same month,

---

184 *The Mining Chronicle*, Nov 16, 1880, 1, 4.

123

the *Mining Chronicle* published a sordid description of opium dens in town, run by and frequented by Chinese.[185]

The different perspectives about Chinese and White working men by the local press reflects the class and racial tensions that abounded in turn of the century U.S. society. Rapid economic growth enriched a new affluent class of elites. At the same time, the middle class that had emerged in the decades prior to the Civil War defined itself as morally superior to the less educated and poorer working class.[186] The post-war industrializing economy exploited workers with long, hard hours, poor working conditions, and wages that were driven lower by newer immigrants who were willing to work for less. The Chinese likewise were being exploited alongside White workers in manual labor, but cultural differences attributed to racial difference created a divide between these large groups that otherwise shared much in common. Perceived racial difference provided industrialists and employers with a powerful weapon against workers' collective action for better pay, benefits, and

---

185   This addiction among working-class Chinese in urban areas had spread in part by British traders (who sold opium to Chinese smugglers) who sought to offset the trade deficit with China in the early nineteenth century when Chinese teas, silks, and other goods were exported to China with very little British goods imported in return. The Chinese government sought to end the import of opium because of its effects on increasing poverty. This economic and moral conflict led to confrontations and, eventually, two Opium Wars with Great Britain. The indemnities charged by Great Britain, as well as other European powers, contributed to the destabilization of China's economy and governing system, which in turn contributed to the larger numbers of Chinese laborers seeking jobs overseas. However, the effects of opium physically have been questioned in recent years. See John R. Haddad, *America's First Adventure in China: Trade, Treaties, Opium, and Salvation* (Philadelphia: Temple University Press, 2013) 113-115. For more information about the effect of the Opium Wars on China see Jonathan Spence, *The Search for Modern China* (NY: WW Norton & Co, 1990), 143-164.

186   See Paul E Johnson, *A Shopkeeper's Millenium: Society and Revivals in Rochester, New York, 1815-1837*, New York: Hill and Wang, 1978; and Mary P. Ryan, *Cradle of the Middle Class: The Family in Oneida County, New York, 1790-1865*, Cambridge, Eng.; Cambridge University Press, 1981.

hours. They could deflect workers' anger at the poor working conditions toward the Chinese instead.[187]

Class divisions also existed within the Chinese immigrant community. The need for large numbers of low-paid workers throughout the Americas and Caribbean had given rise to a new class of Chinese entrepreneurs: the labor recruiters. These men recruited other Chinese from their villages and would contract them out as labor gangs to the railroad companies or plantations. The labor recruiters profited from these contracts that took part of the wages earned by the laborers who suffered poor working conditions. Some Chinese entered the U.S. as merchants, others found opportunities in the U.S. that allowed them to accumulate wealth and become merchants. In large cities, large family associations were central sites where Chinese leaders served as cultural, political, and labor brokers. In small towns, however, Chinese merchants often served as de facto representatives for their community, because they regularly interacted with businessmen and with town leaders.[188] Their greater wealth and social capital gave them power over other Chinese migrants. Given the growth of large-scale industries, the tradition of labor brokers continued as well. "They frequently acted as labor brokers, dealt with the "boss headman"[189] of teams of miners who worked for Chinese owners/investors or Euro American mine owners. Chinese merchants were able to take advantage of ships who would take U.S. goods to China and would bring return shipments of Chinese goods at inexpensive rates. Chinese merchants traditionally sold items on credit which gave them a competitive advantage over other stores.[190] While merchants did not escape anti-Chinese agitation or violence, their class privilege provided

---

187   See Saxton, *Indispensable Enemy*; and David R. Roediger, *The Wages of Whiteness: Race and the Making of the American Working Class*. London; Verso, 1991.

188   Chung, *In Search of Gold*, xviii.

189   Chung, *In Search of Gold*, xviii.

190   Chung, *In Search of Gold*, xviii; Evelyn Hu-Dehart, "5. On Coolies and Shopkeepers: The Chinese as Huagong (Laborers) and Huashang (Merchants) in Latin America/Caribbean." Rutgers University Press, 2019.

some access to respectability and acceptance. What we know of Chinese in Silver City is primarily through this relatively privileged lens.

One merchant who ingratiated himself among the Silver City leaders was Lew Sam. According to the U.S. 1900 Census, Sam was born in China in 1870, arrived in the United States in 1875 as a young boy, and grew up in San Francisco.[191] The earliest record of his presence in Silver City is in the September 2, 1882, issue of the *New Southwest*: "Grabe gave Sam Lew a contract for 200,000 bricks." A Richard Grabe is listed in the 1903 New Mexico Business Directory as a contractor and builder.[192] Fluent in English, Sam may have been a go-between on behalf of one of two Chinese-owned brickyards in Silver City—one owned by Sue Lee "below the old Carrolton mills" and Sam Hop's brickyard "south of town."[193] He himself is not listed as owning a brickyard. Sam also apparently retained connections with the Chinese community in San Francisco through the Chinese Free Masons. Chinese family associations and business organizations were significant not only for business but for staying informed about the national political and economic developments that affected the lives of Chinese throughout the United States; other associations among Chinese settlers took care of burial arrangements.[194] Sam, who served as master of the Chinese Free Masons in the 1890s, was known for hiring out workers; this role may have been related to the Chinese Free Masons whose headquarters was in San Francisco.[195] The Silver City Free Mason Lodge reportedly had "about eighty members, many of whom reside at Pinos Altos and Georgetown," and who probably were laborers for various industries in the county.[196] The Chinese Free Masons in Silver City also may have been a central

191   *Silver City Enterprise,* "DEATH OF LEW SAM, CHINESE MERCHANT," Sept 29, 1905.

192   *New Mexico Business Directory including El Paso, Texas* 1903-1904, Denver, Colorado: The Gazetteer Publishing Co., 1903, 467.

193   *The New Southwest,* May 20, 1882; Sept 2, 1882; and Sept 16, 1882.

194   Chung, *In Search of Gold,* 25-26.

195   *Silver City Enterprise,* Oct 4, 1889.

196   *Silver City Enterprise,* Oct 4, 1889.

source for Chinese in Grant County to learn and share information about the political and social developments that affected Chinese in the U.S.

The U.S. Southwest did not welcome the Chinese any more than the West Coast had. Wunder notes that "Individual non-Chinese attacked Chinese with some frequency." This included beatings of two Chinese in Deming, New Mexico, to prevent their claim on property, and Arizona's town of Bisbee forcing all Chinese out of the city by sundown.[197] In 1880, Chinese men were expelled from Denver by a mob that destroyed their houses and businesses in the city and lynched a Chinese laundryman named Sing Lee.[198] Silver City was not immune to violence. From December 1882 to November 1883, six Chinese men were killed, and one attacked.[199] A December 7, 1882, robbery of seven Chinese stagecoach passengers ended up in a shootout after "the highwaymen began shooting their victims in cold blood." Two Chinese men were killed and two wounded.[200] Three weeks later, the press noted that an unidentified Chinese man was brutally killed during a robbery.[201] The following February in 1883, three Chinese men were shot and killed along Fort Bayard Road, and Koenig noted that law enforcement waited three days to try to locate the killers.[202] Koenig also quotes a November 23, 1883, article in the *Enterprise* about an argument between a Chinese man and a White man, "resulting in the former being knocked down by a blow from a pistol in the hands of the whiteman [*sic*]. No arrest."[203] This violence, taking place right after the passage of Chinese Exclusion at the same time that mobs throughout the western states were forcibly expelling Chinese from their jobs and

---

197   Wunder and Zhu, *Gold Mountain Turned to Dust*, 180.

198   Brent M. S. Campney; "Standing in the Crater of a Volcano": Anti-Chinese Violence and International Diplomacy in the American West. California History 1 August 2021; 98 (3): 2–27, 5.

199   Koenig, "The Chinese of Silver City," 7-8.

200   Koenig, "The Chinese of Silver City," 7.

201   Koenig, "The Chinese of Silver City," 8.

202   Koenig, "The Chinese of Silver City," 7.

203   Koenig, "The Chinese of Silver City," 7.

residences, must have alarmed Chinese throughout Grant County.[204] Koenig suggests complacency in the press about these killings of Chinese; yet the *Enterprise*'s February 8, 1883 report about rustlers killing seven Chinese in Grant County in the past 12 months declared, "It is high time a rustler or two be strung up to a convenient tree." It should be noted that not all the newspapers shared the same perspective.

Although Koenig describes the Chinese as "rather passive,"[205] recirculating a stereotype of Chinese migrants found in the early historiography of the anti-Chinese movement, research by McClain, Salyer, and Pfaelzer, among others have since countered these stereotypes.[206] As McClain and Salyer have noted, Chinese in California became adept at fighting against what they perceived as discriminatory laws in the U.S. legal system. The Chinese Six Companies, the largest family associations to whom Chinese migrants belonged, pooled resources to hire U.S. lawyers to fight their cases in court, most often citing the 14th Amendment. These early cases were key to developing civil rights law including the guarantee of birthright citizenship (even to parents who are non-citizens), and equal protection under the law. From the very beginnings of restrictions, moreover, Lee has described the different ways Chinese fought back against the discriminatory laws that denied them entry by procuring papers for sons or wives who did not exist in fact, so that others might use those papers to enter the United States. These falsified identities based on fictitious kinship resulted in large numbers of "paper sons" and some "paper

---

204   Nicholas W. Mason, "Nonlethal Anti-Chinese Violence in the United States, 1850-1910: Nonlethal violence", 2021. https://www.antichineseviolence.com/nonlethal-violence. "Nonlethal Anti-Chinese Violence in the United States, 1850-1910: Nonlethal violence" lists 13 different riots, assaults, and forced removals from urban and rural locations in Arizona Territory, California, Colorado, Washington, and Montana; New Mexico is not listed.

205   Koenig, "The Chinese of Silver City," 7.

206   See Charles J. McClain, *Chinese Immigrants and American Law.* (NY: Garland Publishing, 1994); Lucy E. Salyer, *Laws Harsh as Tigers: Chinese Immigrants and the Shaping of Modern Immigration Law* (Chapel Hill: University of North Carolina Press, 1995); and Jean Pfaelzer, *Driven Out: The Forgotten War against Chinese Americans* (NY: Random House, 2007).

wives" or "paper daughters" who were related simply on paper.[207] In 1878, the Chinese Six Companies also provided legal counsel for three Chinese men who sought to become naturalized U.S. citizens. Lew-Williams notes that citizenship would protect Chinese Americans' ability to enter and exit the country at will and sidestep any state laws that targeted aliens for additional taxes or prevented them from owning land.[208] Although the court denied the petitions for naturalized citizenship, Lew-Williams has noted over 8,000 naturalized Chinese Americans in the 1900 U.S. census from all classes and occupations.[209]

Lew Sam was one of those naturalized Chinese Americans. The Silver City Enterprise reported, "Lew Sam, the Chinese interpreter of the district court, declared his intentions before the clerk to become a citizen of the United States. The clerk, knowing of no law forbidding a Chinaman to renounce his allegiance to the Emperor Quong Soi, swore Lew Sam to the declaration and issued him a certificate. The query is: Will the district court admit him into full citizenship when he applies to be admitted."[210] The *Enterprise* reporter clearly knew the law, unlike the clerk, and the short answer to their query was yes. The index for declarations of intent lists Sam's declaration on Dec 13, 1884. In the next column is written, "Certificate 20 Apr 1892, Grant, M: 284." [211] Sam's declaration of intent precedes that of other Chinese men in Grant County by a year. One clue for his being naturalized is that Sam by this time was the Chinese interpreter for the very district court that granted him citizenship. After filing a declaration of intent to naturalize in any court—which at the time required no proof of eligibility—applicants had to wait at least two years before filing a petition for naturalization. Sam was granted his papers in 1892,

---

207   Lee, *At America's Gates,* 194-197

208   Beth Lew-Williams, "Chinese Naturalization, Voting, and Other Impossible Acts," *Journal of the Civil War Era,* vol 13(4): 521.

209   Lew-Williams, Chinese Naturalization, 522.

210   *Silver City Enterprise* Dec 19, 1884, 3.

211   "Docket Book 14267, Index to Dec. if Intent, 1867-1908." New Mexico Genealogical Society 2007, vol. II, p. 132. New Mexico State Records Center and Archives, Santa Fe, New Mexico.

"since which he has proudly claimed the rights of citizenship—never failing to vote at party primary or election and served his country in the jury box."[212] As a Chinese American citizen Sam could now purchase property and avoid alien penalties like poll taxes. He also made a point of fully practicing his rights as a citizen, demonstrating that Chinese could be good Americans. Even as a naturalized citizen, however, Sam had to feel vulnerable as increasingly ugly violence took over the anti-Chinese movement on a national scale.

Anti-Chinese resentments against Chinese workers on the basis of economic competition and racial difference soon found expression in "localized grassroots" violence.[213] In February 14, 1885, the *Southwest Sentinel* reported that the Malone Protective Association in Grant County would not allow Chinese to set up business in that town, but no other anti-Chinese organizations were reported until after events in other states. In September 1885, a mob of White miners, railroad workers, and women attacked Chinese miners, killing 28, and burned down the Chinatown in Rock Springs, Wyoming. A month later in Tacoma, Washington, White residents warned Chinese residents to leave by November 3. As a result, 150 left voluntarily, and a mob of citizens drove out 200 more on November 3 and burned down the entire Chinese community.[214] The anti-Chinese tactics that seemed so successful in Wyoming and Washington clearly inspired White miners in Grant County to act.

The rise of anti-Chinese Leagues in the western states and the success of White residents running the Chinese out of Tacoma in 1885, encouraged

---

212 "A Chinese American Daddy," *The Eagle*, Jan 8, 1896. Not coincidentally, the first Chinese American to be naturalized after the repeal of Chinese Exclusion laws in 1943 also was an interpreter for the Immigration and Naturalization Office for thirty-five years. See "Edward Bing Kan: The First Chinese American Naturalized after Repeal of Exclusion," U.S. Citizenship and Immigration Services, Jul 28, 2020. https://www.uscis.gov/about-us/our-history/stories-from-the-archives/edward-bing-kan-the-first-chinese-american-naturalized-after-repeal-of-chinese-exclusion#2

213 Beth Lew-Williams, *The Chinese Must Go: Violence, Exclusion, and the Making of the Alien in America*, Cambridge, MA: Harvard University Press, 2018, 115-117.

214 Lew-Williams, *The Chinese Must Go*, 115.

130

some Silver City citizens to create their own committee toward the end of that year. *The Enterprise* on November 27, 1885, fully supported a boycott of all Chinese businesses. The editorial first explained, "In common with many other towns in the west Silver City is now experiencing ... a strong but subdued anti-Chinese feeling upon the part of a large number of its citizens. This sentiment is no recent growth, yet it has been slow to define itself and it is likely that were it not for the recent occurrences in Wyoming and upon the Pacific coast that it would have slumbered along indifnitly [*sic*]." It then concluded that the Chinese worker "belongs to a race which has nothing in common with us. ... his industry is the industry of avarice, and his slack ways are the ways of cunning. It was in recognition of his unfitness for assimilation in any respect with the people of this country that Congress passed the Chinese Restriction Act. Notwithstanding this he is here and how to get rid of him without violence is a question that has not yet been satisfactorily solved, for without violence it must be done, if done at all. There is but one way and that is to stop patronizing him."[215] The *Southwest Sentinel* also reported a formation of new organization: "The agitation of the Chinese question has resulted in the organization of a secret society ... and is said to be strong in numbers, having for its object the expulsion of Chinamen from our midst." As with other anti-Chinese Leagues, society members took an oath against using violence.[216] An advertisement in the Nov 24, 1885, edition of the *Southwest Sentinel* read:

Attention Citizens!
There will be a meeting of citizens on Tuesday evening at Crown Hall for the purpose of taking into consideration the advisability of ordering the Chinese population to remove, for the following reasons: First, they monopolize work that our needy population desire; second, they have paid but $12 into the treasury as city taxes during the year, and shipped through known sources during the past year $150,000 out of the county; third, they are of no

---

215 *Silver City Enterprise*, Nov 27, 1885.
216 *Southwest Sentinel*, Dec 1, 1885, 2.

benefit to our merchants, importing in the main their food and clothing from China; fourth, they breed pestilence by their filthy habits and their opium dens, and are a source of ruination to the young of both sexes and of all races; lastly, the work they do can be accomplished by our own people in a manner satisfactory to all interested. --- Adv.

The list of complaints against the Chinese did not vary from similar complaints by anti-Chinese leagues and societies, nor from earlier anti-Chinese movements in the 1860s and 1870s. Economic concerns about competition for work and profits motivated much of the agitation, with racial difference accounting for the disease, immorality, and ruin that Chinese brought with them wherever they settled.

But the anti-Chinese movement in Silver City did not unite all White residents across class differences as Lew-Williams suggests it did in other western states; it divided the town. Stark disagreements about the Chinese question were exposed when Silver City's Friends of the Order of Labor society held their first open town meeting at Crown Hall. Their opening resolution proposed that a "committee of ten" be created to order Chinese to leave town in twenty-four hours. Exceptions would be made for those who had declared their intention of becoming American citizens. Those who owned property would be allowed to stay in the city for a month, and for every $1,000 worth of property they would receive another month's reprieve.[217] Certain residents offered counterproposals that suggested efforts to limit the wholesale expulsion of Chinese residents. Dr. Thatcher unsuccessfully proposed that Chinese who had been residents of the city for more than two years be allowed to stay. Judge Bennet's motion that all Chinese be requested to apply for citizenship was tabled, and Judge Ginn who voiced opposition to the resolution was shut down by the audience. John W. Wright—someone who was respected enough to be voted to chair the meeting—also spoke out against the resolutions. He warned against extralegal violence stating that city and county officers would

---

217   *Southwest Sentinel,* Dec 1, 1885.

oppose any violence and might even call in the army to assist. "Before the meeting broke up, Sheriff Woods stepped forward and spoke a word of warning to those present, advising them that at the first violent attempt to make a Chinaman leave town, he would arrest those taking part in it and place them in gaol."[218]

The reluctance of the town leaders and authorities to embrace the anti-Chinese organization's proposal reflected local leaders' vision for Silver City, class differences and distrust, the complicated relationships of federal and state authority, and the larger context of Silver City's diversity and location. The town leaders were highly conscious about Silver City's reputation nationally; the sanatorium and accompanying health industry had emerged as thriving economic boons for the city, but ongoing reports of violence would undermine the city's image as civilized and respectable. By the 1880s, "Attitudes toward lawlessness also changed. In the silver camps, possibly owing to their transient nature, unruly elements thrived. ... But in the copper camps, the companies, local businessmen, and other stabilizing elements of society were eager to see an orderly community. "[219]

City leaders also wanted a stable economy. The mining economy went through surges and lulls; developing other industries was necessary to develop the city into the desirable destination it wanted to become. One of these promising industries was health treatment. Joan Jensen writes that the city "had already achieved a reputation as a place of recovery for TB victims by 1900."[220] She explains, "Town leaders saw healthcare as a growth industry that could cure their "economic blues" and, through good public relations, they helped establish Silver City's reputation as a healthcare retreat.[221] Attracting the affluent clientele able to afford the treatment, however, meant presenting a certain stable, law-abiding community, not one run by "unruly elements." The *Sentinel* emphasized,

---

218   "The Chinese Question," *Southwest Sentinel, Dec* 1, 1885, 2.

219   Robert L. Spude, "Mineral Frontier in Transition: Copper Mining in Arizona, 1880-1885." *New Mexico Historical Review* 51, 1 (1976), 30.

220   Joan Jensen, "Silver City Health Tourism in the Early Twentieth Century: A Case Study." *New Mexico Historical Review* 84, 3 (2009), 325.

221   Jensen, Silver City Health, 325.

"Silver City cannot afford to undergo a scene of bloodshed or violence of any kind. We hope for the welfare of our town that the better elements of the society will control its action, thus preventing any such scenes."[222] Although the society pledged nonviolence and called for an economic boycott, the dominant fears of those opposing the boycott believed that extralegal violence against the Chinese was inevitable. This was supported by anti-Chinese violence erupting through the west and the formation of anti-Chinese societies in New Mexico, but it also suggests different visions for Silver City's future—would the city be governed by business interests or racial interests? Even if businesspersons did not like the Chinese, they relied upon work that the Chinese provided.

The most divisive factor proved to be the economic boycott itself, enacted by the Committee of Ten against not only Chinese-owned businesses but any business that employed Chinese. The *Sentinel* fretted, "We are afraid the movers in this work have carried the thing too far by proposing to boycott all those who by force of circumstances, or otherwise, are compelled to employ Chinamen at times in the absence of other [workers]."[223] The *Enterprise* also described the division sowed by the boycott:

> We do know that they have boycotted several business institutions which did not employ Chinamen in any capacity whatever. ... If boycotting is one of the principles necessary to rid us of the Chinese, as it undoubtedly is, then the association will be indeed short-lived. That principle alone ... will have more of a tendency toward keeping the Chinese with us than all the Friends of Labor can accomplish toward forcing them out. ... The very fact that this boycotting business has arraigned almost all of our best citizens against the association proves that their efforts so far are without avail.[224]

---

222 *Southwest Sentinel,* Dec 1, 1885, 2.
223 *Southwest Sentinel,* Dec 1, 1885, 2.
224 *Silver City Enterprise,* Jan 8, 1886, 1.

Tellingly, even some of those who were members of anti-Chinese organizations decried the boycott. One such person was Dr. G.N. Wood, a commissioner from Georgetown. "He is a leading member of the Friends of Labor at Georgetown but declares if the agitators of this city attempt to dictate where the Georgetown people shall throw their custom that they will get left entirely. While in the city, the doctor put his horse up at a boycotted stable and patronized several other business institutions upon which the death sentence has been passed by the Silver City organization."[225] The *Sentinel* also reported, "So far the movement has met with but slight success, nearly all the merchants, professional men, ranchmen, and mining men absolutely refuse to have anything to do with the organization: Not because they desire the presence of the Chinese, but ... they recognize the fact that as fair-minded men and law-abiding American citizens they cannot attempt to dictate to their fellow citizens, or under the present laws to refuse to foreigners of any nationality the right to live and labor in any part of the United States." The economic boycott violated a fundamental belief in individual freedoms protected by the law and exposed a division of class interests. While the White working class increasingly viewed collective action as the only means of economic survival, White ranchers and businessmen did not want to be told who they could or could not hire. As several historians of the anti-Chinese movement in the United States have noted, the White working class's investment in racial difference blinded them to their common economic interests with non-Whites throughout the United States during the 19th and early 20th centuries.[226]

Another factor that explains Silver City's divided views over the anti-Chinese organizing is that   other issues concerned southern New Mexico at the time. In the same newspaper pages that reported on the anti-Chinese activities of the Friends of the Order of Labor were regular

---

225 *Silver City Enterprise,* Jan 8, 1886, 2.

226 See Saxton, *Indispensable Enemy;* Roediger, *Wages of Whiteness;* Lew-Williams, *The Chinese Must Go;* and Mae M. Ngai, *Impossible Subjects: Illegal Aliens and the Making of Modern America,* new edition (Princeton University Press, 2014).

warnings of "hostiles" near the city. The efforts of the Chiricahua Apache against what they understood as the invasion of their lands by U.S. settlers might have been perceived by town leaders as a more pressing existential threat than that of Chinese workers. Some of the White settlers were not unsympathetic to the Indians. James Hastings, who as a boy moved to Silver City in May 1880, recalled that some of the White male settlers in the county "were just scum, and they by their actions caused the Indians to hate the Whites and that hatred was often taken out on defenseless people."[227] In late November 1885, reports circulated of small bands of Indians "scattered throughout the entire northwest portion of the county." A November 28 communication from Fort Bowie to John M. Wright was published in the newspaper about an "especially malignant" group of "hostiles": "If they succeed in getting away from the various parties now hunting them, they will do all the damage they can. Warn all citizens that there will be constant danger until it is positively known they have left the country."[228] The Indian troubles continued into the new year, alongside anti-Chinese activities. The *Enterprise* on January 8, 1886, reported that a $250 reward for Indian scalps was offered at the Stock Association and Citizens of Grant County meeting held at the Timmer House to discuss "our present Indian troubles." The attendees agreed that a delegate was needed to travel to Washington, DC to speak with the President, Congress, and the Secretaries of War and Interior to share "the true state of Our Indian Troubles and ask that they take immediate action in ridding our sorely afflicted people from the hostile Apache Indians at present devastating our country, killing our unprotected people, and destroying our property." A separate award of $300 to $500 for the scalp of Geronimo was also offered by the Lyons & Campbell Ranch.[229] The editors also suggested on the first page, next to the editorial deploring the anti-Chinese boycott's division of Silver City residents, that the $250 bounty for the killing of

---

227 James K. Hastings, "A Boy's Eye View of the Old Southwest." *New Mexico Historical Review* 26, 4 (1951): 300.

228 *Southwest Sentinel*, Dec 1, 1885, 3.

229 *Silver City Enterprise*, Jan 8, 1886, 2.

136

Indians would be better if raised to $1,000, noting that $1,000 would attract skilled frontiersmen and would still save money for the country versus hostile American Indians' destruction of private property.[230] For town leaders, the division caused by the attempted boycott that targeted not only Chinese but White people's interests was poor timing.

More than a third of the Chinese in Silver City responded to the national and local anti-Chinese efforts by declaring their intent to naturalize. Between December 12, 1885, and July 23, 1886, thirty-two Chinese men residing in Silver City or Grant County went to the court to file their declarations to become naturalized citizens of the United States.[231] Twenty-two Chinese men filed these declarations in December in what appears to have been a coordinated protest of Chinese across the United States against the immigration restrictions. During the same month, over 200 Chinese in El Paso filed their intent to naturalize.[232] The *Enterprise* reported on December 29 that, "A class of Chinese is being taught by Mr. Coates, the Methodist minister, every evening at his house. Quite a number attend and they are making very rapid progress in learning to speak, read and write English." Silver City's Chinese residents communicated their refusal to accept the notion that they were threats to White workers and American society because they were too foreign.

U.S. Congress and the president ultimately concluded that the agitation and vigilantism against the Chinese threatened foreign relations and domestic political stability. China's "most favored nation" treaty status meant that Chinese citizens in the United States were supposed to have the same rights as U.S. citizens. The violence against Chinese had led the Chinese government to demand payments for damages, investigations of crimes that often went unpunished, and greater U.S. federal government protection for Chinese citizens. U.S. politicians also recognized that

---

230   *Silver City Enterprise,* Jan 8, 1886, 2.

231   "Docket Book 14267, Index to Dec. if Intent, 1867-1908." New Mexico Genealogical Society 2007, vol. II, 132. New Mexico State Records Center and Archives, Santa Fe, New Mexico.

232   *Santa Fe Weekly New Mexican,* Dec 24, 1885, as cited by Koenig, *The Chinese of Silver City,* 8.

restricting the Chinese would be a more expedient solution than addressing the structural inequities that existed in the political and economic system of the United States. The political costs of not addressing these concerns compelled significant U.S. diplomatic negotiations with China in order to place greater restrictions on Chinese immigration. Chinese Exclusion was established over a period of six years. The 1888 Scott Act restricted all Chinese workers for twenty years and removed the right of return for Chinese workers, and drastically reduced Chinese entry into the U.S. by 75%.[233] But enforcing the restrictions was not a simple matter, and within four years, the 1892 Geary Act created a system that required Chinese in the US to register as residents as part of a new centralized system of enforcement.[234] 1904 legislation extended Exclusion indefinitely.[235]

Silver City Chinese responded to these geopolitical and political maneuvers by the U.S. government by participating in a national boycott of the registration system and by practicing the politics of respectability in contrast to the anti-Chinese agitators.[236] Some Chinese demonstrated their willingness to integrate by attending English language lessons and Sunday School at the First Methodist Church. The *Enterprise* noted that, "The Chinese school, conducted Sunday afternoons at the Methodist church, is growing at each meeting. The Mongolians are taking not a little interest in the matter."[237] The initial national boycott by the Chinese of the 1892 registration requirement was so successful that the U.S. government was unable to enforce the Geary Act due to the lack of registrations.[238] In November 1893, Congress amended the law to grant Chinese

233   Lew-Williams, Chinese Naturalization, 50.

234   Lew-Williams, *Chinese Must Go*, 135-183; Lee, *At America's Gates*, 225.

235   Lew-Williams, Chinese Naturalization, 53.

236   Lew-Williams, *Chinese Must Go*, 196, 203.

237   *Silver City Enterprise,* Feb 21, 1890. According to an interview with his son, B.E. Pierce, the Reverend Pierce's photographs contain a photograph of Chinese men and the Reverend and other Silver City members in front of the church: B. Edward Pierce Photographs, NMHM Palace of the Governors, Identifier: HP.1976.29-MNM.1976.32-MNM.GA.1677-H. See Benjamin E. Pierce, *Memories of Pierces in Parsonages*, 1975, 8-12.

238   Lew-Williams, *Chinese Must Go*, 205.

migrants six additional months to register and avert mass deportation. To appease ardent exclusionists, the McCreary Amendment also took several new steps to tighten the law: it required two White witnesses to prove a merchant's class, required that certificates of residence include photographs, denied bail to Chinese awaiting deportation, required U.S. marshals to carry out all orders for deportations, and ordered the immediate deportation of all Chinese convicted of felonies.[239] This inspired the *Sentinel* to announce, "Our celestial friends will have to register and be photographed before May 9th or they will have the pleasure of a journey to China at the expense of Uncle Sam."[240]

Silver City and Grant County residents witnessed a surge of federal government agencies enforcing Chinese exclusion laws across the southern New Mexico border. By Spring 1894, a month before the extension ended, "Honorable William Burns, the efficient Deputy Internal Revenue officer under Collector Charles M. Shannon, spent several days in the city this week. He was collecting the photographs of the celestial residents (Chinese) in the city as souvenirs for Uncle Sam's portrait gallery. He procured about 100 of their photographs."[241] This meant that more than half of the Chinese in Grant County were still refusing to register. By 1895, greater resources resulted in more federal enforcement of the exclusion law. In January 1896, "J.H. Behan, an official of the Internal Revenue department, whose special duties are looking after violations of the Chinese exclusion law was in town several days last week, from El Paso [Texas], making pertinent inquiries in regard to the [Mongolian] residents of Silver City."[242] The U.S, Marshals also were activated to investigate and deport Chinese who were in the country with fraudulent or no documentation.[243]

---

239 Lew-Williams, *Chinese Must Go*, 209.
240 *Silver City Enterprise,* Mar 21, 1893.
241 *Silver City Enterprise*, Mar 23, 1894, 3.
242 *The Eagle,* Jan 15, 1896.
243 *Silver City Independent,* Sept 28, 1897.

Some of the White proprietors of Silver City businesses began to advertise that they were not hiring Chinese help with varying degrees of success. In December 1892, Mrs. Julia Black announced she had opened the Broadway Restaurant, promising "No Chinese help will be employed in any capacity."[244] In June 1894, the *Southwest Sentinel* noted, "Broadway room rented to Chin June, "will open restaurant."[245] Starting on April 10, 1895, the Broadway Café in the Broadway Hotel was under the ownership of S.W, Burdick, whose ad in *The Eagle* promised, "No Chinese help will be employed and the culinary department is being looked after by a competent chef from Denver [Colorado]."[246] In case anyone had forgotten, Burdick reminded *The Eagle* readers in May and then June, "No Chinese help employed at the Broadway Café. It is first class in all its appointments."[247] The Timmer House, a hotel owned by Louis Timmer, joined in with nearly weekly disclaimers: "No Chinese help employed at the Timmer House [Louis Timmer, hotel]. A first-class American cook is in charge of the kitchen and the dining room service is excellent."[248] The purchase of these ads, some of which ran almost weekly for three months, indicates that these businesses perceived anti-Chinese sentiment among the visitors and residents of Silver City and Grant County who would stay at their hotels or eat at their restaurant. The ads further implied that a Chinese cook was not as competent as a White cook; and Chinese help somehow devalued the café as less than first class. Louis Timmer also felt compelled to promise that no Chinese cooks or waiters or cleaners worked at the Timmer House. Was this decision based on pressure from others in the city, a personal business decision based on the national dialogue, or a business decision based on the anti-Chinese sentiments?

---

244 *Silver City Enterprise,* Dec 27, 1982.

245 *Southwest Sentinel,* June 26, 1894.

246 *The Eagle,* Apr 10, 1895, 4.

247 *The Eagle,* May 15, 1895, 4.

248 *The Eagle,* Jul 27, 1895.

Timmer House around 1898. Left to right: Dan Long; _____; _____; Solomon S. Sly (from Indiana, grandfather of Mrs. Robt. Judge); Geo. Pelton; _____; _____; Frank Milstead, manager of hotel; Mrs. Milstead; Mrs. Pelton; Mrs. Thomas (mother of Mrs. Judge); Mrs. Sly; Chinese cook. Harlan –collection—courtesy of Mrs. Robert Judge. Silver City Museum.

On April 26, 1898, the following ad appeared in the *Independent:*

Timmer House Dining Room
Is now under new management and has been entirely overhauled.
Meals at all hours.
Board by day or week.
Everything first-class.
Y. FUNG, Prop.

Note that this ad states that Y. Fung is the owner of the Timmer House because Fung is not just advertising the dining room but also daily or weekly room and board. Fung also is using the same language "everything

141

first-class" that several proprietors implied was not possible with Chinese help, much less Chinese ownership. The typewritten caption on the Timmer House photo from 1898 identifies the Chinese man on the far right in the doorway as "Chinese cook." The man is wearing a hat and clean clothing similar to that of the Chinese men pictured attending the Methodist Church. He is wearing a pendant around his neck and a ring on his right hand. Most interestingly, his body language does not demonstrate a subordinate posture. The woman, Mrs. Sly, to his right may be trying to ignore him. But he does not look bothered. Is this truly the cook, or could this actually be the proprietor, Y. Fung?

******

By 1899 more businesswomen actively courted White diners by advertising no Chinese help to varying degrees of success. One was Mrs. Louise Metzger, the very same woman who checked on Chinese male Moor Joe Wee, a longtime Silver City resident and former cook at her Delmonico Restaurant.[249] Somehow hearing of his injuries, "she at her own expense, very charitably procured the professional services of Dr. Wood to alleviate the suffering of the poor friendless wretch."[250] By the end of the year, Mrs. Metzger had sold her restaurant to Mrs. J. Rielinger. This news item in the *Enterprise* provided extensive commentary, possibly from Mrs. Rielinger herself: "The Delmonico Restaurant has changed hands, Mrs. J. Rielinger having leased the business and taken the management of the restaurant. The lady will do everything possible to cater to the tastes of her patrons. This is the only restraurant [*sic*] in the city run under a white persons [*sic*] control, every other is run by Chinamen. White cooks and young lady waitresses in attendance. The prices are less and food and services better than at the Chinese restaurants. Patronize the only American restaurant in the city. Meals only 25 cents."[251] The claim of being the only

249   *Silver City Enterprise*, Mar 23, 1898.
250   *Silver City Enterprise*, Mar 26, 1898.
251   *Silver City Enterprise*, Dec 30, 1898.

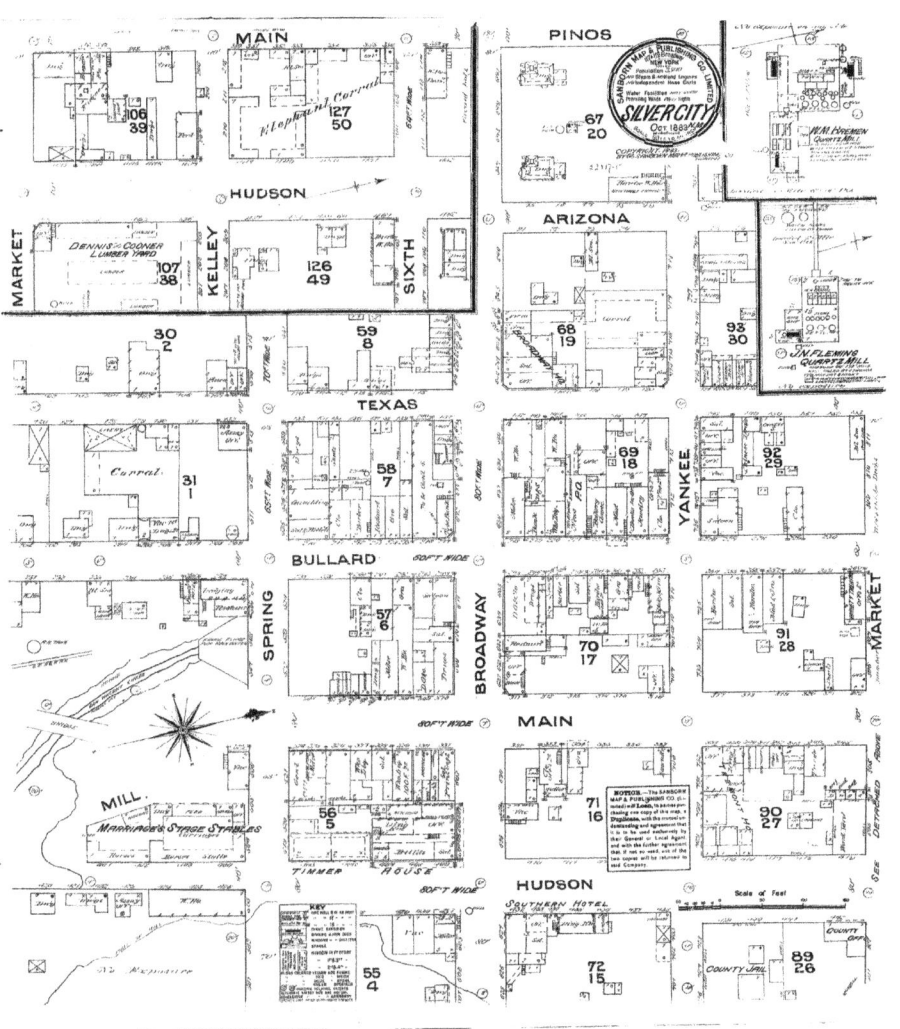

Silver City street map 1883 Source: Silver City Museum

White-owned restaurant in the city (because many Chinese establishments served American food) suggests that Chinese, even during this time of boycotts, were not losing their businesses. After selling Delmonico's, Mrs. Metzger then bought the St. Charles Restaurant (formerly run by Ong Tang) in connection with the Columbia House and advertised "No Chinese help employed in any department."[252] After ten months, she apparently decided a Chinese proprietor would do a better job and sold it to a Chinese man, even knowing it was connected to the lodging house that she retained. "Mrs. Metzger will devote her entire attention to the Columbia lodging house and will in the future erect an addition to the building, containing a large number of elegant rooms."[253] The very same edition noted, "Mrs. Jacob Rielinger has sold out the Delmonico Restaurant (Block 57, Lot 8). The new purchaser will take charge on October 1st and no Chinese help will be employed."[254] This tale of two Silver City restaurants suggests some White residents like Mrs. Louise Metzger, who had relationships with Chinese residents to the point of providing medical care and selling a restaurant attached to her lodging house to a Chinese person, felt pressured in 1898 to perform anti-Chinese hostility by advertising that "No Chinese help" would be employed at her lodging house and restaurant. Within ten months, she apparently felt that a business association with a Chinese restaurateur would not harm her own business. Mrs. J. Rielinger on the other hand, was unhappy that Chinese proprietors dominated the eating establishments in the city and refused to sell her restaurant to anyone other than a White proprietor who would maintain the policy of not hiring Chinese help.

Despite performing acts of citizenship by learning English, attending Christian churches, and declaring their intent to become U.S. citizens, the Chinese in Silver City and Grant County continued to face scrutiny. Of the 33 Chinese from Grant County who declared their intent, only two were naturalized: Lew Sam in April 1892, and Ah Toy, a longtime resident

---

252 *Silver City Enterprise*, Mar 3, 1898.
253 *Silver City Enterprise*, Sep 29, 1899.
254 *Silver City Enterprise*, Sep 29, 1899.

144

of Sierra, in June 1891. As an interpreter for the district court, Sam had to be aware that the 1888 Exclusion Act, "went far beyond its predecessor, forbidding the return of Chinese laborers who had previously resided in the United States, declaring null and void approximately thirty thousand return certificates issued to Chinese laborers since 1882, and rendering thousands of men and women who had temporarily left the United States unable to return."[255] He also had to be cognizant of the growing surveillance of Chinese after the 1902 Geary Act, which required his countrymen without naturalized citizenship to register with U.S. Customs and provide a photograph for visual identification, an attempt to prevent the ongoing immigration fraud. Throughout the late 1890s and early 1900s, Silver City press regularly reported U.S. Marshals coming into Grant County to ensure Chinese had registered, detaining Chinese who did not have their registration papers with them, and deporting Chinese when they were determined to be in the country illegally. Those Chinese who did not have their papers with them when asked to present them were detained in prison until they were able to have their kin or colleagues present their papers on their behalf.

The Silver City newspapers, moreover, seemed to take pride in their only Chinese American resident. As the only naturalized Chinese American they knew, they apparently had to emphasize that Sam was exceptionally capable and deserving of U.S. citizenship. When two years later Sam challenged assumptions that Chinese lacked family, the *Sentinel* approved of the interracial marriage, "Lew Sam, the well-known naturalized Chinaman, was married last Wednesday to Señorita Isabel Lopez by Isaac Givens, J. P. The happy couple have gone to housekeeping in Silver City."[256] the *Western Liberal* proudly shared with its readers that, "A daughter was born to Lew Sam and wife last week. Lew Sam is an American citizen and one of the brightest Chinamen in this part of the country. His wife is a native Mexican and quite a local favorite among her people."[257]

---

255   Lew-Williams, *The Chinese Must Go*, 192.

256   *Southwest Sentinel*, Jul 31, 1894.

257   *Western Liberal*, Lordsburg, NM, Jan 14, 1896.

The *Enterprise* seemed positively tickled that the Sams' daughter was a native-born Chinese American when it announced, "To the wife of Lew Sam, a daughter. Lew Sam is probably the only native of the celestial kingdom who has been admitted to full citizenship and Miss Lew Sam, the only young celestial who can date her American ancestry back one generation."[258] And *The Eagle* proclaimed that Sam had reached "the acme of American citizenship," pronouncing him "A Chinese-American Daddy."[259] Sam was able to marry Lopez because New Mexico lacked a miscegenation law after the legislature repealed the 1857 miscegenation law in 1866.[260] Mexicans were categorized racially as White, but New Mexico was the only western state to not have a law prohibiting interracial or multiracial marriage in 1900. From the 1860s to the 1870s, southern states passed new laws banning marriages between Blacks and Whites, and western states banned multiracial marriages.[261] Arizona's 1865 law in contrast, prohibited marriage between Whites, Blacks, Indians, and Chinese, but did recognize marriages that were legally performed in other states.[262] The lack of Chinese women's ability to enter the United States led male Chinese migrants who married before the 1920s to marry non-Chinese women.

Sam was particularly keen to ensure that his sons also had their birthright citizenship documented. He did not do this for his three daughters. On November 20, 1902, he filed this statement with the district court:

> To all whom it many concern: Greetings: I, Lew Sam a citizen and resident of the County of Grant and Territory of New Mexico, do hereby certify that by birth I am a native of the Empire of China, and that on the Eleventh day of April A.D. 1892, I was duly and fully naturalized as a citizen of the United States of America and

258   *Silver City Enterprise,* Jan 10, 1896.

259   "A Chinese American Daddy," *The Eagle,* Jan 8, 1896.

260   Peggy Pascoe, *What Comes Naturally: Miscegenation Law and the Making of Race in America* (Oxford University Press, 2009), 40.

261   Pascoe, *What Comes Naturally,* 197-8.

262   Sal Acosta, "Against the Odds. Chinese Mexican Marriages in Southern Arizona," *1880-1930,* New *Mexico Historical Review* 89, 2 (2014): 182-3.

146

received my final certificate therefor, in the District Court of the third Judicial District of the Territory of New Mexico, sitting in and for the County of Grant and that I had at the time of receiving said certificate, I had then resided in the United States for the period of Twenty-one (21) years; and furthermore, that subsequent to my said naturalization, I was, married to a mexican [*sic*] woman, who is now my wife, and subsequently, to-wit: - On March 22nd. A. D. 1902, there was born to myself and my wife, Sabel Sam, a son who has been christened Yuan Loy Sam, who is still living at Silver City, Grant County, New Mexico, his place of his birth.[263]

Sam's assertive declaration is remarkable for at least two reasons. First, Sam applied for and received naturalized citizenship in 1892, ten years after the Chinese Exclusion Act clearly stated that foreign-born Chinese were not eligible for naturalized citizenship. Second, Sam returned to the courthouse on each occasion of his two son's births in 1902 and 1905 to certify in court that they were native-born in Silver City. Sam made sure to reiterate in writing his own naturalization, his lawful marriage with Isabela Lopez (listed as Sabelito in the 1900 census), and his sons' birthright U.S. citizenship. This paper trail indicates Sam's acute awareness that his presence in the United States was subject to ongoing surveillance and might be revoked at any moment. Lew-Williams reminds us, "Naturalized Chinese always faced the possibility of denaturalization, and with denaturalization came the threat of disenfranchisement, deportation, and exclusion."[264]

Chinese Americans in 20th Century Silver City

The twentieth century brought changes to Silver City's Chinese American community. Even though the federal decennial census numbers are not fully accurate, they still demonstrate certain population patterns. 1885 marked the high point of the Chinese population recorded in Grant County, which

---

263 *Index to Book of Deeds,* vol 44, p. 15, Grant County Records Office, Silver City, New Mexico.

264 Lew-Williams, *Chinese Must Go,* 189.

slowly declined until a large drop to 58 in 1920. The ratio of Chinese men to women was still highly imbalanced for several decades. Adam McKeown's analysis of Chinese migration found "in the United States, the proportion of women rose from about 2 percent of all arrivals in 1881 (the year before exclusion) to 5 percent in the late 1880s, and 14 percent in 1889, the highest proportion of any year until the 1920s."[265] This explains why Chinese American children were not very common in Silver City's Chinese community until the 20th century. Silver City's Chinese population peaked in 1900 at 95, dropped to a low of 25 in 1920, but then rose to hover in the mid-40s in 1930, 1940, and 1950. As the overall population numbers dropped, the number of women and children increased, but more and more native-born Chinese Americans left Silver City for other parts of the United States.

One of the Chinese American families with deep roots in Grant County and Silver City was that of M.F. Lime of Silver City and Sue Lew of Deming. Their story illuminates the importance of the agricultural knowledge that Chinese immigrants brought with them to the United States and to southern New Mexico, and the role of Chinese Americans in contributing to Silver City's economy with restaurants, vegetable farming, and grocery and mercantile stores.

Ma Foon Lime was born in Guangzhou (Canton), China, on April 1898.[266] He originally used the name Foon Lim when he and his brother Yat Lim sailed from Hong Kong on the S.S. Mongolia in September 1911. They arrived in the United States at the port of San Francisco on October 18, 1914, where they were met by Lim Shee Poon who identified as their father.[267] That same year he was a mess boy at Fort Huachuca, Arizona.[268] The census records do not provide any further information for Lim until the 1930 census reports him living in Precinct 3 of Grant, New Mexico. He states his employment

---

265   Adam McKeown, "Chinese Emigration in Global Context, 1850–1940," *Journal of global history* 5, no. 1 (2010): 95–124, p. 112.

266   Ma Foon Lime draft card, 1942. Silver City Museum Unprocessed Lime Family Collection, Silver City, New Mexico.

267   State Immigration Office, List 4, San Francisco, Oct 15, 1914. Retrieved from ancestry.com.

268   *Silver City Enterprise*, Apr 29, 1938.

148

as ownership of a truck farm and says that he was born in California.[269] Lime's name and birth year kept changing, which may be why he avoided the census takers as much as possible. By 1919, Lime was known as Mah Foon Lime or M.F. Lime. According to Susan Berry, Mah was Lime's true surname; he and his brother had bought papers from the Lim family to enter the United States. He apparently also had to pretend he was three to four years older than he actually was.[270] In the 1917-1918 city directory for Silver City, Lim Foon is listed as a waiter for American Kitchen located at 203-205 Broadway and owned by O.D. Wing (See a list of all Chinese residents listed in Silver City in the 1917-1918 city directory in Table 1).[271] Lime's obituary stated that he started work for the French Kitchen in 1918 and later owned the business, documentation for which has not been found.[272]

Table 1. Chinese residents & businesses
Hudspeth Directory Co's 1917-18 Directory of Silver City

Name	Occupation Place of residence (wks=works for; lab = laborer for; rms same = rooms at place of work; r = rooms at; mdse= merchandise; prop=proprietor)
Aing Ahtoy	cook English Kitchen rms same
American Kitchen	OD Wing prop, open day and night, private dining rooms, quick service 203-205 Broadway, phone 38 (see adv left top lines)
Ah Hing	cook rms 100 (500) E Kelly
Ah Lee	gardener r es A T & S F tracks 3 blks bey pass depot
Don Chee	wks Sing Lee rms 113 (208) Market
Eagle Café	Wah Hop prop 202 Broadway
English Kitchen	(AT Fawn, Hong Tong) 104-6 E Broadway
Fawn A T	(English Kitchen) r 104-6 E Broadway

269   1930 U.S. Census. Grant Co, New Mexico, Pop. Schedule. Precinct 3 part of, Apr 11, 1930. Enumeration Dist. No. 9-6. Sheet No. 3B. Lime, M.F. Dwelling no. 72, Family no. 73. Retrieved from ancestry.com

270   Susan Berry Interview, Susan Berry, Interviewee; Karen J. Leong, Interviewer; Javer Maruffo, Interviewer. Dec 15, 2023, Silver City Museum, Silver City, New Mexico.

271   Hudspeth Directory Company's Directory for Silver City 1917-1918 (Denver Co: 2017), 88.

272   *Silver City Enterprise,* Jul 7, 1977.

Fong Ben	Gardener r es A T & S F Ry ¼ mile bey depot
Fong Fook	waiter Eagle Cafe rms Fong Sing
Fong Kim	waiter Eagle Cafe
Fong Ming	cook Eagle Cafe
Fong Quon	rms 100 (500) E Kelly
Fong Sing	Chinese mdse ss Kelly 1 e Bullard r same
Fong Yick	cook French Kitchen rms same
French Kitchen	L C Wong prop 202 Bullard
Hom Yok	lab Fong Ben r same
Hong Tong	(English Kitchen) rms 103 E Broadway
Leo Ti	cook English Kitchen rms same
Lew Pow	lab Fong Ben r same
Lim Foon	waiter American Kitchen
Lo Huang	rms Fong Sing
Lou Quet	r 104 (504) E Kelly
Lou Sai	waiter r 100 (500) E Kelly
Mox Sue	wks Sing Lee rms 110 (208) Market
Ong Guy	waiter American Kitchen 100 Market
Ong Sing	hlpr American Kitchen rms rear same
Ong Wing	wks Sing Lee r 110 (208) Market
Sing Lee	laundry 110 (208) Market r same
Sing Maw	cook American Kitchen rms same
Song Ting	waiter English Kitchen rms same
Wah Hop	prop Eagle Café r same
Wing O.D.	prop American Kitchenw
Wing Wah	laundry 108 E 6th r same
Wong L.C.	prop French Kitchen r 105 1/2 E Broadway
Yee N. Fung	Chinese mdse 309 Bullard r same
Ying Wing	wks Sing Lee 110 (208) Market

Caption: Names of all Chinese residents and businesses identified by a Silver City Museum staff member from Hudspeth Directory Company's *Directory for Silver City 1917-1918* (Denver Co: 2017). List compiled by author from photocopied pages found in Vertical File, Silver City Public Library.

Based on existing records, it appears that the Golden Farm Company that operated Chinese Gardens in Silver City was founded in 1919 by Gee Hoy with partners Lee Lang, M.G. Fong, and M.F. Lime. This is based on a notice posted in the *Enterprise* on February 15, 1924, dissolving the company, with Hoy liable for all debts owed and payments due the company. Ming Fong, cook at the Eagle Café, possibly could refer to Lime's business partner M.G. Gong, but Gong does not appear in the Silver City census records (see Table 1.) In 1919, there is a record of M.F. Lime leasing 40 acres of land from Nicholas Grenfell beginning January 1, 1919. The lease filed on February 19, 2019, describes the 40 acres:

> ... one of said tracts of land and garden comprising about six (6) acres and being north of the railroad bridge of the A.T. & S.F. Ry. across Badger Creek, and lying just east of the home of [Nicholas Grenfell]; the other tract of land and garden comprising about thirty-six (36) acres and being just south of the said Badger Creek and west of the said railroad right-of-way, and just south of the home of [Nicholas Grenfell], about six (6) acres of which are claimed by the A.T. & S.F. Ry. Co and which are leased by [Nicholas Grenfell] from said A.T. & S.F. Ry Co ... together with that certain gasoline engine and pumping plant, and all the agricultural tools of [Nicholas Grenfell] to be used with the above described and leased premises, with the right of [M.F. Lime] to the well upon said lands and used for pumping water to irrigate the premises hereby leased , and with the rights to use all the water in said well in connection with this lease; and also, the right to the use of the two (2) houses now situate on said premises and the right to the use of all improvements hereafter placed thereon.[273]

---

273   Lease L.R. Greenfell, Admr., to M.F. Lime. Feb 7, 1927. Miscellaneous Deeds vol 72 p 597-9. Grant County Records Office, Silver City, New Mexico. The 1927 Lease between M.F. Lime and L.R. Grenfell, administrator of Nicholas Grenfell's estate, states that the leased lands are located "in Sections Eleven (11) and Fourteen (14), Township 18 South (T. 18 s), Range Fourteen West (R. 14 W) , N.M.P.M." Nicholas Grenfell had purchased 80 acres from John F. Fleming for a total of $200, the first 40 acre parcel in 1910 (the south half of the south half of the southwest corner of Section 14 Township 18 south range 14 New Mexico principal meridian) and the second 40 acre parcel in 1915 (the south half of the south half of the Northwest corner of Section 14 Township 18 South Range 14 West, New Mexico Principal Meridian). He apparently also leased acreage from the Atchison Topeka & Santa Fe Railway Company for his own farm. The Grant County 1920 Assessor Records list his estate as SE 1/4 SW 1/4, W 1/2, SW 1/4, and NW 1/4.

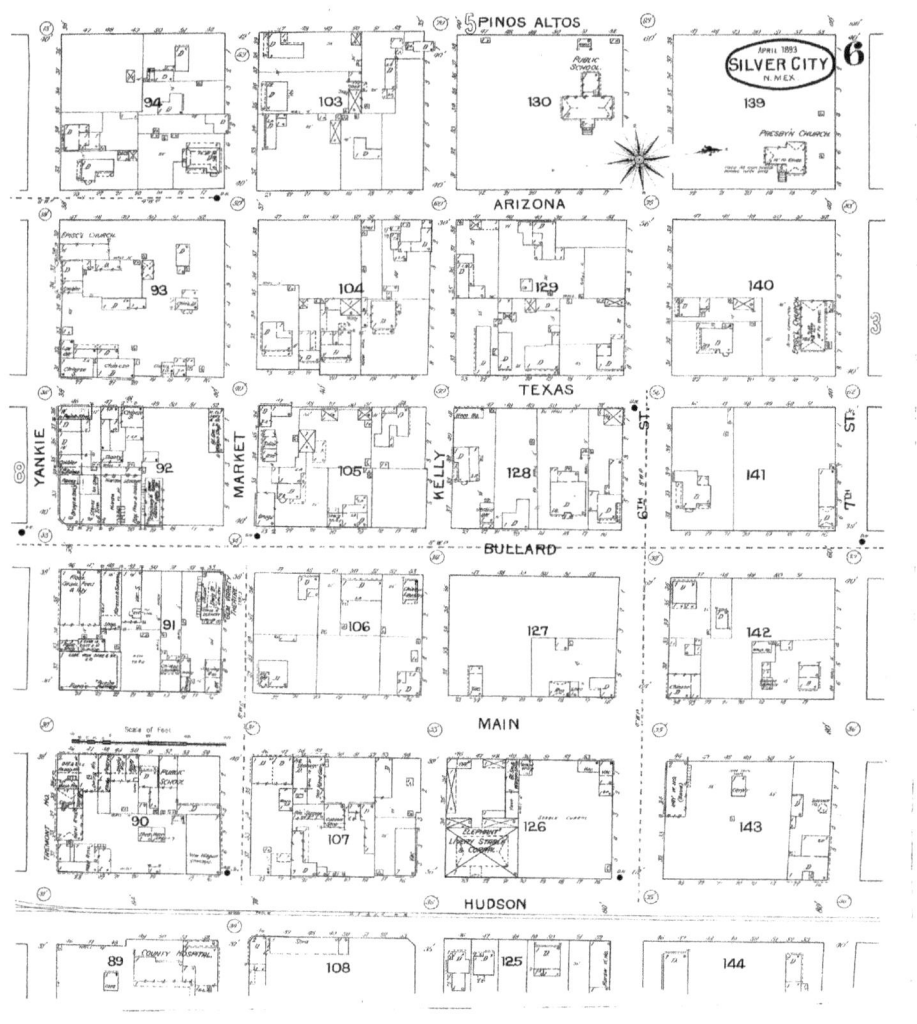

Sanborn Map Silver City1893 Sheet #6 Source: Silver City Museum

This lease lasted from January 1, 1919, to January 1, 1924, at a cost of $345 a year and granted M.F. Lime the option to renew the lease for five more years.[274]

---

274   Miscellaneous Deeds, vol 63, p. 399. Grant County Records Office, Silver City, New Mexico.

The Chinese Gardens were part of Silver City's economy early on. Because so many of the earlier migrants from China were from farming communities in areas that had learned how to successfully irrigate the poor soil, many were skilled in farming vegetables.[275] Whereas Smith assumes that miners did not have time to garden and thus instead purchased vegetables from others,[276] Chung notes that Chinese miners often supplemented their mining wages by growing and selling vegetables.[277] According to Chung, "By the 1880s, the Chinese [in the American West] had established themselves in truck farming or "gardening ..." [278] These "truck farms" were large enough to produce vegetables for local markets. O.W. Williams, cited earlier, described former Chinese railroad workers taking over the gardens south of Silver City after the railroads were completed in the early 1880s.

Fresh vegetables were valuable to Silver City from its beginning not just because they supplied nutrients, but also because of the unreliability of food deliveries. In a student research paper about food production and supply in Silver City, Michael J. Rock explains these food shortages. Before the railroad was built linking the main lines to Silver City, ox-drawn wagons would run "regular month-long routes between Silver City and the Chihuahuan towns of Jasno and Case Grandes; others followed a ten-day route between Silver City and La Mesilla."[279] Wagon trains or coaches making deliveries from the railroad, moreover, could be delayed by fears of being ambushed by Mescalero Apache.[280] For this reason, the raising and selling of vegetables could be profitable, and the areas south of Silver City clearly supported successful farms. According to Rock, "One of the

---

275   Chung, *In Search of Gold*, 144-5.

276   Duane A. Smith, *Rocky Mountain Mining Camps. The Urban Frontier*, Indiana University Press 1967, 6 as cited by Michael J. Rock, "Supplying Food and Drink to Early Silver City," History 514 paper, Western New Mexico University, May 1991, Silver City Public Library, Silver City, New Mexico, 3.

277   Chung, *In Search for Gold*, 144.

278   Chung, *In Search for Gold*, 29.

279   Rock, "Supplying Food and Drink," 8.

280   James K. Hastings, "A Birds Eye View," 289.

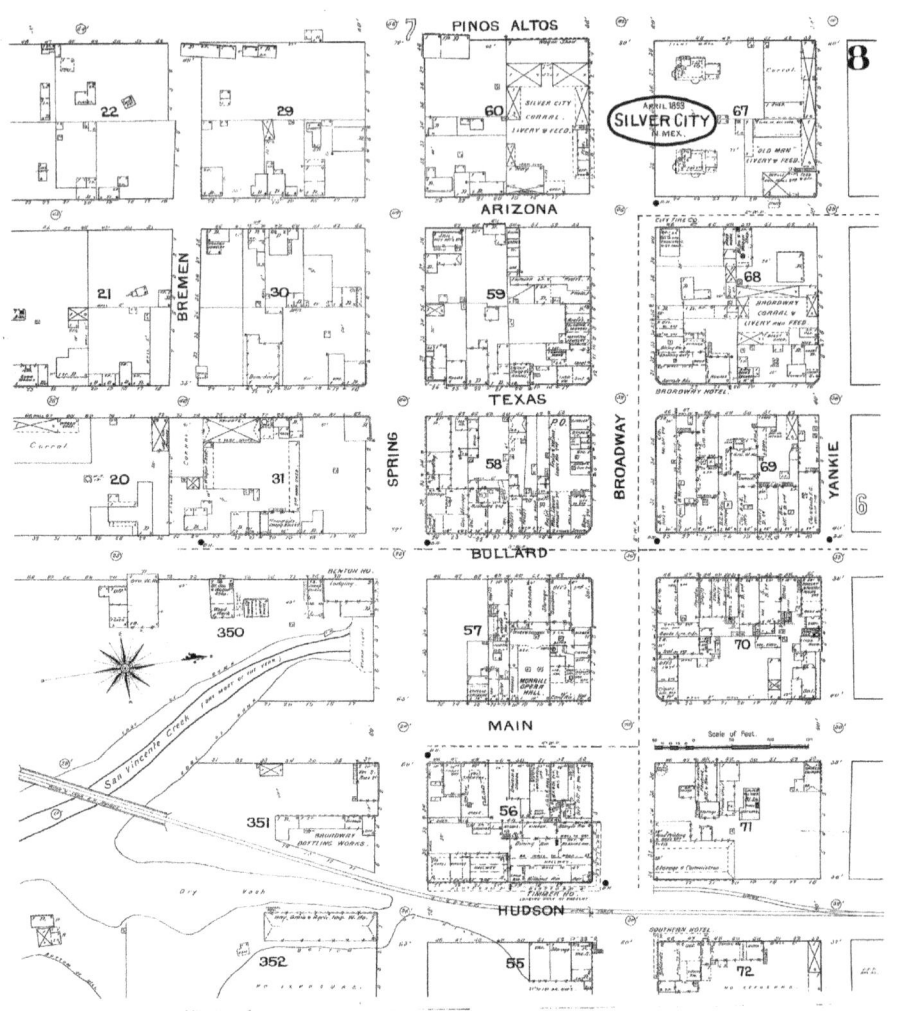

Sanborn Map Silver City 1893 Sheet #8 Source: Silver City Museum

earliest documented gardens ... was that of Isaac Stevens, a lawyer. In the plot south of town, he grew cabbage and tomatoes. Another garden was tended by William McGary, a barkeep for a local saloon."[281] In 1875, a year after arriving in Silver City, Sam Chung rented Mr. Stevens's garden south

---

281   Rock, "Supplying Food and Drink," 4.

of town in order to sell vegetables[282] to Silver City. Lin Chop, who operated a retail store in Silver City is credited with supplying large amounts of vegetables, but there is no documentation to clarify whether Chop actually grew the vegetables or contracted to sell them.[283] In 1881, a news story about H.J. and H.W. Loomis's two ranches, mentions that "Chinese gardeners are cultivating a large tract, and are making it pay. All of this produce is marketed in Silver City and Pinos Altos."[284] Here it is not clear whether Chinese gardeners were working for the Loomis family's business interests or if they were renting the land.

The number of gardeners listed in the Silver City census records from 1880 to 1930 averaged six. Koenig notes that more gardeners are listed in the 1885 Territorial Census of Central and suggests that this may have been closer to the Chinese Gardens near Fort Bayard.[285] The lower numbers of gardeners also may indicate that, as with farms, laborers were hired for labor intensive but seasonal jobs such as harvesting the produce while gardeners oversaw the gardens daily. M.F. Lime, for example, was reported to employ "from 10 to 15 men at different seasons of the year." [286] The *Southwest Sentinel* in March 1883 observed that Chinese had started a vegetable garden below town as if this were a new location. In May 1900, officials announced their intent to relocate the Santa Fe Depot "to foot of Bullard Street near rock quarry. It is intention of officials to move roundhouse down below the Chinese gardens."[287] A year later, *Enterprise* in 1909 noted that Louie Jung had grown vegetables in his "truck patches below the smelter and has ... been supplying Silver City housewives with fresh vegetables for the last quarter of a century ..."[288] There apparently was

---

282   *Grant County Herald*, April 11, 1875.

283   Carm Sandoval,"Chinese in Silver City. Excerpts from a Paper by Carm Sandoval," n.d., 16-17, 17. Chinese Documents- School Museum Project, Silver City Museum.

284   *Silver City Enterprise* Jul 31, 1881.

285   "Chinese of Silver City," 9

286   *Silver City Independent*, Oct 15, 1929.

287   *Silver City Enterprise*, May 4, 1900.

288   *Silver City Enterprise*, May 14,1909.

land consisting of "the lower Chinese Gardens" [289] on "the other side of the Bremen mill" as early as 1890.[290] The rent supported Abigail Bremen, and perhaps this was the location for Jung's truck patches. Another eleven-acre garden used by Ong Ting Fong, south of the Santa Fe Station and by the tracks, was sold in 1920 to build a 500-foot railroad stub track.[291]

M.F. Lime's landlord, Nicholas Grenfell, also was a successful gardener. The *Enterprise* in early 1908 described how Grenfell, an immigrant from Cornish, England had begun growing crops

> in the Silver City draw about two miles below town. Nicholas Grenfell has a large acreage under cultivation and is now engaged in clearing some raw land preparatory to putting in crops this spring. The Chinese gardens are also now located in the Silver City draw about three miles south of the city and most of the produce is raised without irrigation. The soil in the draw is a rich black loam carried down from the mountains by the floods and is capable of producing the finest crops without irrigation. Someday the entire valley between Silver City and Deming will be settled up with happy, prosperous homes and country produce will be so plentiful that fresh ranch eggs will no longer be placed in the same class with automobiles and other expensive luxuries.[292]

The phrasing "are also now located in the Silver City draw" suggests that the Chinese gardens were not always located there. Thus, the land that M.F. Lime and his partners began leasing in 1919 included the land that had been established as a Chinese truck farm by, if not before, 1908. Although M.F. Lime was growing vegetables and apples on fifty acres, the entire tract Lime leased from Santa Fe Railway and Nick Grenfell totaled 75 acres and was divided by the Santa Fe Railway bridge. Grenfell's tracts contained the

---

289   *Silver City Independent*, Apr 13,1933.
290   *Silver City Enterprise*, Jul 18, 1890.
291   *Silver City Enterprise*, Mar 5, 1920, and Mar 19, 1920.
292   "Dry Farming Close to Silver City," *Silver City Enterprise*, Feb 28, 1908.

"80-foot well" that filled a reservoir for the crops, and a shed equipped with a water tank for washing the vegetables. What made Lime's venture so profitable were his contracts with the U.S. Veterans Bureau Hospital at Fort Bayad and with "three of the leading groceries in Silver City." The truck farm raised and distributed, "celery, carrots, beets, cauliflower, lettuce, radishes, onions, tomatoes, mustard greens, cucumbers, squash, turnips, chili, bell peppers, corn, cabbage, peas, string beans, chard, spinach and many other things for the dining room table."[293] The assessor valuations for Golden Farm listed two livestock.[294] The two livestock may have referred to the two mules that Lime would hitch to a wagon to deliver vegetables during the 1920s.[295]

Chinese vegetable gardens along Santa Fe railroad tracks just south of Silver City depot, about 1912. Courtesy Mrs. Robt. Jackson – Harlan Collection, Silver City Museum.

This was not the only venture that Lime developed. He and Sam Ting started a partnership in the Manhattan Café on Bullard Street in downtown Silver City beginning in October 1923 with a loan of $750 to purchase

---

293   "M.F. Lime Cultivates Fifty Acres at Farm South of the City," *Silver City Independent*, Oct 15, 1929.

294   Assessors Records 1928, 1929-30, 1931, Grant County Assessor's Office, Silver City, New Mexico.

295   Susan Berry Interview, Dec 15, 2023.

furniture, fixtures, and equipment for the restaurant.[296] The Manhattan Café was an upscale establishment with white tablecloths and a dramatic painted front window.[297] The 1929 assessor records for Grant County also suggest that this restaurant was fancier than most; in comparison with English Kitchen and French Kitchen whose improvements were valued at $300 and $1,000, respectively. Manhattan Café's improvements were valued at $1,500.[298]

Sue Lew grew up in Deming, the only daughter of the Lew family of Deming. The Lew family was one branch of Chinese brothers who had immigrated to the United States. Although they reportedly began the Chinese Gardens in Deming in 1900, it is very difficult to locate them in the census records, partly because the romanization of the names seems to have varied greatly. Lew See for example, only shows up in the 1900 Census. According to his daughter, "He and his two brothers had come together as the three Wah brothers into the Mimbres River Valley in the mid-1870s." One brother lived near the City of Rocks before moving to Madero Mexico. "My father then moved to a site three miles east of Deming in the early 1880s—before the coming of the railroads. The homestead became known as "Tai You Yuen—the Chinese Gardens. It was located between the Southern Pacific Line and the Santa Fe Railroad." They delivered produce locally and to surrounding areas by horse and wagon, and even sold it to merchants from Morenci, Arizona.[299] The gardens had a fifty-foot-diameter, eight-foot-deep earth tank for irrigation that looked like a pond and was stocked with fish. The pond was surrounded by willow trees. The gardens were sectioned off by fruit trees. An adobe tower overlooked the garden for security.[300]

---

296   Agreement Crescent Lumber Co. and Silver City Beer & Ice Co and M.F. Lime and Sam Ting, Jul 11, 1924, Miscellaneous Deeds vol 63, p 633-4. Grant County Records Office, Silver City, New Mexico.

297   Susan Berry Interview, Dec 15, 2023.

298   Assessor's Records 1929, Grant County Assessor's Office, Silver City, New Mexico.

299   Sue Lew Lime, "SEE LEW Chinese Gardens," [unknown publication],16-17, Chinese Gardens file, Deming Luna Mimbres Museum Archive. Deming, New Mexico.

300   *Deming Graphic*, Jun 9, 1929, Chinese Gardens file, Deming Luna Mimbres Museum Archive. Deming, New Mexico.

Yee Lime standing in front of cart, Chinese Gardens Source: Silver City Museum, Lime Family Collection

Sue Lew and her mother Wong Yat Lew were rarities as women born in the United States, but their experiences were very different. Wong Yat was born in California where she did not attend school and was married at age 18 to Lew See, who was thirty years her elder.[301] Sadly, the success of the Chinese Gardens provided Wong Yat with little comfort. Much of her early married life was focusing on raising her children and taking care of the home. "Years later, [Sue] confided to one woman that her mother cried herself to sleep every night with depression and worry."[302] Lew See still was married to his first wife in China, something not uncommon among some early Chinese migrants. The first wife traditionally had control over other wives and their children. In 1911, when China became a Republic, Lew See took Wong Yat and their children back to his home where his first wife still lived but had no children of her own. After arriving in China,

---

301   Sue Lew Lim, "SEE LEW Chinese Gardens."

302   Nancy Johnson, "Lew See's Secret," NM History and Beyond, *Deming Headlight,* May 2, 2007, 4, Chinese Gardens file, Deming Luna Mimbres Museum Archive. Deming, New Mexico.

Wong Yat gave birth to a daughter, Suey Heung, who remained behind to be raised by the first wife. The fourth son, Hinn died in 1916 while in China from smallpox. In 1921, the family returned with Sue, whom Wong Yat insisted on bringing back.[303] Back in Deming, Wong Yat gave birth to five more sons. Her husband decided to return to China in 1934 with his two oldest sons, Fon and Himm, leaving Wong Yat with five boys, ages 13 to 4.[304] Lew See died three years later. Wong Yat and her four youngest sons moved in with her daughter and son-in-law, Sue and M.F. Lime, and their infant son. She eventually moved to Los Angeles in 1940 with four of her sons. But her worry may have continued as her first son died in a car accident in China in 1935, and her second son Himm did not return from China until 1948, right before the Communists ousted the Nationalists. The Chinese Gardens in Deming closed during the Depression, and in 1955 were covered by a manganese stockpile.[305]

Sue Lew Lime enjoyed more choices than her mother, but their lives also were similar in some respects. Wong Yat's life was dictated by her family and then her husband, a not uncommon experience for women living in the U.S. and China in the 1930s and 40s. Sue's experience of returning to China after 11 years away meant that she was fluent in Chinese. But it also meant she would need to start kindergarten in Deming at the age of eleven. She learned English from her classmates and learned Spanish from the workers at the garden. After completing 8th grade when she was 19, Sue attended high school for one more year. She appears to have spent time in Arizona before returning to New Mexico where she met M.F. Lime. In 1934, M.F. and Sue's marriage was a major community

---

303   "Some Lew Family Chronicles," transcribed for Wong Yat Lim, Mar 6, 1982, 3 pp, The Silver City Museum Unprocessed Lime Family Collection Silver City, New Mexico.

304   Nancy Johnson, "Lew See's secret," NM History and Beyond, *Deming Headlight*, May 2, 2007, 4, Deming Luna Mimbres Museum Archive. Deming, New Mexico.

305   Julie Cordova, "Chinese Gardens...A unique showcase northeast of Deming," *Desert Winds Magazine*, Sept 1988, 18, Chinese Gardens file, Deming Luna Mimbres Museum Archive. Deming, New Mexico.

occasion, hosted in the Borenstein home and officiated by Judge George W. Hay. The circumstances of Lew's life were affected by her father's desire to return to China in 1911, but her mother demanded that Sue return with them to the States in 1921.

Sue's own experience as a U.S.-born Chinese American woman is distinct from the histories that have been told of other second-generation Chinese American women in the urban, large Chinese communities of San Francisco and Los Angeles. Having been taken to China at the age of one, and then being brought back to the US at the age of 11, Sue's experiences are more similar to those of the 1.5 generation, a term often used to describe immigrants from Asia who are brought to the United States before their early teens. "Through the process of relocating from traditional [Chinese] culture, and negotiating with the host culture, the 1.5 generation creates a "separate" group identity that is different from the identities of the first and second generations."[306] Given that she may have been her mother's primary confidant because her mother was socially isolated, and she and her mother were both raising young children at the same time, Sue's own identity may have been shaped even more by her mother's experiences than most 1.5 immigrants. Yet Sue was not as isolated as her mother appears to have been. Being able to speak multiple languages, Sue seemed able to occupy diverse social spaces, enjoying good relationships with Mexican employees of Chef's Grill, other congregants at the Church of the Good Shepherd, and the middle-class members of the Town and Country Garden Club.[307] This was the expected role women played in their community. But social expectations for women were finally catching up to women like Sue, as evident in a letter Olive Lime Streit wrote to the journalist Becky Billings who had authored a series of articles about Women in Grant County. Olive encouraged Billings to speak with her mother. Her reflections as a daughter who lived through a series of

306   Mary Yu Danico, "Internalized Stereotypes and Shame: The Struggles of 1.5-Generation Korean Americans in Hawai`i", Linda Trinh Vo and Rick Bonus, eds. Contemporary Asian American Communities: Intersections and Divergences. Temple University Press, 2009.

307   "LIME Obituary," *Silver City Daily Press*, Jan 11, 1995.

social movements in the late 1960s and early 1970s and grew up seeing her mother being an active partner with her father in sustaining the family business are telling: "It is satisfying to feel some consciousness-raising is taking place regarding the value and roles women carry in our society. So often women are publicized only as appendages of successful men." Olive knew her mother did "so many many additional things that deserve recognition and credit," but recognized that she might also need "validity and a feeling of worth."[308]

We do not know how Sue made sense of her situation, but she seemed determined to make things work for her family and their business. In her recollections of growing up in Deming she recalled, "In 1934 I moved to Silver City and married May[*sic*] Foon Lime—and also married his restaurant which we ran until 1978. I continued with my education at Teacher's College."[309] She emphasized that she continued her classes even while pregnant with her third son, which indicates how important her education was to her. M.F. Lime in the late 1930s ended his lease agreement for the Chinese Gardens, and the Manhattan Café became their sole source of income. She was serious when she said she married M.F.'s restaurant—as with many family businesses, family labor was expected. Children as they grew older would contribute to the business. Nathan, the youngest of the six Lime children, was "tasked with peeling potatoes as soon as he was able to safely hold a knife. With five older siblings, he learned five different "best" ways to peel those potatoes and adapted the method preferred by whichever sibling came to check on him."[310] Being active in the restaurant business, while strenuous work, also allowed her to be more present in the community. She and M.F Lime operated the Manhattan Café in the historic Swift Building until 1952, when the building was bought by an Arizona company that terminated their lease. Sue and M.F. then opened

308   Image. Letter to Becky Billings from Olive Lime Streit. Silver City Daily Press. Mar 2, 1976, 4.

309   Sue Lew Lim, "SEE LEW Chinese Gardens", n.d., 16-17, Chinese Gardens file, Deming Luna Mimbres Museum Archive. Deming, New Mexico.

310   "A Celebration of Life. Geoffrey Nathan Lime 1947-2021," 6 pp., 4. Silver City Museum Unprocessed Lime Family Collection, Silver City, New Mexico.

up a smaller, more casual eatery on Texas Street, The Chef Grill. The compact 31-seat restaurant would have a staff of four during the busiest times when up to 200 people would eat lunch, and familiarity and personal taste were honored and remembered by the chefs.[311] Sue and her staff created that sense of community in how they interacted with each other and the customers. People recalled her generosity in providing students with meals when they couldn't pay.[312] What many people may not have known is that Sue was managing the grill without M.F., who had been hospitalized for several years.[313] After closing The Chef Grill in 1976 and after M.F.'s death in 1977, Sue tried to reopen Chef Grill with Isabel Eaton in a couple of places, including the coffee shop of the Murray Hotel.[314] In 1979, however, Sue officially retired from the restaurant business.

Necessarily limited in scope, this chapter has provided the historical context national discourse about Chinese immigration to the United States and examined the different ways Silver City residents responded. Exploring the experiences of Chinese entrepreneurs, workers, and their Chinese American children from early 1920s through the 1980s requires further research and a second chapter. Some of the research questions to guide future research are offered below.

Future Research Questions

What caused some Chinese American families to move to or depart Silver City? Y.D. Toy Grocery and Market at the corner of Market and Arizona was owned and managed by Yee Do Toy and Rose Toy. Toy formerly owned and managed grocery with two partners in Morenci, Arizona, but decided to move to Silver City during the Great Depression as the mines were closing and workers were laid off. One of his former partners, Bow Yee, moved almost at the same time to Silver City and set up Bow's Market in

---

311   Olive Streit, "Twenty-Six Years at the Chef Grill," Dec 20, 1976, 4 pp., 4. Silver City Museum Unprocessed Lime Family Collection, Silver City, New Mexico.

312   Susan Berry Interview. Dec 15, 2023.

313   Image. Letter to Becky Billings from Olive Lime Streit. *Silver City Daily Press*, Mar 2, 1976, 4.

314   *Silver City Daily Press,* May 19, 1977.

the Murray Hotel. Hing Lee in 1925 had started the Hing Lee Grocery on Broadway that survived the Depression. Herbert Toy, in an oral history about his family's market, noted that the three Chinese markets in town would help each other out when they were short on certain items. Why did these families start markets in Silver City in the 1920s, who were their customers, and how did their businesses change as the city and the national economy changed from the 1920s through the 1970s and 1980s?

What more can we learn about second-generation Chinese American and Asian American women, particularly outside of large metropolitan areas? Shirley Lim's *Girls Just Want to Have Fun*, Judy Tzu-Chun Wu's *Mom Chung of the Fair-Haired Bastards*, and Judy Yung's *Unbound Feet* all center around California, with the former focusing on U.S.-born Asian American high school and college-aged women in Los Angeles and their engagements with U.S. popular youth culture, and Yung's work focusing on Chinese American women growing up in San Francisco's Chinese American community. Wu's work focuses on the first Chinese American doctor and the borders she crosses, not only spatially but also socially and culturally. But there are many more stories to tell.[315] Susan Berry's acquisition of the Lime family papers and items provides an opportunity to explore a Chinese American woman's choices and decisions growing up in Deming with a Chinese immigrant father maintaining a split-family household with her mother, his second wife, and how her experiences affected the decisions her children made.[316] Once processed, the collection will provide a rare opportunity to explore the generational shifts and different choices her daughters and sons experienced.

The ways that certain Chinese organizations and leaders structured Chinese merchants and workers' lives in turn of the century Silver City raises questions about the family, village, and other social networks that

---

315 Shirley Lim, *A Feeling of Belonging: Asian American Women's Public Culture, 1930-1960* (New York University Press, 2005); Judy Yung, *Unbound Feet*, 1995; Judy Tzu-Chun Wu, *Doctor Mom Chung of the Fair-Haired Bastards the Life of a Wartime Celebrity* (University of California Press, 2005).

316 This collection of family items is unavailable until processed. Silver City Unprocessed Lime Family Collection, Silver City, New Mexico.

Chef Grill interior c. 1960 Source: Silver City Museum

connect Silver City Chinese Americans with other Chinese Americans in El Paso, Deming, Lordsburg, and Clifton Morenci, and possibly throughout the United States. How were these networks built and sustained, and what did they accomplish?

The Mexican names provided by individuals of Chinese descent in census and other documents beg further genealogical and transnational analyses to determine whether, as Julian Lim mentions in her book, these were Chinese passing as Mexicans to cross the border into New Mexico, or if these individuals were Chinese and/or Mexican Chinese children of earlier settlers in Mexico seeking wage work or opportunities in the United States. Rich scholarship exists about Chinese in Mexico and Chinese Mexicans and more can be done by those with the appropriate language and research skills as well as the tenacity to map out the many possible pathways and border crossings that undoubtedly have taken place in this region.

This demographic shift from rural to urban areas reflected national patterns, and second-generation Chinese Americans were not the only ones to not return. But little has been researched about Chinese American rural experiences in the U.S., nor about Chinese Americans in rural areas who moved to urban spaces. It may also be worth exploring how the Chinese Americans who remained in Silver City contributed to the community during the Cold War era. Some of the Mexican youth growing up in the 1960s recalled that The Rainbow was one of the few places they felt welcomed downtown. Several Silver City residents worked for Chinese American-owned businesses when they were teenagers. What can they tell us that might help us further understand different Chinese American experiences in Silver City and Grant County?

KAREN LEONG, PH.D., UNM Department of History, Ph.D. from University of California, Berkeley. Research Interests: History of Women, Gender and Sexuality, Asian American History, American West History, 20th Century U.S. History, Cultural History, Critical Race and Relational Ethnic Studies

CHAPTER 5:

Captives, Hostages, and Indian Slaves in Southwestern New Mexico

By Andy Hernández, WNMU

In October 1837, a New Mexican who had been taken captive by a group of Mescalero Apaches entered El Paso in order to bring an offer from his former captors of peaceful relations in exchange for trading rights. His interrogation offered remarkable insights into a series of highly complex and fluid trading and raiding relationships between the Mexican government and its citizens, Apaches, and Anglo-Americans. The group that held this captive for nearly two years had maintained peaceful trading relationships with northern New Mexican settlements in the vicinity of Cebolleta while frequently raiding New Mexican settlements further to the south, in some cases trading goods they had taken by raiding with northern New Mexican communities. These Mescaleros further relied on trade with unspecified Anglo-American partners who provided firearms and gunpowder in exchange for mules, with the added benefit that these partners sometimes joined Mescalero raids. Recent violence had perhaps encouraged these Mescaleros to pursue peaceful relations with their Mexican neighbors in the vicinity of El Paso, as Comanches had just attacked this band of Mescaleros and taken seven captives of their own.[317]

While we might naturally expect that independence from Spain brought considerable changes to Mexico and to New Mexico, this incident underscores just how thoroughly events had disrupted an equilibrium that had been in place for centuries. The taking of captives by Spanish authorities had long been a part of a strategy to ostensibly assimilate or to at least detribalize Apaches, Comanches, Utes, Navajos, among some of the other Indigenous groups in the region.[318] While such captives might sometimes be referred to as "cautivos" or "amados," in many cases their status could more readily been encapsulated by the term "slave," even though this form of slavery was quite different from the perhaps more familiar practice of chattel slavery in the United States. At the same time, Native societies in the regions and throughout the Americas also had long-standing practices tied to taking captives, with some of those even becoming fully assimilated by their captors. The 1837 incident in El Paso, however, highlights the rapid fluctuation between war and peace between Euro-American groups and Indigenous peoples as well as fundamental shifts in the practices or raiding and captive taking that had been such a crucial element of the frontier political economy.

To this point, I've emphasized the taking of captives by Mexican forces and by Native American groups. The practice of either ransoming prisoners of war or taking them as slaves is an ancient one that dates back to some of history's earliest records. I routinely use the image below

---

317   Interrogation at Santos Horcasitas, El Paso, October 16, 1837; Cayetano Justiniani, El Paso, to the Secretary of Government, October 20, 1837; *El Noticioso*, No. 136, November 9, 1837, in *Mexico: Periodico Oficial de Chihuahua*, October 7, 1834 – October 21, 1840, Reel One of the Francisco Almada Collection, University of Texas at El Paso, hereafter referred to as FAC.

318   Ned Blackhawk, *Violence over the Land: Indians and Empires in the Early American West* (Cambridge and London: Harvard University Press, 2006); Brian DeLay, *War of a Thousand Deserts: Indian Raids and the U.S.-Mexican War* (New Haven and London: Yale University Press, 2008); James F. Brooks, *Captives and Cousins: Slavery, Kinship, and Community in the Southwest Borderlands* (Chapel Hill: Omohundro Institute of Early American History and Culture, 2002).

168

in courses on Western Civilization and the Institution of Slavery as an important example of this conceptualization. Here we have the Standard of Ur, a piece dating to approximately 2500 BCE and presently housed in the British Museum. The piece is a box approximately 20 inches in length and inlaid with lapis lazuli and red limestone. The two largest sides depict scenes of "War" and "Peace" respectively, and I've included the image of the "War" side below. In the upper right corner of this side, we see war captives brought before the king of the Mesopotamian city-state of Ur. These prisoners had been enslaved and are distinct not least due to their size and stature, their shabby clothing, and the fresh wounds that some of them display.[319]

Middle Eastern slave depiction Source: British Museum

In the northern borderlands, the effects of distance upon law enforcement and the erosion of Crown authority were especially pronounced. In the vicinity of northern mining towns, officials constantly repeated regulations that made the unauthorized enslavement of Native Americans a criminal act. Despite these attempts, illegal enslavement of Natives continued. Indeed, the conflict between local, regional, and viceregal levels of Crown officials over the issue of slavery produced confusion and hostility

---

319   "The Standard of Ur, box, Early Dynastic III, Ur, Royal Cemetery." Courtesy of the British Museum.

among the Native populations, further weakening Spanish control over the northern periphery.

From ancient Mesopotamia to 19th century New Mexico and in so many places and times in between, captives taken as prisoners of war were commonly enslaved. While the expectation of forced labor might be for a lifetime or even passed on to children, as was the case with the institution of chattel slavery in the 19th century United States, or whether captives were limited to shorter terms of forced labor as was the case for some Indigenous peoples in New Mexico, the status of enslavement carried other common characteristics across place and time. Slaves were culturally alienated, as evidenced by the fact that they were taken from their Native cultures by force. They also faced social and natal alienation, as they were taken from their families, frequently forced to speak new and unfamiliar languages, and may even have been forced to take on new names as a measure designed to erase their lives as free people. Slavery for such peoples was also a deferred death sentence to be enforced at the discretion of the owner, a status that justified the cruel treatment of slaves.[320]

Finally, slavery was most certainly not a cultural artifact unique to Western civilization or to their colonial descendants. Aside from the vignette that I used to begin this chapter, Francisco Vázquez de Coronado's account of this expedition to New Mexico includes a moment in which he accepted a gift of four Indian slaves including Isopete while at the Pueblo of Cicúye, or present-day Pecos. He further noted the presence of other Native slaves among the peoples of this pueblo.[321] Separately, as one fascinating aspect of the 18th century reconceptualization of the Indian slave trade as an institution controlled at the direction of Crown officials, a bando promulgated by Governor Cruzat y Góngora declared that the sale of Apache captives to Puebloans was illegal.[322] He made no mention of the

320   Orlando Patterson, *Slavery and Social Death: A Comparative Study*, 2 ed. (Cambridge and London: Harvard University Press, 2018).

321   Frederick Webb Hodge and Theodore H. Lewis, eds., *Spanish Explorers of the Southern United States*, 1528-1543 (New York: Scribner: 1907).

322   Cruzat y Gongora, December 6, 1732. Spanish Archives of New Mexico II, #378, 6:1243.

sale of slaves to New Mexicans. Apparently, by the time of Cruzat's administration, merchants or other commercial interests had begun to expand the market for Indian slaves to the various Pueblos. Even though this trade likely continued after Cruzat's *bando*, it seems clear that the Indian slave trade, to the extent that was permitted, was for Spanish settlers only.

In any case, the scope and severity of the enslavement of Indians in New Mexico varied greatly over time, as did the degree to which Indigenous groups-initiated reprisals in an attempt to recapture their kin or take captives of their own. Oñate's suppression of resistance at Acoma stands as a significant early example, with an estimated six hundred Acomans killed.[323] After all Acomans were judged guilty of rebellion against the Spanish, Oñate ordered the amputation of one foot for adult males over twenty-five years of age and sentenced men and women above the age of twelve to a twenty-year term of slavery. Women judged to have been not guilty of rebellion faced a separate form of alienation, as they were remanded to convents in Mexico City.[324]

For the remainder of the 17th century, Franciscans and Crown officials squabbled over control of the labor of Native peoples in New Mexico, with each group at various points charging the other of enslaving Indigenous peoples. Fray Alonso de Benavides saw the hand of Satan at work in aligning an Indian captain with New Mexico governor in order to take Natives as slaves.[325] A few years later in his 1634 report, Benavides placed the popu-

---

323 Ward Alan Minge, *Acoma: Pueblo in the Sky* (Albuquerque: University of New Mexico Press, 1991), 47-54.

324 *Don Juan de Oñate*, 428-480; Gaspar Pérez de Villagra, *History of New Mexico*, ed. F.W. Hodge and trans. Gilbert Espinosa (Los Angeles: The Quivira Society, 1933), 268; Oñate was subsequently judged to have acted cruelly against both colonists and Native people, and ultimately traveled to Spain to clear his name. His nephew Vicente de Zaldivar remained in New Mexico and was one of many colonists to complain just a few years later that many of their slaves had escaped. *Oñate Documents* 2:815, 822; Testimony of Marcos Leandro, July 30, 1601, *México*, 26, in Archivo General de las Indias, cited in Jack D. Forbes, *Apache, Navaho and Spaniard* (Norman: University of Oklahoma Press, 1960), 91.

325 Morrow indicates that the identity of this unnamed governor is unclear, possibly being either Admiral Don Phelipe Sotelo Osario, (1625-1629), or Captain don Francisco Manuel de Silva Nieto, (1629-1632). Baker H. Morrow, ed., *A Harvest of Reluctant Souls: The Memorial of Fray Alonso de Benavides, 1630*, trans. by the editor (Niwot: University Press of Colorado, 1996), 75.

lation of Santa Fe at 250 Spaniards and 700 servants and slaves of mixed or Indian blood, thereby offering important insights into the scope of the enslavement of Indians during these years.[326]

Governor Bernardo López de Mendizábal was perhaps the most notorious slaver among New Mexico's officials during the 17th century and profited greatly from the forced labor of slaves in his textile obrajes. Countering Franciscan criticisms of his conduct, Mendizábal responded in 1662 that the Franciscans had only taught Indian laborers "how to guard and herd an infinite number of livestock, serve as slaves, and to fill the barns with grain, cultivated and harvested with their own blood, not for their humble homes, but for those of the friars."[327] Though Mendizábal was subsequently recalled to Mexico City, the continued practice of slavery in the colony heightened Native resentments even as feuding between officials and clergy generally undermined the legitimacy of their authority.

Indian slavery was among the tensions that continued to smolder in New Mexico, ultimately igniting in the Pueblo Revolt of 1680. In the opening events of the revolt, some Natives showed considerable interest in liberating captives from Spanish settlers. Maestre de Campo Francisco Gómez, for example, claimed that thirty people of unknown ethnic origin had been killed or captured in the Pueblos of Nambé and Pojoaque.[328] One Native of Las Salinas, Pedro García, reported that three captives had been taken from the families of Captains John Nieto, Juan de Leiva, and Nicolás

---

326 George P. Hammond and Agapito Rey, eds., *Fray Alonso de Benavides' Revised Memorial of 1634*, trans. by the editors (Albuquerque: University of New Mexico Press, 1945), 23-24.

327 Reply of López de Mendizábal Charles Wilson, ed. *Historical Documents relating to New Mexico, Nueva Vizcaya, and Approaches Thereto, to 1773*, three volumes, Translated by Adolph F.A. Bandelier and Fanny R. Bandelier. (Washington, D.C.: The Carnegie Institution of Washington, 1923), 3:213.

328 "Auto and Declaration of Maestre de Campo Francisco Gómez", Santa Fe, August 12, 1680, in Hackett, *Revolt of the Pueblo Indians of New Mexico and Otermin's Attempted Reconquest, 1680-1682*, two volumes, translated by Charmion Clair Shelby. (Albuquerque: University of New Mexico Press, 1942) I:10. Hereafter referred to as RPI.

de Leiva.[329] These two reports are representative of the claims of many surviving New Mexicans who reported the loss of their servants or the capture of family members upon reaching sanctuary in El Paso.

The Indian goal of liberating captives in the Pueblo Revolt was further underscored by their actions in besieging Santa Fe. In negotiations with one of the Native leaders, Governor Otermín revealed that the fate of captured Indian slaves was at the forefront of Native concerns, even though the governor was quick to dismiss demands for the freedom of such captives. One Native leader demanded that all Native slaves be handed over to the rebel army. This particular leader specifically requested the return of his wife and children, as well as the return of all Apache men and women.[330] Viewing these demands as a delaying tactic to allow more Natives to join the rebelling army from other areas of the kingdom, Otermín refused.

Decades after Vargas' Reconquest, the Pueblo Revolt gradually began to pass from living memory in New Mexico. Many officials continued to believe, however, that Apaches had instigated the revolt. Clinging to this belief proved all the more necessary as officials and settlers attempted to forge a long-term peaceful co-existence with Puebloans. Ultimately, the enduring belief in Apache guilt convinced eighteenth-century governors to attempt to forge a similar peace with the newly arrived Comanches, as well as with Navajos and Utes, who were not similarly tainted with perceived guilt for any role in the revolt. A long-term peace between Utes, Comanches, Navajos, and New Mexicans, though, would be decades in the

---

329 "Declaration of Pedro García, and Indian of the Tano nation, a native of Las Salinas", August 25, 1680, in Hackett, RPI, I: 25.

330 The particular emphasis on Apaches lay in the fact that many Apaches comprised the rebel army and wished to ensure that any captive family members would be returned to them. This emphasis on Apache slaves and the presence of Apaches in the rebel army, though, would in part lead Otermín and others to conclude that Apache agitators were solely responsible for the Pueblo Revolt. After Vargas's Reconquest, New Mexican officials would organize most of their campaigns against Apaches as a result of these assumptions. "Letter of the governor and captain-general, Don Antonio de Otermín, from New Mexico [to Fray Francisco de Ayeta], in which he gives a full account of what has happened to him since the day the Indians surrounded him." September 8, 1680, in Hackett, RPI, I:99.

making. At all points in this process, the acquisition and exchange of slaves remained a pivotal component of Spanish-Native relations.

During this period, baptismal records also emerged as an excellent determinant in assessing the extent of slaving. As Crown officials began to cement the sale of Indian slaves as a function of officially sanctioned attacks against Indigenous peoples deemed to be recalcitrant or of the purchase of Indian captives taken by other Indigenous groups, they set the expectation that captives be baptized, taught the core tenets of Catholicism, and educated in the Spanish language. Accordingly, the noted ethnographer David M. Brugge's analysis of baptismal records from the Archdiocese of Santa Fe and other Catholic archives lends itself to visualizing the shifts in the enslavement of Indians in New Mexico as depicted in the chart below.

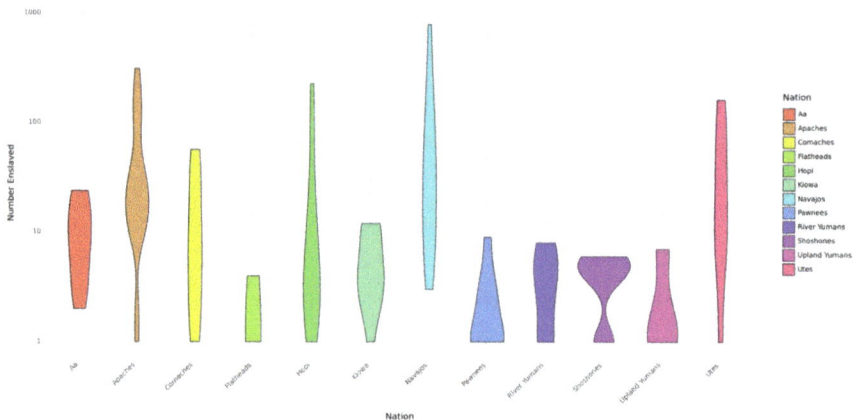

Indian Baptisms in New Mexico from 1694 to 1875. Source: Author

Violin plot of data compiled from David M. Brugge's *Navajos in the Catholic Church Records of New Mexico, 1694-1875*. This plot has four pieces of data embedded in it including the name of individual Native groups and the total number of captives documented as being baptized from 1694-1880. The length of each column shows the time span, while the bowing and slimming gives us a look at captives taken by year.

In the course of most of the 18th century, the Indian slave trade in New Mexico focused much less on the exploitation of forced labor and more on "reducing" Indigenous populations deemed hostile by Crown authorities. This period further saw the broadened application of the term *genízaro*. The frequently used definition of "detribalized Indians" is especially poignant for our purposes as the construction of fictive kin relationships through the conceptualization of ransoming Natives into adoptive New Mexican families led to forms of social alienation that left former slaves as a new category of person who generally did not fit into the societies of their former Indigenous kin nor that of New Mexican families, but instead emerged as intermediaries who were granted land to settle into newly established communities such as Abiquiú, Tomé, and Las Trampas on the periphery of New Mexico's more established villages.[331]

While serving as New Mexico's governor, Juan Bautista de Anza perhaps best formulated the combination of religious impetus and colonial project embedded with the evolving practice of buying captives in a letter to Jacobo Ugarte y Loyola, then Commandant of the Internal Provinces. In this letter, Anza framed such efforts as part of "a useful and Christian thought . . . to stipulate in another article that prisoners whom they [Comanches] should take from these barbarous nations [Apaches], if they be less than fourteen years old, will be ransomed from the Comanches for a small price . . . to stimulate our allies to search and capture because of interest in this ransom . . ."

For as much as Anza's recommendations set in place something akin to a potential bounty system while also defining the purchase

---

331   The term "genízaro" itself is adopted from the Turkish concept of Janissaries, or Christian children taken as captives or hostages, forced to convert to Islam, and subsequently placed in trusted positions in the Ottoman bureaucracy or put into infantry units comprising the sultan's household guard. Robert Platt and Moises Gonzales, *Slavery in the Southwest: Genízaro Identity, Dignity, and the Law* (Carolina Academic Press), 2019; Moises Gonzales and Enrique R. Madrid, *Nación Genízara: Ethnogenesis, Place, and Identity in New Mexico* (Albuquerque: University of New Mexico Press), 2021; Paul Conrad, *The Apache Diaspora: Four Centuries of Displacement and Survival* (Philadelphia: University of Pennsylvania Press, 2021), 94-97.

of captives as part of a Christianizing mission. Even so, the administrations of Anza and his contemporaries led to a period of relative stability in which some New Mexicans began to look once again outside of their boundaries. The new wave of explorations led by men such as Rivera, Domínguez, and Escalante embodied a spirit of optimism that had begun to manifest itself throughout New Mexico in the wake of generally successful peace treaties with Apaches, Comanches, Utes, and Navajos.[332] The success of these explorations quickly turned bittersweet as it became increasingly clear that the knowledge brought by these explorers would be used illegally to circumvent restrictions against Indian slavery. As New Mexican traders began to look to the Great Basin as a source of lucrative trade opportunities that included the purchase of Indian slaves in the late 18th and early 19th centuries, they inadvertently created a cycle of escalation in which the demand for slaves fueled increased raiding between Indigenous groups, which then further fueled reprisals by those groups that had been raided. The upending of the equilibrium that had defined much of 18th-century New Mexico itself also fell exactly as the era of Mexican independence brought that nation's frontier into increasing contact with Anglo-American trappers and traders. The introduction of a new population itself represented an additional destabilizing element, as it brought the increased potential for new conflicts with Native peoples as well as a new population to add to the demand for the capture and sale of Indian slaves.

332 Ross Frank identifies cultural manifestations of this new spirit of optimism in the depiction of various *Santos* during this period. Most particularly, he points to *santeros* of Job, the biblical figure whose religious faith was tested through years of torment and loss. Drawing parallels between the life of Job and the crises faced by eighteenth century New Mexicans, Frank concludes that "War against the nomadic Indians and smallpox had challenged the growth and prosperity of the province and had placed its population in almost continual jeopardy ... At the same time, a marked improvement in material conditions within the province at the end of the eighteenth century and the beginning of the nineteenth served to complete the self-identification of New Mexican vecinos with Job." Ross Frank, *From Settler to Citizen: New Mexican Economic Development and the Creation of Vecino Society, 1750-1820* (Berkeley, Los Angeles, and London: University of California Press, 2000), 232-233.

Indeed, the text of one will from this period sheds numerous insights into the commodification of slaves resulting from these broader changes. In David Weber's study of the Martínez hacienda in Taos, two Ute girls who likely had been ransomed decades earlier were granted land in the will of Severino Martínez in 1827.[333] The family traditions of the Martínez clan, at the same time, recall the presence of "Indian slaves, born on the hacienda, the descendants of Navajos who had been captured in early colonial campaigns."[334] If true, then this testimony further indicates that ransoming was no longer the only source of slaves and further that one could now be born into the condition of slavery. In this respect, the condition of slavery for Indians in New Mexico had evolved into slaves becoming a type of property that could be passed across generations, signaling the erosion of long-standing precedents that limited the terms of service required of slaves. In contrast, however, even slaves who were so unambiguously treated as property could still, in turn, inherit property through the wills of deceased owners.

As demonstrated in the opening example used in this chapter, changes to the political economy of the former Internal Provinces also contributed to significant fluidity in the shifts between peaceful relations and warfare, and between raiding and trading. Continued raids in the Mexican north regularly yielded confirmation that many attacks were intended as retaliation or as part of a larger effort to rescue other slaves who had been taken previously. In the vicinity of Nuevo Casas Grandes on August 29, 1837, a Mexican boy was taken captive by an unidentified group of Apaches. He soon learned that at least three other Mexicans had been taken captive in earlier raids, including his first cousin, who had married an Apache woman. Upon being interrogated by his captors, the boy learned that the Apaches were most interested in learning the fates of two other Apaches who had themselves been

---

333 David J. Weber, *On the Edge of Empire: The Taos Hacienda of Los Martínez* (Santa Fe: Museum of New Mexico Press, 1996), 27.

334 Weber, 73.

taken as slaves in a Mexican reprisal conducted in March of 1837.[335]

The following year, a New Mexican who had also been held by Apaches reported large numbers of Mexican captives in Apache rancherías within present-day southern New Mexico and northern Mexico, including two women, two small girls, and seven boys who had been taken from several northern settlements including Carmen, Carrizal, and San Antonio de Satevó.[336] Felipe de Jesús Fernandez, who escaped from Gileño Apaches in June 1838 noted that the Gileños were encamped in the Florida Mountains.[337] Another former captive, Juan Mancha, indicated that he had been taken to an Apache encampment near El Gallego and that he saw eleven other captives taken from Carrizal and other nearby settlements. Mancha further related that his captors had not just taken captives but also continued to raid for foodstuffs such as wheat and cattle.[338] Taken together, these accounts place Apache rancherías from the Gila River to the Florida Mountains to El Gallego and on to Casas Grandes as firmly integrated in the ever evolving trading and raiding economy even as they fluctuated between states of war and peace.

One major factor that contributed to such fluctuations was the growing tendency of the Mexican government to hire mercenaries and scalp

---

335 Captives taken by Apaches and ultimately freed by Mexican troops included a resident of Valle de San Buenaventura as well as a Tarahumara woman. Partes Oficiales sobre Incursiones de Enemigos, José Morales, Casas Grandes, to subprefect of Galeana, June 15, 1837: *El Noticioso*, No. 116, June 16, 1837, FAC. Copy of Interrogation, Gabriel Carrasco, Concepción, August 8, 1837; "Partes Oficiales Sobre Incursiones de Enemigos," José María de Yrigoyen, Chihuahua, to Secretary of State, August 14, 1837, *El Noticioso*, No. 125, August 20, 1837, FAC; William B. Griffen, *Utmost Good Faith: Patterns of Apache Mexican Hostilities in Northern Chihuahua Border Warfare, 1821-1848* (Albuquerque: University of New Mexico Press, 1989), 51-53.

336 "Ocurrencias de Indios Barbaros," Rafael Guerrero, Encinillas, to Commandant General, July 23, 1838, *El Noticioso*, No. 173, July 26, 1838, FAC.

337 "Ocurrencias de Indios Barbaros," Benito Colomo, Carmen, to Commandant General, June 19, 1838 in *El Noticioso*, No. 169, June 28, 1838; Interrogation of Felipe de Jesús Fuentese, José Patricio Varela, Janos, July 1, 1838 in *El Noticioso*, No. 172, July 19, 1838, FAC.

338 "Ocurrencias de Indios Barbaros," Rafael Guerrero, Encinillas, to Commandant General, July 23, 1838; *El Noticioso* No. 173, July 28, 1838, FAC.

hunters to carry out campaigns against some Apache groups. One of the more notorious of these men was James Kirker, who signed a contract in 1839 providing him with bounties to bring in Apache captives or scalps. Kirker had initially established friendly relations with some Apache groups in the region by trading cattle and firearms. Any goodwill he may have established was lost as a result of his massacre of Juan José Compa and other Mimbreño Apaches in the vicinity of Santa Rita del Cobre in 1837. Proving to be indiscriminate in his attacks, Kirker and his men subsequently attacked a band of Apaches near Janos who had encamped under a flag of truce. His group took perhaps twenty captives after leaving as many as eleven dead.[339]

Kirker's actions themselves set the stage for long-standing hostilities between Mimbreño Apaches, their kin among other Apache groups, the Mexican government, and later the United States government. Mangas Coloradas, who had himself earlier married a Mexican captive named Carmen that he had taken around 1815, thereafter became leader of one of the surviving groups of Mimbreños and carried out numerous raids against Mexican settlements over the next two decades.[340] Mangas Coloradas allied with Chiricahua Apaches to deal Mexican forces their most devastating defeat of that nation's Apache Wars near Hermosillo in January 1851. After carrying out additional raids in the area, which included the taking of Mexican captives, Mangas Coloradas and his men, including Geronimo who was himself a Bedonkohe band of the Ndendahe Apaches, traveled to Janos in Chihuahua to trade the following month.

Subsequent events vividly demonstrated how the cycle of violence between these various groups became self-sustaining. Colonel José Maria

---

339   Ocurrencias de Apaches, *El Antenor*, No.13, January 21, 1840; "Ocurrencias de Apaches," Santiago Kirker, Carmen, April 27, 1840: *El Antenor*, No.28, May 5, 1840; Santiago Kirker, Barranco Colorado, to Commandant General, May 13, 1840; "Ocurrencias de Apaches," Francisco García Conde, Chihuahua, May 18, 1840: *El Antenor*, May 19, 1840 in FAC; William S. Kiser, "The Business of Killing Indians: Contract Warfare and Genocide in the U.S.-Mexico Borderlands," *Journal of American History* 110 (2023): 15-39.

340   Andrés Reséndez, *The Other Slavery: The Uncovered Story of Indian Enslavement in America* (First Mariner Books, 2016), 231.

Carrasco had been appointed military commander in Sonora after the defeat of his comrades at arms and learned that Mangas Coloradas and his men had entered Janos. Carrasco led his unit to Janos, where he attacked the nearby encamped Apaches while Mangas, Geronimo, and other warriors were within Janos. Among others, Carrasco and his men killed Geronimo's wife, mother, and children. Geronimo later recalled that for the rest of his life he "never ceased to plan for their [the Mexicans] punishment."[341]

A few months later, Mangas reached a peace agreement with U.S. representatives and returned to the Pinos Altos area. Over the course of the next decade, however, the reopening of Santa Rita del Cobre and the influx of Anglo-American miners led to a gradual increase in tensions between miners and Apaches. In December 1860, these tensions erupted into violence as a group of miners killed four Apache Indians and captured thirteen women and children after ambushing an encampment on the Mimbres River.

Mangas's raids against nearby communities coincided with the Bascom Affair of early 1861. On January 27th, Tonto Apaches raided John Ward's Ranch near Sonoita, stole cattle, and took Ward's twelve-year-old stepson Felix captive. Lieutenant George Bascom led a detachment of U.S. infantry to search unsuccessfully for Felix. Not realizing that Felix had been taken by a different group of Apaches, Bascom believed that nearby Chiricahuas had carried out the attack and took Cochise and members of his family prisoner after Cochise denied knowledge of the attack.[342]

Cochise was able to escape and took three U.S. and nine Mexican teamsters as prisoners to be used as hostages, hopefully to be exchanged for his family in a manner similar to Bascom taking Cochise's family members as hostages. Cochise tortured and killed the Mexicans but offered to release the U.S. teamsters in exchange for his family. Realizing that this portion of his plan was unlikely to succeed, Cochise fled to Sonora and killed his

---

341   Turner, *Geronimo: His Own Story*, 90091, 102; Reséndez, 237.

342   Edwin R. Sweeney, *Cochise: Chiricahua Apache Chief* (Norman: University of Oklahoma Press, 1995), 144-46.

hostages along the way. On February 19th Lieutenant Isaiah Moore, who had led cavalry reinforcements to Apache Pass, executed Cochise's brother Coyuntwa and Cochise's nephews in retaliation.[343]

As a result of these two events, Mangas Coloradas and Cochise began to raid U.S. encampments and troops detachments with a ferocity that they had reserved for Mexican soldiers and civilians just a decade earlier. The cycle of attack and counterattack continued until Geronimo's surrender in 1886 but left so many taken captive or dead along the way.[344] Attempts to resolve the conflict peacefully frequently led to treachery, as was the case for Mangas Coloradas himself. In January 1863, Mangas traveled to Fort McLane near present-day Hurley to meet with General Joseph West. Though Mangas arrived under a flag of truce, West ordered his execution while reporting Mangas's death as an escape attempt.[345] Mangas's torture and execution ensured that there would be no quick end to the conflict between Apaches and U.S. forces.

Reminding readers of the inextricable connections between these conflicts and slavery, Geronimo also shared his recollections of the taking of captives. He noted, for example, that expectations varied quite a bit for men who had been taken captive as compared with those for women and children. While Mexican men were expected to "cut wood and herd horses, Mexican women and children were treated as our own people."[346]

While Geronimo might have idealized these events later in life, such memories stand in marked contrast to the place of Apache children taken captive in the region. Before his death in an Apache attack in 1871, John Bullard reputedly captured an Apache child and gave the young boy to the Benavides family in Silver City. After discovering the child holding an

---

343 Sweeney, 163.

344 Helge Ingstad, trans. By Janine K. Stenehjem, *The Apache Indians: In Search of the Missing Tribe* (Lincoln and London: University of Nebraska Press, 2004), xxvii.

345 Geronimo and S.M. Barrett, *Geronimo: The True Story of America's Most Ferocious Warrior* (Skyhorse, 2011), 73-4.

346 Turner, *Geronimo: His Own Story*, 90-91, 102; Reséndez, 237.

axe over another of their infant children a few years later, the Benavides family sent the Apache child to the San Carlos reservation.[347]

In a separate instance in August 1885 the Silver City *Enterprise* published the story of an Apache "papoose" that had been captured after the battle of Doubtful Canyon. Noting that the child's support might "cause an outbreak among the whites," the writer called on "Indian loving eastern cranks [to] show their devotion to the 'poor Indian' by adopting this young vagrant."[348]

Just over a year after Geronimo's surrender, the *Enterprise* also reported on a four-year-old Apache boy who had been captured at the age of approximately 18 months and was "in the possession of a gentleman by the name of Adams" who was then living near Duncan, Arizona. In unflattering terms foreshadowing the likelihood that this child would never quite be able to fit into his fictive parent's world, the writer shared that:

"He can smoke and chew. He looks like Geronimo, and it is thought that he is related to the old warrior. He seldom talks but he is a fighter worthy of a more noble race. He came near cutting one little boy to death, as small as he is, and would have succeeded but for the interference of older people. He carries a knife and will use it at the slightest provocation."[349]

The capture and possible longevity of Charley McComas proved to be perhaps the most enduring narrative of possible lives led by a captive. Charley's father, Judge Hamilton McComas of Silver City, had been called to Lordsburg in March of 1883, and he elected to travel along with his wife Juniata and Charley who was six at the time. The family was attacked near the mouth of Thompson Canyon by a group of Apaches under the leadership of Chatto, who left Hamilton and Juniata dead while taking Charley as a captive, possibly "as a pawn or bargaining chip against the day when they might have to recross the border and seek terms."[350]

---

347   "Silver City, New Mexico" (8 pages). Fray Angélico Chávez History Library, New Mexico State Records Center and Archives.

348   Silver City *Enterprise*, Friday, August 14, 1885.

349   Silver City *Enterprise*, Friday, September 30, 1887.

350   Marc Simmons *Massacre on the Lordsburg Road: A Tragedy of the Apache Wars* (College Station: Texas A&M Press), 160.

The resulting search for Charley may have been the largest of the Apache Wars with members of Charley's family offering a reward of $500 for his safe return.[351] Learning that Chatto's band had returned to Mexico, General George Crook received permission from Mexican authorities to send detachments of cavalry and Apache scouts in pursuit. The group included an interpreter named Mickey Free, who had himself been taken captive by Apaches as a young boy.

Subsequent events left conflicting accounts as to Charley's death. In some versions, he had been killed by survivors of an attack by Captain Emmet Crawford on an encampment that included members of Chatto's family. And yet, stories of his survival continued to capture the imaginations of readers in the United States. At least one small band of Apaches attacked a ranch near Deming in 1892, near Animas in 1924, and a small village on the Chihuahuan-Sonora border in 1930. Members of the posse that gave chase in 1924 reported that the bronco (wild or free) Apaches were led by a man with a blond beard. Since Charley McComas had been blond, speculation endured that he may have been the leader of this remaining group of raiders.[352] Whether Charley McComas or some other person entirely, the suggestion that Apache raiders in the 20th century were led by a blond man points to the enduring legacy of captive taking and assimilation in the southwestern borderlands.

While the line between captive and slave blurs in some contexts, the underlying and unifying element remains that captives and slaves were taken violently as a direct consequence of warfare. This trend remains incontrovertibly true from the conquest of New Mexico through the end of the Apache Wars. Across time, the enslavement of Indians may have evolved but it stands fundamentally tied to colonial projects, be they the

---

351   *Arizona Weekly Citizen*, April 21, 1883; Dan L. Thrapp, *Al Sieber, Chief of Scouts* (Norman: University of Oklahoma Press, 1964), 269.

352   Simmons, 175; "Horrible Outbreak of Apaches," *Alamogordo Daily News*, Thursday September 18, 1924, p.2; Paul Salopek, "Mexican Recalls Last Apaches Living in Sierra," *The Seattle Times*, September 7, 1997; Simmons, "White chief may have led last free Apaches into the 20th century," *Santa Fe New Mexican*, April 10, 2015.

extraction of Native labor or the attempts at assimilating or detribalizing Indigenous peoples such as Apaches. Equally important, as the closing examples above demomstrate, these acts cannot be set in a comfortably distant past. Instead, the lifespans of captives and slaves taken in the closing years of the Apache Wars take us quite uncomfortably proximate to the realm of living memory while serving as a reminder that the legacy of the enslavement of Indians in New Mexico continues to echo among us today.

ANDREW HERNANDEZ, PH.D., WNMU; Ph.D. US History; Professor of Latin American Studies Ph.D. in History, University of New Mexico (2003); Doctoral Dissertation: "The Indian Slave Trade in New Mexico: Escalating Conflicts and the Limits of State Power" M.B.A., Western New Mexico University (May 2009), M.A. in History, New Mexico State University (1996); M.A. Thesis: "On the Defensive: Foreign Military Assistance to the Sandinistas in Nicaragua, 1979-1993", B.A. in History, Texas Christian University (1993)

CHAPTER 6:

Of Cows and Men: Cattle Ranching in Grant County Since 1870

By Stephen Fox, PhD

Silver City and Grant County began in a rush of mining claims for gold, silver, and copper. Within a few years, most of those claims had played out and subsided. Some of the miners left Grant County, but many of them stayed and became cattle ranchers instead. Ranching was always difficult and unpredictable, dependent on the whims of weather and large, undisciplined animals—but even it was considered a safer, surer bet than mining. Both pursuits were retarded for some years by sporadic, last-ditch fights with Indigenous raiders, mainly Apache.

Grant County in the 1870s was a cow's paradise. The grama grass was everywhere, growing as high as a horse's belly, providing a dense pasturage of thick mats and tufts. "That grass was high enough," John Allred recalled, "that it would drag my feet in the stirrups all day long. And thick, it was just like a mattress on the ground." The range between Silver City and Deming stretched for fifty miles from north to south, reaching the horizon in every direction, as yet unimpeded by any arroyos or canyons. "That was the prettiest grazing country you ever seen," a rancher said later. Even the rural roads were paved with grass, somehow impervious to hooves and wagon wheels. Grama grass was especially well adapted to arid conditions and was actually more nutritious than farmer-grown hay.[353]

To the north of Silver City, grama grass covered the mountains and valleys that would not become the Gila National Forest until decades later. The land was all quite vulnerable and unprotected and free for the taking. The takers were not shy. "You could go wherever you please and settle where you wanted and raise as many head as you wanted or you could afford," a ranchwoman named Emma Trotter remembered. "There was no limit to ya at all."[354]

The breeds of cattle were gradually improved. The original Spanish or Mexican cattle were small and half wild. They gave little milk and did not fatten well. Longhorns from Mexico and Texas were bigger and smarter. In their behavior, they were short-tempered and alert; at night, their eyes seemed to glitter. When being driven among different breeds on the trail, Longhorns would take the lead, always the same ones in front every day. "They took care of themselves better than any graded stock," the rancher Stokley Ligon recalled. "They'd fight for their young where there were wolves. ... They were so much more active and self-sustaining. They were wonderful cattle."[355]

Longhorns in turn yielded to Durham cattle, first brought to Silver City from Missouri by Harvey Whitehill in the 1870s. Fifteen cows and a bull, brought in ox-drawn wagons, arrived in bad shape. Set loose on the grama range south of town, in four years they had increased to 120 cattle. Hereford breeds came along a few years later; they did well in a dry climate. Both Durhams and Herefords gave more milk than Longhorns, and their

---

353 John W. Allred, transcript 3, p. 14, *Pioneers Foundation Oral History Collection* (PFOHC), Miller Library, Western New Mexico University; Wayne Whitehill, transcript 502, pp. 11-12, PFOHC; *Silver City Enterprise*, March 27, 1885.

354 Emma Trotter, transcript 206, p. 30, PFOHC

355 Clara M. Love, "*History of the Cattle Industry in the Southwest,*" *Southwestern Historical Quarterly* (April 1916), p. 374; J. Stokly Ligon, transcript 198, p. 5, PFOHC.

186

beef had a higher fat content and thus better flavor for the demanding markets in Kansas City and points east.[356]

Of the humans tending to these cattle, Vic Culberson ultimately became the most prominent rancher in Grant County, repeatedly elected to leadership positions in cattlemen's organizations. His early life had been a picaresque series of ventures and false starts, typical for a young cowboy of that time.

He was born in Atlanta, Georgia, in 1863, during the Civil War. In its tangled aftermath, he and his family moved to southwestern Texas when he was 13. "I would dream of being manager of a big cow outfit in some part of the West," he remembered. "The remote West called me. I loved it for its vastness, its beauty, its color, and its life—for its wildness and violence." The Wild West had all those things, and more.[357]

At age 18, Culberson left home with not much money, maybe no money, and headed west. "I was always able to find some kind of work, although not invariably to my liking." His first job was carrying drinking water for a railroad crew for fifty cents a day. He somehow saved enough money to buy a horse and saddle. With them, he got his first ranch job as a horse wrangler. He soon felt stuck. "It was almost impossible for a lad without money or influence ever to become the manager of one of those Texas ranches."

So he decided to try New Mexico. Vic stopped in El Paso with fifty dollars from selling his horse and saddle. "Work was a little hard to get," so he tried waiting tables in a restaurant, which he had never done. "I held this job for a week, got my pay, but disagreed with the cook." Yes, you could call it a disagreement. "After throwing a tray of dishes in his face, I drifted."

---

356 *Silver City Independent*, December 21, 1915; J. J. Wagoner, "Development of the Cattle Industry in Southern Arizona, 1870s and '80s," New Mexico Historical Review (July 1951), pp. 220-22; Kenneth Fordyce, "History of Cattle in the Southwest," in Ann Lacy and Anne Valley-Fox, eds., *Cowboys, Ranching & Cattle Trails* (2013), pp. 268-72.

357 These nine paragraphs about Vic Culberson are drawn from his memoir, published in the *Silver City Independent*, December 3, 1929; and see Representative New Mexicans (1912), p. 67 in Culberson folder, Vertical File, Silver City Public Library; *Enterprise*, October 3, 1930, and January 23, 1958.

Without money or prospects, Vic walked the hundred miles from El Paso to Deming, New Mexico. There he met Dick Hudson, the owner of Faywood Hot Springs. They rode back to Faywood and Culberson stuck around for a while, doing chores for his board. Hudson told him about a prosperous silver-mining camp, Georgetown, 65 miles away, where he might find work. Vic made his way there, again on foot.

In Georgetown he made the most important connection of his life. George O. Smith ran the mining operations. A native of New York state, Smith had headed west at age sixteen and reached Grant County in 1875. He gave the young Culberson a job in one of his shafts. Vic had never worked as an underground miner. On his fifteenth day below ground, he was buried by a sudden landslide. "I was taken out very much bruised—in fact, more dead than alive. This thoroughly convinced me that I was not a miner." He never tried it again.[358]

"Mr. Smith was very kind and began to take a keen interest in me." The boss wanted to switch from mining to ranching. He had bought 121 head of cattle and needed someone to look after them. Culberson offered himself. "As soon as I was able, we went out and looked the situation over. The country was wonderful grass everywhere, and plenty of water." They agreed that Culberson would work the cattle for three years, after which Smith would take back 121 head and the two would split the proceeds from any additional cows. "I was a happy lad; for was I not to be the manager of an outfit in what I considered a wonderful cow country?"

Vic leased a place with a small cabin, eight by ten feet, where he lived alone for three years. "I now felt quite well-to-do. I had a home consisting of a log cabin, a dog, a cat, 121 head of cattle running on a well-watered range, covered with the best grass in the world for cattle (black grama), all equipment necessary for a cowpuncher, and three good ponies." For six weeks at a time, he might not hear another human voice. One afternoon he killed three bears with his pistol. Another time, he stood in his door and watched Apache raiders steal two of his ponies—but they left him alone.

---

358 *Enterprise*, June 8, 1900. On the GOS Ranch, see Lacy and Valley-Fox, Cowboys, pp. 160-61 and *Enterprise*, December 2, 1982.

After three years, both men were well pleased. Smith could see a future for himself in cattle ranching. He launched the GOS Cattle Company, named for his initials, with Culberson as the manager. Their Turkey Cienega ranch on the Mimbres River had plenty of water, always an issue in Grant County. After the failure of H.B. Ailman's bank in Silver City in 1887, for an agreeable price they bought his thousand head of cattle and 320 acres of patented land.

"We had free range, no grazing fees of any kind to pay, and practically no taxes," Culberson recalled. "Our range was fine, with grass everywhere and an abundance of water." He bought some thoroughbred bulls, first Longhorns, then Shorthorns ("they were not the cattle for a rough mountain range"), and finally Herefords, well suited for mountainous terrain. Still in his twenties, Vic took charge of the GOS spread, a few miles northeast of Georgetown, and started building it into one of the biggest ranches in Grant County.

George Hearst of California, who controlled the largest private mining company in the United States, started buying ranch properties in southwest New Mexico in 1882. Eventually, his enormous Diamond A ranch stretched all the way from Hurley southward to fifteen miles beyond the Mexican border, as well as other spreads in Grant and Luna counties. Hearst himself only came here a few times, in September 1882 and June 1884. His partners took charge of their holdings in New Mexico.[359]

Today Hearst is best known as the father of William Randolph Hearst— and as one of the rampant sociopaths in the fictional HBO series *Deadwood*, which ran from 2004 to 2006. His associates in Grant County gained only superficial impressions of Hearst; but, for what it's worth, they liked him. "A great big rawboned man with a big, gray beard," as Henry Brock, a Diamond A foreman, remembered Hearst. He was generous to any ranchers and miners who were down on their luck. "A big, broad-minded, big-hearted man," Brock insisted, some sixty years after Hearst's death.[360]

---

359   *Silver City New Southwest*, September 16, 1882; *Enterprise*, June 20, 1884.
360   Henry Brock, transcript 93, p. 15 and transcript 103, p. 2, PFOHC.

The acknowledged leader among Grant County ranchers was a remarkable man named John Brockman. Born in Germany in 1841, at age seven he came to America with his family. They settled on a farm in Rock Island, Illinois. When the Civil War began, he enlisted at once in an Illinois regiment, twenty years old, and saw combat for the next four years. (A classic pattern, often seen in American history, of immigrants proving their loyalty to the new country by serving in its armed forces.) Brockman fought in all the major battles of the Army of Tennessee and in Sherman's march to the sea.[361]

After the war, he joined the hordes of young men seeking their fortunes out west. Eventually, he found his way to Pinos Altos. He tried panning for gold, not successfully, and took up ranching. Somehow, he bought a ranch and farm along the Mimbres River. By 1869 he was running over 3,000 head on a thousand acres. Gradually he specialized as a stock breeder, buying fancy Angus and Galloway bulls from an outfit in Mount Pleasant, Missouri, and selling them to other ranchers in Grant County. Soon his ranch was declared "a great success," supplying "nearly all" the local ranches with those coveted calf-makers.[362]

Given the normally unlimited water from the river, the ranch was also a thriving farm. Brockman's farmers raised alfalfa, corn, apples, peaches, pears, cherries, and grapes. Aside from food for everybody at the ranch, these cash crops yielded an annual profit of about $10,000 (equivalent to well over $300,000 today.)

In 1885, Brockman moved his ranch headquarters to Silver City. He took a leading role in founding the Silver City National Bank, the first bank in town, and served as its president. He was then, at just forty-four years old, the best-connected rancher in the county.[363]

In Grant County and elsewhere in New Mexico, some of the larger and more successful ranchers were organizing themselves into groups

361   *Notables of the West: Being the Portraits and Biographies of the Progressive Men of the West* (1915), 2: 137.

362   Ibid.; *New Mexico Stock Grower*, April 4, 1885, and October 3, 1885.

363   *Notables of the West*, 2: 137; *New Mexico Stock Grower*, August 8, 1885.

for mutual support. The first such group, the Southwestern Stockmen's Association, was started in Silver City in November 1881, essentially to encourage cooperation in roundups and branding practices and to deal with the perennial problem of rustling. "We now have something," said the *Grant County Herald,* "that will protect the interests of the stockman." With John Brockman, W.W. Wines, Richard Hudson, and R.N. Newsham among its leaders, it was soon deemed "one of the best regulated associations in the territory."[364]

These groups also started to address the heedless, suicidal practice of overstocking their ranges. With no fences, the unsupervised cattle were allowed to roam freely, always following the grama grass, gouging out arroyos and canyons, draining the streams, and doing enormous, permanent damage to the land because they ate and trampled the roots that would normally provide seeds for next year's grass. In August 1885, the *New Mexico Stock Grower,* the weekly newspaper for the state's ranchers, deplored "the insane policy which is being pursued by tenderfeet in placing cattle on already stocked ranges." In other words, the newer, smaller ranchers were just following the same bad practices that older, bigger ranchers had pursued. "Grant County ranges are becoming overcrowded," the *Stock Grower* warned two weeks later. We must "deter any further influx of cattle."[365]

None of this had any discernible effect. The well-established ranchers had no credibility in urging new ranchers to adopt more prudent practices than the older ranchers themselves had deployed. Too many of them put too many cows on too little range. The lush, beautiful fifty miles of grama grass between Silver City and Deming were doomed.

*****

364 *New Mexico Stock Grower,* August 8 and 29, 1885; *Grant County Herald,* November 22, 1881; *Enterprise,* August 28, 1885.

365 *New Mexico Stock Grower,* August 8 and 22, 1885.

The cowboys worked hard, especially during roundups and on the trail when herds were being driven somewhere. On the Diamond A, the rule of thumb was one man for every thousand head, and about seven horses for every man. The pay varied, twenty to thirty dollars a month plus room and board, depending on the size of the ranch and a man's experience. Every cowboy had to provide his own guns, a necessary tool of the time, usually a Colt revolver and a Winchester rifle.[366]

Whether at home or on the trail, the food did not vary much. Vic Culberson's wife, Mary Agee Culberson, cooked for the ranch hands on the GOS spread. It was hearty, basic fare: canned corn and tomatoes, dried apples, peaches, and apricots, sourdough biscuits baked in a Dutch oven, oceans of black coffee, and always beef, fresh and recently butchered. "We et good" on the trail, Ben Avery recalled, savoring the memory. Beef three times a day, beans, sourdough biscuits six inches high, and the usual coffee and dried fruits. "That was the happiest days of my life," Avery said.[367]

For most of the year, cowboys lived at the ranch, riding the local range, doing various routine chores, and sleeping in their own beds in their own bunkhouse. The more difficult, unpredictable, even dangerous times came on the trail and during the spring and fall roundups. The cattle had wandered wherever they pleased, always in search of grass and water. "My god, there was no end to the range then," John Allred said. "There was no fences. ... The cattle drifted and mixed up and went in every direction. ... During the winter they scattered awful bad." Unsupervised for most of the year, the herds from different ranches would mingle together, spread into unknown mountains and valleys, produce calves of mixed, vague ancestry, and wander hither and yon.[368]

Roundups imposed some order on this chaotic situation. Often far from the home ranch, the men and their chuck wagon were camped near

---

366   Henry Brock, transcript 100, pp. 4-5, PFOHC.

367   Mrs. Victor Culberson (Mary Agee Culberson), transcript 125, p. 18, PFOHC; Ben Avery, transcript 10, pp. 14-16, PFOHC.

368   John W. Allred, transcript 3, p. 8, PFOHC

where they thought their particular cattle, or most of them, would be found. The day began early, at four o'clock. After eating a quick but hearty breakfast, and hearing the foreman's plans for the day, the cowboys were mounted and riding by daybreak at five.

The wagon boss had in mind a very large, rough circle within which he expected his cattle would be found. The boss took some cowboys and rode in one direction around the circle; another bunch of cowboys went in the other direction. At regular intervals, a man would be dropped off and stationed at the edge of the circle. As they ran across their own cows, they drove them toward the center. When the herd was thus surrounded, more or less, all hands came inward to a point and started to sort out what they had gathered.[369]

After letting the cattle settle for a while, the cowboys began the cutting process of examining their brands and extracting the cows that belonged to somebody else. In this process, a good cutting horse was the star. A cowboy would point his horse toward a particular cow, and the horse would take over. "A cutting horse," Henry Brock explained, "is a horse that's about as smart as a man is—or a little smarter because they're keen ... bright and active." The horse would put his ears down and keep his eyes riveted on the target cow. "You never got to rein one to do what he's got to do because he's doin that the instant he sees it. You've got to ride him, that's all."[370]

The new calves had to be roped and coaxed from their mothers. The mothers sometimes did not cooperate. Brought close to the fire and the branding irons, the calves were branded, ear-marked, and castrated (if necessary.) Sometimes the men would pick up stray unbranded cattle and add their own brands. "It was a pretty common custom," Charley Holson said. "It wasn't much of a crime. If you found a calf that wasn't branded and he was old enough to get along without his mother, why you'd grab onto him."[371]

---

369   Henry Brock, transcript 100, pp. 20-22, PFOHC.
370   Henry Brock, transcript 108, p. 15, PFOHC.
371   Charley Holson, transcript 164, p. 12, PFOHC.

Out on the frontier, far from any lawmen, legal niceties could be quite adjustable. "Lots of men got rich from brandin other people's cattle," Clark Hust explained. "Everybody wasn't thieves, but everybody had dealings with thieves." During these years, the Southwestern Stockmen's Association often deplored the problem of rustling; but it was just talk, leading to few apparent actions. "My life was threatened," the rancher Montague Stevens recalled. "I used to get anonymous letters all the time."[372]

Every cowboy story needs a bad guy—and the ranchers of Grant County in these years included a really, really bad guy. Tom Lyons, a British immigrant of Irish background, came to Silver City in 1872. A boilermaker and machinist by trade, at first he provided those skills to the many mines that surrounded the town. With his partner, Angus Campbell, he then made some money in mining. They bought a spread on the Gila River southwest of Silver City. The Lyons and Campbell Ranch quickly became a bristling empire. By the fall of 1885, the LC took in 1.5 million acres of owned and leased land, 20,000 graded Durham cattle, and 250 horses; the largest ranch in Grant County. Lyons "came to Grant County as a poor boy," the *New Mexico Stock Grower* exclaimed that year, and by pluck and hard work he had become "the cattle king of that section."[373]

Local rumors whispered that Lyons had reached that pinnacle, in part, by sometimes having his smaller ranching rivals killed. Nobody dared to say that out loud in public, or for publication in the newspapers. Who would have dared accuse Lyons on the record of such crimes? If any smaller ranchers homesteaded spreads near the borders of his ranch, Lyons wanted their land and cattle—and would commit murder to get them. These stories, never written down and published during his lifetime, have persisted even to the present day. A local man told me that his grandfather told his father the name of one of Lyons's regular killers, Red John.[374]

---

372 Clark Hust, transcript 168, pp. 22-24, PFOHC; Montague Stevens, transcript 302, p. 9, PFOHC.

373 *New Mexico Stock Grower*, June 20, 1885.

374 Confidential interview in Silver City.

Recently discovered historical evidence confirms that the rumors were true. In the late 1940s and 1950s, the oral historian Louis Blachly conducted hundreds of interviews with senior citizens here about their memories of the late 1800s in Grant County. Montague Stevens knew Lyons as both a partner and rival. "He was one of the bad men of the West. ... I knew him well," Stevens said. If anybody dared to claim ranch land on the edges of the LC, "He hired killers to kill them. ... I knew the killers, some of them. ... Tom was a mean man. Not only a thief and a murderer but he was mean as he could be."[375]

chuck wagon and its cook, Source: Silver City Museum

Agnes Meador Snider lived with her family at a ranch on the San Francisco River. Her father worked for Lyons, and they became "pretty good friends ... quite intimate." But what about those small ranchers near the LC? "Tom Lyons hired these men to go out and kill these little ranchers and get 'em away off of the land because he wanted it." Snider remembered the names of two of the hired guns, Childers or Childress and Red John or

---

375   Montague Stevens, transcript 292, pp. 4 and 7, PFOHC.

195

Red Johnson. (Men in that line of work often changed their names.) "Tom Lyons hired 'em and paid 'em so much for every man that they killed."[376]

Marvin Powe remembered Lyons as "quite a nice-lookin man ... and a mighty pleasant man to meet." However. "He had a bad reputation from the little cowman. Whenever a man come in there and got anywhere near on what Tom Lyons called his range, which he didn't have any more right to than anybody else, why he made every effort in the world to get them off even if it come to killin 'em. ... If he couldn't run 'em off, why he'd hire killers and kill 'em!"[377]

These three people were contemporaries of Lyons. They knew him and heard the stories about him—not years later, but at the time. "There was quite a few men killed," Henry Graham told Blachly. It's impossible now to say how many were murdered, or who they all were.[378]

Along with these and seven other Blachly interviews, there is a signed, confidential, first-hand, contemporary document about Lyons and his killings.

The four Hall brothers had small ranches near the southwest border of the LC. Bob and Dick Hall were kidnapped and beaten to death in September 1892. Johnny Johnson was then the foreman of the LC, with private inside knowledge of Lyons and his practices. Two years later, Johnson signed a ten- page affidavit about what he knew. He revealed that two of Lyons's "most trusted employees and friends" and another man had killed the Halls; that Lyons sent men to the murder site to hide any evidence of the crimes; that Lyons ordered Johnson to kill the two surviving Hall brothers, their father, and another man; and that Johnson "pretended to agree" with that plot for quadruple murder but did not carry it out. Johnson quit the LC six months later in March 1893.[379]

---

376 Agnes Meador Snider, transcript 274, p. 11; transcript 277, p. 14; and transcript 279, p. 9, PFOHC.

377 Marvin Powe, transcript 241, pp. 1-4, PFOHC.

378 Henry Graham, transcript 151, p. 12, PFOHC.

379 Affidavit of John M. Johnson, May 21, 1894, in the pardon file for Peter Hall Jr., folder 78, box 14058, William T. Thornton Papers, State Records and Archives of New Mexico, Santa Fe.

None of that credible, damning, secret testimony led to any legal troubles for Lyons, then or later. It would have been difficult to get anybody to come forward in public and tell the truth about him. But we can now say that he was not "perhaps" a killer or "probably" a killer. He was a killer, period. The evidence is overwhelming. Lyons was beaten to death under mysterious circumstances in 1917. It was simple justice, long delayed.

*****

Tom Lyons, the murderous cattle baron of Grant County,
Source: : Silver City Museum

When cowboys reminisced about those early times from the long distance of the 1950s, their memories were layered, ambiguous. As old men recalling their vigorous, healthy youths, when their lives seemed wide open and full of possibilities, they liked to relive those times with long, perhaps rose-tinted stories. But they also did not neglect the darker, tugging undertows.

"As I look back to those rugged days, I recall many pleasant memories, also many hardships," Charley Holson wrote in a memoir for his family. "A cowboy's life was not for weaklings. The hours were from daylight until dark at best. The chuck was sometimes not too good, and often the cook was a broken-down cowboy. Often the weather was bad. At times, rain would fall in our plates or the wind would blow dust and sand all over our grub. ... Our means of entertainment were quite limited, consisting principally of an occasional country dance where the floor space was inadequate or the ladies too few."[380]

The old cowboys often remembered those times as more honest, more straightforward compared with the devious complexities of modernity. A man would look you in the eye and shake your hand—and that was better than any signed and sealed legal document. "They were good days," Reed Dean said to Lou Blachly. "I'll tell ya when a man told ya something you never questioned it. ... Those were the days that we had and that's what made life worthwhile."[381]

By the 1950s, everyday life for a cowboy had changed so much from those faraway times. Automobiles, airplanes, movies, radio, television. Pickups instead of horses. Indoor plumbing, rural electrification, central heating. Yet life seemed more vivid, more exciting, even more happy back then. "I look back to these days with the greatest pleasure," A.B. Wadleigh, an old rancher from southwest New Mexico, wrote in the *New Mexico Historical Review,* "and am proud of the fact that, in a small way at least, I helped to build up the country. I never expect to get again a thrill or the same enjoyment like those of the old days. ... When men

---

380   *The Life Story of Charles W. Holson* (1958), pp. 5-8, in the Charles W. Holson folder, Vertical File, Miller Library, Western New Mexico University.

381   Reed Dean, transcript 4, p. 22, PFOHC.

were men and the incentive to do and see were not softened, when travel was not easy and when life was hard. I enjoy the modern comforts, but not for much would I miss the satisfaction that I feel when I think of the days gone by, with their primitive pleasures, their hardships and above all their joy of living."[382]

*****

The American conservation movement, started by hunters and fishermen in the 1870s, was not significantly engaged until two decades later. In 1891, Congress authorized the president to create "forest reserves" by withdrawing land from the public domain. Most of these reserves were carved from large swatches of underused federal land in the West.[383]

Conservation came to Grant County in March 1899 when the Gila River Forest Reserve was established on the northern part of the county, including the Mogollon mountains. For years ranchers, miners, and timber cutters had been using that land, sometimes even living there, all for free and with no regulations. Now they had to pay fees and follow rules set by the faraway Interior Department in Washington. So began the feud between aggrieved locals and distant outsiders that has waxed and waned ever since.

"The people of the Mogollon mining districts are rightfully indignant," the *Silver City Enterprise* declared in October 1899, "at the interdictions placed upon their business interests by the regulations established for the forest reserve." Mining companies needed reliable sources of wood for their mine shafts and to light their stoves and steam engines. "Now an attempt is being made to paralyze the mining industry," the *Enterprise* continued, "for the sole purpose of furnishing places to a few political hangers on. It is an outrageously unjust and also

---

382   A. B. Wadleigh, "Ranching in New Mexico, 1886-90," *New Mexico Historical Review* (January 1952), p. 28.

383   Roderick Nash, *Wilderness, and the American Mind* (Third edition, 1982), pp. 133-34.

illegal measure." Similar reactions came from ranchers over paying the new grazing fees and being told where their cows could graze. The old days of the open range and no rules were over.[384]

The early rules were quite generous, as though to ease the ranchers into the novel notion of taking orders. In 1902, up to 250,000 sheep were allowed, with no limits on cattle and horses because, it was explained, "they do no injury to the reserves." The grazing fees in 1905 were only 35 cents a head for cattle, twelve cents for goats, and five cents for sheep.

The name "forest reserves" was soon changed to "national forests"; a subtle shift implying that the forests were still to be used, not just reserved. That was the essential purpose of the US Forest Service, established in 1905, and its ambitious young director, Gifford Pinchot. He always insisted that conservation meant more prudent, wiser use, not absolute bans. But just in case, by an act of Congress, the Forest Service rangers were given police powers and the right to arrest anybody without a warrant. Pinchot's extended hand included a few cudgels.[385]

Grant County ranchers slowly began to accept the situation, and at times even to like it. Vic Culberson's GOS Ranch lay entirely within the Gila National Forest, so he had to pay large grazing fees. "This seemed quite a hardship at first," he recalled, "as it added much to the cost of producing an animal. But I soon learned that it was a benefit to be on the forest, rather than a detriment, notwithstanding that we had to pay a fee"—because troublesome homesteading farmers were now denied access to that land. "Anyone who owns a cow knows what a nuisance the dry farmer is to the cow range. Under the regulations of the Forest Service, only the man with a grazing privilege can be on the forest, which is a great benefit."[386]

A future leader of Grant County ranchers arrived here in 1896 from a most unlikely background. Hugh Lenox Hodge, the son of a wealthy Philadelphia surgeon, graduated from Princeton University in 1895.

---

384 *Enterprise*, October 29, 1899.

385 *Independent*, February 25, 1902; *Enterprise*, December 15, and April 14, 1905.

386 *Independent*, December 3, 1929.

He seemed to have no interest in the city-bound, conventional careers being launched by his classmates. In 1896, on his way from Cuba and Mexico to California, he visited a college friend who had moved to Silver City for his health. Eureka! Less than a month later, "I was back again prepared to stay."[387]

Presumably with help from his father, Hodge bought the Diamond Bar Ranch, 65 miles northeast of Silver City, near the national forest. "Out in the mountains," he reported to his classmates, "thirty miles from the nearest post office and fifty-five from the railway, without a neighbor within twenty miles." The local weather, he wrote, was "always perfect" except for two months of the year. A recent rise in cattle prices had even made his ranch profitable. "The outdoor life in the saddle is most enjoyable," Hodge concluded. "Wishing you could all enjoy the free life out here with us." (I wonder how many of his Ivy League classmates, dressed in proper suits and toiling at entry-level office jobs, thought about lighting out for the territory.)[388]

The Southwestern Stockmen's Association, founded in Silver City in 1881, had at some point ceased to exist, perhaps during the prolonged hard times of the 1890s. In November 1914, a new such group was started, again in Silver City, under the cumbersome name of the Southwestern New Mexico Cattle and Horse Growers' Association. Forty ranchers from Grant, Sierra, and Socorro counties, after a meeting with the supervisor of the Gila National Forest, joined together for focused measures and mutual support.

In 1916, the group's office was moved from Deming to Albuquerque. Three of its first five presidents ranched in Grant County: Calvin Glenn of Pinos Altos (1914-16), Vic Culberson of Fierro (1918-20), and Hugh L. Hodge of Silver City (1922-24). Gradually, the organization broadened its range to include the entire state and to exclude horses, as reflected in its streamlined name, the New Mexico Cattle Growers' Association.

---

387   *Enterprise*, November 12, 1937; Princeton Alumni Weekly, November 26, 1937.
388   Andrew Clark Imrie, ed., *Triennial Record of the Class of 1895 of Princeton University* (1898), p. 67.

By that handle it has continued, through good times and bad, down to the present.[389]

At its annual meeting in Las Vegas, New Mexico, in March 1918, President Culberson was introduced before his speech as "one of the best known and best liked men in the cattle business." The world war was then in its fourth year; the United States had entered the fray a year earlier. The mood at the meeting was understandably somber. "We have been hurled into one of the most cruel and bloodiest wars in the history of the world," Culberson said. "We must furnish men and we must furnish food." The usual supplies of meat for Europe from Australia and South America, and of wheat and corn from the United States, had been cut off. "All the bravery of the world cannot conquer on empty stomachs," he said. "We are called upon to feed the world, and we must do it if we win the war."

So New Mexico's ranchers had to adopt special measures. They had just passed through one of the worst droughts in years. They could not increase the herds on their ranges, Culberson said, "for the most of them are stocked to their full capacity." But they could improve the quality of their herds by deploying better bulls. "The scrub is a cheap animal which never sells well on account of its poor killing qualities, and it takes just as much grass, if not more, to feed him." As to the workforce, many of their foremen and best cowboys had been drafted into the armed forces. "It is next to impossible to handle a stock of cattle in rough mountain ranges with novice labor," so they should bring all the pressure possible to have their foremen exempted from the draft.

"To feed the millions of soldiers which are now upon us is the biggest job we ever undertook," Culberson wound up. "It is up to us to furnish the Allies the great bulk of their meat; no matter how much we produce there is bound to be a great demand as long as the war lasts. We do not want our army to starve."[390]

---

389 Steve Cormier, "*'Times Were Not Easy': A History of New Mexico Ranching and Its Culture, 1900-1960*" (PhD dissertation, University of New Mexico, 1998), pp. 23-24. Robert K. Mortensen, *In the Cause of Progress: A History of the New Mexico Cattle Growers' Association* (1983).

390 *Proceedings of the...Annual Meeting of the New Mexico Cattle Growers' Association* (March 1918), pp. 26-28.

Vic Culberson, an early leader among Grant County ranchers,
Source: Representative New Mexicans (1912)

A year later, with the war over, the association met in Albuquerque. "Our country has played a most important part in bringing to a close the most terrible war that was ever waged in the history of the world," Culberson said in his presidential address. "Our brave sons have so willingly given their lives, if necessary, to crush the military despotism that threatened the peace of the world. ... I am positive that there is not a cowman in the State of New Mexico who did not do his bit in bringing this terrible struggle to a glorious end."[391]

---

391 *Proceedings* (March 1919), p. 17.

Hugh Lenox Hodge, the Ivy League cowboy,
Source: Special Collections, University of Arizona

*****

From that exultant height, back down to certain hard realities. For the ranchers of Grant County, the immediate postwar years brought a jarring alternation of boom and bust. During the war, the price for a good steer had gone from thirty to as high as forty-five dollars, a sudden increase of 50%. Cowmen were becoming rich, and many tenderfeet rushed to get into the cow business. Bankers were handing out easy loans to anybody who wanted to buy cattle.[392]

392 *Independent*, December 2, 1929.

The one aspect of cattle ranching in New Mexico that nobody could control was the rainfall. A severe three-year drought began in 1922. The cows were stricken, and many died without enough water. Ranchers could not pay off the loans they had undertaken during the plush times; therefore, many local banks failed. The prices for cattle plummeted. In Grant County, ranchers in Tyrone were offering cows for thirty-five dollars and steers for just twenty-five. At the start of 1922, New Mexico had about 1,132,000 cattle, far too many for the available grass and water. Over the next twelve months, desperate ranchers shipped almost 58%—58%!—of those cows to feedlots, slaughterhouses, and ranges in neighboring states. More than half of them were dumped during the last three months of the year.[393]

It would be no exaggeration to call this a cattle and human apocalypse. The rainy season of 1923 again brought no relief. In November 1923, Hugh Hodge, the current president of the Cattle Growers' Association—perhaps sounding more optimistic than he actually felt—gave a cheerleading report. "We have grass," he said. "We have water. We have still some cows left, and those same cows are going to pull us through yet." "Trying to build up quality," the Grant County correspondent reported to the association, "and reduce numbers, as range has been badly abused. Need more cooperation."[394]

The epic drought lasted two more years. Late in 1924, a worried report from Grant County did not mince words. "The southern part of the county never looked worse at this time of year," it said. "A dry winter will finish us sure this time." Finally, finally, the summer of 1925 brought adequate rainfall. The monsoons continued into September. Grant County ranchers could finally exhale. "The rains have been very heavy," one relieved man wrote, "and sufficient to put the range in excellent condition. The cattle are going into the winter in good shape. There is an excellent demand for steers and calves, a good demand for cows and a fair demand for heifers."[395]

---

393 Mortensen, *In the Cause of Progress*, p.12; *Quarterly Bulletin...Issued by the New Mexico Cattle Growers' Association* (May 1923).

394 *Quarterly Bulletin* (November 1923).

395 *Quarterly Bulletin* (November 1924), (November 1925); Mortensen, In the Cause of Progress, p. 16.

The winter and spring of 1926 brought more good news. "Cattle have wintered better than for many years," a man wrote from Silver City. "Winter range has been first class and spring grass is very good. More winter moisture than for many years and more than five inches of rain has fallen since the first of March. Winter losses have been very light." "Everything now points to a very prosperous season for the cattlemen," a correspondent wrote from Tyrone. "Plenty of feed in sight and for the first time in years a feeling of optimism prevails."[396]

Within the year-to-year fluctuations, the broad patterns never changed. Grant County ranchers spent a lot of time looking up at the sky, hoping and praying. In that sense, the cattle business had a timeless quality of cowmen dancing with nature—but always at its mercy in an unequal minuet.

In the same way, a cowboy's life had not yet changed much from the old days. The best account that I have found of New Mexico cowboying in these years was written by John Sinclair (1902-1993). He was later called "the dean of New Mexico authors," a major figure in the literary history of the state. In the 1920s and '30s he was just another cowboy on the Diamond A ranch in southwestern Chaves County, about fifteen miles west of Roswell. The Diamond A was at the same latitude as northern Grant County, with similar conditions of grama grass and a hot, dry climate of little rainfall. What he said about the Diamond A also describes Grant County ranching at that time. The particular value of Sinclair's recollections is his application of an acute writerly sensibility to the everyday doings of a typical cowboy.[397]

John Sinclair was a Scots immigrant with a permanent burr in his voice. In Scotland he had grown up among pedigreed Scottish stocks of horses, cows, and sheep. "Anything that grazed," he explained. At 21, newly arrived in America and headed to Vancouver, he got off the train in Roswell and had a shock of recognition. "I knew this was where I wanted to be." Not

396   *Quarterly Bulletin* (November 1926).
397   Steve Beesley, "Master Storyteller Captures Essence of the West," *New Mexico Magazine* (March 1990).

206

yet a writer, he already had a classic writer's personality of craving a lot of time alone, reading, thinking, and, later, writing. Sinclair never felt like a typical cowboy. "The cowboy was not of the earth," he said later. "He was in the business of raising beef from horseback, and he put a whole lot of acrobatics into it. He wasn't my kind of person." Although not drawn to cowboys themselves, he liked how they lived. "All my life I've loved solitude. Cowboying gave me the opportunity to observe that rugged type of life as well as live far off by myself."[398]

This Diamond A gave him plenty of room for solitude. It was an enormous spread, fifty miles long and twelve miles at its widest, 450 square miles in all. That much range required four wagon bosses, "the most expert cowboys ever to ride for wages in New Mexico, and who will live in legend for their riding, roping, and 'horse sense' abilities." At a roundup in 1926, they branded 7,000 calves. About 400 wild horses munched nearby on the grama grass, mostly "mockeys" (mares) and "condemns" (unbreakable hooligans with dangerous habits.)[399]

Sinclair rented a small cabin—good for solitude—and rode into the town of Capitan for supplies. All the foodstuffs were basic, fresh, dried, or canned and free of chemicals. "To the cowboy trade the words genuine, undoctored, honest, pure, were the truly important words in the English dictionary, even if the cowboy was a sorry hand at putting words together." In Capitan he might get a haircut and shave, and a country-style meal at Mother Julian's Boarding House, "eat all you can hold" for thirty cents.[400]

"Money, or the lack of it, was the least of the cowboy's worries," Sinclair wrote. "Independence and the dignity of his vocation was all. He was a horseman, which gave him pride, a high perch to look down on the world. With a few exceptions to the rule, he was honest; and the environment that was his to live and work in was the cleanest in America. His string of saddle horses was his utmost concern—for without a good

---

398   Ibid.

399   John Sinclair, *Cowboy Riding Country* (1982), p. 44.

400   Ibid., p. 70.

mount a good cowboy is no cowboy at all. If he could find a paying job, what the hell! And if he couldn't, what the hell!"[401]

John Sinclair, first a cowboy and then a writer, at home later on.
Source: New Mexico Magazine

---

401   Ibid., p. 70

When he had a job, the work was long and unforgiving, in weather often too hot in the summer and too cold in the winter. At times, it was done at a slow walk or easy trot, with time to dismount and let the saddle cool, to roll a cigarette and let the horse drag its reins to a stray patch of grass. At other times, it was hard riding, man and horse pushed to their limits, charging over elevated baldies and alkali sinks, across or up or down arroyos. The sounds of nickering and bellowing, whistling and shouting, and always the choking clouds of dust kicked up by all those clattering hooves.[402]

At the spring or fall roundup, the crucial tools were the branding iron, castration knife, vaccine syringe, and lariat rope. The roper dragged any unbranded calves to the fire of red-hot coals and the focused attentions of two flankers and the man with the iron. "There's the bawl of a creature in agony when the brand is applied, and the knife put to surgery, converting little bulls into little steers, and the ear marked with an officially recorded crop, split, or swallow fork for further identification." The horses were changed frequently all day long. The men just kept working. No time to waste.[403]

The absolute monarch of a roundup was the chuck wagon cook. He took orders from nobody. "Roll out you beauties," he would bellow very early in the morning, long before daylight. "Come to life and earn your wages. The grub pile is waiting. Come and get it." The horse wrangler was the next man up. After a quick breakfast, he went to tend to the remuda of horses. The cowboys slowly came to life. A big coffee pot offered thick, black Arbuckle's coffee. The grub included fried steaks, crisply fried potatoes, frijole beans for those who liked them for breakfast, a bucket of sugar, a can of molasses, canned peaches or prunes, and a Dutch oven full of golden-crusted sourdough biscuits.[404]

The cook was usually grouchy and irritable. Cowboys approached him carefully, trying to gauge his mood, not wanting to annoy him. So much depended on the volume and quality of his food. The cook knew

---

402   Ibid., p. 101.

403   Ibid., p. 102.

404   John L. Sinclair, "Chuck Wagon Chow," *New Mexico Magazine* (March 1938).

that his gnarly reputation encouraged an easy acquiescence from all hands. Behind his back, the men called him coosie, cookie, dough wrangler, biscuit shooter, belly cheater, sally, the old woman, grease puncher, pot-slinger, and other, less printable names.[405]

With the roundup over, and back at the ranch headquarters, Sinclair settled into a bunkhouse shared with other cowboys in the mid-1920s. It was dark and small, with rock walls, a concrete floor, a low ceiling, and one small window that gave little relief from the prevailing odors of stale cigarette smoke, tobacco spit, and unwashed men. In the center of the room, a wood- burning cast iron stove provided heat. The men spat at it for good luck. A small table hosted the blackjack and poker games, with the men sitting on nail kegs, and a coal-oil lamp for illumination. The conversation was mostly about sports and the prostitutes in Roswell. No decorations on the walls, no feminine touches at all, but plenty of randomly placed nails for hanging clothes and belongings. The beds had no mattresses and no sheets, just blankets and quilts between upper and lower layers of canvas tarp.[406]

None of these details of cowboy life had changed since the nineteenth century. The only trace of modernity for the cowboys on the Diamond A was an elderly Model T pickup truck. Otherwise, all these scenes were frozen in time from long ago. After fourteen years as a cowboy, John Sinclair quit the life. He sold his first story to *New Mexico Magazine,* for $13.50, and became a writer. But he often thought about those old days and wrote about them. Some fifty years later, his measured judgment was succinct and balanced. "The loneliness, the grueling hardships, the ever-present danger," he wrote. "And the exquisite joys and freedom that fired the blood and mind of the old- time cowboy."[407]

*****

---

405   Ibid.

406   Sinclair, *Cowboy Riding Country*, p. 106; John Sinclair, *A Cowboy Writer in New Mexico: The Memoirs of John L. Sinclair* (1996), p. 62.

407   Sinclair, *Cowboy Riding Country*, p. 107.

Vic Culberson as the third president of the New Mexico Cattle, Growers' Association (1918-20), Source: James Culberson

The 1930s brought the longest and most sustained period of economic depression in American history. It affected everyone, leaving millions and millions of people baffled and desperate. Under such prolonged pressures, Franklin D. Roosevelt and his New Deal pushed through many innovative measures to regulate and stimulate the economy. But prosperity did not really return until the bloody demands of the Second World War.

At the annual convention of the New Mexico Cattle Growers' Association in January 1933, the current president, Albert K. Mitchell of Harding County, said that he was speaking at "the lowest ebb in the tide of the cattle industry in the history of the association." A year later, things looked even worse: "About the only reason I know of that a cowman could feel elated would be the fact that the year 1933 is now a matter of history." The annual cash income of the state's ranchers, which had peaked at $34.5 million in 1928, had plunged to only $7.4 million in 1933. "With the optimism that has saved us in the past," Mitchell bravely asserted, "we look to 1934 for a ray of hope."[408]

Among other problems, ranchers were producing too much beef for the reduced demand from consumers, many of whom could not afford to eat cow meat. The tightening vice of less demand and more supply was collapsing the price of beef on the hoof, from $46.50 a head in 1929 to $14.20 in 1934. "In passing from a free-range business of light overhead, small calf crops and heavy losses," Mitchell explained, "to the current day of controlled ranges and high-quality cattle, there have been successive increases in the cost of production." What to do?[409]

Hugh Hodge, 61 years old in 1934, was still among the leaders of Grant County and New Mexico stockmen. In his four decades of ranching, he had navigated the sometimes-testy relations with the Forest Service men on the Gila National Forest. Early in 1934 he wrote an exasperated challenge to a new Forest Service plan to fence strips of canyon bottom lands, up to a mile in length, and to prohibit grazing on them in order to prevent erosion and increase the stream flow. "It seems the policy of the so-called 'higher ups' in charge of National Forests, in their infinite knowledge of the range cow, to rather laugh at objections to this new restriction and to claim we exaggerate its importance."[410]

Hodge called it "The Last Straw" among many provocations. Given his years of dealing with the Forest Service, now complicated by the Great Depression and the New Deal's expansion of rules and regulations from Washington, Hodge took refuge in sardonic humor. "In spite of ribald laughter to the contrary," he continued, "we believe the average permittee

---

408 *Quarterly Bulletin* (January 1934); New Mexico Stockman (June 1939).
409 *Quarterly Bulletin* (January 1934); Mortensen, In the Cause of Progress, p. 19.
410 *Quarterly Bulletin* (May 1934).

212

on our National Forests is influenced not only by the natural desire to continue his home and business, if possible as heretofore on a more or less profitable basis, but also by the sincere wish to assist in whatever plans may be for the best interest of the natural resources of our National Forests."[411]

The surging federal tide was irresistible. Later that year, Congress passed the Taylor Grazing Act, the most significant legislation in the history of cattle ranching. Brought to the House by Edward T. Taylor, a Democrat from Colorado, it was the first federal measure to regulate grazing on federal lands (not including the national forests and parks). It was riding on political urgency from the Dust Bowl when heedless land practices had caused much of the American prairie land to blow away. "While this bill does not give us what we wanted," Albert Mitchell explained, "it seems to be the only one possible of passage at this time." Most western stockmen opposed it, but the New Mexico Cattle Growers' Association played "a most important part" in getting the bill passed.[412]

The Taylor Act removed all remaining federal land from homesteading claims. (Ranchers had long argued that the troublesome small homesteaders were the main cause of overgrazing and erosion.) The act put 80 million acres—and later more—of that land into grazing districts to be administered by a new Grazing Bureau within the Interior Department. The bureau set the fees and enforced regulations, and it required more fences to control where the cattle grazed. As a typical New Deal measure, it established government mandates over the last vestiges of the old free range. For the fiscal year 1938, New Mexico led all other states in the number of licenses, 1,962, granted under the Taylor Grazing Act.[413]

At the 25th annual convention of the Cattle Growers' Association in Clovis in 1939, Governor John E. Miles denied the widespread impression that the livestock business was tumbling into a long-term decline in the state. Sales and profits were rebounding from the bottom of the

---

411 Ibid.

412 *Quarterly Bulletin* (January 1934).

413 *New Mexico Stockman* (June 1939).

Depression, he said. Venturing carefully into the political aspects, he allowed that "some of my more conservative friends among the cattlemen are not particularly fond of the New Deal's planned economy." Well, yes. "Yet I often have wished that in the early days there had been some measure of control, regulation and planned economy for our range lands in the West." Ranchers might not have plowed up range lands for farming empires, on land that was suitable only for livestock, which then blew away in dust storms. "Perhaps if we had had in those days some measure of planned economy and more foresight, fewer cattleman would have gone broke, and today our ranges would have been greener with grass, instead of browner with sand."[414]

After brutal droughts in the first half of the 1930s, enough rain came at the end of the decade. "Cattle have wintered better than for many years," a man reported from Grant County in May 1940. More than five inches of rain had fallen since the first of March. "General soaking rains" arrived in late summer, making for "excellent" range conditions, cattle fattened for the winter, and better prices. The hardest decade in the history of Grant County ranching was closing with some grounds for hope.[415]

*****

And then a second world war, only two decades after the first one, and actually caused by the botched peace of the first one. Like most Americans, Grant County ranchers turned to World War II with a certain weary, resigned determination. Three months after Pearl Harbor, 1,400 New Mexico cattle growers met in Albuquerque for their annual convention. "It was a meeting in which there was a minimum of flag waving," the *New Mexico Stockman* reported, "and a maximum of quietly and soberly expressed support for all those fundamentals of freedom for which the flag of the United States stands." The banquet included no speeches but did offer entertainment and a floor show. "Entertainment, however,

---

414 *New Mexico Stockman* (April 1939).
415 *New Mexico Stockman* (May 1940).

was secondary to the serious business of the convention," the *Stockman* continued. "The shadow of war was seen on the faces of many fathers and mothers. The problems brought on by the war were reflected in all faces. The will to win found convincing expression."[416]

After the war, and the postwar adjustments, the country could finally relax into its first extended period of normal life in twenty years. Wartime needs and pressures had accelerated certain new technologies which now had peacetime applications, for ranchers and everybody. Cowboys had always been slow to adopt new gadgets and machines; they were wedded to their horses and old ways of doing things. But even they could see some merit in tractors and pickup trucks.

A survey of the membership of the New Mexico Cattle Growers' Association in 1950 found that 30% of them were connected to central power lines and another 35% were plugged into some private source of electricity. Thus, two-thirds of these ranchers were electrified, many through the federal Rural Electrification Administration—yet another gift from the New Deal.

Seventy percent of the ranchers listened to the radio on a regular basis, bridging their usual isolation and bringing instant news into their homes. A few decades earlier, very few ranchers had also been farmers; the two callings were quite separate and, in fact, often disdainful of each other. The Cattle Growers' survey found that 64% of the state's ranchers were now tilling some farmland aside from their general range land operations.[417]

Electricity eased many of the daily chores such as milking cows and churning butter, and powered the pumps and wells that were addressing the endemic worries about water rights and rainfall. Ranch women especially welcomed electricity to their traditional domain of the kitchen. "Today's kitchen is the result of the multitude of electric appliances available," the *Stockman* celebrated in 1950, "with plenty of workspace and time saving arrangement built into it." Cooking and heating the water, rooms,

---

416 *New Mexico Stockman* (March 1942).
417 *New Mexico Stockman* (February 1950).

and flatirons—once provided by a kitchen stove that needed frequent tending of its coal or wood—were now there at the flip of a switch. The old icebox, with its daily, dripping bother, had become electric. Even dishwashing, the most mundane and inevitable daily chore in a kitchen, could be electrified.[418]

Here's a tour of twenty-five Grant County ranches in the summer of 1954, from the smallest to the largest. Notice the long family ties for most of these outfits, and the recent innovations in ranching practices such as grazing leases from the Taylor Act, and the new wells, farms, and better ways of managing the land.[419]

Fred W. Foster, the incumbent Grant County superintendent of schools, had one of the oldest ranches in the county, established in the late 1860s by his wife's grandfather, James Metcalf, on about six sections of land (or six square miles), 18 miles northwest of Silver City. Their house was built in 1868. They kept a herd of about sixty polled Herefords. James Metcalf's son, O.B. Metcalf, was one of the first local men to bring in that breed. If the ranch had enough feed, the young cattle were held over and sold as yearlings. If feed was scarce, they were sold as calves.

The Cureton ranch consisted of an 80-acre farm and 40-acre leased irrigated pasture in Gila, and a 30-section ranch in Lordsburg. George H. Cureton established the ranch in about 1905; a half-century later it was run by his son, Jim, and son-in-law, George Jackson. The farm was added in 1948. The Curetons brought their calves to the farm when they were weaned in the fall. They munched through the winter on pasture and feed grown on the farm. In the spring, the bulls were sold, and the heifers returned to the ranch. The Curetons maintained about 85 head in a typical year.

Mike Hughes ran about 90 head on his three-section ranch a few miles north of San Lorenzo. The place had been in his family since the

---

418 "Grandma Never Would Recognize the Modern Push-Button Farm or Ranch Kitchen of Today," *New Mexico Stockman* (May 1950).

419 The twenty-five Grant County ranches were described in the *New Mexico Stockman* (August 1954).

1870s. His adoptive father, Alex MacGregor, had a claim on some land in the mountain country to the north which he traded to George O. Smith for some mining property; and that, according to family lore, was the start of the enormous GOS Ranch. Hughes gave the ranch only part of his time. He also had a job at the Chino open-pit copper mine in Santa Rita.

The Little Oak Ranch was ten miles south of Silver City on the road to Lordsburg. Owned by Howard and Aloha Burris, who had previously ranched in nearby counties, the Little Oak ran about 125 cows on 4,000 acres, all deeded land. Water was "somewhat hard to come by" on the place; their three wells, 600 feet deep, supplied the stock water. Howard Burris sent calves every fall to buyers in Dodge City, Kansas.

The Royall Hereford Ranch ran about 150 head of Herefords on 20 sections of land, 25 miles southeast of Silver City. Robert Royall came to New Mexico from North Carolina in 1910 and bought the old 7XV spread in the rolling hills of the White Signal country. The grama grass was still lush and stirrup-high, and by good husbandry Bob and his brother William kept it that way. Bob Royall was a charter member of the New Mexico Stock Growers' Association and one of its most active leaders, serving as president from 1930 to 1932. Some of his Hereford bulls achieved their own kind of fame: Real Square, Husker Mischief, Young Mischief, Shorty Domino, Don Blanchard, and Beau Resolute. Most of Royall's bulls were sold as weaner calves in southwestern New Mexico, but some went as far away as New Hampshire. Any heifers not retained for replacement were sold to local neighbors.

J.S. Mitchell started ranching his place on the Mimbres River, some nine miles northwest of San Lorenzo, in about 1900. His memories went back even farther to the days when Geronimo was roaming the country. Mitchell ran 150 head on 20 sections of national forest land and a few more of deeded land. He also cultivated 40 acres of farm fields, raising feed crops for his cattle. Water was supplied by springs, some of which had of late been drying up for the first time ever. And more bad luck: a few months ago, his ranch home burned to the ground.

Noel Rankin bought his first ranch on a twelve-section place about 15 miles southwest of Cliff in 1935, and he had recently bought a farm in the Gila Valley, a few miles northeast of Cliff. The ranch consisted of patented, state, and Taylor lease land. Rankin usually shipped yearlings to Kansas and to the West Coast. With the farm, Rankin planned to bring his calves from the ranch in the fall and to feed them on the farm till spring. He had about 200 acres under irrigated cultivation on the farm, all of it in feed crops. As long as the Gila River kept flowing, Rankin had created a self-contained, integrated system of cows, crops, and water, complete with a 500-ton silo. Horace L. Bounds and his wife operated the Wigwam Ranch, ten miles east of Santa Rita. It consisted of about six sections, mostly deeded land.

They were currently running about 150 registered Herefords and 50 more commercial cows. Most of the calves from the Herefords were sold in Arizona. The family, including their son, Jupe, had won prizes at the Phoenix National competition. They were also farming 300 acres to feed their cattle.

Starting in the early 1900s, Tom Foy and his brothers ran a ranch and lumber yard near Santa Clara. In about 1929 he bought out his brothers, and in 1954 Tom was running the outfit with his four children: Rosemary Stewart of Santa Clara, J. Franey Foy of Bayard, Winifred Ann Munson of El Paso, and Thomas P. Foy of Bayard. (Thomas was also the president of the Grant County State Bank in Bayard and the incumbent Grant County district attorney.) This well-connected family usually ran about 250 head on six sections. The Foys bought most of their registered bulls from Robert Royall and sold them to Noel Rankin or a packing company in El Paso.

Forrest Delk ran about 300 head on the ranch five miles east of Santa Rita that was homesteaded by his father in 1914. The ranch consisted of about 30 sections, mostly deeded land with some state and private leases.

Delk bought most of his registered bulls from the Cureton ranch in Lordsburg. He usually held his steer calves to sell as yearlings when they were fattened to 650 pounds. Most of them were shipped to Phoenix.

Forrest Delk also fronted a popular western-music band, Delk's Gully Jumpers, made up entirely of local ranchers indulging their hobbies. They were scheduled to play for the Hereford Tour dance in Silver City in September.

Eddie L. Allison and his (unnamed) wife ran the Iryvenir Ranch on 40 sections about 23 miles northwest of Silver City. They had been working that land—from the national forest, state, and a Taylor grant—for about 15 years. With about 350 head, they bought most of their registered bulls from Robert Royall. As ranching conservationists, they were trying to restore parts of their abused range by stocking it conservatively and letting some sections rest for a year or more. Most of their calf crop was shipped to the West Coast as weaner calves.

James B. Turner's ranch bordered Silver City to the west and south, and his headquarters was about two and a half miles from the heart of town. His father, Burke Turner, had homesteaded the place in 1912 with a single partial section of 160 acres. Since then, the ranch had grown to about 24 sections, most of it deeded and with some state and Taylor land. James Turner was currently running about 450 cows. His main bull, MW Larry Domino 127th, was famous in his own, prolific way. Raised by the Sellman Brothers of Watrous, New Mexico, he had been declared the first-place senior calf at the New Mexico State Fair in 1951. Turner's grazing ranges in foothill country were used all year, even in the dry season, with water from eleven wells and ten surface tanks.

The XXX Ranch, on the Mimbres River just north of the town of Mimbres, dated back to 1877. Ace Christmas bought the place in 1937 and gave it to his son, Ace Jr., five years ago. He ran 500 Hereford cows on some 35,000 acres of deeded and national forest land. In the last two years, they had bought some bulls from the Curetons. They generally used a ratio of ten bulls to 100 cows. The Mimbres River ran through the ranch for eight miles, giving most of their stock water along with wells and springs.

In 1883, D.C. McMillen started the AT Cross Ranch, about 15 miles west of Silver City, and thus began one of the oldest family lines among Grant County ranchers. Two of his sons, the brothers John T. and Elmo

McMillen, split up the ranch in 1941. John took 40 sections, 11 miles west of Silver City on Highway 260, and ran about 500 cows on them. Water for his stock came from springs, wells, and surface tanks. John's adult children also went into ranching. Elmo got a bigger share of the family ranch, 100 sections, and ran more cattle, about 1,000. His water supplies included surface tanks, springs, wells, and the Gila River. Both brothers shipped their weaner calves to Kansas City.

The Y6 Hereford Ranch was five miles south of Mule Creek, which was 46 miles northwest of Silver City. Sam Means had owned it since 1917, recently with Mr. and Mrs. George C. Schale as partners and managers. The ranch embraced about 70 sections of which 8,000 acres was national forest land. They ran 600 head, half of whom were purebreds that produced 75 to 100 range bulls each year. Most of the annual production went as yearlings to Arizona feeders.

Randolf Franks had a ranch about six miles west of Silver City. It was first homesteaded by his father, Will Franks, and Randolf had lived there his entire life. It took in about 80 sections of deeded, state, national forest, and Taylor land. The herd of about 650 mother cows was serviced by registered bulls from George Cureton's ranch in Gila. At Cliff, Franks also had a 100-acre farm on which he grew feed crops for his own use. His two daughters were members of the Grant County Registered Hereford Heifer Club, and each was looking after eight registered cows: the third generation on that ranch.

The famous GOS Ranch was run by Vic Culberson until his death in 1930. At its peak, it included 400 sections and 5,000 cattle. One large piece of that empire, at the head of the Mimbres River in the Mogollon and Black Range mountains, was bought by Hub Estes in 1931. He ran about 700 cows on 100 sections. In the lush valley at his ranch headquarters, Estes had about 100 cultivated acres, raising oats for his horses and cattle—yielding 150 to 200 tons a year. Estes shipped his calves to Texas and Oklahoma.

The three McDonald brothers—Bartley, Taylor, and John—had a place in White Signal, about 20 miles southwest of Silver City, that was established in 1903 by their father, Jerry J. McDonald. It consisted of 50 sections

220

of deeded, state, and Taylor land with about 800 head. The brothers used only Hereford bulls from Robert Royall's adjoining ranch. In 1948, Royall and the McDonalds built an eight-mile water pipeline to supply both of their ranches. The two-inch pipe drew water from three wells and was connected to six stock tanks at various points.

The H-Y Ranch was about 45 miles northwest of Silver City, just east of Mule Creek. Huling Means bought the place in 1916. Its 30,000 acres were mostly deeded land with some state and Taylor leases. It normally carried about 1,000 cows. Means kept a small herd of purebred Herefords for his supply of bulls. In recent years, he had been using Angus bulls on his yearling heifers. Means sold his calf crop as yearlings except in very dry years. The ranch currently depended on surface tanks and a creek for water, but Means was drilling wells to tap into a more reliable source.

J.L. McCauley and his sons—James, Harry, and Frank—ranched 104 sections about 17 miles south of Silver City, near Tyrone. The father had been working that land since 1908. At times of normal moisture, they ran about 1,000 head, including 180 registered Herefords bred by Robert Royall and the Curetons. Most of their calf crop was sold to Kansas, Iowa, or California. Almost all of their stock water came from wells.

On his 65 sections located on Bear Creek, four miles east of Gila, Joe Hooker raised about 1,000 Herefords only. Half his land was patented, and the rest from state, national forest, and Taylor leases. Joe's father, Horace Hooker, came to the Gila country in 1875 and worked as a cowboy; Joe grew up in Grant County and inherited the calling. His ranch lay entirely in foothill and mountain country. The water came from springs, wells, and ground tanks. Most of the registered bulls were bought from Hub Estes of the GOS Ranch. Hooker's calves were sold to various places in New Mexico, Texas, and Oklahoma.

The Moon Ranch of 90 sections in southwestern Grant County was only a small chunk of Tom Lyons's old LC Ranch. Its seven miles of pipeline were a relic of the piped water system that Lyons had installed for the LC in 1886. L.R. Spires, a relative newcomer, had bought the Moon in 1951.

Spires also had ranches in Santa Rosa and Capitan, New Mexico. On the Moon he ran about 1,200 head of Hereford and Angus cows, but he did not crossbreed them. He sold his stock as calves, yearlings, or even older, depending on current market trends, to buyers in Iowa and California. Aside from his pipeline, Spires also drew water from surface tanks, springs, and wells.

The Mangas Cattle Company was located five miles north of Tyrone, in the Big Burro mountains. Managed by Roy Wilmeth, it ran 1,400 head on 100 sections of deeded, state, national forest, and Taylor land, lying on both sides of the Continental Divide. Given the recent drought, Wilmeth had been hauling 5,000 gallons of water a day to keep the cattle spread out and away from the water holes where the feed was exhausted. For the past three years, the company had been buying their registered bulls from Robert Royall.

And finally: On the ranch land near Cliff first established by their father, Fred McCauley, in 1903, the four McCauley brothers—Tom, Hap, Dale, and Fate—ran about 1,600 cows on 165 sections. They had divided the original ranch into four linked operations in 1948. Their holdings embraced state, patented, national forest, and Taylor land. That included about 1,500 acres of irrigated farmland growing feed crops for the cattle. Fate McCauley also ran a feedlot that could handle about a thousand head. The brothers sold their cattle to the Deming Packing Company and to the West Coast.

These twenty-five ranches in 1954—counting the old AT Cross Ranch as two ranches after it was split between the McMillen brothers, John T. and Elmo—provide a sense of recent changes in Grant County ranching. On the twentieth anniversary of the Taylor Grazing Act, nine of these ranches included some Taylor land. Nine also had become less dependent on the unreliable rainfall by digging and pumping wells. In what earlier might have seemed an act of heresy, seven of these ranchers had also become farmers— although the food they raised was generally for cows, not for humans. One great continuity remained: seventeen of these ranches were built on family ties, through two or even three generations by 1954. Despite all the trials and endemic uncertainties of ranching, it was still often passed down from parents to their children. That must suggest something about the attractions and the everyday grounded stability between humans and their cattle.

*****

Noel Rankin was a major leader among Grant County's ranchers, in the traditions of Vic Culberson, Hugh Hodge, and Robert Royall. Noel was born in 1897 in Throckmorton, a town in central Texas. When he was five, his family moved across the line to eastern New Mexico, then to Grant County fourteen years later. After serving in the Navy during the world war, he was mustered out in 1919, 22 years old, and looked for a ranching job. Huling Means hired him to work on his H-Y Ranch east of Mule Creek. After two years he made Rankin the foreman.[420]

On a trip to El Paso, Noel met Carrie Ricker, a Mississippi girl who, it was said, "hardly knew a horse from a cow." Nevertheless, he married her.

One morning, Noel asked her to check on the ranch's water holes and report back to him. Carrie had never bridled or saddled a horse, and she received no instruction from her husband. She sweated, fussed, and cried but finally got it done. Noel allowed later tongue in cheek that his wife "was game and eventually made a good hand on the ranch."

In 1935, they bought a spread on twelve sections southwest of Cliff. Taking a large risk, Noel sold all his cattle to provide the cash to drill for water. Huling Means, wishing to help the young couple, brought a woman from El Paso who supposedly had the gift of water dowsing, of finding underground water with the magic of a forked stick. This "water witcher" walked around a part of the ranch, dowsing, and finally stopped and piled up some rocks. "It's here," she said. And it was. The drillers found a steady supply of water at 438 feet down.

420   The fullest account of Noel Rankin's life is the six-page typed biography in folder 5, box 1 of the Noel Rankin Papers, Special Collections, Branson Library, New Mexico State University, Las Cruces. The first four paragraphs of this section draw from that source. And see *El Paso Times*, April 14, 1970.

The Soil Conservation Service, another New Deal measure, was created in 1935 to help ranchers and farmers take better care of their land. Rankin joined the Grant County Soil and Water Conservation District in 1950 and remained an active member for years, spreading this conservation gospel to other ranchers. In general, the word "conservation" began to appear more often during the 1950s in the *New Mexico Stockman,* the monthly magazine of the New Mexico Cattle Growers' Association. Rankin served a term as president of the association, and he was named its Cattleman of the Year in 1970. He also gave time to many other boards and civic organizations, both local and state-wide.[421]

However, he parted company with most conservationists over the touchy, perennial issue of grazing cattle in the national forests and wilderness areas. Ever since the first wilderness area within the Gila National Forest, spearheaded by Aldo Leopold in 1924, many such areas had been created.

But they lacked legislative permanence and could be undone at any time by an unfriendly Congress or presidential administration. Howard Zahniser of the Wilderness Society spent the last fifteen years of his life flogging his bill in Congress to pass the Wilderness Act and protect those areas forever.

Zahniser's bill struggled through endless hearings and revisions. In some versions, it banned all stock grazing in wilderness areas. Ranchers quite understandably saw that as a threat to their livelihoods. In January 1959 Noel Rankin joined six other speakers at a protest meeting in Glenwood attended by over one hundred ranchers, farmers, and others. Among his contentions, he said the bill would eliminate thousands of dollars of income from national forest leases, money that helped support local schools. Later that year, Rankin and two other members of the New Mexico Farm Bureau board warned that the bill would especially hurt small ranchers who were dependent on grazing in the Gila Forest. Over

---

421 Unidentified clipping [1970?] in folder 5, box 1, Rankin Papers; "conservation" appearing in *New Mexico Stockman*: for example, in August 1950, November 1954, and September 1958.

half of Grant County's ranchers, they said, held grazing rights in the forest and its wilderness areas. The bill would curtail these rights with "a disastrous effect on the value of ranch lands in Grant County" and would "result in economic ruin" for many of its stockmen.[422]

The final version of the bill, passed in 1964, allowed grazing in wilderness areas "where those practices have already become well-established." The crucial Interior committees of both houses of Congress were controlled by lawmakers from ranching states in the West, and the bill could not have passed without that change. But it left the wilderness areas still vulnerable to overgrazing by any careless stockmen.[423]

The conservation movement was about to explode into the modern environmental movement. Rachel Carson's bellwether book of 1962, *Silent Spring,* had directed attention to threats to humans as well as the dangers to non-human aspects of nature which had previously engaged conservationists. When humans were themselves threatened, that, of course, interested humans much more. A new term, "environmentalism," caught this new, broader, more ecological focus: We're all in this together. The conservation movement had always been tiny, just a small group of people reading each other's magazines and muttering in their corner. Suddenly, in the years around 1970, it was transformed into the mass movement that we have known ever since.

Between 1966 and 1975, the membership of the Wilderness Society grew from 35,000 to 87,000; of the Sierra Club, from 35,000 to 147,000; of the National Audubon Society, from 45,000 to 321,500; and of the National Wildlife Federation, from 271,800 to 612,100. It was generally conceded that the newly energized Sierra Club was leading the way, in the spirit of its co- founder and first president, John Muir.[424]

---

422 *Enterprise,* January 8, 1959; Albuquerque Journal, July 29, 1959, and a two-page typed statement in folder 6, box 1, Rankin Papers.

423 Mark Harvey, *Wilderness Forever: Howard Zahniser and the Path to the Wilderness Act* (2005), pp. 204-06; James Morton Turner, The Promise of Wilderness: American Environmental Politics Since 1964 (2012), pp. 30-31.

424 Stephen Fox, *John Muir and His Legacy: The American Conservation Movement* (1981), p. 315.

*****

The story of Grant County ranching since 1970 is essentially the story of ranchers responding to this new environmental consciousness. Among the local ranchers—as among the local residents in general—there is a schism, subtle and at times not so subtle, between the lifelong residents and the newcomers who have moved to Grant County as adults. The newcomers are more politically liberal, in general, than the lifers, which can lead to some sharp resentments. (Full disclosure: I am one of those newcomers, having lived here since 2008, and you should probably bear that in mind.)

Judged by the new environmental standards, Gene Simon and David Ogilvie were two of the most enlightened Grant County ranchers in recent history. (They were both newcomers.) They demonstrated that, even under our stringent conditions of rainfall and terrain, cattle could be raised here successfully without abusing the land. Simon came to ranching late in life and mostly had a small ranch here; Ogilvie grew up ranching in Arizona and ran a large spread near Cliff. It made no difference. The essential principles were the same.

Eugene A. Simon was born in 1916 in Burlington, Iowa. He graduated from Baldwin Wallace University in Berea, Ohio, then took a master's in political science at the University of Pennsylvania. While teaching at Penn State, he met his wife, Elisabeth Howe, known as Libby. During the Second World War he served for three years on the attack carrier USS *Belleau Wood* in the Pacific theater, narrowly surviving a kamikaze attack during the Okinawa campaign. When the *Belleau Wood* limped into San Francisco for repairs, Gene and Libby got together for the first time in those three years.[425]

After the war, he settled into a long career with a family newspaper, the *Valley News Dispatch,* in Tarentum, Pennsylvania, a small town outside

---

425 *Silver City Daily Press*, May 10, 2012; Bill Pippin, "Gene Simon," *New Mexico Magazine* (June 2002).

Pittsburgh. He and Libby raised their children there. The *Dispatch* took on organized crime, which was flourishing in Pittsburgh. "I was advised not to park my car in the same place twice," he recalled. "An anonymous caller actually threatened our two kids." Over the years, Gene also conducted interviews with many world leaders, including Fidel Castro, Nasser of Egypt, Nehru of India, and the Shah of Iran.[426]

Like many kids, as a child he was besotted with cowboys and boyish dreams of riding the range out West. His chance came when the *Dispatch*, as an investment, bought a ranch in southwestern New Mexico. After three decades with the newspaper, and no experience of working the land beyond his backyard in Tarentum, Gene, at the age of 62, decided to move to Grant County and become a rancher. (I wonder how Libby at first reacted to this startling plan.) "Some of my friends and peers thought I was crazy for doing that," he said later, "but it was the best decision I ever made."[427]

They moved to the Ponderosa Highlands Ranch, 45 miles north of Silver City, near Lake Roberts. It ran about 700 head on a 67,000-acre grazing lease in the Gila Wilderness, nine miles north of the ranch. Libby learned to cook large meals for the hired hands, and Gene loved his new cowboy life, mostly. In the summer of 1979, after a long roundup day, the men were riding back to the ranch when they saw two coyotes chasing their dogs. "It is highly unusual for coyotes to chase dogs," Gene noted. "Usually, it's the other way around." Gene was worried about his young dog, Tippy, so he moved diagonally toward the coyotes, cutting them off. The larger coyote backed away, lifted his head, "and let out the most eerie howl of frustration I've ever heard. It made your spine tingle." Resuming the ride home, they ran into a big flock of turkeys, then some cow elk and calves, and a small herd of deer "on a nearby ridge sharply outlined against a red-streaked western sky at sunset. With two golden eagles soaring overhead, that was the frosting on the cake for a truly memorable day."[428]

---

426   Ibid.

427   *Daily Press*, April 22, 2011.

428   Larry Godfrey, ed., *Cows and Columns: Gene Simon's "Think about It"* (2008), pp. 218-19.

Gene Simon, a newspaperman and rancher in Grant County., Source: New Mexico Magazine

Gene still worked part-time as a journalist, writing columns for the local papers, including the biweekly, bilingual *El Reportero* newspaper published by Gregorio Mesa and edited by Luis Quiñones in the late 1980s. Appalled by the excesses of the Reagan presidency, Gene finally renounced the ancestral Iowa Republicanism of his parents and registered as a maverick Democrat. He reversed the usual pattern by becoming more liberal, not less, as he aged. "Liberal and conservative don't mean a thing to me," he insisted. "I'm only interested in what's right or wrong." Increasingly, he found what's right on the left.[429]

429 Godfrey, *Cows and Columns*, p. 11; Pippin, "Gene Simon."

He expressed many liberal Democratic opinions that few local ranchers would have agreed with for wolves, energy conservation, alternatives to oil, and solar power, and against the National Rifle Association, the theft of the 2000 presidential election, the Iraq War, capital punishment, global warming, pesticides, and corporate farms. Unlike many ranchers, he allowed no hunting or trapping of coyotes on his land. He knew these "predators" would control the rodent population naturally, without having to trap or poison them, and in 34 years he never had a coyote problem on his ranches.[430]

As an engaged rancher, he could walk the walk as well as talk the talk.

After a few years, starting to feel his age, he and Libby moved to a smaller spread, the 80-acre Rancho del Rio along the Mimbres River near Faywood. To that he added 7,600 acres bought from neighboring ranchers. "The climate here is the best in America," Gene exulted. "I think the people are too. When we first moved to the Mimbres Valley, even though anyone from east of El Paso was considered an Easterner, our neighbors' main concern was whether or not we liked the place."[431]

All his life, Gene had loved to take care of animals and observe their behaviors. He noticed that they often behaved better than humans. He praised the steadfast mothering by his cows and hens; never a case of child abuse among them. Of all his animals, he liked the horses best. "I don't think there's any animal much smarter than a smart horse," he maintained. "I've got some that can open gate bolts and latches, and they've got fantastic memories as to where the good grub is or where a gate is open. But even more impressive is how well they get along together. My best cow horse is *numero uno* of the four, and all he has to do to get into another's stall is merely touch his rump. But he never does it in a nasty way and the others never resent it. … I know danged well that my horse wouldn't be gullible and dumb enough to get taken in by the likes of Rush Limbaugh."[432]

---

430   Godfrey, *Cows and Columns*, pp. xvii-xx, 34-203.
431   Pippin, "Gene Simon."
432   Godfrey, *Cows and Columns*, pp. 228-29.

Gene ran his ranches along the principles expressed in his columns. He learned how to keep all the elements—land, plants, animals, and water—in proper balance without violating the natural processes, which otherwise could become punitive. "Being blessed is doing what you want to do, where you want to do it," he wrote in 2002, "and being able to do it—even crowding 86. And come to think of it, being able to get reactionary right-wing extremists riled up once in a while with a newspaper column!"[433]

Gene and Libby sold a thousand acres to the State Parks division to expand the City of Rocks State Park. Later they gave permanent protection to their land by granting a conservation easement to the New Mexico Land Conservancy. A future owner could still ranch that land. "After living in this beautiful valley for so long," Gene said, "and coming to know all the natural and cultural treasures on this ranch, I couldn't stand the thought of breaking up the integrity of this incredible place." Gene died in 2012, 96 years old.

Libby died three years later; 95 years old. Two lives well lived.[434]

*****

David Ogilvie was born in 1957 on a cattle ranch southeast of Flagstaff, Arizona. His paternal grandfather had emigrated from Scotland in 1898; he followed a relative to central Arizona and started ranching. His sons and their sons and their sons stayed in ranching through four generations of Ogilvies.

David's father worked at that ranch for 46 years, for much of that time as the foreman. He always mused about owning his own spread, but as a child of the Great Depression, he was reluctant to take risky chances and incur debts.[435]

From the age of five, David cowboyed and rode a horse. He always expected to stay in ranching. At the University of Arizona he majored

---

433 Ibid., p. 224.

434 *Daily Press*, April 22, 2011.

435 David Ogilvie, interview by author, Silver City, August 24, 2023.

in Animal Science, took many courses in ranch management, and met his wife, Tammy, who had grown up on a cotton farm. After graduating in 1980, and his father's retirement as foreman of the ranch, David and Tammy returned there. They had three kids and David worked as the foreman for six years.

David Ogilvie a third-generation rancher, Source the author.

Wishing to become their own boss, and willing to assume the inherent risks, the young couple started to think about a place of their own. They considered many different locales across the American West.[436]

They first saw the Cliff/Gila Valley in the spring of 1985. Arizona was in the midst of a huge population explosion which did not include ranchers. "Thousands of people from all over had moved there," David recalled, "for its beautiful scenery, climate, wide open spaces, or for many other

---

436　Ibid.

231

reasons I'm not sure of! The rural nature of the place had disappeared, and we were looking for a place to escape the people." On this first exposure to that part of the Gila River, David was most struck by its lack of development. "Here was a river valley in a rural setting that had not been taken over by Californians ... The Cliff/Gila Valley landscape was virtually intact. The activities of ranching and farming were still active and were an important part of the economy, not banished from the river, not replaced by expensive homes with fancy foreign cars."[437]

With Arizona in a headlong embrace of modernity, David and Tammy turned the clock back. In the spring of 1988, they bought a spread of 16,000 acres, about ten miles from downtown Silver City; Tammy's parents cosigned on the mortgage. The property was part of the old AT Cross Ranch that had been owned by the McMillen family. With three children to educate, the Ogilvies liked its proximity to town. (David's boyhood ranch was seventy miles from town.) A few years later, with the mining company Phelps Dodge getting out of the cow business, the Ogilvies leased its adjacent land. That enormously increased their holdings by about 290 sections and formed the U Bar Ranch. It stretched 90 miles from north to south and included nine miles along the Gila River.[438]

All over the West, the 1990s brought a nasty, rancorous, ill-tempered showdown among cattle ranchers, environmentalists, the Forest Service, and other federal agencies. Many environmentalists wanted to ban cattle ranching entirely as an unnecessary blight on the land. Many ranchers wanted to ban environmentalists. The federal agencies, caught between these two factions, pleased nobody. In Grant County, this squabbling was sharpened by the existing generational and political divisions between the newly arrived, often younger environmentalists and the entrenched, more conservative ranchers.

The Quivira Coalition, founded in Santa Fe in 1997, hoped to find a "radical center" among these combatants and get them to stop shouting at each

---

437   David Ogilvie, "The Cliff/Gila Valley," *Quivira Coalition Newsletter* (September 2002).

438   Ogilvie interview.

other. The coalition was started by Courtney White (a green writer), Jim Winder (a green rancher near Nutt, New Mexico, about 20 miles south of Hatch), and Barbara Johnson (another green writer). In Grant County, the coalition attracted support from local environmentalists such as Dutch Salmon, Sally Smith, Jack Carter, Peter Russell—and David Ogilvie.

As it happened, the canary in the coal mine here was a small, rather obscure bird named the southwestern willow flycatcher. Phelps Dodge still owned some land along the Gila River. In cooperation with the U Bar Ranch, they restored some long-unused earthen breastworks and then irrigated land on the banks of the river. That restored the riparian plants and trees, which attracted Ogilvie's grazing cattle, which worried environmentalists.[439]

The flycatcher was thought to be nearly extinct and had never been seen along that stretch of the Gila. David arranged for a population survey done from May to July of 1994, conducted by qualified biologists using an established U.S. Fish and Wildlife Service protocol. To everyone's surprised astonishment, it found a high population of 64 pairs of flycatchers. Their nesting habitats, instead of the expected young, dense stands of willow and cottonwood trees, were mostly flood plain patches of box elder and older, mature cottonwood and willow. Later annual surveys found 107, 138, 174, and 186 pairs. Meantime, the U Bar was increasing its riparian land under irrigation, and the number of cattle grazing it.[440]

"The ranch can be considered an environmental paradox," Ogilvie wrote in the September 1998 issue of the Quivira Coalition's newsletter, "because the largest known and most successful population of southwestern willow flycatchers is found on the private land that we graze and farm." Agriculture and, specifically, cattle grazing had been considered the main cause of the flycatcher's declining numbers. Yet the bird was prospering despite these high and growing densities of livestock. "U Bar Ranch's livestock management," David continued, "in association with

---

439 Ibid.
440 David Ogilvie, "The Southwestern Willow Flycatcher and Me," *Quivira Coalition Newsletter* (September 1998).

the occupied habitat, has always been flexible, with some of the pastures being grazed strictly in the dormant season, while others are used in a rest/rotation system in direct association with nesting bird activity. Most farming activities in close proximity to nesting bird habitats are minimized during the active nesting season."[441]

Without so intending, David Ogilvie and the U Bar had become a model for how to calm the civil war between ranchers and environmentalists. In 2000, Courtney White praised the man and his ranch for being open to new ideas such as grazing their bird habitat only during the dormant season. "Ogilvie's environmental ethic is large," White declared, "and his managerial abilities skillful." Two years later, the coalition gave its first annual Clarence Burch Award, named in honor of a pioneering rancher and conservationist from Oklahoma, to Ogilvie and six of his associates in the flycatcher project—"for their integrity, dedication, and unfailing good humor, sometimes in the face of adversity." Those associates included a rancher, a college professor, biologists, and people from the Forest Service.[442]

David, in his early forties, was part of a new generation of cattle ranchers, college graduates who were not bound to any ancient notions of how to raise livestock. He practiced rest/rotation grazing throughout the U Bar, not just in flycatcher territory. The ranch was divided into eighteen pastures. The cattle were rotated through sixteen pastures during the growing season, and the other two pastures were grazed only during the dormant winter season. During the growing season, grazing periods ranged from one to four weeks, and then a pasture was rested for about a year. The following year's rotation was different to make sure the pasture would not receive the same impact every year. Ogilvie believed, in general, that recovery was a more important goal than productivity.[443]

---

441 Ibid.

442 *Quivira Coalition Newsletter* (August 2000), (January 2002).

443 Nathan F. Sayre, *The New Ranch Handbook: A Guide to Restoring Western Rangelands* (2001), pp. 19-20; Ogilvie interview.

He was characteristically willing to try different measures, and not everything worked. Concerned that piñon-juniper trees were crowding out desirable grasses, perhaps because of more flooding and sedimentation in lower areas, David tried burning one section of his land. He rested that area for three growing seasons before ignition to allow fuel to accumulate. But the results of the fires were disappointing and inconsistent. In some parts, the trees were wiped out, but in others not so much. In the well-burned areas, some grass came back, but also less desirable browse such as willow, sumac, and mulberry. He did notice an increase in elk and deer on the burned areas.[444]

As of 2023, sixty-six years old, David is still agreeably engaged in the perennial rhythms of the ranching life. A typical year is highlighted by two intense two-month periods. In the spring they gather and brand the new calves; in the fall they wean the calves and ship them. That provides most of the ranch's income. Ever since buying his own place, he has only run Angus cattle, and since 1988 he has never actually bought a cow. All his cattle are descended from those originals. On occasion, he has to purge any cows that turn out to be unproductive. He has kept a favorite horse, Buck, now 30 years old and blind, allowing him to live out his life on the ranch.[445]

"I don't know a rancher that is rich," David said. "They may be land- rich, but they don't have a large bank account." Tammy has a job in town, teaching in the education program at Western New Mexico University. Their son Ryan, 42 years old, runs the 35,000-acre ranch north of Lordsburg that David bought in 2014. Their son Andrew, 40 years old, has a farm near Benson, Arizona, with some livestock. Their daughter, Erin Kartchner, is a neonatal nurse married to a civil engineer in Las Cruces. The current flycatcher population on the Gila is about 300.[446]

---

444 Ogilvie interview.

445 Ibid.

446 Ibid.

David likes to insist that his attitudes and practices are now typical of most Grant County ranchers. He proudly locates himself in the middle among the five generations of Ogilvie ranchers that today include his grandson. "I consider myself an environmentalist," he said, not flinching from the word. "If you're a third-generation rancher, you've seen it when it was good and when it was bad. If you're in it for the long term like we are, you want to treat the land as best you can."[447]

*****

In the high, dry terrain of Grant County, cattle ranching has never been an easy way to make a living. Over the last half-century, and despite the ongoing flood of new gadgets and machinery designed to lighten a rancher's load, it has become even more difficult to make ends meet. On the McDonald ranch in White Signal, run in the 1950s by the brothers Bartley, Taylor, and Jonny of the second generation, Jonny's son Jerry and his wife, Linda Nielson McDonald, eventually urged their six children—of the fourth generation—to leave the ranch and find employment elsewhere. "There's nothing for you here," they said. Only Niel of the fourth generation stayed where he was. "I have an absolute passion for cattle ranching," he explained.[448]

Ty Bays grew up on a Grant County ranch with 120 head of cattle. "We made a living," Ty recalled. "We scraped by." Now he has a ranch near North Hurley with 250 head, more than twice as many, but he has to work a full- time job at the mining company Freeport McMoRan to get by. Niel goes to his job at an Edward Jones office in Silver City five days a week, and indulges his passion for ranching in the evenings and weekends. On the Bays ranch, his wife is the ranch cook and his two sons are the ranch hands. Ty can't pay any other salaries. Niel and Ty are both smart, aware, educated men with two college degrees each. They would love to be ranching full time. But today only much bigger ranches, such

---

447 Ibid.
448 Niel McDonald, interview by author, Silver City, June 10, 2021

236

as the Ogilvie and the Billings spreads, can attain the economies of scale to be reliably profitable.[449]

The problem comes down to this: Since about 1970, the costs of ranching have skyrocketed, far surpassing what most ranchers can get for their cattle. A pickup truck, that essential tool on a ranch, has gone from an old price of $6,000 up to the current model, with many additional if not necessary bells and whistles, that costs $50,000. The prices of land, feed, and equipment have also zoomed out of sight and reach. Those new gadgets and machinery look beguiling—but they're expensive. Modern transportation across oceans and continents has brought more foreign competition in beef providers that are not subject to American labor costs and regulations. Small and medium-sized ranchers in Grant County are being squeezed from many sides of this contracting landscape.[450]

Grant County has so far avoided the massive immigration of outsiders that pushed David and Tammy Ogilvie out of Arizona and into the Cliff/Gila Valley. Thanks to heroic efforts by the county's environmentalists, the Gila River remains the last free-flowing river in the area, a reliable boon for both ranchers and recreationists. And while it must be said that pessimists have been predicting the decline and fall of Grant County ranching for many years, especially during prolonged droughts and hard times, the ranchers, some of them, are still here.

Yes, but fewer of them as time passes. Americans believe, more than anything else, in what they call Progress. To most of us, that usually means "subduing" the land and establishing "dominion" over its creatures, in the aggressive spirit of the first chapter of Genesis. Ranchers, with their many thousands of unpaved acres and large, unbridled animals, seem to belong to an earlier time in our history, an age of cowboys and horses. Americans still love their hamburgers, and the meatless versions of those items offer tasteless insults to the American palate. Ranchers, their cattle, and their beloved burgers will continue to ride horses into our national image and imagination.

---

449   Ty Bays, interview by author, Silver City, June 11, 2021.
450   Ibid.

STEPHEN FOX... PH.D. is a historian from Boston. He studied US history at Williams College and Brown University. He is the author of *John Muir and His Legacy: The American Conservation Movement* (1981) and other books. Steve and his wife, Alexandra Dundas Todd, fled the Boston winters and moved to Silver City in 2008. His article on "Jaime Crow in New Mexico: Mexicans and Whites in Grant County Since 1870" appeared in the Spring 2019 issue of the *New Mexico Historical Review*.

CHAPTER 7

Booms and Busts, 1870-1952: The History of Business in Silver City

By Scott Fritz, Ph.D.

This essay examines the business history of Silver City and Grant County, New Mexico. Its purpose is to assist the Silver City Museum in constructing future exhibits on the economic history of southwestern New Mexico. It will argue that there were three economic linkages to the larger U.S. economy that brought money into Grant County and sustained Silver City's businesses during the late nineteenth and early twentieth centuries. The primary linkage was mining; the secondary linkage was ranching; and the third linkage was government spending and healthcare. Exports of minerals and cattle were the most important sources of wealth in the region, and the economy was dependent on the sale of these commodities outside New Mexico. Prices for cattle and metals were highly volatile. A "boom" occurred when prices were high for these products, and a "bust" occurred when those prices fell. The region's economy was rural and undiversified and was susceptible to periods of economic decline. Nevertheless, Silver City did not become a "ghost town" like many mining towns in the American West because it was the center of distribution for the region, was the county seat where government spending trickled into the economy, and a growing number of tuberculosis patients moved to the town and spent their money locally.

Early Mines as a Primary Linkage

Santa Rita Copper Mines: Early Booms and Busts

In 1799, several Apache led Jose Manuel Carrasco, a Spanish officer stationed at the presidio of Janos, Mexico to the Santa Rita Mountains, 500 miles Northeast of Chihuahua in today's New Mexico. Carrasco learned that the area had valuable outcrops of native copper that could be mined and minted into Spanish coins. He filed a mining claim with the Deputacion de Mineria in Chihuahua and was able to obtain a mining grant. Carrasco relied on money invested by Chihuahua merchant Ramos de Verea to develop the mines. He also brought the first miners into the region. He hired Mexicans and Apache, and used a dual-wage system in which Apache were paid less than Mexicans. He also used prison labor from jails in Janos and Chihuahua. He exported the copper by mule along the "Janos Trail" to Janos, where it was further shipped to mints in Chihuahua and Mexico City. The Spanish "rations system" paid the Apache for their friendship and this allowed him to mine in the area. However, he did not make great profits because of the remoteness of the region, the interest payment on Verea's investments, and Spanish taxes.[451]

In 1803, facing financial difficulties, Carrasco sold his claim to a wealthy Chihuahua merchant, Francisco Manuel Elguea. Spanish merchants like Elguea made great profits from government contracts to supply Spanish forts, and they often had additional sources of income through livestock and mineral production and transporting products along El Camino Real to Mexico City. His Hacienda de Torreon near Chihuahua produced numerous mules for his transportation business that allowed him to also ship copper easily to Janos and Mexico City. While Elgua continued the practice of using prison labor, a community developed that would be called Santa Rita del Cobre, a name derived from a gold mine four miles to the west of the copper mines called Santa Rita de Cascia; the miners simply replaced "Cascia" with "Cobre," the Spanish word for "copper." He also began the construction of a fort to house the prisoners and to provide

---

451   Christopher Huggard, *Santa Rita Del Cobre: A Copper Mining Community in New Mexico* (Boulder: University of Colorado Press, 2013), 7-13.

protection from Apache attacks, as seen in Figure 1. Elguea died in 1806 and the mine passed to his heirs. Profits from the mines were not great due to the same factors that had affected Carassco some years earlier. Furthermore, in 1810 the War of Mexican Independence began and the Viceroyalty in Mexico City could no longer maintain the rations system that had allowed Carrasco and Elguea to mine on the Apache's land. Production stopped for several

Figure 1: Remnants of the Spanish fort first built in the early 1800s heirs of the Elguea estate. Photo is courtesy of the Silver City Museum.

years, but resumed in 1812 when the Elguea's heirs hired military protection, which forced Chiricahua Apache chief Juan Diego Compa to negotiate a peace which lasted till 1819 when the War of Mexican Independence intensified and the Spanish abandoned Santa Rita.[452]

Mexico's independence in 1821 opened New Mexico to Anglos from the United States. The old policy of Spanish mercantilism, that forbad trade with the United States, was ended and individuals like Robert McKnight and James Ohio Pattie came into the region to trap beaver. Such individuals sought employment at the mines and some like McKnight and Pattie leased the property. But again, the region's remoteness made transportation costs high, and intermittent Apache attacks hampered copper production. Apache raids intensified following the Johnson Massacre of 1837, when U.S. beaver trapper John Johnson murdered several Apache chiefs and their families in the Animas Mountains of Southwestern New Mexico. Mining stopped for ten years, until the United States took over the region following the Mexican-American War (1846-1848). In the 1850s, the U.S Army established Fort Webster to protect the area, and small scale

---

452   Ibid., 13-18.

241

mining resumed. While the 1850s would not see many problems with the Apache, the Apache wars against the United States intensified in 1860 following the Bascom Affair in Arizona, in which some family members of Chiricahua chief Cochise were murdered by the U.S. Army. Copper production was impacted negatively in the 1860s, though the establishment of nearby Fort Mclane in 1860 and Fort Bayard in 1866 provided military protection that allowed miners to go back to work. It was not until 1873 that mining resumed to full production.[453]

Pinos Altos Gold Mines

Gold mining in Grant County began with Spanish miners operating several placers four miles west of Santa Rita, at Santa Rita de Cascia. It is also believed that Mexican miners panned the placer deposits of San Domingo Arroyo in the Pinos Altos Mountains 20 miles west of Santa Rita in the 1820s and 1830s, but were driven away by the Apache. In 1860, a group of Anglo prospectors associated with the Walker Party discovered rich placers at the confluence of Cherry and Bear creeks in the Pinos Altos Mountains. The discovery of gold coincided with the Bascom Affair in Arizona in 1860 when the U.S. Army killed some family members of Chiricahua Apache chief Cochise and sparked an Apache war. This explains why the Apache attached the miners in Pinos Altos repeatedly in the early 1860s. On September 22, 1861, for example, the Apache attacked several miners, including Thomas Mastin. Mining was further hampered when the Confederate Army invaded New Mexico in 1861. The Apache threat subsided in 1863, when Chiricahua Apache chief Mangas Coloradas travelled to the mining camp to negotiate a truce, was captured by the miners, and murdered by U.S. soldiers at Fort Mclane in 1863. Mining resumed when the Civil War ended in 1865. The mining camp's name, "Birchfield," was changed to "Pinos Altos" and the community grew into a small mining town. In 1866, four merchants from Santa Fe and Mesilla established the Pinos Altos Mining Company, and by 1868 there were

---

453 Susan Berry, *Built to Last: An Architectural History of Silver City, New Mexico* (Santa Fe: New Mexico Historical Preservation Division, 1986), 7-9.

some 600 miners working in the nearby mountains. The town had several stores, saloons, and hotels. Grant County was created that same year with the town of Central, next to Fort Bayard, being the first county seat. The county seat was moved to Pinos Altos the following year. The growing town of Pinos Altos created a demand for locally grown food which came from a small agricultural community nine miles south of Pinos Altos on the banks of Saint Vincent Creek, which local Hispanos called "La Cienaga de San Vicente."[454]

The area around La Cienega de San Vicente was lush and nestled between several hills. The various farmers, sheepherders and Indian traders lived there but did not know of any mineral deposits other than at Pinos Altos and Santa Rita. That changed when news of a discovery of silver in the Pyramid Mountains, some 60 to the south, spread north. Several Anglo farmers at the "Cienaga" travelled south to inspect the ore at the new mining camp of Ralston, including two brothers from Missouri, John and James Bullard. John Bullard (as seen in Figure 2) reportedly said, "...if that is silver ore, I know where there's plenty of it!"[455] He quickly located his Legal Tender Claim, at the base

Figure 2: John Bullard was killed by the Apache in 1871. Photo is courtesy of the Silver City Museum.

of a hill one quarter of a mile west of the "Cienaga." That hill would later be called Legal Tender Hill, named after his claim. Miners from Pinos Altos also staked their claims and two mining districts developed: Silver Flat Mining District that encompassed the Legal Tender Hill and Chloride Flat

---

454 Ibid., 8.

455 Ibid., 9; See also Henry Ailman, *Pioneering in Territorial Silver City* (Albuquerque: University of New Mexico Press, 1983), 38.

Mining District located a one mile to the west. The peaceful community of farmers on La Cienega de San Vicente quickly became a mining camp.[456]

Some of the first miners like John Swisshelm, Joseph Yankie, and the Bullard brothers (who formed the Bullard Mining Co.) decided to name the mining camp "Silver City." It grew into a town and became the seat of Grant County in 1871. When prospector Henry Ailman arrived in 1871, he noted in his memoir, *Pioneering in Territorial Silver City*, that there were already several stores and cabins built along the new streets, [and] the "Mexican people" built adobe smelters that "were in all parts of town."[457] Lorenzo Carraco operated many of those smelters. His father, Nepomuceno "Juan" Carrasco and his extended family had experience working the silver mines of Mexico and they had the knowledge to build small adobe-made smelters and file claims on some of the best ores in the Chloride Flat District. The majority of their smelters were located at the southern end of the town and it is said that the Carrascos earned some $200,000 in profits from their silver mines and smelting operations. [458]

Anglos established the first stamp mills in Silver City. Such machinery crushed ore into small particles and allowed for greater amounts of silver to be produced. Martin Bremen, born in New York in 1840, came to Pinos Altos after the Civil War where he homesteaded in 1866. He built a steam powered saw mill and sold timber to miners and the U.S. Army at Fort Bayard. In 1871, he bought an old stamp mill in Pinos Altos and set it up on San Vincente Creek, just south of Silver City. He improved it by using wooden barrels turned by a leather belt attached to a steam engine. This allowed him to further refined silver. Even though the stamp mill was worn-out, his operations were profitable. In one week, for example he produced $2,422 worth of silver. Merchants were some of the first

---

456   "This is Silver City," Vertical Files, Folder "Silver City – History," Miller Library, WNMU. John Bullard was killed by Apache on the San Francisco River in 1871.

457   Ailman, 39.

458   Helen Lundwall, "History of Silver City" (1970), Vertical Files, Folder "Silver City – History," Miller Library, WNMU. James Bullard owned the St. Louis Mine in the Burros Mountains.

individuals to install modern stamp mills in Silver City. Henry M. Porter was a prosperous merchant from the gold mining town of Elizabeth, New Mexico. He opened a store in Silver City and established the Tennessee Reduction Co. in 1873 with other local investors like Thomas Lyons, Richard Hudson, and Valentine S. Shelby. The latter had purchased a processing mill from Lucien Maxwell, the owner of the Maxwell Land Grant in northeastern New Mexico. The mill was shipped to Silver City in 1873 which the company operated until 1877 when it was sold to Martin Bremen.[459]

Development of a Merchant-Capitalist Economy

General merchants established the first businesses in Silver City. They sold manufactured goods on credit to farmers and miners who paid their bills with agricultural and mineral products. Gold, silver, and copper were highly liquid assets that could be sold for cash back east where they sold the metals to the U.S. Treasury to be minted in coins. Copper was often sold to eastern factories for the purposes of industrial production and America's fledgling electrical industry. Merchants' stores had assay office where they determined the value of the ores and metals being delivered by their customers. These same merchants also bought food locally and sold it to miners and the U.S. Army, though their trade in mineral products was more significant.

Mesilla Valley Merchants and Silver City's Economy in the 1870s
Merchants in Las Cruces and Mesilla dominated the trade in Silver City prior to the coming of the railroad in 1883. They owned stores and wagon teams that moved goods from the terminus of the Atchison, Topeka, and Santa Fe Railroad as it was being built into New Mexico. They also had the wagons needed to export mineral products out of the territory. For this reason, they were able to transport manufactured goods easily to Silver City and export

459   Ailman, 152, and 158-159. Martin Bremen bought the "76" mine in Chloride Flats and in 1887 he sold his mining properties and smelting facilities, went to Globe Arizona, and returned to Silver City, committing suicide by drinking morphine in 1887. C. P.Crawford was the manager of H. M. Porter and Co.

mineral products from Grant County. Moreover, these merchants partic-ipated in a barter-based, agricultural economy. They sought to diversify their business by also doing business with to miners who paid their bills in gold, silver and copper. These were highly liquid commodities that could be sold quickly for cash. For these reasons, merchants from Las Cruces and Mesilla sought to open stores in Grant County.[460]

Mesilla Valley merchants opened stores in the region after 1860 when gold was discovered in the Pinos Altos Mountains. James Griggs and Joseph Reynolds, merchants from the town of Mesilla, helped establish the Pinos Altos Mining Co., in 1866. The company drafted

Figure 3: The Bennett Bros. store in the 1870s.
Photo is courtesy of the Silver City Museum.

---

460   William Parish, *The Charles Ilfeld Company: A Study of the Rise and Fall of Merchant Capitalism in New Mexico* (Cambridge: Harvard University Press, 1961), 42. Parish wrote that "the most consistent, reliable and profitable method of acquiring eastern credit, against which drafts could be drawn, was through the shipment of raw materials. Wool, hides, and metals comprise the bulk of these commodities."

246

articles of incorporation and opened a store where they supplied their employees with products. The store also sold goods on credit to independent miners who paid their bills with gold. By February 1872, the Pinos Altos Mining Company had taken out $200,000 in gold. Some historians believe that the company's mine was on the west side of the Pinos Altos Mountains, at the Cleaveland Mine site. There were several other businesses that opened in Pinos Altos, including the store of Thomas Bull, a merchant from Mesilla. In 1872, Reynolds and Griggs opened a store in the new mining town of Silver City. Alexander H. Morehead, who was a post-trader at Fort Selden in the Mesilla Valley, served as the manager for the Reynolds and Griggs store in Silver City before opening his own store in 1875 called A. H. Morehead and Co. It was at this time that Reynolds moved to Silver City to run the Reynolds and Griggs store, but in 1877 that firm was dissolved when Reynolds bought out Griggs.[461]

When Silver City was founded in 1870, some of the first merchants to open shops were from the Mesilla Valley. This would include the firm Reynolds and Griggs. It would also include H. Lesinsky and Co. In 1872, Henry Lesinksy, a Las Cruces wholesaler, and Joseph Bennet, a Civil War veteran and Mesilla stage operator, and his brother Cornelius, opened the wholesale/retail firm of J. F. Bennett and Co., which also operated the Southern Overland Express Company. Their store building was completed in 1872, as seen in Figure 3, on the northeast corner of what would later become Hudson and Broadway streets. Another early firm that had connections to the Mesilla Valley was Amador, Macias and Co. In 1873, Las Cruces merchant and freighter, Martin Amador, went into business with Jose Macias, from Mexico who was a colonel in Maximilian's Army during

---

461   Amberg and Elsberg had acquired claims in the area as early as 1861, and Amberg's cousin managed those properties. When the Apache stole some mules in 1861, the cousin and some 12 men were ambushed and killed trying to get the mules back, see Parish, *The Charles Ilfeld Company*, 9-10; *Borderer*, September 27, 1871; December 13, 1871; Ailman,166. By February 1872, the Pinos Altos Mining Company had taken out $200,000 in gold, see *Borderer*, February 21, 1872. The practice of selling goods on credit to miners is sometimes referred to as "grubstaking."

the French Intervention, and together opened the store that specialized in freighting and selling grocery items.[462]

Merchants in the Mesilla Valley often traveled back East to buy products and they had developed relationships with wholesalers and bankers in New York, Philadelphia, and St. Louis that allowed them to acquire sufficient capital to buy goods in bulk and transport them by rail and wagon to southern New Mexico. Lesinsky's uncle, Julius Freudenthal, lived in New York and acted as the firm's purchasing agent. Las Cruces merchant Louis Rosenbaum, who was a partner in the Silver City firm of J. B. Morill and Co., made seasonal trips to purchase goods in the East and Europe. The firm of Reynolds and Griggs likewise made season trips to the East to buy goods. Joseph Reynolds managed affairs in New Mexico, while his partner James Griggs traveled eastward to deal with financial matters and make purchases.[463]

These merchants employed commission firms operating on the Atlantic, Topeka, and Santa Fe Railroad as it was being built into New Mexico. These companies charged a commission for assisting New Mexico merchants in the purchase of manufactured goods and transferring products to and from the railroad terminus. The largest commission firms were Browne, Manzanar and Co., Otero, Sellar and Co., and Chicke, Browne and Co. Wholesalers like Henry Lesinsky shipped eastern goods to commission merchants' warehouses on the railroad terminus and had the products forwarded to New Mexico

---

462   *Borderer*, June 15, 1871; July 19, 1871; August 16, 1871; March 16, 1871; April 24, 1871; February 21, 1872; February 28, 1872; October 14, 1871; April 13, 1871; and July 26, 1871. The *Arizona Daily Citizen*, November 30, 1872 reported that Lesinsky's Tucson store closed in late 1872. See also the obituary of Nehemiah Bennett in the *Mesilla News*, February 12, 1876; New Mexico Census, 1870. The Rio Grande Historical Collection's summary of the Amador Collection says that Amador, Macias and Co. was established in 1871; Ailman, 148. *Mesilla Valley Independent*, July 14, 1877 reported that Mesilla Valley merchant George Maxwell owned the Providencia Mine near Silver City. *Thirty Four*, March 26, 1879 reported that Henry Lesinsky owned a stamp mill in Grant County. The 1870 census reported that Richard Ziggman of Canada owned a grocery store in Silver City,

463   *Borderer*, May 15, 1872; July 10, 1872; April 13, 1871; June 15, 1871; June 19, 1872; March 16, 1871, October 25, 1871; *Grant County Herald*, April 1, 1876.

248

where they picked up their goods at the end of the railroad and used wagons to transport them into southern New Mexico. Smaller merchants like Martin Amador also purchased products back east and had them shipped by train with the help of these firms. For example, in Spring 1877, Brookmill and Renken of St. Louis, sold Amador tobacco, grease, coffee, sugar, molasses, tea, tobacco, baking powder, candy, chocolate, and canned fish. The goods were transported along the Missouri Pacific and the Atchison, Topeka, and Santa Fe railroads and deposited at the warehouses of Chick, Brown, and Co. in El Moro, Colorado. Amador's ox wagons then took the goods to Las Cruces and Silver City. Because Amador was able to obtain a Grant County liquor license in 1873, he also employed these commission firms to a transfer bulk amounts of alcohol, including fine whiskeys purchased in the East, onto his wagons destined for his stores in Las Cruces and Silver City.[464]

Hispano merchants in the Mesilla Valley often freighted goods to Grant County. Among the largest were Martin Amador, Guadalupe Ascarate, Cisto Garcia, Rafael Bermudes, Mariano Barela, and Ramon Gonzales. Almost all freighters owned stores from which they managed their freighting enterprises. Amador's Las Cruces store, for example, was part of the Amador Transfer Co. and had livery stables patronized by travelers and his teamsters. Hispano freighters were often noted in local papers. In 1880, for example, it was noted in the *Thirty Four* that Guadalupe Ascarate's freighting teams had camped only a thousand yards from a group of Indians. The Apache posed no threat, however. He was with thirty five men accompanying two freight trains,

---

464 "Bill of Lading, Missouri Pacific Railway Co.," April 26, 1877, Box 2, folder 1 and "Bill of Sale," March 7, 1876 and January 17, 1877, Box 2, folder 1, AFP. Liquor License is found in Box 27, folder 1, June 1873.

and five of the wagons were loaded with guns and ammunition for Grant County merchants.[465]

Many of the goods that Martin Amador and other Mesilla Valley merchants were shipping into Grant County were destined for other merchants. Cor. E. Goldsmith and Co., wholesale and retail merchants of Silver City, received 9,000 pounds in one week. Much of this merchandise was sold to smaller merchants operating in the nearby community of Georgetown. Often, freight coming from the Mesilla Valley to Silver City was destined for communities in Eastern Arizona, and vice versa. Morrill and Kellner of Silver City received in June 1878, twenty-seven thousand pounds of goods, 10,000 of which was destined for Globe City, Arizona. The Silver City firm of I. N. Cohen and Co., owned wagon teams and plied the roads connecting Las Cruces with Clifton. The Silver City newspaper, the *Grant County Herald*, noted in 1878 that the firm received 103,000 pounds of pig copper from Clifton, Arizona which it shipped to the railroad terminus in Colorado. J. F. Bennett and Co. transported 35,000 feet of lumber in 1876 to Henry Lesinsky's Longfellow Copper Mine.[466]

Wholesale merchants in Las Cruces and Mesilla also were major transporter of mineral products from Grant County. The Las Cruces newspaper the *Borderer* noted that in 1871 Bennett Brothers and Co. of Silver City shipped to Henry Lesinsky's store in Las Cruces in one week 1400 ounces of silver and 50 ounces of gold, all of which was then sent by wagon north to the Atchison, Topeka and Santa Fe Railroad terminus in Kansas, to be shipped east. The *Borderer* in March 1871also noted that Lesinsky

---

465   New Mexico Census, 1870; *Mining Life*, December 6, 1873; December 27, 1873. Anglo freighters, although fewer in number, included Charles Ellis of Texas, George D. Maxwell of New York, and Bradford Daily of Missouri. They ran freight out of Las Cruces, see *Borderer*, February 28, 1872; May 18, 1871; May 25, 1871; May 27, 1871; *Mesilla News*, March 28, 1874; June 19, 1875; September 18, 1875; September 26, 1874; October 2, 1875. Amador Papers, RGHC, MS 4. See *Borderer*, September 27, 1871 for a description of Amador's freighting activities. Las Cruces retailer, George D. Maxwell and Co. also owned a store, warehouse, and stables located in Las Cruces.

466   *Grant County Herald*, April 1, 1876; and June 15, 1878; and *Tucson Weekly Citizen*, January 10, 1874; and October 11, 1873.

exported silver ore which was smelted in New Jersey. On October 9, 1875, the *Mesilla News* reported that some 30,000 pounds of copper was shipped from Lesinky's Longfellow Copper mines near Clifton, Arizona, which he acquired in 1873, to be exported to New Jersey via Silver City. Lesinsky did not own his own wagons, but hired Las Cruces storekeepers like Mariano Barela to freight his copper to the Atchison, Topeka, and Santa Fe depot. Merchants who bought, sold and transported bullion from Grant County on a regular basis included James Griggs, Joseph Reynolds, and Thomas Bull. These merchants sold gold and silver to the U.S. Treasury to be minted into U.S. coins. While some of the copper got into the money supply, most of the copper was purchased by eastern factory owners.[467]

Mesilla Valley merchants' penetration of Grant County and eastern Arizona was also based on the mines and smelting equipment that they owned in the region. Their direct investments in mineral production stimulated the mining sector. One of the largest firms to invest in the production of precious metals in eastern Arizona was the firm of H. Lesinsky and Co. In 1873, the firm bought the Longfellow copper mine near Morenci, built a smelter, and started to export thousands of pounds of copper, through his partner's Silver City store, to the Atchison, Topeka, and Santa Fe Railroad each year. Lesinsky also invested in Joseph Bennett's Cibola Reduction Works in Silver City and processed copper, silver, and gold ores in its stamp mills.[468]

The waning dominance of Mesilla Valley merchants in Silver City can be explained by an economic downturn following the Panic of 1873, when over-speculation in western railroads resulted in a series of

---

467   *Borderer*, March 23, 1871; April 27, 1871; May 29, 1872; May 8, 1872; May 22, 1872; October 4, 1871, May 18, 1871; May 30, 1874; May 1, 1875; October 24, 1874; December 12, 1874; September 5, 1875; October 9, 1875;September 27, 1871; May 29, 1872; May 8, 1872; May 22, 1872; October 4, 1871; September 5, 1875; October 9, 1875, March 23, 1871; *Mesilla News*, August 8, 1874; August 22, 1874; and September 18, 1875; October 9, 1875; *Arizona Citizen*, October 10, 1873. Henry Ailman forwarded bulk minerals from the Silver Bar Mine in Grant County to Denver where the ore was refined into silver bullion, see Ailman, 70.

468   *Tucson Weekly Citizen*, January 10, 1874; October 11, 1873; and *Grant County Herald*, April 1, 1876; and June 15, 1878.

eastern banks failing. An economic depression ensued and merchants had a difficult time earning profits, particularly from their trade with farmers. That was why Mesilla Valley merchants wanted to trade with miners in the 1870s because they paid in gold, silver and copper that could be sold for cash and used to liquidate debts easily. Even though the Coinage Act of 1873 stopped the U.S. Treasury from buying silver, miners still purchased their goods with gold and copper, and even with low silver prices, merchants could make some profits. However, the 1870s was a difficult time to be in business for some merchants. Martin Amador and Jose Macias were increasingly in debt by that latter half of the 1870s. In fall of 1877, Dodd, Brown and Co. of St. Louis sent two correspondences urging Amador to pay a debt totaling $1,474. Amador held a liquidation sale in December and dissolved his partnership with Macias on January 8, 1878. During this period of time, Henry Lesinsky terminated his partnership with the Bennett Brothers and James Griggs liquidated his investments in the firm of Reynolds and Griggs in 1877. These Mesilla Valley merchants also knew that with the coming of the railroad, they would have to compete with other merchants who could now get their goods to Silver City direct by train. Ultimately, the Deming, Silver City, and Pacific Railroad arrived in 1883 signaling an end to the dominance that Las Cruces and Mesilla merchants once enjoyed in transporting products to and from Grant County.[469]

Jewish Merchants

Historian William Parrish, in his book *The Charles Ilfeld Company: The Rise of Merchant Capitalism in New Mexico*, argued that Jewish merchants radically changed the business structure of New Mexico by establishing the first large general stores. As can be seen in Figure 4, these stores were the latest in design and often had two counters where customers and clerks traded with each other. Parish's work led to a profusion of other historical studies focusing on the Southwest's Jewish population, including Floyd S.

---

469 Amador Papers, RGHC, Box 15, folder 1. For more information, see Box 16 and Box 27. In 1880, there were 68 farms in Mimbres and Gila Valleys, see Ailman, 166.

Fierman's publications on the Freudenthal-Lesinsky-Solomon clan who were active in Southwestern New Mexico and Southeastern Arizona. Taken together, Parish's books and articles argue that Jewish merchants initiated a commercial revolution in the Southwest in the late 1840s and that they had important connections with eastern financiers and the government that allowed them to buy goods in bulk, extend capital into the region through selling products on credit, and find markets for their customers' products, including with nearby military installations. [470]

Jewish merchants were some of the first business people to open stores in Silver City, and that would include Henry Lesinsky. Henry Lesinksy was born in Prussia, learned the trade of woodcarving and stone work in London, and moved to Australia to mine gold. He later moved to San Francisco. Lesinsky had an uncle, Julius Freudenthal,

Figure 4: This Silver City store, ca. 1880s, shows what the latest type of store looked like. Photo is courtesy of the Silver City Museum.

who lived in New Mexico and contracted with the U.S. Army to provide food and forage to army forts. In 1859, Freudenthal wrote a letter to Lesinsky regarding the potential gold mines that awaited him in New Mexico. Propelled by visions of gold, Lesinsky traveled to Albuquerque the following year. Instead of mining, Lesinky joined his uncle in a business partnership supplying grain to the United States Army. After the Civil War was over, he opened up H. Lesinsky and Co. in Las Cruces with a branch in Silver City (operated by the Bennett Brothers) by 1873. [471]

470   Scott Fritz, "Merchants and Modernity: Market Transformation in New Mexico and the Southwest," (Dissertation: Northern Arizona University, 2004), 15-17.

471   Fritz, 45. The first merchant in Silver City was Eugene Golding, who was probably of Jewish descent.

253

Figure 5: Isaac Cohen, ca. 1880. Photo is courtesy of the Silver City Museum.

Another Jewish merchant of note was Isaac Cohen. As seen in Figure 5, Isaac N. Cohen came to New Mexico around 1868 and clerked for Lesinsky's Las Cruces store. Because Lesinksy conducted business in Grant County,

Cohen learned that the region had the potential for great profits. Accordingly, he relocated to Silver City and opened his own store in 1872. With silver prices being propped up by the Bland Allison Act of 1878 (which required the government to purchase between $2 and $4

Figure 6: Isaac Cohen's building, ca. early 1900s. It is where today's Little Toad Brewery is located. Photo is courtesy of the Silver City Museum.

million ounces of silver per month) Cohen had sufficient capital to invest in a new building in 1881, on the corner of Bullard and Broadway Streets. (See Figure 6.) He later was instrumental in bringing the railroad to Silver City and served on the railroad's board of director before moving back to New York City a couple of years later. Max Schutz was also a merchant of Jewish descent who with his brother Solomon, operated several businesses, including in El Paso and Silver City. Indeed, the Schutz family was part of a close-nit Jewish community helping to explains why Henry Lesinksy's son, Charles, married into the Schutz family in the 1890s.[472]

Merchants and Fort Bayard

The military supply system allowed merchants to liquidate their customers' debts by selling their agricultural products to Fort Bayard. Soldiers at

---

472　*Thirty Four*, June 4, 1879; July 30, 1879; February 4, 1880; February 11, 1880; May 12, 1880; June 9, 1880; Ailman, 97 and 99. Further research into the Schutz family is needed, including how their stores in El Paso and Solomon Schutz who was a commercial agent at El Paso del Norte in the 1870s, see Scott Fritz, "Mesilla Valley Merchants, 1870-1881: History of Hispano and Anglo Involvement in the Santa Fe Trade of Southern New Mexico (Thesis: New Mexico State University, 1997), 40.

Fort Bayard enforced a government policy intended to remove the Apache from their ancestral lands and prevent them from roaming freely and possibly controlling valuable resources. The policy was good for business at the expense of Apache sovereignty. It opened up Apache lands to homesteading, timber extraction, ranching, and mining. It also benefited merchants and civilians living near military installations because the government employed civilian construction workers, wood haulers, and wagon freighters, and bought products from local farmers, ranchers, and merchants. The largest merchants received contracts from the government to supply produce, forage, and freighting services. Such contracts gave them the opportunity to earn greater profits, which in turn, enable them to buy more of their customers' products. Military contracts provided merchants the extra capital they needed to encourage their customers to increase the production of raw commodities and bring about a capitalist approach to farming. Government contracts were paid in U.S. currency, which helped to transform Grant County's barter economy into a cash economy. Soldiers also spent money in local businesses, thereby serving as an economic benefit to businesses in nearby towns like Central.[473]

Mesilla Valley merchants who had businesses in Grant County were often awarded contracts to supply Fort Bayard. Much of food sold to the military was acquired from farmers in the Mesilla Valley and along the Mimbres River, and through trade with Mexican merchants. Contractors included merchant Thomas Bull, whose son purchased food from farmers at his store in the town of Rio Mimbres, located 45 miles east of Silver City. James Griggs also won military contracts to supply grain and corn to Fort Bayard. Merchant based in the region sought to serve as forage agents and post-traders for Fort Bayard. Alexander Bull, the son of Thomas Bull and an up and coming merchant, worked for his father's stores in Mesilla and in Rio Mimbres. In 1876, Alexander applied for the position of forage agent at Fort Bayard. His father wrote the chief quartermaster urging acceptance of his son, believing that he could easily receive grain

---

473   Fritz, 95-119.

at the Rio Mimbres store. There was competition for the job, however. Other merchants applying for the job included Johnson, Kohn and Co. of Silver City and Staab and Co. of Santa Fe. The position of post-sutler was also desirous, explaining why Ailman, Meridith and Co. in Silver City had invested in Fort Bayard's sutler store in the early 1880s. Darlis Miller wrote in *Soldiers and Settlers: Military Supply in the Southwest* that by 1880 Grant County was "the second largest producer of barley in New Mexico and raised modest amounts of corn and wheat ...[and] many local residents found employment at the post [e.g. Fort Bayard] and others would supply it with building materials, hay, charcoal, and limited amounts of cattle, grain and other commodities."[474]

Mining Boom in the 1880s

The price of silver dropped throughout the late nineteenth century. However, government purchases of silver and the completion of railroads made mining in Grant County profitable in the 1880s. The Bland Allison Act of 1878 stabilized silver prices because the government made monthly purchases silver for the purpose of coinage. The cost to transport ores out of the territory dropped due to the completion of the Southern Pacific Railroad, which was joined with the Atchison Topeka and Santa Fe Railroad in Deming in 1881. Direct rail service between Silver City and Deming began when the Deming, Silver City, and Pacific Railroad was completed in 1883. Grant County miners could now easily sell their silver at a profit. This created a boom in silver production resulting in new mining camps being established in the region. Growing silver production created demand for new smelters, such as the Silver City Reduction Works, built in Silver City by Florida real estate developer, Henry Flagler, and local investors in 1884. In Figure 7, the reader can see how the plant had a railroad connecting it with nearby mines by 1906. Another factor explaining

---

474 Darlis Miller, *Soldiers and Settlers: Military Supply in the Southwest, 1865-1881* (Albuquerque: University of New Mexico Pres, 1989), 59-60; "Thomas Bull to J. A. Belcher," *Letters Received*, September 11, 1876, roll 28. Louis Rosenbaum's Rio Mimbres store is mentioned in the *Mesilla Valley Independent*, June 30, 1877. Ailman, 171.

Figure 7: Silver City Works, ca 1906. photo courtesy of the Silver City Museum.

the mining boom of the 1880s was the end of the Apache Wars, which contributed to the ability for miners to freely prospect in the mountains of southwestern New Mexico. With stable silver prices, easy transportation, and peaceful social conditions, it was a good time to be in businesses in Silver City.

Georgetown was established as a mining camp in 1874 when George Magruder discovered silver twenty-five miles northeast of Silver City. Mining in Georgetown was benefited by the construction of the Mimbres Reduction Works, owned by Magruder and his business partner James Fresh. That mill, established 3 miles east of Georgetown on the Mimbres River and managed by Fresh, was water powered and process ores from Georgetown and Santa Rita. By 1888, Georgetown had 1200 people, and a brewery, hotel, theatre, a Chinese restaurant, a billiard hall, several stores, and twenty saloons. Sid Lindaur's Georgetown store was one of several that the family would operate in Silver City and Deming several years later. Other mining camps were established. In 1883, prospectors discovered valuable silver ore ten miles west of Silver City and established the mining camp of Fleming near the Old Man Mine. It was named after one of

258

its founders, John Fleming. Within three months of the camp's establishment, town lots had been surveyed and 200 men lived there. Its businesses included a meat market, bakery, corral, blacksmith, two general stores, and five saloons, and three restaurants. Municipal laws were also enacted that limited the freedom of certain ethnic groups. There was a prohibition on the Chinese from entering in town and Hispanics could not own stores, but could be employed in the mines. African Americans like John Woods were not prohibited from opening businesses. Woods opened one of the first bakeries in the town, though he was murdered in his tent following a botched robbery in 1883. Fleming would continue to be a boom town until 1888, when silver prices once again started their precipitous fall.[475]

Indeed, both Grant County and Silver City would experience a boom that began in the late 1870s. In 1873, Silver City had about 1,000 people, and seven years later that number grew to about 2,000, with two-thirds of the population being Hispanic. Grant County itself grew about 300% from 1870 to 1880, with the U.S. Census declaring in 1880 that there were 4539 people living in the whole county. Silver City's business community had grown. As early as 1882, the town had two banks, twelve retail stores, two meat markets, four restaurants, three billiard halls, several dance halls and brothels, and fifteen saloons.[476]

Silver City's merchants sold products according to regional needs. Prospecting and mining equipment were in constant need. Advertisements in local newspapers often included mention of mining supplies. G. W. Holt and Co., retailers in general merchandise, specialized in mining outfits. The company advertised in local newspapers that they sold tools, explosives, canned food, and work clothing. Louis Rosenbaum, whose Las Cruces store supplied his Silver City outlet (i.e. J.B. Morril and Co.) advertised in the *Grant County Herald* in June of 1878: "The particular attention of the mining population of Silver City and vicinity is called to my assorted stock of all kinds of mining tools, steel, powder, fuse, miner's

---

475   "Fire, disease [and the] 'Crime of 93" and "Answer Book," Vertical Files, Folder "Georgetown," Miller Library, WNMU.

476   Miller, 60.

clothing, etc." [477] Neff, Bell and Stevens, wholesalers and retailers of hardware advertised in *The Enterprise* in early 1880s indicating that they sold dynamite, iron and steel. Dennis and Coomer and Co. sold lumber and specialized in mining and mill timber.[478]

Miners needed food, and in the 1870s merchants supplied the region with corn, beans, and wheat grown along the Mimbres River, in the Mesilla Valley, and in Mexico. Henry Lesinsky was one of the first merchants to sell flour in Silver City. E. E. Burlingame, an up and coming entrepreneur, noted in the *Mining Life* in 1873 that Lesinsky sold flour for fifteen dollars per sack while the same amount went for $10.50 in Rio Mimbres, some 50 miles east of Silver City. Silver City storeowners who had partners operating stores in the Mesilla Valley purchased produce from farmers along the Rio Grande and as far south as San Elizario, Texas, some twenty miles southeast of El Paso. In fact, food was in such high demand that Mexican merchants traveled to Silver City every year in large caravans and sold corn, beans, potatoes, flour, sugar, lemons, cheese, and candy. In fact, Silver City was where Mexican merchants cleared U.S. customs before Deming was founded in 1881.[479] Henry Ailman wrote in his memoirs, *Pioneering in Territorial Silver City* that "Mexican merchants moved in groups of up to forty pack mules each and that on arrival, "their first move would be to see who would make them the best price on manta (unbleached muslin). Whoever purchased that would get all trade."[480]

Lumber mills benefited from the existence of mining and a growing population in Silver City. Martin Bremen's lumber mill near Pinos Altos was not the only one he owned; he also built another mill in the 1860s ten miles northeast of Fort Bayard to provide timber for miners and the U.S. Army. However, because of Apache attacks he moved it to the outskirts of

---

477   *Grant County Herald*, June 15, 1878.

478   Ibid., April 1, 1876; Pattie Unger, *True Tales: 1882 & 1883* (Silver City: SunDog Publishing, 1991), 153; 193. Thomas Lyons, an owner of the L. C. Ranch and Cattle Co. came to Silver City in the 1870s as a mining equipment engineer

479   *Mesilla Valley Independent*, December 1, 1877; *Mining Life*, September 20, 1873; and Ailman, 70. Lundall, "History of Silver City."

480   Ailman, *Pioneering in Territorial Silver City*, 70.

Silver City in 1871. Wood cutters were always in demand, both in Silver City and in nearby mining camps. *The Enterprise* on Dec. 28, 1882 noted that there were 300 individuals living in Burro Mountains mining camp of Oak Grove and they were principally miners and wood cutters. Christopher Huggard, in the *Santa Rita Del Cobre: A Copper Mining Community in New Mexico* wrote that the forests surrounding Santa Rita were largely cut down to provide fuel to the town's smelters. The mining camp of Parshall was established in the Burro Mountains in the early 1880s and was the location of the Denver Company Reduction Works. Local newspapers noted that the Denver Company's mill consumed large quantities of fuel, resulting in the forests surrounding the camp being cut down. Indeed, mining increased the demand for wood which contributed to seasonal flooding, including in Silver City where the famous floods of 1895 and 1902 destroyed Main Street. Because of the denuding of the forest, furthermore, rainfall did not soak into the soil sufficiently, resulting in Silver City's water table dropping through the 1880s and 1890s.[481]

The mining boom of 1880s started a vibrant building construction industry. Robert Black was an important contractor in Silver City. He was born in Massachusetts in 1840, where he learned carpentry and the construction business; he also studied architecture at Harvard. He came to Silver City in 1872 to construct a building for a stamp mill. After completing the job, he stayed and opened a carpentry shop with his brother, Thomas. Shortly thereafter, Black formed a partnership with hardware store owner Eugene Cosgrove and started a lumberyard. They bought a steam powered saw mill and had it transported to Silver City. During the late 1870s and 1880s they sold lumber to miners, the military and town residents. They also constructed buildings in Silver City, Fort Bayard, Hillsboro, and Georgetown. To meet the demand for timber, Black established a second saw mill in the Burro Mountains in 1876. Black also built many homes in the 1880s, particularly in the neighborhoods west of

481 Berry, 11; Huggard, 38; Unger, 44; *Desert Exposure*, May 2002 in Vertical Files, Folder "Silver City- History," Miller Library, WNMU. *Silver City Enterprise*, January. 19, 1984, in Vertical Files, Folder "Fleming, NM." . Vertical Files, Folder "Burro Mountain Homestead," Miller Library, WNMU.

downtown, in what was dubbed Black's Addition. He also built homes for two merchants, Henry Ailman and Hartford Meredith, for which in return Black was given a third saw mill that the merchants owned in the Burro Mountains.[482] Another contractor, George Grabe, and his cousin Richard Grabe, came to Silver City in the 1880s and constructed several buildings, including the Peter Wagner block in 1884. When another builder, William Laizure, came to Silver City in 1884, the Grabe brothers formed the firm of Laizure, Grabe and Co., and purchased the planning mill of John A. Miller. The firm built several important buildings, including the Episcopal Church and St. Joseph's Hospital and Sanitarium, prior to dissolving their firm in 1897. In Figure 8, one can see Richard Grabe's carpentry shop that he established following the dissolution of Laizure, Grabe and Co. His shop was located at the north end of Bullard.[483]

The mining boom created a demand for hotels. One of the first hotels in the early 1870s was built on the southwest corner of Yankie and Main streets. It was Joseph Yankie's Keystone House, which was purchased by Peter Ott and renamed the Tremont House. Ott invested in several

Figure 8: Richard Grabe's carpentry shop, ca. late 1890s-early 1900s. Photo is courtesy of the Silver City Museum.

hotels over the course of his life, including a hotel in the mining camp of Fleming in 1883. After the railroad was built to Silver City in 1883, several hotels would be built on the east side of Main, along Hudson Street where the railroad ended. They would include the Timmer House and the Southern Hotel. The Southern Hotel was

---

482   Ailman,162. The Ailman-Meridith sawmill was acquired when they bought Joseph Reynolds store in 1880.

483   Ibid., 36, and 42-43.

established in the 1880s at the site of the old Bennett Bros. mercantile store. The new owner, David Abraham, employed Robert Black to renovate the building's second floor in 1888 making it one of the nicest hotels in town, as seen in Figure 9. While some of the nicer hotels were located along the track on the east side of Main Street, other hotels would still be established in other parts of town, like the Benton House and the Palace Hotel built by Max Schutz in 1900.[484]

Figure 9: The Southern Hotel, ca. mid 1880s. Notice the railroad track in front. Photo is courtesy of the Silver City Museum.

Hotels created demand for launderers, a trade that was largely controlled by the Chinese. Hotels needed to clean linens every day to keep their rooms clean. There were several Chinese owned washhouses, including one that was attached to the Broadway Hotel in the 1890s that was operated by a Chinese man that locals dubbed, "Crazy Horse." Sing-Kee owned a laundry nearby, which the *Silver City Enterprise* indicated was destroyed by a flood in town in August of 1893 because it was made of

---

484   Unger, 155. Peter Ott is mentioned in the *Silver City Enterprise*, January 19, 1884; and *Silver City Daily Press*, July 9, 2010, Vertical File, Folder "Silver City – History," Miller Library, WNMU.

adobe. Many of these laundries were in adobe buildings and were easy to broken into. In September of 1875, Henry McCarty (i.e. Billy the Kid) broke into the laundry of Sam Chung and Charley Sun and stole some cloths. Charley Sun is considered to be the first Chinese person in Silver City and lived with a growing number of Chinese in Silver City's "Chinatown," which was centered in the area of Texas and Yankie streets. Mutual aid societies called "tongs" helped Chinese like Sun and Chung relocate to Silver City and open businesses. [485]

Silver City visitors and residents created a demand for restaurants, bakeries, and saloons. In the early years, hotels often hired professional hunters to provide venison and other wild meats to its customers. This included hotels not only in Silver City, but also in Shakespeare, New Mexico where the Grant House advertised antelope steaks every Sunday. Hotels often had restaurants associated with them, like the restaurant next to the Benton House. Restaurants included the Broadway Restaurant which for a short time was managed by Lottie Deno, a famous gambler of Kingston, Georgetown, and Hillsboro, who had come to Silver City in 1878. One of the earliest saloons was the Exchange Saloon. Another famous saloon opened in the late 1890s was the Cave Saloon. Its owner, Stephen Uhli, got his start in Silver City working for McMillan's Meat Market, which was an outlet for cattle produced on the AT Ranch located 20 miles west of Silver City in the Mangas Valley. Uhli also constructed the "Uhli Block" on Broadway where he located his saloon. [486]

The Chinese found an economic niche selling food. The Chinese entered the restaurant business because they engaged in truck farming. This was a practice when farmers produced small amounts of vegetables for a nearby urban market and "trucked" (i.e. transported) the food

---

485 Vertical Files, Folder "Silver City – History." Charley Sun died in China in 1883. In 1885, there were 1,872 whites, 74 Chinese, and 28 blacks in Silver City. Hotels also created demand for furniture stores. These would include Derbyshire's Furniture Store, Cox's Furniture, and O.C. Hinman's Furniture store.

486 See Grant House in *This is Silver City, 1888-1889-1890*. Lottie Deno is mentioned in the *Silver City Daily Press*, February 5, 2004; Photo of the Benton House includes restaurant next to it, see Unger, 155.

into nearby towns. The Chinese had farms in Grant County, which were usually called "Chinese Gardens." One existed near Lone Mountain, five miles southeast of Fort Bayard, and another one was located downstream from Silver City, on San Vincent Creek. There is some indication that the Chinese rented these agricultural lands, since it was known that Martin Bremen had owned the Chinese Gardens and that his wife collected rents from it after her husband's death in the late 1880s. Moreover, local newspapers refer to the Chinese at the "Carwile Place," which was a property near the Chinese Gardens owned by the Carwile family. Nevertheless, the existence of Chinese farmers explains why several of them owned restaurants and grocery stores. In spite of seasonal flooding and possible contamination from the Silver City Reduction Works, they continued to farm there well into the twentieth century.[487]

Silver City became the center of transportation and distribution. Most of the early wagon transporters had corrals at the southern end of town, like the Tenderfoot Corrals owned by Levi Miller in the 1870s. Wagon corrals continued to exist in that part of town even after the railroad arrived in 1883. In fact, the railroad did not end the need for wagon transportation and stage coach companies. Instead, it increased the demand for waggoneers. The railroad made mining more profitable by lowering transportation costs and that helped to create a mining boom. As the number of mining camps increased so did the number of wagon teams servicing those areas. There were several important wagon transporters in the 1880s. The White Elephant Corral was owned by P.C. Chase and was sold to C. Chapman where Sheriff Dan Tucker once worked. Perhaps, one

---

487   Berry, 44; The EPA in the 1990s sought to prevent seepage of arsenic and lead from the old Silver City Reduction, see *Silver City Daily Press*, November 28, 2008, Vertical Files, Folder "Silver City – History," Miller Library, WNMU. Vertical Files, Folder "Silver City – History," Miller Library, WNMU. Charley Sun died in China in 1883. In 1885, there were 1,872 whites, 74 Chinese, and 28 blacks in Silver City In 1885, the Chinese made up 3.75% of the population and operated not only farms, grocery businesses, and laundries, but also small general stores. Following the Chinese Exclusion Act of 1882, some Chinese might have entered the U.S. illegally by crossing the U.S. and Mexico border, making Silver City as logical destination. There was also some fear expressed in newspapers about their stores serving as fronts in an illegal trade in opium.

3042
Ten Mule Ore
Team.
Silver City,
N. Mex.

Figure 10: W.A. Tenney's freight team, getting ready to leave to Mogollon, ca. 1880s. Photo is courtesy of the Silver City Museum.

of the largest wagon freighters in the 1880s and 1890s was W.A. Tenney. As one can see in Figure 10, he had wagon teams that had up to 8 mules pulling a wagon. Freighters increased demand for black smiths, such as William Carvil who opened a blacksmith shop in Silver City in 1883 and advertised in the *Silver City Enterprise* that he specialized in repairing wagon. Stage line operators increased in number to provide service to regional mining towns, and included companies like Ed Marriage and Co. that operated stages connecting Silver City with Mogollon. Another stage company in the 1880s was owned by Richard Hudson. He ran stages from his Hudson Hot Springs to Santa Rita and Deming. Stage operators in the Mesilla Valley also provided service to Silver City, including Mariano Barela's stagecoach company.[488]

---

488   Unger, 124; and Fritz, "Mesilla Valley Merchants," 76-77.

266

The mining boom of the 1880s gave rise to a growing number of banks. Historically, Silver City merchants were the first "bankers" because they sold goods on credit to miners, who paid their bills in gold, silver and copper. Because metals could easily be shipped back and converted into currency, there was a relatively high level of species in circulation. Accordingly, the largest merchants in Silver City during the 1870s often advertise themselves as being both general merchants and bankers. Large companies like the Silver City firms of H. M. Porter and Co. and J. F. Bennett and Co. advertised themselves as merchants and bankers. H. M. Porter and Co., for example, in the winter of 1874 advertised in the Mining Life: "Banker and Wholesale and Retail Dealer in General Merchandise." [489] Similarly, J. F. Bennet and Co., received deposits, issued certificates of deposit bearing interest payable in four, six, or twelve months, remitted drafts, and draw sights drafts on Santa Fe and New York." [490]Such businesses engaged in a variety of banking service and exchange gold and silver dust and bullion for cash, received deposits from savers, issued promissory notes, and sold sight drafts on Santa Fe and New York. For instance, in 1881 merchant Henry B. Ailman provided $800 to miner Mike Cooney, who used his cash to develop his Silver Bar Mine near the town of Mogollon. [491]

Meridith, Ailman and Co.

The firm of Meridith, Ailman, and Co. was an important bank in the 1880s that is well-document, largely due to the fact that one of its owners, Henry Ailman wrote a memoir titled *Pioneering in Territorial Silver City*. From that autobiography, once can appreciate how the owners of this bank came to Silver City to mine, and later went into merchandising and then

---

489   *Mining Life*, December 19, 1874.

490   *Grant County Herald*, April 1, 1876; Charles Lesinsky opened a bank in Silver City, but only for one year, see Ailman 173.

491   *Mining Life*, June 14, 1873; Commission merchants operating on the ATSF Railroad Chick, Browne and Co., advertised themselves as bankers, see Santa Fe New Mexican, January 28, 1873 and Mesilla News, August 30, 1875. *The Biography of Gideon Truesdell* (Article Copyright: Richard Fritz, 625 North Michigan Ave. – Suite 600, Illinois 60611); and Ailman, 70.

banking. Their story is a case study in the rise of banking in Silver City and deserves special attention.

Henry Ailman was born in Pennsylvania in 1845 and as a youth had received a good public education. He was teacher for several years and then was employed by a local railroad company for five years. He saved his money. He went west to Kansas, and after a couple of failed business attempts, he got a job on the Atchison, Topeka and Santa Fe Railroad as it was being built in Colorado. In 1871, he joined a group of prospectors in Kit Carson, Colorado, looking for mineral deposits in Arizona. The prospector got lost and ended up finding their way to Pinos Altos, where the groups split up. Ailman settled in Silver City, trying to find a profitable mine. He moved to Santa Rita where he learned of a recent discovery of silver near what would become Georgetown, located twenty miles north of Santa Rita. He traveled there to the new mining camp of Georgetown and was employed by George Magruder as a mine worker. He met another miner by the name of Hartford Meridith. Meridith was from Kentucky and had prospected in Montana, Nevada, and California.

Figure 11: Theodora Ailman, ca. 1880s. Photo is courtesy of the Silver City Museum.

He owned a valuable mine east of San Diego. He came to New Mexico when he heard of the silver strike in Ralston in 1870, and later found his way to Georgetown. The two men met ultimately leased part of Magruder's claim and shortly thereafter staked their own claim which proved to be quite profitable. They named it the Queen Naiad Mine, which they soon learned could produce on average 7,000 ounces of silver per ton. It should be noted that the

268

management of the mine also included the wife of Ailman, Theodora Ailman (as seen in Figure 11). She had come to Santa Rita as a young adult with her parents, having travelled across the Santa Fe Trail in the early 1870s. She kept the mine company's accounts, including managing the payroll of some 40 employees. Their mining company was profitable since silver prices were stable in the late 1870s due to the Bland Allison Act. In 1880, they sold the mine to the Mimbres Mining Co. at a profit and invested in a general store. They purchased it from Joseph Reynolds, of the Las Cruces firm of Reynolds and Griggs in 1880. [492]

They had up to five clerks at a time, responsible for daily operations, including the filling of orders from customers. They also opened an outlet in Georgetown. They purchased wheat from local farmers and sold it to miners, like in Mogollon. In one instance, their wagon carrying wheat was attacked by Indians, who killed the teamster and took the food. This was during Victorio's Uprising of 1880-1881. They imported manufactured goods into the territory using the services of the commission merchant firm of Browne, Manzanares and Co. located on the railroad terminus. They also exported metals using the firm, and that included shipments of high quality ores to smelters in Colorado.[493]

Ailman and Meridith and Co. specialized in banking starting in 1883 when they sold their entire stock of merchandise to German immigrant Max Schutz in March of that year. They did so at an opportune time. Several banks had gone out of business, including the C. P. Crawford Bank and Newton Bradley's Grant County Bank. So, with the closure of the two banks, they decided to go into banking fulltime because there was less competition. Ailman and Meridtith prospered as bankers during the boom years of the mid-1880s, as seen in Figure 12. Cattle and silver prices were stable. Their customers included miners like James Cooney, and Stanton Brannin, who borrowed $5.000 to expand his holdings.

---

492   Ailman, 50-51, 69, and 165; Unger, 83, 129; Mimbres Mining Co. was first mining company in Georgetown to be owned by eastern capitalists, Ailman, 40. Note: Some sources indicate that Black owned a sawmill in the Burro Mountains in 1876, making one wonder if he now owned a second mill.

493   Ibid.

Figure 12: Meridith and Ailman Bank, ca. 1880s.
Photo is courtesy of the Silver City Museum.

Eventually, their bank failed when they had over extended their loans to ranchers. When the drought of 1886-1887 started and ranchers could not pay of their debts. Furthermore, silver dropped from $1.20 to $.55 due to the short-lived impact of the Bland-Allison Act and the mines closed, resulting in their bank going out of business in 1887.[494]

---

494   C. P. Crawford mined gold in Elizabethtown, before becoming a clerk for H.M. Porter and Co.. He later become a business partner in the general mercantile firm of H. M. Porter and Co. in 1880. However, two year later he bought out Porter's share in the business and opened a bank, which failed shortly thereafter, see Alice Kirchman Hanson, "Commodore Perry Crawford, 1844-1907," (Published by author, copy at the Silver City Museum), 1-97; and 131-144. Crawford and Porter met in Elizabethtown, in Colfax County, see "Silver Boom Town, New Mexico," July 1951 in Vertical Files, Folder "Georgetown," WNMU. Max Schutz was born in Essen, Germany in 1845. He jumped a German naval ship, and came to the Southwest where his relatives taught him merchandising.

Ranching as a Secondary Linkage

Like the mining boom of the 1880s, there was a ranching boom in 1880s. It was partly driven by the growing number of miners in the region who needed food, but the most significant reason was the growing immigrant population in the eastern United States. This helps to explain why some of the most important ranches that were established exported most of their cattle out of the territory. These ranches included the Apache Tejo ranch that extended from Hurley southwest into Animas Valley and S.E. Arizona and the Diamond A Ranch, which later became Gray's Ranch near what today is the Playas Smelter. The Scott Ranch was located just south of Silver City and was owned by an African American rancher. Ranches along the Mimbres River included the Mattocks Ranch and the NAN Ranch. Daniel C. McMillan's AT Ranch was located in the Mangas Valley. The Patterson, McDonald, and McCauley ranches were located in the White Signal area. Several ranches were established in the Gila Mountains, like the G. W. Dub Evans Ranch which was in the Beaverhead area, and Joseph and Jerden Rogers' T.J. Ranch near the Gila Cliff Dwellings on the middle and west forks of the Gila River. The Warm Springs Ranch ran cattle in the Gila Mountains, just upriver from the town of Gila. There were also several large ranches that were owned by corporations, such as the Victorio Land and Cattle Co. which was owned by George Hearst. Many of these ranches shipped their cattle to the Silver City stockyards just south of Chihuahua Hill prior to being transported by railroad to the East.[495]

Often, ranchers got their start in Grant County by coming to the region to engage in the mining sector. This included Daniel C. McMillan who came to Silver City in 1876 as a prospector and worked at Martin Bremen's '76 Mine. He later homesteaded northwest of Silver City, started the AT Cross Ranch, and opened a butcher shop in Silver City to sell his meats. He later acquired more ranches and became one of the largest ranchers in Grant

---

495   "Slash Ranch Hounds" Vertical Files, Folder "White Signal," Miller Library, WNMU. See also *Silver City Daily Press*, June 16, 2007 in Vertical File Folder "Gila Cliff Dwellings." Research is still needed to be conducted on the Warm Springs Ranch and the Scott Ranch, south of town, which might have been owned by an African American.

County. Another rancher who originally came to mine was John Fleming. Born in Massachusetts, at the age of 19 he moved to Cripple Creek, Colorado to prospect. He left Colorado in 1877, and prospected in Arizona, New Mexico and Mexico, before moving to the gold mining town of Hillsboro later that year. He found work in Hillsborough and was responsible for digging the first shaft in that town's mining district. However, he wanted to develop his own mine, and shortly thereafter he partnered with John Swisshelm to prospect in Arizona, where they developed a valuable mine. The two men sold the property for $90,000, and divided the profits. With that money, Fleming went to Silver City. He acquired the Warm Springs Ranch on the Upper Gila, near Turkey Creek. In a bet, he won the Duck Creek Ranch near the Gila River, giving him the nick name "Lucky Jack." He then sold that ranch to two miners, Thomas Lyons and Angus Campbell for $100,000, which allowed him to buy more cattle for his Warm Springs Ranch.[496]

The largest ranch to be operated in Southwestern New Mexico, the Lyons and Campbell Ranch and Cattle Co. was also founded by individuals who first came to Silver City to participate in the mining industry. Thomas Lyons and Angus Campbell came originally as mining engineers. Lyons himself was a machinist and had started a foundry with John Swisshelm, manufacturing parts for mining equipment like boilers and providing repair services. Lyons and Campbell later invested in a lead mine near Lone Mountain called the Cosette Mine, which they sold for $50,000. With that money, they invested in cattle. They incorporated the L.C. Ranch and Cattle Co. in New Jersey in 1884, and generated a capital stock of $1.5 million. The capital that was generated allowed them to purchase the Duck Ranch from John Fleming, which included the ranch house dubbed the White House. Eventually, they moved the headquarters to the nearby town of Gila. Unlike other ranchers who primary exported their cattle eastward and to Colorado, Lyons and Campbell would also ship cattle to the growing towns in Southern California by 1888. Their ranges stretch

---

496   Terrence Humble, *Images of America – Silver City* (Charleston: Arcadia Publishing, 2013), 62; and Ralf Adcock, "Brief History of John W. Fleming," Vertical Files, Folder "Fleming, John," Miller Library, WNMU.

as far south as Lordsburg and it was from that railroad town that they shipped cattle westward. For cattle that were shipped eastward and to Colorado, Deming was used.

Campbell and Lyons also invested in other related pursuits. Like Daniel McMillan, they opened a meat market in Silver City as an outlet, which they called the L.C. Meat Market. They also had a vast farm along the Gila River, near the town of Gila, that was operated as a subsidiary of the L.C. Ranch and Cattle Co. called the Gila Farm Co. Following the death of Angus Campbell, Lyons established the Gila Farm Store in 1892 (as seen in Figure 13) at their headquarters where manu-factured goods were bartered for agricultural products in the region. It was a company store, similar to those that were established in mining communities. The only differ-

Figure 13: The L.C. Ranch Company store in Gila, ca. early 1900s. From *The Cattlemen's Empire* (National Survey of Historic Sites and Buildings), p. 17

ence was that it was part of a larger corporation that produced agricultural products and cattle, and its employees (i.e. cowboys and farmer workers) would often cash their paychecks and obtain manufactured goods. The Gila Farm Store was also where Hispanic sharecroppers who rented land from Lyons could obtain tools and seed on credit and also deliver their crops to the store to fulfill their sharecropping contracts. The ranch was also a real estate company and bought and sold ranches throughout the region, helping to explain why the ranch's "range" extended south from the Gila River to Lordsburg. By the early 1900s the company was increasingly engaged in the commission businesses and would buy and sell cattle for other ranchers and arrange for ranchers' cattle to be shipped to Colorado where they were often "fattened" before being shipped to slaughter pens and meat packing plants back east.

273

Public Role of Business Owners in the 19th Century

Business owners played an important public role and provided community leadership. Merchants served as mayors and county commissioners. They participated in fraternal organizations and helped established the territory's first normal school in Silver City. They represented local residents in times of social upheaval and organized community meetings regarding the future prosperity of Grant County. For some, it was true altruism and they wanted to help people. For the others, it was out of their own self-interest to promote their economic activities, to make themselves look good to the public, and to influence government policy to benefit their businesses.

Merchants in the Mesilla Valley who had businesses in Grant County were some of the first individuals to help Silver City when it was first established. This was particularly the case when the number of Apache attacks increased in the early 1870s. By 1871, Apache warriors had murdered several miners, including John Bullard, and stolen livestock throughout the region. Merchants in the Mesilla Valley were concerned that their new customers might go hungry. In April 1871, Henry Lesinsky was appointed treasurer overseeing donations to the besieged citizens of Silver City. Both Lesinsky and Joseph Bennett contributed $50. Other merchants supplied flour, such as George D. Maxwell, Guadalupe Ascarate, and Louis Rosenbaum. Coffee was provided by Martin Amador and J. F. Bennett and Co. Reynolds and Griggs supplied one hundred pounds of bacon.[497]

Mesilla Valley merchants also wanted to develop the region's economy and accordingly they advocated for the construction of a telegraph connecting Fort Bayard with Santa Fe. In October 1875, James Griggs hosted a convention at his house in Las Cruces concerning the construction of the telegraph. Among the numerous guests were several merchants who had investments in Grant County: Joseph Reynolds, Thomas Bull, and Louis Rosenbaum. They believed that the telegraph would benefit their businesses in Grant County and they agreed to donate 1500 poles to the

---

497   *Borderer*, April 6, 1871; April 13, 1871; April 20, 1871; January 31, 1872.

government so long as the army agreed to construct it through the Mesilla Valley. Telegraph poles were bought on the open market and supplied by merchants and common citizens. The specifications called for pine, oak or cedar, twenty four feet long, not less than eight inches at the bottom and six inches at the top, and the bark had to be peeled off. That telegraph was completed in 1876.[498]

Perhaps, the greatest public attention surrounding business owners was their participation in local politics. For example, many participated in the 1876 Convention that voted for Grant County to secede from New Mexico and join Arizona Territory. Many storekeepers felt that the Santa Fe Ring had too much power and were preventing Grant County from having equitable representation in Santa Fe. Ultimately, Grant County did not secede from the territory because the bill died in congressional committees in Washington D.C., but it did result in Santa Fe realizing that they should allow Silver City's autonomy to prevent any future moves to secede. Accordingly, Silver City was granted its own charter and the first municipal election was held in 1878. Building contractor Robert Black was elected as the town's first mayor. He would continue as mayor through the late 1870s and 1880s. He was also a member of New Mexico's Territorial Legislature and was elected to County Board of Commissioners, serving in that capacity from 1891 to 1892. Another mayor of Silver City was miner John Fleming who became mayor in 1888 and stayed in office till 1906. Fleming was also a delegate to the Grant County Democratic Convention. Numerous business owners engaged in politics, including Henry Ailman who served as the City Treasurer in the early 1880s.[499]

Business owners in the region helped with efforts to provide law enforcement. John Fleming, a local miner and rancher, helped established the Grant County Volunteer Militia, to control the apache and

---

498   *Mesilla News*, October 9, 1875; October 30, 1875.

499   Ailman 96, and 162. Silver City Charter allowed city to tax businesses to support public education. Black also served as president of the Silver City School Board for over 20 years. Black died in 1910 from a stroke.

look for rustlers. Similarly, Lyons and Campbell were members of the Grant County Stock Association. In January of 1886, when the Board of County Commissioners agreed to reward anyone with $250 for apprehending an Apache, Lyons and Campbell agreed to pay an additional $500 for the scalp of Geronimo. Moreover, the association and other leaders in Silver City met at the Timmer Hotel on January 8 of that year, and formed a committee that would travel to Washington D.C. to discuss the Indian problem. The committee included Lyons and several other ranchers. The Grant County Stock Association did other things as well including the control of rustling and overseeing the branding of cattle on the public domain.[500]

Business owners participated in Free Masonry and other fraternal organizations. For example, officers in the Silver City Lodge in 1888 were: W. C. Porterfield, J.W. Fleming, C. Bennett, E. Cosgrove, Hyman Abraham, Robert Black, Alexander H. Morehead, and Max Schutz. Fleming himself was also a member of the Knights of Pythias of the World, Eastern Star, and B.P.O Elks. Indeed, both Anglo and Jewish business owners were often members of freemasonry, though few Hispanics merchants were. [501]

Business owners helped to establish New Mexico Normal School and oversee its management. In 1893, Robert Black traveled to Santa Fe to lobby for a normal school, spent his own money to influence legislators, and Mayor John Fleming donatedhis land to the west of downtown for the school. In 1893, members of these groups, including the Odd Fellows, led a procession to lay the corner stone for Old Main at New Mexico Normal School in 1893. Fleming served on the college's Board of Trustees and its Board of Regents. Robert Black also served as a member of school's Board

---

500   Adcock, "Brief History of John W. Fleming," 5; Campbell, 80-81.

501   "List of Lodges" in *Western's Early Days*, Vertical Files, Folder "WNMU-History," Miller Library, WNMU; Fleming married Petra Romero of Silver City, who died in 1900, see Adcock, 6. In the late 1880s, John Fleming donated his 2 story house near the courthouse to the Sisters of Mercy, which began St. Joseph's Hospital and Sanitarium. Elizabeth Warren also helped with hospitals and helped with one of the first operations in her building. See Berry, 38.

of Regents. He also served on the Board of Regents of the Agricultural College at Las Cruces.[502]

Times were changing by the 1890s for business owners. The repeal of the Sherman Silver Purchase Act in 1893 resulted in silver prices continuing its historic fall. Nearby mining towns too were impacted by falling silver prices. Georgetown stopped producing silver in that year, and by 1903 would largely be deserted. Furthermore, the financial panic of that year created a five year economic depression, and rising unemployment meant that less people were buying goods at the stores. Persistent overcutting of the surrounding hills to meet the demand for mining timbers and fuel had resulted in the denuding of the land and the growing instances of flooding in the town. Indeed, business owners hoped that the establishment of the normal school might help to bring students to Silver City who would spend money locally. As the decade came to an end, business owners were embracing the growing ethos toward progressivism and the belief that working together in league with the government would be good for business. This spirit of progressivism would carry into the twentieth century.[503]

The Twentieth Century

The twentieth century continued to see mining as the primary linkage to the larger U.S. economy that would sustain Grant County's economy. Eastern capital increasingly financed mineral production and large mining corporations emerged. New types of metal were mined, like zinc, iron, and manganese. Cattle ranching continued to grow in dominance and exports of cattle to California increased. Government spending also benefited the region's businesses, particularly in the 1930s during the Great Depression when federal work programs like the Works Progress Administration (WPA) pumped money into the local economy. A growing health care industry developed that was largely based on the

---

502   Adcock, 5-6; and Ailman 162.

503   "Fire, Disease, [and the] Crime of '93," *Independent*, January 25, 2005, Vertical Files, Folder "Georgetown" Miller Library, WNMU.

establishment of sanitariums treating of tuberculosis patients and hot springs that attracted to the area patients suffering from arthritis. The 1900s also saw greater levels of cash in circulation, the rise of specialization in the retail and service sectors, and growing opportunities for women to open businesses.

Growth of the Mining Corporations

Mining in Grant County in the 20th Century was increasingly becoming dominated by corporations. Perhaps, the best known person reflective of this change in Grant County would be George Hearst, a California Senator and millionaire, who had investments throughout the U.S. His invest-

Figure 14: The Neff Store in Pinos Altos, early 1900s. From *The Pinos Altos Story*.

ments in the region began with the Victorio Land and Cattle Co., which operated south of Silver City. As a result of his ranching investments, he learned of the valuable deposits of minerals in the territory. He started acquiring mining claims in the 1890s, which included copper claims in Santa Rita and mines in the Chloride Flats District. His company also had plans to invest in the Pinos Altos gold mines but was put on hold when he died in 1897.

His wife Pheobe directed the Hearst Co. to buy mines Pinos Altos in 1897. This would create a "boom" in Pinos Altos, resulting in new businesses opening up, like the Neff Store, as seen in Figure 14. The company also bought a ranch near Ft. Bayard for its water rights, and pumped water up to Pinos Altos. They also bought the Silver City Reduction Works, though it burned down several years later. They also started plans for a railroad to connect their mines to the Silver City railhead. Indeed, these investments occurred in a good economic environment as the Depression of the 1890s was coming to an end. In 1906, the company sold their holdings to Comanche Mining and Smelting Co. The company built the Silver City, Pinos Altos, and Mogollon Railroad the following year that connected their mines in the Silver Flat and Chloride Flats mining districts and in Pinos Altos with the company's reduction plant in Silver City. However, they went bankrupt shortly thereafter, and all the properties were acquired by the Savanna Copper Co. in 1909.[504]

When Hearst sold their mining properties, it had already sold most of its leases in the Santa Rita Mining District, which the Santa Rita Copper and Iron Company acquired by 1900. This was beginnings of the Santa Rita Mining District being increasingly controlled by

Figure 15: The Santa Rita Company Store, early 1900s. Photo courtesy of the Silver City Museum.

several different companies, including the Santa Rita Copper Company which acquired the Santa Rita Copper and Iron Company in 1901. The mining company employed workers for its several mines; it also leased its properties to independent miners.

The Santa Rita Copper Company also acquired the Santa Rita Company Store, established in the 1890s. As seen in Figure 15, this 5,000 square foot building housed a variety of manufactured products, and the company issued script or coupons that the Hispanic workers called "boletas" that forced employees to shop there since that was the only place where the script could be redeemed for products. The store adopted a policy of extending just enough credit to company employees to keep

---

504   Berry, 43; *Los Angeles Herald*, numbers 18 and 19, October 1909.

279

them perpetually in debt, forcing them to continue working for the mining company. The company also tried to drive out other businesses and take-over other individuals' mining claims. This effort was aimed particularly at businesses located on the nearby Pinder-Slip claim. The claim was originally called the James Pinder Claim and was acquired by the Hearst Estate, but due to a lack of assessment work being done, it converted to the public domain in 1898, at which time it was acquired by Ayrus Hamilton. Hamilton acquired the claim because it was on the main wagon road paralleling Santa Rita Creek leading from Santa Rita to Hanover Junction (i.e. San Jose) and it was an ideal location to establish a business. He also knew that the railroad connecting Hanover Junction would be soon completed. He opened a saloon, but following a shooting that he was involved in, he decided to sell the claim and saloon to John M. Storz, who built a new saloon and allowed Benno Rosenfeld to establish a general store. Other businesses were established, including a barbershop and butchery. The site was dubbed "Storzville" and had a small railroad station following the completion of the locomotive by 1899.[505]

The Santa Rita Copper and Iron Company sought to drive out the businesses at Storzville and acquire the Pinder-Slip Claim. They alleged that the claim was actually part of their holdings and filed a law suit in the Third District Court in Silver City, which was thrown out. In the meantime, the Santa Rita Copper and Iron Company was acquired by the Santa Rita Copper Company and the businesses in Storzville grew to include a gambling hall and a new mercantile, G. L. Turner and Son. They also tried to drive out the businesses on the Pinder-Slip Claim by adopting a policy that said that employees could not to shop at other stores, particularly that of G. L. Turner and Son, or they would be fired. At the same time, the company filed for a patent on the Pinder-Slip Claim, but was denied. Turner also sued the Santa Rita Mining Company for restraint of trade under the Sherman Anti-Trust Act of 1890 because they forced its employees to shop only at the Santa Rita Company Store. Turner won the case, though his original demand of $50,000 in compensation was reduced to

---

505   Huggard, 49.

$2,000. Ultimately, the Santa Rita Mining Co. purchased the Pinder-Slip claim for $15,000 in 1908. When the Chino Copper Co. acquired the properties of the Santa Rita Mining Company in 1909, they also acquired the Pinder-Slip Claim and the Turners and other businesses were forced to close their shops in 1910.[506]

Figure 16: P.W. Samaniego's Shoe Store, ca. early 1900s.
Photo courtesy of the Silver City Museum.

The Chino Copper Co. would come to dominate mining in Santa Rita for the next two decades, and in so doing would begin the process of open-pit mining. This company transformed Santa Rita into a company town, and employed John M. Sully to manage the company's mining operations and the administration of Santa Rita. He not only determined that the low grade copper ore could be mined profitably through open pit methods, but he also oversaw a policy that segregated Hispano workers from Anglo employees. He instituted a dual wage system where the latter workers were paid more than Hispano workers. To keep its workers happy, he allowed independent businesses to open up, so long as they were not in direct competition with the Santa Rita Company Store. These businesses

---

506   Ibid., 50-52.

281

Figure 17: Porterfield Manganese Co. wagons, ca. 1920s.
Photo courtesy of the Silver City Museum.

included the Manhattan Confectionary and Candy Shop, Carillo's Saloon, the Santa Rita Garage, and other businesses like butcher shops and stage lines. Al Owen and his brother were liked by company officials due to their assistance in the acquisition of the Pinder-Slip claim, and accordingly, they were given the opportunity to open a bar and the best hotel in town that had electric lights, running water, and individual bathrooms. There was a considerable number of Hispanic owned businesses like those P.W. Samaniego, as seen in Figure 16. He owned zapeteria (as seen in this photo) and a bunk house. Jose Cosmo opened a shoe shop after Samaniego sold his business. While many of these Hispanic owned businesses catered to the Spanish speaking population, Pedro "Pete" Gomez operated the Orpheum Theatre. This movie house was open to both Anglos and Hispanics, though the seats were segregated; that policy continued when it was torn down and replaced with El Cobre Theatre in the early 1940s. El Cobre Theatre also provided a separate "Spanish Program" on Mondays and Tuesdays that included movies in Spanish. Just like company policy of segregation, the businesses in Santa Rita too were segregated. For example, the San Nicolas Café was for Hispanics only), while the Santa Rita Café (i.e. the Elite Café) was for Anglos only.[507]

Mining corporations were formed to mine new type of minerals and metals during the early twentieth century. Small companies were formed, like those operating the Grandview Mine and the Royal John Mine in the Black Range that mined lead, zinc and some silver. Manganese was first mined on the Legal Tender Hill in 1880 by the Massachusetts and New Mexico Mining Co. Though it was short-lived, the fact that the company's headquarters were in Boston resulted in the locals starting to call the Legal Tender Hill, "Boston Hill." Other companies would continue mining manganese on Boston Hill, including the Porterfield Manganese Co. starting in the 1910s, as illustrated in Figure 17. Manganese mining continued through the 1930s and 1940s and one of the last mines, the Luck Mine, would continue shipping manganese by railroad till the 1950s.[508]

Of all the new minerals being mined, uranium was the most unique. It is often overlooked that uranium mining started in Grant County in the 1920s. In the late 1910s, Mrs. A. A. Leach with her husband discovered uranium ore in the White Signal Mining District. News of the discovery spread and other individuals started mining for the mineral too. By the 1930s, the Tyrone-based Ra-Tor Mining Co. developed a market

Figure 18: Ra-Tor Mining Company trade mark, ca. 1920s.

507 Ibid., 121-122. Other companies operating at Santa Rita: Santa Rita Copper and Iron Co., Ray Consolidate Copper Co.(1924), and Nevada Consolidated Copper Co. (1926). Ultimately, Kennecott acquired the mine in 1933, and invested $10 million to build Hurley as smelter town. Another company that should be included is the Phelps Dodge Co. that invested in the copper mines in the Burro Mountains in what would be the town of Tyrone by 1913. Tyrone was considered a model company town.

508 *Stories from Our Streets*, (Silver City: Murray Ryan Visitor Center), 3.

for facial creams and mineral water containing uranium. People believed in the early 1900s that uranium had certain health benefits. In Figure 18, the reader can see one their logos used to sell their beauty clay. It would not be until World War II that uranium prospectors found large quantities of uranium just north of Grants, New Mexico and sold it to the U. S. Nuclear Regulatory Commission. Small mining companies in Silver City continued prospecting for uranium in the White Signal area in the 1950s that included Robert Mathis, the owner of Mathis and Mathis. This small mining company had several pet claims, but large amounts of uranium were never found locally.[509]

Silver City Commercial Center in the 20th Century
Unlike Santa Rita and Tyrone, Silver City was not a company town. It would continue into the twentieth century as the center of commerce for Grant County. It remained the county seat, where the courts and municipal offices were, and was the location for the New Mexico Teachers College. It also saw the construction of a new depot for the Deming, Silver City, and Pacific Railroad in 1915 where most of the region's mineral products were exported from. It still had several smelters and reductions works and its business community would become more diverse and developed than those found the nearby company towns.[510]

The layout of Silver City's commercial center had changed at the dawn of the twentieth century. Indeed, the overcutting and overgrazing of lands upstream from Silver City contributed to a series of floods in the 1890s and early 1900s. The flood of 1902 was the worst and it inundated the Chinese Gardens, eroded the foundation of several businesses, like the Hotel San Vincent, and destroyed the railroad bridge. Because the bridge was washed out, hotels were no longer as profitable along Hudson Street as they once were, and new hotels west of Main Street like the Palace Hotel and later the Murray Hotel would service the needs of travelers. Even Main Street was destroyed, resulting in it becoming "the Ditch." New businesses would

---

509   Vertical Files, Folder "Royal John Mine," Miller Library, WNMU
510   In 1910, Grant Co. had 15,000 people, see 1910 Census.

be built along Broadway, as well as buildings, such as the Uhli Block. The firm of Lindaur and Burnside was also established along Broadway Street.

The amount of cash in circulation increased in the early 20th century which facilitated economic transactions and created a vibrant retail sector.

Figure 19: C.W. Cox Furniture Co., early 1900s. Photo courtesy of the Silver City Museum.

Compared to agricultural communities, Silver City had more cash in circulation because gold, silver, and copper were highly liquid assets. Levels of cash increased also because the Federal Reserve was created in 1913 and the printing of more money increased nationally. Also, the overall U.S. economy continued to grow helping to explain Grant County's economic development and why the days of bartering at the general store were coming to an end.

Growing levels of cash contributed to specialization in the retail sector. No longer did an individual have to find someone that was willing to barter with them for their products. Instead, businesses selling a limited type of product or service had sufficient demand because more people had money that could be spent anywhere. Indeed, the era of the general merchant was coming to an end, and in its place there would be a proliferation of specialized stores, like W.S. Cox's furniture store (see Figure 19), Bower Monument Co. who sold headstones, the J. D. Parker Shoe Shop, the Silver Horse Shoe Tea Room, and a growing number of theatres by the 1930s like the famous El Sol Theatre and the Silco Theatre. What were called "cash-stores"[511] grew in number as early as the 1890s, like the "New Cash Store" that gave customers a discount for paying in cash. These cash stores

---

511 Good photo in museum collection showing the "New Cash Store," which was operated by Mr. and Mrs. H. D. Gilbert, see in Unger, p. 91.

Figure 20: Yee N. Fung's store, ca. 1920s.
Photo courtesy of the Silver City Museum.

were transformed into "five and dime stores" in the 20th Century. This included Yee N. Fung's store, located on Bullard, as seen in Figure 20, in which he advertised that he also sold products for 5 cents, 10 cents, and 25 cents and that he specialized in candy, toys, and Japanese products. As seen in Figure 21, another Chinese owned business who specialized in Chinese and Japanese products was Yee Lung and Co. whose store was on Yankie St. [512]

The growth of the retail sector afforded Chinese immigrants continued business opportunities. Their community was tight nit and they maintained close ties with Chinese businesses all throughout New Mexico. The International Directory of Chinese Businesses included business names, owners, and addresses for Chinese businesses in all the major towns in New Mexico. The directory indicated that there were nine Chinese owned businesses in Silver City in 1900: two restaurants, four general merchants, and three grocers. Indeed, engaging in food production and running restaurants continued to provide a sustainable income for the Chinese in the early twentieth century. This included truck farming in the area, like that of the Wah Brothers whose farm northeast of Deming allowed them to have a ready source of food to open restaurants. The Chinese Gardens in Silver City also allowed for Chinese to readily open restaurants. Mah Foon Lime who farmed in the Chinese Gardens in the 1920s married Lan Lew Lime in 1934. They ran the Manhattan Café, with the help of their children including Donna Lee. Barker's Café was owned by Yat Lim (a.k.a. Charlie Mah) who was beaten to death in 1945 by several Anglos who were acquitted of the crime. The Wang family owned their own restaurant too. Yee Toy and Bow families ran a grocery store.

---

512   Berry, 43.

286

Figure 21: Yee Lung and Co. store, ca. early 1900s.
Photo courtesy of the Silver City Museum.

Indeed, the sustainability of Chinese businesses was largely based on that fact that everyone needs to eat.[513]

Businesswomen

The development of Silver City's economy also opened up more opportunities for women to establish businesses. Indeed, the history of business women in Silver City began in the late nineteenth century with wives working behind the scenes running the day-to-day operations of their families' businesses. They also ran brothels and clothing stores in the late 1800s. That trend continued in the early twentieth century, and they came to operate new types of businesses in this period as well.

Elizabeth Warren came to Silver City with her husband, Orange Scott Warren, in 1882. Together, they operated an insurance company that sold policies in Silver City, Mogollon, and Georgetown. Her husband died in 1885, and she took over the business. She insured homes, businesses, and mines. When the Silver City Reduction Works burned down in 1903, she

---

513   International Chinese Directory, 1900. This was found online in 2015; Donna Lee was the daughter of Mah Foon and Lan Lew Lime, see Elan Head "When East Met Old West," *Desert Exposure*, September 2014, Vertical Files, Folder "Silver City – History," Miler Library, WNMU.

Figure 22: Hotel San Vincent, ca. 1902.
Photo courtesy of the Silver City Museum.

paid out their claim that amounted to about $15,000 which allowed the Hearst Estate to rebuild it two years later. Several years later, she started the Grant County Abstract Co. that provided notary services and processed paperwork for real estate transactions and mining claims. It is said that on any given day, there would be long lines of miners filing their mining claim location notices who needed her services as a public notary. Indeed, she would be the first woman in New Mexico history to be a certified insurance agent and to own an abstract company. Because her abstract business involved overseeing other peoples' real estate transactions, she naturally began investing in real estate, coming to own several properties in town. In 1902, she purchased the Timmer House and renamed it Hotel San Vicente, as one can see in Figure 22. However, the flood of that year destroyed the foundation and she eventually had to demolish the hotel. [514]

514 *Silver City Independent*, June 30, 1903.

Warren had many properties and this helps to explain why she went into the construction business. In 1907, a city ordinance was passed requiring all property owners to build sidewalks in front of their buildings. Since she had many properties, she knew it would be expensive for her to hire cement workers, and she was having a hard time finding men to construct them. Around this time she met Matilda Koehler. Koehler had come to Silver City to serve as superintendent of the normal school. Her brother was in the cement business and knew how to lay cement. Accordingly she resigned her position at the school 1907 to go into business with Warren full time. Accordingly, Warren learned how to mix cement and make her own sidewalks. As she completed her sidewalks, she realized that there was demand for more sidewalks, and she went into cement manufacturing. She acquired some vacant land near the northern edge of Bullard and installed a rock crusher and cement plant. She began laying down those first sidewalks in 1907, which naturally led to her investing into construction-related businesses. Near her rock crusher, Warren built a saw mill, and shops for carpentry, blacksmithing, and paint. Koehler serve as a crew boss, overseeing men building sidewalks and buildings. Some of her early buildings included structures she built at the southern end of town 1914 where the railroad planned to build a new depot. On top of her numerous projects in town, she also built retaining walls along the "Ditch" near her house that protected it from the continued threat of monsoonal flooding. [515]

Silver City's economic development opened up more opportunities for brothels. Since Silver City was a mining town, it historically had larger amounts of cash in circulations in the 1800s, giving rise to brothels, like those owned by an early madam by the name of Kate Stewart in the 1880s.

---

515   Emma Muir, "The Vision of Pioneers, in New Mexico" (March 1952), found in "This is Silver City, 1888, 1889, 1890," Vertical Files, Folder "Silver City – History," Miller Library, WNMU. Linda Harris, "The Warren House," New Mexico Magazine, April 1996, vertical files, WNMU, folder "Silver City – History." The Corner of 9th and Bullard historically had lumber yards. Continental Lumber Co. 1907, Silver City Lumber Co., Marke Lumber Co., Crescent Lumber Co., Leonard Lumber Co.. Elizabeth Warren used area for her rock crusher. -Richard Grabe in 1899 started planning mill and carpentry shop in this area. Galbraith – Fox started in Deming.

The number of brothels grew in the twentieth century, particularly east of the Ditch, where a new Red Light district emerged along Hudson Street. Mildred Cusey, who was known to the locals as "Madam Millie" operated several brothels on that street starting in the 1930s. Cusey was born back east and came out west with her sister who was suffering from tuberculosis. They moved to El Paso. To make money, Cusey for a time worked for railroad concessionaire Fred Harvey as a "Harvey Girl" serving food to travelers along the Southern Pacific Railroad. She learned that she could make more money as a prostitute and went to Silver City. However, law enforcement informed her that she was too young and she would have to leave town. She said that, "when I come back, she will buy that brothel." That is what she did some years later, after having started her first brothel in Deming. By the 1930s, she had three brothels on Hudson Street, one of which was the old McComas House. She also opened brothels in Lordsburg and Laramie, Wyoming. In all, she operated six houses. She was a shrewd businesswoman and diversified her investments by also operating a ranch, parking lot, taxi service, and several bars and restaurants.[516]

Women often owned clothing shops. One of the first was Mrs. G. Truesdell, a Silver City dressmaker of fashionable clothing and fabrics, who in the *Grant County Herald* in April of 1876 personally invited "the ladies of Silver City and vicinity to visit her store."[517] As the economy developed in the early 1900s, the number of female-owned clothing stores increased. Mrs. O'Bera Click and her husband Al moved the family to Silver City in 1941 because Al suffered from tuberculosis. Five years later, she purchased "The Model Shop", a high-end clothing boutique in the C. T. Ross Building. Another store was the Specialty Shop, owned by Mrs. Walter Gibbs in the Schutz-Brent Building, and in the 1940s, next to the Murray Hotel, there was a female-run store called "Minnie Shops."[518]

---

516   C. A. Gustufson, "Mildred Cusey – Madam Entrepreneur." Vertical Files, Folder "Mildred Cusey," Miller Library, WNMU.

517   *Grant County Herald*, April 1, 1876.

518   *Stories from Our Streets*; and Humble, 107.

Transportation and Distribution in the 20th Century

Silver City continued to serve as the regional transportation hub in the 20th century. The Deming, Silver City, and Pacific Railroad allowed for the ready exportation of cattle and mineral products and importation of manufactured goods. Until the railroad's closure, the southern end of town had many warehouses where goods were stored and transferred from. Silver City would also become the region's center for automobile sales and services, and the growing use of trucks would aid in the distribution of small parcels and dairy products throughout Grant County.

Coal distribution became an important part of the economy as corporate-finance mining increased in the 20th Century. Furthermore, the days of relying on wood to fuel stamp mills had largely come to an end due to overcutting and the establishment of the Gila National Forest in 1907 that minimized the amount of timber that could be cut. Coal was imported into Grant County from Colorado and transported to Silver City by the Atchison Topeka and Santa Fe Railroad and the Deming, Silver City, and Pacific

Figure 23: Rosedale Dairy delivery truck, ca. 1920s-1930s. Photo from *Images of America: Silver City.*

Railroad. While the Phelps Dodge Corporation and the Chino Copper Co. used their own trains to supply coal, smaller mines like those mining manganese on Boston Hill got their coal in Silver City. The Lowe and Hann Coal, Transfer, and Storage Co. met the need for coal by mine owners in the area. It was established by Thomas L. Lowe and Edward T. Hann, who had purchased the entire block at south of town in 1914 across from the proposed location of the new Silver City depot. The firm also owned a large warehouse and charged a commission to house and transfer products for other businesses, including mineral products. Ultimately, in 1924 Lowe was convicted of banking improprieties and paid a $750 fine. He left Silver City and relocated to Los Angeles, where he died in a car accident in 1926.[519]

---

519 *Stories from Our Streets.*

291

The Silver City area was also the center of distributing dairy products. The Rosedale Dairy is the old dairy in Grant County. It was established in 1890 by C. G. Jenks just off what is today's Rosedale Street. It comprised much of the land to the east of Silver City. For a short time, it was operated by Agnes Morley Cleavelend, who is famous for her autobiography *No Life for a Lady*, in which she wrote that her ownership of the dairy was short-lived (e.g. from 1907-1908) because she was using the incorrect ratio of water to butter, resulting in her butter turning pink and the townspeople thinking they were being poisoned. Accordingly, she sold it to Philip Harsh in 1908. When a descendent, Fiske Harsh took over management of the dairy in 1927, he purchased delivery trucks (as seen in Figure 23), and made deliveries all throughout the region. Their distribution of dairy products continued when they moved the dairy to the Gila-Cliff area after World War II.[520]

Silver City also became the center of automobile related businesses. Some of the earliest automobile shops were located at the southern end of town, which historically was where corrals and wagon transport companies had been located in the 19th century. In 1914, Elizabeth Warren, built a Ford motorcar agency building which was said to have had "show rooms in a commodious building."[521] In 1915, the Overland Auto Salesroom was established nearby at 311 West Broadway. At the corner of Arizona and San Vicente streets, Leo Wray's blacksmith shop was active in the 1920s, and was known for tightening the spokes of car rims. However, quickly, the northern blocks of Bullard became the center of automobile related businesses, often next to the lumber companies. In 1911, Frank Houre opened an automobile shop next to the Continental Lumber Co, at the corner of Bullard and 7th. At the corner of 9th and Bullard, there was a Ford garage, established in 1914. Before it was destroyed by fire in 1918, it was also where Charlie McAninch operated the town's first taxicab. It is interesting to note that his taxi business was located near auto garages because it shows how automobiles at the time were new and liable to malfunctioning and

---

520   Interview of Alexis Harsh, in 2017 and 2021.
521   *Stories from Our Streets.*

292

this would allow McAninch's cars to be fixed in a timely manner. It is also likely that his taxi company drove customers to and from their houses as they were getting their cars repaired. Nearby, Bennett Motor Transit Co. was established in 1916 that sold high-end cars like Marmons, Hupmobiles, Nashes, and Studebakers. The company also transported small packages and mail to outlying communities. In the 1930s, W. H. Emerick had a service station on the corner of 7th and Bullard, and on the S. E. Corner of 9th St. and Bullard, Dick's College Service Station was located. [522]

The Health Industry and Government Sector as Tertiary Linkages

The health industry in Southwestern New Mexico can be considered as a third economic linkage that brought money into the region. As early as the 1880s, Silver City was promoting itself as the "World's Sanitarium."[523] Indeed, the American West was always considered an area conducive to the treatment of tuberculosis because of the dry air. Southern New Mexico was ideal because it not only had dry air, but had a relatively mild climate during the winter. There were several sanatoriums that opened up in southern New Mexico, serving particularly easterners suffering from tuberculosis. This would include Van Patten's "Mountain Camp" in the Organ Mountains ten miles east of Las Cruces that was sold to Dr. Nathan Boyd in 1915 who made it into a proper tuberculosis sanatorium. When Fort Bayard was closed down in 1899, it was converted to an army hospital to treat soldiers with tuberculosis. Sanitariums catered to easterners, many of whom had money, and they traveled to Silver City for treatment, thus injecting more money into the local economy.

Silver city would come to have several tuberculosis sanatoriums, one of the first being Cottage Sanatoriums. Cottage Sans was founded by Dr. Earl Sprague Bullock who originally worked at Fort Bayard who believed that he had a superior way of healing tuberculosis patients. Instead of a lot of food, he believed that minimizing food intake, resting and breathing

---

522 Humble, 97.

523 "World Sanitarium: Silver City," (Silver City Bureau of Immigration, 1887), Vertical Files, Folder "Silver City-History," Miller Library, WNMU.

fresh air was the solution. He needed money. One of the patients Wayne McVeigh Wilson came from a wealthy family, whose mother Nellie Wilson, felt obliged to help Dr. Bullock. His mother was able to get letters of introduction from Woodrow Wilson and Grover Cleveland, which she used to solicit funds from Andrew Carnegie to establish a sanatorium based on Dr. Bullock's ideas. Perhaps, it was because of Carnegie's *Gospel of Wealth* idea that she was able to get a generous loan from him. She also was able to get money from the president of the Baldwin Locomotive Works, John Converse. Some of the money she got was in the form of a $15,000 endowment to be used to pay for the $80 month cost for patients who could not afford it. She gave the money to the doctor, who used it to buy 280 acres of land about 3 miles north of Silver City and start his business, Cottage Sanatorium in 1905. It had its own kitchen, prepared food grown by Chinese who tended its gardens, and by the time it was sold, it had a post office and small store.[524]

Cottage Sanatorium set an example for others to follow. The Sunnyside Sanitarium was established in 1909 near the Cottage Sanatorium and its name was changed in 1915 to the National Methodist Sanatorium. Two other sanatoriums were built in Silver City, one near the waterworks and the other at the old Lyons and Campbell Mansion to the north of town. For African American patients, the Africo-Sanitarium was established in 1910 on the east side of town. The "Pines" was established near Tyrone in the Burro Mountains in 1904. There were also other parts of town that patients paid to live in tents and be attended to. There was also a hope that a health resort could be developed at White Signal due to the belief that the uranium in the area might be conducive to health. These sanitariums pumped money into the economy. One estimate is that they contributed some $75,000 into the economy each year. Indeed, the patients that arrived were often well-to-do and spent money locally and some, like Robert Munroe Ferguson, who was a business partner and personal secretary with Theodore Roosevelt and

---

524   Berry, 46; *Silver City Daily Press*, August 4, 1987, Vertical Files, Folder "Silver City – History," Miller Library, WNMU.

294

served under Roosevelt in the Rough Riders, would stay because of the dry air. In the case of Ferguson, he would acquire land on the northern flank of the Burro Mountains and build his home, the Burro Mountain Homestead. Another tuberculosis patient was Alford Colley, who also knew Roosevelt and who had been Assistant U.S. Attorney General. He came with his wife and even entertained Theodore Roosevelt and his wife. It is said that when the Roosevelts visited, Mrs. Roosevelt had been taken to Schadel's Restaurant, but since she wanted tea, the owners had to scramble around town to find tea.[525]

Figure 24: McDermott's mineral water bottle. Photo was found on the internet.

The history of hot springs can include Dr. Richard Stovall's Mimbres Hot Springs at the turn of the century, but a more important spring in Grant County was the Faywood Hot Springs which was well-known as a place where people went to heal, particularly from rheumatoid arthritis. The springs were originally called Hudson Springs, named after Richard Hudson who visited it in 1870. Hudson purchased the springs and in 1875 he built a 50 room hotel. He also operated a wagon and stage line running between Fort Cummings and Silver city. The hotel burned down in 1892. The new owner, A. E. Graham rebuilt the hotel and called it Casa de Consuelo. It was later purchased by J.C. Fay, William Lockwood, and T.C. McDermott. Fay and Lockwood's names were combined to create the "Faywood" name. They improved the old Casa de Consuelo and called it the Faywood Hot Springs Hotel. It was a one-story building that could hold 125 guests and had a three-sided courtyard with 900 foot long veranda. It also included a large dining

525 Vertical Files, Folder "Burro Mountain Homestead," Miller Library, WNMU. The Timmer House also appealed to health seekers before the building was demolished following the 1902 flood, see *Silver City Daily Press*, August 4, 1987, Vertical Files, Folder "Silver City – History," Miller Library, WNMU; and Berry 60.

room, parlors, a writing room, a barber shop, gun room, and billiard room. Spring water was cooled and piped into the hotel rooms and bath houses. McDermott became the sole owner of the hot springs and by the 1920s, he was selling mineral water from the springs om specially made bottles with "Faywood" on them as seen in Figure 24. [526]

Conclusion

The purpose of this paper has been to provide historical content that will assist the Silver City Museum in its efforts to develop exhibits showcasing Grant County's economic history chronologically and thematically. It began with the early mines during the Spanish, Mexican and early territorial periods, and then focused on the development of mining starting in the 1870s. The essay argued that mining served as the main economic linkage brining money into the economy and sustaining a business community in Silver city. Ranching was also an important linkage that brought wealth into the region. This economy was dependent on the exportation of mineral products and cattle, and as such, was susceptible to volatile swings in commodity prices. When cattle and mineral prices were high, the region experienced a "boom." When prices fell, the businesses of Grant County experienced a "bust." The price volatility of the commodities exported from this region was moderated by government spending and health care in the Twentieth Century, which brought additional money into the region. The period covered in the paper shows that there was an economic transformation from a merchant-capitalist economic order based on bartering to a modern to a cash-based economy that gave rise to greater levels of specialization and a growing number of retail businesses being established.

---

526 Drug stores found a demand on the part of patients and local residents and some of these products would have been sold there. Drug stores Howell Drugs was in the old Cohen building. There was also Aggies Drugs.

Epilogue: Future Research

The history of business is immense and research on Silver City's business history will continue into the future. This essay will evolve and its author (Scott Fritz) will be available to assist in the researching of upcoming museum exhibits. In this section, readers will find a summary of the author's latest research regarding the following themes: 1) Government spending benefiting businesses; 2) business during the 1920s; 3) the impact of the Great Depression and the New Deal; 5) the impact of World War I and World War II; 6) the growing tourism industry; and 7) the growing labor movement that culminated in the Empire Zinc Strike of 1950-1952 in Fierro, New Mexico. This section will also include comments related to future directions that this research may take.

Government spending benefited Silver City and the larger region of southwestern New Mexico. Federal, territorial/state, county, and municipal governments introduced money into the economy that helped sustain businesses in the twentieth century. While this paper has included some information on Fort Bayard, more research is needed on how the existence of the New Mexico Teachers College benefited local businesses. For example, the government employed contractors and construction workers to build the college's first buildings, like the firm of Laizure and Grabe that received a contract to build Old Main. The college brought students and teachers to Silver City, who spent their money locally. Since there were no college bookstores in the early 1900s, students went bought their books in town, like at Blackwell's Books. Phillips Gifts advertised that they sold textbooks for the Teacher's College. Another example of the government's support of public school resulting in money tricking into the local economy was in the construction of the new public school on 6th Street, of which Elizabeth Warren's construction company graded the land prior to the school being built in 1910.[527] During the Great Depression, New Deal work programs bene-fited businesses. This was particularly the case for the Works Progress Administration because it paid local men to work on projects, and unlike the CCC which required its workers to send most of their pay checks back home (in the East), WPA workers spent their money locally. The WPA built Western High School on the campus of the New Mexico Teacher's College. It also reinforced the walls along "the Ditch," including up Silva Creek to what later would be the 12th St. Bridge. The WPA funded the construction of Swift Memorial Hospital by contracting with Fred Tatsch. It also built numerous sidewalks in town. The WPA also paid workers in the larger region of Grant and Catron counties, including the "Catwalk" which use to be part of the water delivery system of the Graham Mill on Whitewater Creek that closed in 1915. It should also be noted that the CCC built some 14,000 check dams and planted trees north of Silver City to help end the flooding that historically plagued Silver City's business community.[528]

More research into the Gila National Forest's impact on business is needed. Ideally, this topic would start by looking at the early economic interests using forest resources, like lumber companies. Research ques-tions include: Where did the lumber companies, like those owned by John A. Miller and George Grabe, get their timber? Did they get it from the forests north of town? This topic naturally leads to the question of why the Gila Forest Reserve was created in 1899 and why the forest was transferred to the new Forest Service when the Gila National Forest was created in 1907. That is, forest reserves and national forests were intended to prevent overcutting so as to protect watersheds but also prevent an over-abundance of timber on the market that tended to drive lumber

---

527 Humble, 76; Frank Tatch built Silver City Woman's Club building. Mrs. James Gilchrist organized effort to buy land and build the building, see *Desert Exposure* April 2009, Vertical Files, Folder "Silver City – History," Miller Library, WNMU. Questions to be research: Did business support Statehood? How city spending benefited business, like when Fred Tasch built 12 street bridge? Did the digging of wells in the Franks Wellfield and Wordward Wellfield in Mimbres, added in 1950, benefit businesses?

528 *Desert Exposure*, May 2012, Vertical File, Folder "Silver City – History," Miller Library, WNMU; and Humble,104.

prices below what companies needed to charge in order to make a profit. Did lumber companies in town and nearby ranchers and farmers support the creation of Gila National Forest? Indeed, the national forest took these lands out of the public domain and employed "forest guards" and rangers like Henry Woodrow to evict "squatters." They also oversaw permits for local homesteaders to graze cattle and herd sheep, assisted ranchers by keeping sheep out of cattle pastures, and oversaw the implementation of the Forest Homestead Act of 1906. Other economic interests include predator hunters like Ben Lilly (1856-1936) and Nat Straw (1857-1941), who sold wolves, grizzly bear, and mountain lion hides to ranchers and government. Did these men make more money selling hides to the government than to local ranchers? The Gila Wilderness was created in 1924 that sought to limit humans' impact on the forest and included the policy of not building roads in the wilderness. Did local ranchers and farmers oppose the creation of the wilderness? And, did the benefit from the wilderness being created? Indeed, local residents benefit financially from the forest, through gaining employment cabins for ranger stations, like at Little Dry Creek and telephone lines, like the ones that stretched from Little Dry Ranger Station to Center Baldy. Contracts were also awarded to build fire lookouts, like at Granite Peak in 1917. What were the business interests that benefited from such contracts? Also, research needs to be done on the impact that the Grazing Service (which was the result of the Taylor Grazing Act of 1934) had on local ranchers. As of now, more research will be conducted into how the Gila Forest became a tourist destination after World War II. For example, in 1950s, the *Silver City Daily Press* put at top "Gateway to the Great Gila Wilderness Area."[529]

Examining the public role that business owners played is still needed, particularly for the twentieth century. The following information has been compiled for this section so far. Thomas Lowe, who owned Lowe and Hann Coal, Transfer and Storage Co., was a regent for NM Normal School.

---

529 *Daily Press*, July 30, 1959. See also "Brief History of the Gila Wilderness," and *Silver City Daily Press*, June 4, 1999, Vertical Files, Folder "Gila National Forest," Miller Library, WNMU.

He was also a member of Chamber of Commerce, as well as a member of the Elks Lodge and he was a Mason. Often stores served as social centers where residents met to gossip, get their mail, make phone calls, etc. This was particularly the case in small, rural communities like Hanover, Gila, Pinos Altos, etc. For example, Tom McCoy's store in Hanover during the 1920s and 1930s was where the only phone in town was located, and it was noted that people went to the store to talk and gossip. The McCoy store also had an employee who was a judge and apparently he held court there in a room attached to the store. The history of archaeology is well-documented here in Grant County. However, little has been research on the role that business played in archaeological research. This would include members of the Cosgrove family, who owned a hardware store, that dug up Mimbres Pottery for the Peabody Museum in the 1910s and 1920s, and that would include C. Burton Cosgrove and his wife Harriet. Moreover, this paper has also found evidence that sons of business owners served in the U.S. Army during World War II and helped with the war effort in other ways too. For example, during WWII, the Navy bought the tools of Bennet Motor Transit Co., and shipped them to New Mexico State University. The Navy also had Ernest Bennett be instructor. Sons of Chinese-owned business served in the war, and included brothers Yolk Lew, Sin Lew, and Joe Lew. In the case of philanthropy, some business owners were noted for their public good works, like brothel owner Mildred Cusey who was known to help individual pay their medical bills, and would feed families whose husbands and fathers were on strike, and paying students' tuition.[530]

Another topic to be assessed in the future is the history of local businesses in the 1920s. Generally, historians talk about the "Roaring 20s" as a time of prosperity in the cities. However, the decade was not good for businesses in rural communities, and that would include Silver City to some extent. When World War I ended in 1918, government military spending also ended. No longer was the government buying wool, food, copper and lead. Research into this topic has already discovered that beef prices

---

530 *New Mexico Magazine*, March 2002, 25-26, Vertical File, Folder "Fierro" Miller Library, WNMU; and Images of America, 14, 95 and 110.

fell and there was a severe drought in 1921, which together drove many ranches in Grant County out of business. Mining slowed down as well, due to the lack of demand for metals for industrial production. The decline in mining will need more research, since there was large scale manufacturing of consumer goods like automobiles during this decade. Furthermore, discussing twentieth century banking in Silver City could be part of the section on the 1920s. For example, in 1924, Silver City National Bank, American National Bank, Bank of Tyrone and the People's Savings Bank failed. They were consolidated through recapitalization and reopened as American National Bank. Perhaps, the burning down of Robert Black's Mill and Lumber Co. and the death of his wife was an analogy for this decade.[531]

Similarly, the impact of the Great Depression on Grant County businesses will need to be assessed. There are examples of economic difficulties during this time period. The Cottage Sanatorium went out of business in 1930 for two reasons: The Great Depression resulted in less people traveling to the reason to be treated for Tuberculosis and new treatments were developed that did not require people to go to dry air. George Pennington bought the sanatorium in 1931. He tried to make it profitable. He maintained the post office and grocery store that was located on the property, and he rented his medical equipment to doctors. However, he kept losing money and was forced to sell his medical equipment and even some of the property's buildings. Economic difficulties were seen in the mining district. Celia Reyes of Fiero noted in an interview that her father was laid off from the mines, and they had one last pay check left. The only problem was that they did not have enough money to drive into Silver City to shop at the Safeway. Instead, they relied on the nearby general store in Hanover owned by Tom McCoy. The locals called it "La Tienda de Tom" and the business would sell on credit to customers. She noted that her father relied too much on credit and eventually was cut off. The family instead, bought food from local farmers in the Mimbres Valley. They were able to save money by buying direct from the producers (i.e.

---

531 Black's Mill and Lumber Co. was located on Market Street. Palace Hotel changed name to Clark Hotel in 1920s.

the farmers). This topic still begs at least one question: Did those farmers extend credit to families living in the mining district? Since men were unemployed, there was a mining boom in Pinos Altos for placer gold in the 1930s. How significant was the gold mining boom of the 1930? It is known that unemployed men during the Great Depression started placer mining throughout many areas of the American West. Indeed, some individuals were able to sell their stocks before the stock market crash of October 1929, helping to explain why there was a country club at Bear Mountain Lodge during this time.[532]

Some of the latest research for this paper has found that Silver City began promoting itself as a tourist destination starting in the 1930s. It was during this time the WPA-funded Federal Writers Project created a series of guidebooks, for each of the states. Also, the continued improvement of roads through the Federal Highway Act of 1917 that included the building of Route 66 made city business hopeful that people might drive to Silver City for vacations. Philip's Bookstore, for example, sold "Kneeling Nun Novelties." Most likely, these were small gift-items that played into people's fascination with the myth of the Kneeling Nun that brought some tourists to see the rock formation above the town of Santa Rita. Doing a little research into the stories of the Kneeling Nun would be important to assess whether tourists came to Grant County to see the formation. Of course, it began with Spanish miners at Santa Rita in the early 1800s telling stories of a nun, who fell in love with a Spanish soldier and lost her virginity. She was turned in to stone as a punishment. Anglos started publishing fictive accounts and poems romanticizing the story which became popular and might have play a role in bringing tourist into the region starting in the 1930s. These romanticized versions of the story were published by Harry Burgess in 1899, including his Poem "The Kneeling Nun" and by Lou Curtis Foster who published his works in the early 1900s. The

---

532 *New Mexico Magazine*, March 2002, 25-26, Vertical Files, Folder "Fierro;" Miller Library, WNMU. Bear Mountain Lodge was originally homesteaded in 1910, converted into Rocky Mountain Ranch School (for unruly boys) in 1928, and then made into a country club. The club had a pool, tennis court, and golf field. It became a guest ranch in 1959

growth in automobile tourism increased after World War II when numerous car "courts" were established, like: Pueblo Court (on Silver Heights Rd.), Clark Courts (on Silver Heights Rd), as well as several more on Pope St.: Jennings Camp (12th Street and Pope) and Silver Court (located at 1005 Pope St.) Moreover, surplus army jeeps after WWII gave hunters, fishermen, and campers greater access to the forest, resulting in destruction of land and a movement to improve roads. Two new roads were built. The Copperas Extension was from Highway 35 north to Gila Hot Springs and the North Star Road was built further to the east, connecting Highway 35 with Beaverhead and roads leading to Hot Springs, New Mexico (later called Truth or Consequences). Many supported these roads because they felt it would keep automobiles from driving over forest land in an unorganized way, while others feared that they would encourage more use in the forest and that the North Star Road would divide the wilderness into two halve. Today, the Copperas Extension is named the Clinton Anderson Highway, though evidence was found for this paper that he opposed the road. The question should be asked: Did he oppose the extension? And, if yes: why did he oppose it and why is the road named after him?[533]

The history of entertainment-related businesses should also be expanded. Current secondary sources have a lot of good information on the following modern theatres: Silco Theatre, El Sol Theatre, and the Gila Theatre. The Silco Theatre was the first to be established around 1923 on the site of an earlier theatrical hall called the Airdome. The building was owned by the Freemasons, and they made money renting spaces in the building for the theatre and stores. The theatre was purchased by Lessee Ward in 1931, and by the 1940s there was a small café next to the theatre called the Silco Confectionary. The theatre called El Sol was built in the 1930s and the Gila Theatre was built in 1949. More research is needed into Eddie W. Ward because he would come to own all the theatres in town.

---

533 Vertical files "Kneeling Nun") (Silver City Sun News clipping, Vertical file Silver City- History) "Brief History of the Gila Wilderness," and *Silver City Daily Press*, June 4, 1999, Vertical Files, Folder "Gila National Forest," Miller Library, WNMU.

Ward came to Silver City in the 1890s, was mayor for several terms, and owned the Silco, the Gila, and El Sol. He also owned theatres in Hurley like, Sky Vue Drive Theatre and El Tejo; he also operated the El Cobre Theatre in Santa Rita. Apparently, he and other New Mexico and Colorado theatre owners created Gibralter Enterprises and operated their theatres under that company's incorporation.[534]

More information will be needed for the post-World War II era. The following information has already been collected. Increasing number of students after World War II, using the GI Bill to go to the New Mexico Teacher's College, must have been a boon to local businesses. There were so many new students in the late 1940s, that the college built "The Campus Village" which housed students and their wives in some 20 army surplus barracks. There was a famous murder at the Barker Café that needs to be included in this part of the essay. Charlie Mah (i.e. Yat Lim) was most likely a part owner of the café with several other Chinese. Mah was killed in a fight when he was thrown to the ground at the café. Ultimately, George McNight and Roy L. Mahoney were charged but found not guilty. Other Chinese would own business in this period, like Yee Toy who operated Y. Toy Grocery on Market St. and Hing Lee who owned Hing Lee Grocery. Information has been found on the Bow brothers, but the question is: Did the Bow brothers owned businesses? Another question that needs to be ask is: Did the number of Chinese-owned business begin to decline by the 1950s and 1960s? Other historic businesses of the 1950s include: Parish Stage Lines who provided bus service to El Paso and Jessie's Café. In the 1950s, the first cash and carry stores were opened, where customers selected you goods and checked them at the register. More research is needed with the Empire Zinc Mine Strike of 1950-1952 and how union activist Clinton Jenks worked with Hisapnic mine workers in Hanover, Fierro and Santa Rita to end the dual wage system that had paid Hispanic workers less than Anglo workers who were doing the same job. This is

---

534   *Silver City Sun New* June 30, 2008 and Aug. 18, 2007 in Vertical Files "Silver City – History"; 3) Shadel's Bakers that was located in the Schutz-Brent Building. The Gila Theatre was built by Tatsch Construction

important because evidence has been found that businesses in near Hurley allowed families participating in strikes to pay their bills later. Ideally, this paper would end in the 1960s with the continued growth in nation-wide chain stores and how that impacted small, family owned businesses. Phillip Parotti wrote that K-Mart opened up in Silver City in 1974, and small stores closed.[535]

SCOTT FRITZ, PH.D. in US History and now Associate Professor of History at Western New Mexico University, specializing in the history of the American Southwest. He teaches US History, New Mexico, Native American and History of the American Southwest. Current research on small businesses of New Mexico from ca. 1900 – 1967.

---

535 *Desert Exposure*, article The Campus Village May 2008 vertical files Silver City – history). (Silver city daily press, 12/6/03 Mah had left china as a youth, Charlie Mah was born in China and emigrated to the United States. Did Chinese like Mah still benefit from mutual aid societies called "tongs" in the mid twenti-eth century?) (Phillip Parotti, Desert Exposure May 2012, Vertical Files "Silver City-History"); and Laura Krol, *Images of America: Deming*, (Charleston: Arcadia Publishing, 2012), 60.

CHAPTER 8:

Popular Culture: Silver City and the Enduring Legend of Billy the Kid

James L. Smith

INTRODUCTION

The Undocumented Life of Billy the Kid

When Pat Garrett killed Billy the Kid on a hot July night in 1881, he not only ended the short and violent life of a notorious outlaw, but he also helped spark one of history's most enduring legends. Today, the Kid's place as an American legend has been solidified by the countless number of items in his media catalog: motion pictures, songs, television shows, plays, comic books, short stories, documentaries, video games, orchestral works, and more than one thousand books (both fiction and nonfiction). Abraham Lincoln may be the most written-about person in United States history, but Billy the Kid is the topic of more media than any other character from the American West.[536]

As a subject for academic historians, the Kid's biography is a limited topic for research. He died young (age twenty-one, possibly only nineteen), and he left little documentary evidence of his life. We know nothing about his father and little about his mother. We don't know the date of his birth (possibly 1859), the age of his brother (most likely younger), the

---

536 Stephen Tatum, *Inventing Billy the Kid*, pp. 3-9. Richard W. Etulain, *Billy the Kid: A Reader's Guide*, Loc. 57, Loc. 4962 (Kindle version).

307

name given to him at birth (probably Henry McCarty), or the source of his name at the time of his death (William H. Bonney). As Frederick Nolan wrote in *The West of Billy the Kid*, "It is almost as if he decided at birth to leave behind as little documentary trace as he could of his entry into, and passage through, the world."[537]

We know a fair amount about the Lincoln County War of 1878, a range war in which he fought. However, he was not a major player in the conflict, and if he had died at any time during the five-month war, he would most likely be little more than a footnote in today's history books.

What made the Kid famous took place during the three years after the war when his exploits as a revenge-seeking bandit from the losing side placed him in the headlines of New Mexico's newspapers. The character of "Billy the Kid," as the newspapers called him, was a creation of the media, the local news reporters, and national fiction writers looking to sell a good story. The sobriquet was a winner for the media, a name that allowed writers to romanticize and sensationalize the exploits of a young outlaw.

Whether he deserved all the attention is open to debate. In the minds of some, he represented the lawlessness and violence of a vanishing way of life. For others, stories about the Kid were simply a means of deflecting attention away from the rampant corruption in New Mexico's territorial government.

In either case, his three years as a postwar outlaw are difficult for historians to document. We are left with a few letters he wrote to the governor of territorial New Mexico, the transcribed testimony he gave to a grand jury, a handful of interviews he conducted with reporters, and sketchy court records of his trial for murder.

In the final analysis, most of what we know about Billy the Kid comes from interviews with people who knew him personally. With a few notable exceptions—such as Pat Garrett himself—those who knew the Kid did not tell their stories for the record until the mid-1920s or later, decades after the Kid had died. Historians can't help but be skeptical about the accuracy of memories reaching more than forty-five years into the past.

---

537   Frederick Nolan, *The West of Billy the Kid*, p. 3.

So where does this leave us? As a subject for serious historical research, Billy the Kid, as one might say, is all foam and no beer. Academic historians might even ask themselves whether the Kid is worth the effort. How much time, after all, does someone want to spend researching a teenage outlaw from more than 140 years ago who left so little reliable documentation of his life?

From another perspective, however, the Kid is endlessly fascinating and worthy of much research. He was an uncommon outlaw who left a durable legend that provides remarkable insight into changes in American culture. Rather than focusing on the details of the Kid's biography, historians can be well served by researching and writing about how people have told the Kid's story and what those stories say about the historical context in which they were created. How, for example, do stories about the Kid from the 1920s, the 1960s, or the 1980s differ according to the time in which they were told? What, if anything, do the ever-changing stories about Billy the Kid tell us about how US history has changed over the decades?

As a subject of both entertainment and art, the Kid is a chameleon, a character who can be anything a creative mind desires. For someone telling a fictional tale—or even a historian attempting to get the story right—the Kid's life can be painted in a variety of colors. He can be portrayed as the devil's meat, a satanic outlaw who delivered much

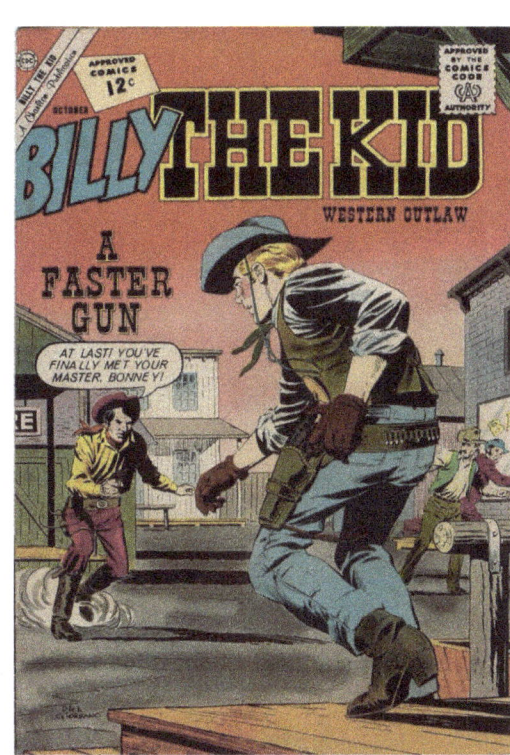

Source: kickstarter.com

309

grief into the world. He can be the subject of a story about a good boy gone bad or a rebellious young man at odds with society. He can be a revolutionary, a freedom fighter on the side of the downtrodden and oppressed. He can be used to tell the story of what happens to someone who is a victim of false accusations or someone who is a victim of the media, a celebrity whose fame got him killed. He can also be a tragic figure, a boy who lost his mother and never had a chance to make it in this world. The possibilities for storytelling and mythmaking are endless.

In stories about Billy the Kid, we can see who we once were and who we are today. The people of the 1890s, for example, were open to accepting different legends and myths than the people of the 1930s, the 1960s, and the 2020s. The Kid's legend is dynamic, ever changing, and often contentious, and what we think about the Kid reveals more about who we are at different times in history than it reveals about the Kid himself. As stated in the Talmud, "We do not see things as they are, we see them as we are.

PHASE ONE OF THE KID'S LEGEND (1881-1925)
"A Low-Down Vulgar Cutthroat"

The Kid's legend began months before he died on July 14, 1881. Newspapers had been describing him as the leader of a dangerous gang of outlaws terrorizing the New Mexico Territory, an outlaw who represented lawlessness and violence, a symbol of everything wrong with the American West. As the *Grant County Herald* stated two weeks after his death, "He was a low-down vulgar cutthroat with probably not one redeeming quality."[538]

His death was described in newspapers nationwide as an event to be greeted with relief and celebration. After killing the Kid, Pat Garrett gained overnight fame, becoming a national hero, a representative of law and order who had freed the world from a notorious killer. Newspapers praised Garrett for what he had done, and the people of New Mexico's Grant County made a cane out of wood from the Kid's old home in Silver

---

538   Stephen Tatum, *Inventing Billy the Kid*, p. 38. Peter Hertzog, *Little Known Facts about Billy the Kid*, pp. 20-21. *The New Southwest and the Grant County Herald*, July 23, 1881.

310

City, topping it with a gold ball and an inscription before sending it to Garrett as a gift.[539]

In 1882, Garrett published *The Authentic Life of Billy the* Kid, telling not only the story of the Kid's life (much of it falsified), but also how Garrett arrested and killed the Kid. In portraying the Kid as a charming, although sometimes brutally violent, young man, Garrett's book confirmed many long-lasting myths about the Kid's murderous nature, including the story of him killing a man in Silver City for insulting his mother. This myth and many others from Garrett's book (via the pen of his ghostwriter, Ash Upson) lasted almost nine decades until historians began to debunk them in the 1950s and 1960s.

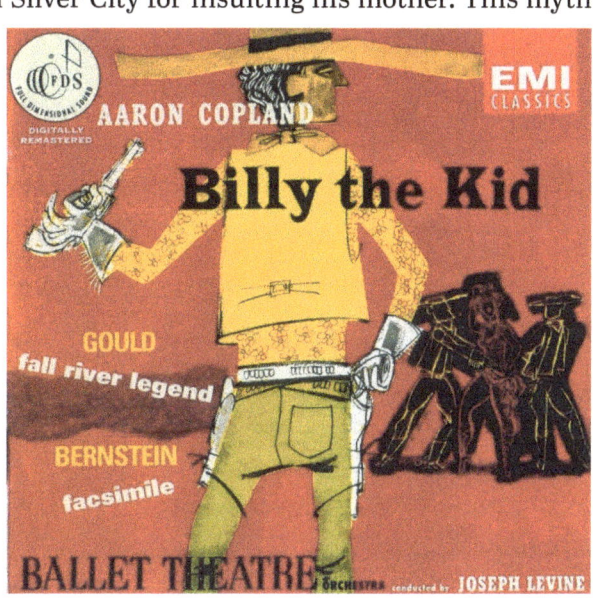

Source: duckduckgo.com

Meanwhile, the dime novels of the late 1800s, which romanticized and sensationalized activities in the American West, used the Kid to tell stories of a boy who was a satanic killer, a boy who dipped his fingers into the blood of his victims, a boy who kicked a man's corpse over a cliff as his family watched in horror. In dime novels, the Kid was a bloodthirsty murderer, a boy who represented the worst of all human beings, violently assaulting his opponents, and killing on a whim. In short, he was a blight on humanity and needed to be destroyed. Pat Garrett, on the other hand, was portrayed as strong and honest, a hero who represented the best of a law abiding

---

539 Frederick Nolan, *The West of Billy the Kid,* p. 291. Leon Metz, *Pat Garrett: The Story of a Western Lawman,* p. 127. *Daily New Mexican,* March 31, 1883.

Price 25 Cents.

BILLY THE KID

A ROMANTIC STORY FOUNDED UPON WALTER WOOD'S AND JOSEPH SANTLEY'S SUCCESSFUL PLAY OF THE SAME NAME.

BY ARDA LACROIX.

Source: duckduckgo.com

nation, the man who saved the nation from the devilish Billy the Kid.[540]

Although stories about the Kid as a scourge on society continued well into the early 1900s, by the 1910s and 1920s, the stories about his wicked deeds began to evaporate. In 1925, Harvey Fergusson, a New Mexico-born journalist and novelist, published an article in *The American Mercury* asking, "Who remembers Billy the Kid?" Fergusson described the Kid as "the key figure of an epoch" who had been "forgotten and overlooked by history," Despite a few dissenting voices, including Fergusson himself who described the Kid as a "quixotic romantic, who cared nothing for money,"[541]it appeared the Kid by the mid-1920s would be remembered as little more than a notorious outlaw, if he was remembered at all.

In the context of the time, the United States in the late 1800s and early 1900s was redefining itself after a period of dramatic transformation brought about by an Industrial Revolution fueled by massive waves of immigration and the creation of big cities. In the midst of dramatic social, cultural, and economic changes, Billy the Kid represented the anarchy and violence of an old world, the "evil" that needed to be purged before the

---

540   Stephen Tatum, *Inventing Billy the Kid,* pp. 45-46.
541   Stephen Tatum, *Inventing Billy the Kid,* p 86.

nation could move forward as a civilized society. It made sense that people wanted to forget the Kid and leave him behind. Good riddance to the Old West and its culture of anarchy and violence. Good riddance, Billy the Kid.

PHASE TWO OF THE KID'S LEGEND (1926-1954)
"Robin Hood of the West"

Everything changed for Billy the Kid's legend when Walter Noble Burns published *The Saga of Billy the Kid* in 1926. Burns, a Chicago journalist and historian of the West, was old enough in the 1920s to remember stories about the Kid, and on a trip to New Mexico, he interviewed people who were old enough to have known the Kid personally. Although digging into memories that were almost fifty years old, Burns heard a different

description of the Kid than what he heard from the media of his youth. Rather than hearing about a black-hearted thief and killer, Burns heard the Kid described as charismatic and good-humored. The people Bums interviewed were generally sympathetic to the Kid.

As a reporter, Burns knew he had a story and returned to Chicago to write *The Saga of Billy the Kid.* In the book, Burns describes the Kid as handsome, generous, and daring, a young man who was a champion of the oppressed, a warrior against a corrupt political machine in the New Mexico Territory, a "Robin Hood of the West."[542]

Source: wp.com

---

542   Stephen Tatum, *Inventing Billy the Kid*, p. 101.

313

In 1926, the newly inaugurated Book of the Month Club featured *The Saga of Billy the Kid* as its first main selection, and it became a bestseller. Burns's book not only transformed the public's image of the Kid, but it also made the Kid famous again, setting off a firestorm of new books and articles about the almost-forgotten outlaw. After the publication of Burns's book, the Kid was generally portrayed as a heroic young man who had the courage to fight corruption and help the downtrodden. He may have been an outlaw, but his fight against villainous bankers and landowners was justified.

In 1930, Hollywood released *Billy the Kid,* its first feature-length movie about the Kid. With a college football star named Johnny Mack Brown in the starring role, the movie romanticized the Kid's fight for the oppressed, and when a preview audience was shown the movie before its release, audience members expressed dismay that the Kid died at the end. The producers, therefore, changed the ending. Instead of killing the Kid, Pat Garrett allows him to escape to Mexico with his girlfriend.[543]

In response to the movie, the New Mexico governor, Richard Dillon, wrote an open letter stating his belief that the Kid had fought for personal liberty.[544] Then, in 1936, Miguel Antonio Otero, governor of the New Mexico Territory from 1897 to 1906, wrote a biography titled *The Real Billy the Kid* portraying the young outlaw in a positive light. According to Otero, who had met the Kid in 1880, the Kid was much adored by New Mexico's Hispanic population. He was considerate of the old, the young, and the poor, and he was loyal to his friends.[545]

In 1938, the Kid's story turned into a piece of orchestral music when the great American composer, Aaron Copland, wrote the score for a ballet titled *Billy the Kid.* In Copland's ballet, the Kid is a good boy who becomes an outlaw after the death of his mother. Copland's music evokes much sorrow and grief when the Kid dies at the end. In mourning the loss of the Kid as a tragic figure, Copland's music rejected

---

543   Johnny Boggs, *Billy the Kid on Film,* lac. 600 (Kindle version).

544   Stephen Tatum, *Inventing Billy the Kid,* p. 107.

545   Richard Etulain. *Billy the Kid: A Reader's Guide,* Loe. 1929 (Kindle version)

the late nineteenth century view of the Kid as a black hearted villain whose death should be celebrated.

The Kid's place in American culture as a heroic figure was also embraced by the Producers.

Releasing Corporation (PRC) when it released fifty-two movies between 1940 and 1946 portraying the Kid as a gunfighter who saves the day fighting bad guys. In late 1943, the PRC announced it wanted to eliminate any "suggestion of gangsterism or outlawism" and changed the Kid's name to "Billy Carson" for the final twenty-three films in the series. Even so, the successful formula of a heroic outlaw fighting for justice remained the same.[546]

The PRC films were followed by numerous comic books published in the 1950s featuring the Kid fighting for widows and orphans. In the *Masked* Raider series, published by Charlton Comics beginning in 1957, the Kid wore a black mask as he fought against bankers and land barons.[547]

Source: media-amazon.com

Source: media-amazon.com

546   *The Billy the Kid (and Billy Carson) Series from the Producers Releasing Corporation (PRC)* bttp-www b westerns com/billykid htm)

547   *Billy the Kid (Charlton Comics)* https://en.wikipedia.org/wiki/Billy_the_Kid_(Charlton_Comics)

All told, the second phase of the Kid's legend—from the mid-1920s to the mid-1950s—contained portrayals of the Kid as a good Samaritan, a well-mannered gentleman who fought for just causes. This image of the Kid can be seen as a product of the times, an era of political corruption and gangsterism in the 1920s, the Great Depression in the 1930s, and World War II in the 1940s. The Kid represented a principled individual fighting against corruption, injustice, and tyranny. He was, in short, a hero for the times. Although he often turned to violence when fighting evil, his personal code aligned with the best interests of the community.

PHASE THREE OF THE KID'S LEGEND (1955-1980)
"Rebel without a Cause"
The third phase of the Kid's legend began in July 1955 when a teleplay written by Gore Vidal was broadcast on the NBC network. With Paul Newman starring as the Kid, Vidal's play told the story of a social outcast who simply wanted to be free and live his own life. As a young man who did not care what anyone thought of him, he became a victim of the media, destroyed by his own fame.

In 1957, Vidal's teleplay became a Hollywood motion picture titled *The Left-Handed Gun.* As an A-list western directed by Arthur Penn, the film starred Paul Newman in reprisal of his role as the Kid. James Dean, the star of *Rebel Without a Cause,* had originally been signed to play the Kid, but died in a car accident before filming began. The casting of James Dean, an icon of rebellious youth in the 1950s, speaks volumes about how the Kid's image had changed and how the legend would be framed through the 1970s.[548]

Vidal's teleplay and the film it inspired set the Kid's legend on a new path. Rather than portraying the Kid as a villainous outlaw or heroic champion of the oppressed, books and movies began portraying the Kid as a symbol of rebellious youth, a free soul fighting against conformity and social convention. One can easily add Billy the Kid to the pantheon

---

548   Johnny Boggs, *Billy the Kid on Film,* lac. 3026 (Kindle version). David Quinlan, *Quinlan's Illustrated Guide to Film Directors,* pp. 229-230.

of legendary rebellious characters of the time, both fictional
and real, that included Holden
Caulfield, Dean Moriarty, and
Abbie Hoffman.

During this third phase, the
Kid also became the subject of
serious artists who used him
to express ideas about what
they may have perceived as the
moral bankruptcy of the times.
In 1970, for example, the Sri
Lankan-born poet and novelist Michael Ondaatje published
The Collected Works of Billy Kid.
In a work of literary fiction,
Ondaatje uses a series of short
writings to reimagine the Kid as
a poet who is also an outlaw and

Source: media-amazon.com

killer. In Ondaatje's book, the Kid is a free spirit who will not be controlled
by the rules of society, a sexually liberated alcoholic who hallucinates
about Jesus.

This book was followed in the early 1970s by several motion pictures
embracing the Kid's credentials as a counterculture icon. In *Chisum,* a
film released in 1970, the character of John Chisum, a cattleman fighting
on the same side as the Kid, debates the Kid about the merits of vigilante justice. Chisum, played by John Wayne, argues for justice within
the law while the Kid argues for achieving justice outside the system. The
by-any-means-necessary philosophy expressed by the movie's version of
the Kid coincided with the philosophy of many social and political activists of the time. The film, of course, gives John Wayne's character the final
word, and the Kid is shown to be a dangerous anachronism in his desire
to live outside the law.

In *Dirty Little Billy,* released in 1973, the Kid is shown as a moronic punk living in squalid conditions. The Kid is a social outcast, but he is also a lazy and cowardly young man living in a world of filth and corruption. This humorless film not only destroys romanticized myths about Billy the Kid, but it also destroys the romanticized myth of the Old West as developed through several decades of Hollywood motion pictures.

Another film released in 1973, *Pat Garrett and Billy the Kid,* was directed by Sam Peckinpah. The film advances the myth that Pat Garrett and the Kid were friends who became estranged after Garrett sold out to powerful business interests. The Kid, as played by Kris Kristofferson, is a long-haired rebel fighting against the Santa Fe Ring, a collection of powerful attorneys, land speculators, and politicians controlling the New Mexico Territory. Not only is the Kid at war with corruption, but he is also disturbed about what is happening to the West, the West that had once allowed people to roam free.

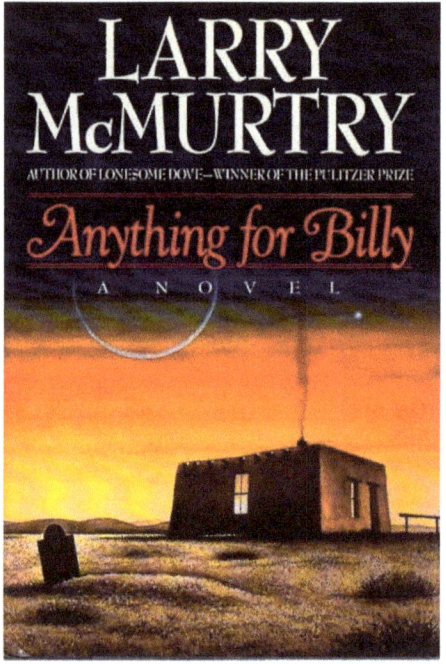

Source: media-amazon.com

All told, the third phase of the Kid's legend, from the mid-1950s to the late 1970s was dominated by stories showing the Kid as a rebel, a social outcast and nonconformist. At odds with conformity and the power of the media, the Kid is an idealist who perceives the world as corrupt and phony. This portrayal of the Kid can be explained in the context of the mass media that emerged in the 1950s and 1960s, a time also characterized by a general distrust of the system that was exacerbated by the Vietnam War and Watergate. It was an era of rebellion and protest

318

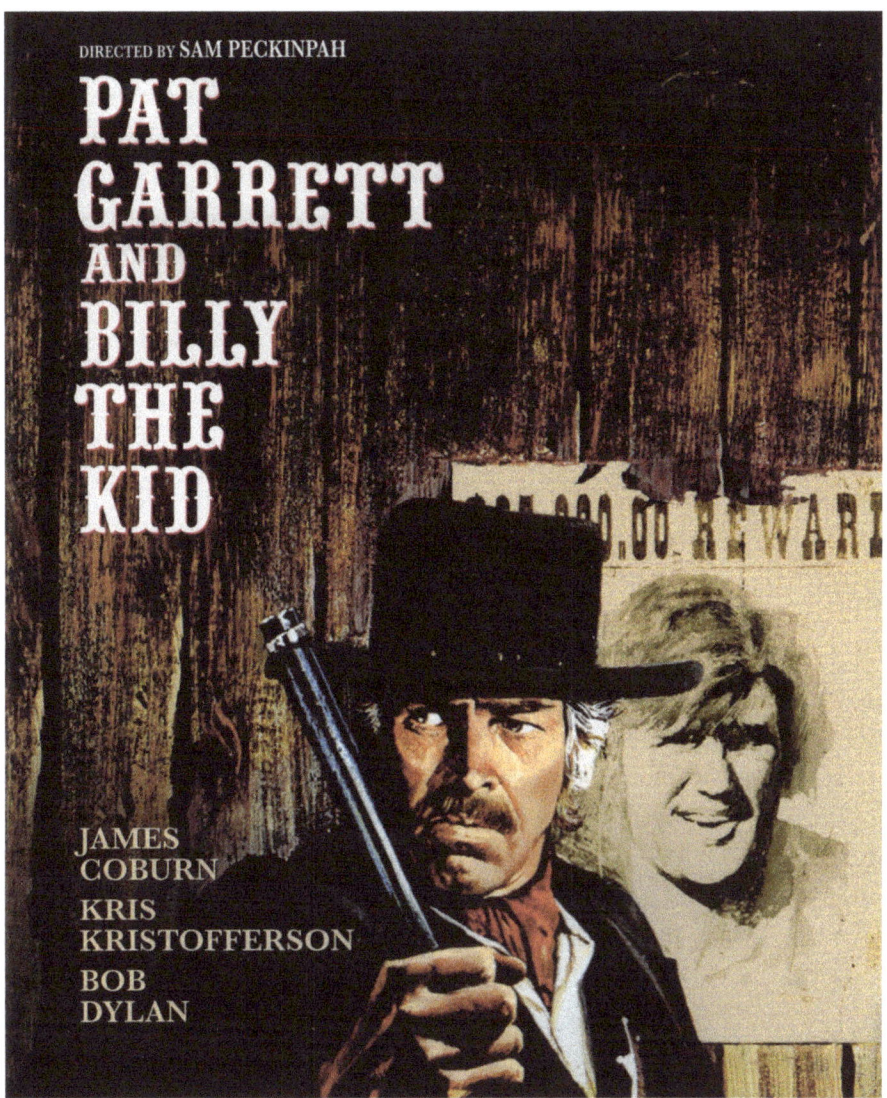

Source: media-amazon.com

as seen in the civil rights movement, the protest against the Vietnam War and the emerging counterculture. As an alienated radical individualist living at odds with society, Billy the Kid provided entertainers and artists with a legend that fit the times.

PHASE FOUR OF THE KID'S LEGEND (1981 TO THE PRESENT)
"The More Versions There Are, the Truer It Is"

The year 1981 marked the centennial of the Kid's death, as well as a turning point for those telling the Kid's story. The Kid's legend in previous eras can be described in terms of a general theme running through a time period: the Kid as a villainous outlaw (the 1880s), the Kid as a champion of the oppressed (the 1930s), the Kid as an iconic rebel (the 1960s). From the early 1980s to the present, however, identifying a general theme is difficult, if not impossible. The Kid's legend spreads across a wide spectrum of creative possibilities. When Phil Lesh, bassist of the Grateful Dead, was asked which version of a song performed by the Dead, a song never played the same way twice, was the "true" version, Lesh replied, "Like fairy tales or folk songs, all versions are true. The more versions there are, the truer it is." During the fourth phase of the Kid's legend, the tale is never told the same way twice and all versions are true—not as history, but as legends.

In recent years, the United States has entered a period of cultural and political division that might loosely be labeled "postmodernism." The absence of a single philosophy to coalesce the nation, a unifying theme for our time, has seemingly created a society marked by the phenomenon that "anything goes." People can say or believe anything, no matter how outrageous or conspiratorial. American culture is, therefore, characterized in part by the creation of all types of art and entertainment, and every issue, political or cultural, no matter how seemingly insignificant, can spark disagreements and arguments. Stories about Billy the Kid are only one example of this postmodernist chaos.

In 1988, the motion picture *Young Guns* did not portray the Kid as either a black-hearted villain, a champion of the oppressed, or a rebellious youth. Instead, the movie shows the Kid as an insolent young man making arbitrary decisions, unwilling to listen to more reasonable people.

Through his irrational behavior, he keeps escalating events during the Lincoln War. As portrayed in the movie, the Kid is a young man with no clear moral compass and few admirable traits. He serves as the hero of the story only because the people he is shooting are clearly corrupt.

Due to the success of *Young Guns,* Hollywood released *Young Guns II* in 1990. The sequel portrays the Kid in the same light as the first movie, but also advances the myth that Pat Garrett did not kill the Kid in 1881. According to myth, the Kid lived a long life and did not die until 1950 when he was living as Brushy Bill Roberts in Hico, Texas. In our postmodernist era, a seemingly factual statement such as "Pat Garrett killed Billy the Kid" has become a topic for debate, and Hollywood showed its willingness in *Young Guns II* to thrust itself into the debate.

With no single, unifying theme running through stories about Billy the Kid, the current era of the Kid's legend contains seemingly unlimited ways to tell his story in film. A French documentary released in 2007 titled *Requiem for Billy the Kid* compares the Kid favorably to Arthur Rimbaud, a French poet of the nineteenth century who celebrated the bohemian lifestyle, attacking social snobbery and conventional religious beliefs. In 2012, a PBS documentary explores the Kid's heroic status in the American Hispanic community. In 2019, a film titled *The Kid,* starring Dane DeHaan as the Kid and Ethan Hawke as Pat Garrett, portrays the Kid as a generally likable and self-aware young man who did not want to hurt people. He is, however, a survivor living at a time when he has to kill to stay alive, and his willingness to use violence is nothing compared to other characters in the film.

The Kid also made an appearance in two books by Pulitzer Prize-winning novelists. In N. Scott Momaday's *The Ancient Child,* published in 1989, the Kid materializes in the dreams of a Native American medicine women as a courageous, articulate, and good-humored young man. In Larry McMurtry's *Anything for Billy,* released in 2001, the Kid is portrayed as an ugly, filthy, murderous moron with no conscience. He kills people without remorse so he can maintain his villainous reputation in dime novels.

Several other novels also used the Kid to create fictional ways of interpreting his life. In *Billy the Kid: The Legend of El Chivato,* the author Elizabeth Fackler provides a romanticized view of the Kid that focuses on the women in his life. Meanwhile, Gale Cooper's *Joy of the Birds* provides a psychological study of the Kid in which he confronts his guilt over the life he has led. In John Vernon's *Lucky Billy,* the Kid is shown to be a profane and alcoholic product of a lawless society. Most recently, in a novel published in 2021 titled *The Gospel According to Billy the Kid,* Dennis McCarthy explores the possibility of a middle-aged Billy the Kid given a second chance to learn from the mistakes he had made as a young man.

As a subject for both entertainment and serious art, the Kid's legend has been ubiquitous in media produced over the last forty years, and a complete examination of all this media is beyond the scope of this chapter. However, it should be emphasized that media about the Kid lacks a common theme in how the Kid is portrayed. Indeed, the legend seems to change with each new book or film featuring the Kid as its subject. In our postmodernist era, anything goes, and the divisions are deep, a phenomenon found not only in American politics and culture, but all elements of American society—the legend of Billy the Kid included.

BILLY THE KID IN SILVER CITY
The Origin Story of an American Legend and *a* New Mexican Town

Over the last 140 years, the Kid's legend has taken many forms and adopted a variety of themes. As with any legend, the subject of the legend has an origin story, and any attempt to tell the Kid's origin story will necessarily include information about time he spent in Silver City, New Mexico. Billy the Kid and Silver City are linked together forever, and it is impossible to tell the story of one without the other. The Kid spent two and a half years in Silver City (1873-1875), and the time he spent in the town not only stretches the imagination of creative minds wanting to write a novel or make a film, but also the skills of historians with limited documentation hoping to create an accurate narrative of the Kid's life.

Even so, the Kid's time in Silver City raises two significant questions. First, how much can we know with certainty about Billy the Kid himself during the time he lived in the town? Second, to what extent can we accurately create a description of the town itself during the time the Kid lived there?

In answering the first question, we must confront the problem that we actually know very little about the Kid during the time he lived in Silver

City. Beyond a land deed marking the location of his family's home, a list of children attending school, a newspaper story describing his mother's death, and another newspaper story describing his escape from jail, we have little documentation about his life in Silver City.

Everything else we know about the Kid's time in Silver City comes from interviews with those who knew him, and the memories of those who were interviewed are not necessarily credible. In most cases, for example, they were interviewed forty-five or more years after he died, and Henry McCarty, as he was known at the time, would most likely have been forgotten by those who knew him in Silver City had he not later become famous.

What those being interviewed knew about the famous "Billy the Kid" was likely derived from newspapers or dime novels, and their memories of young Henry McCarty were possibly clouded by what they were getting from the media. If, for example, they were interviewed in the 1890s, a decade after he died, they were being asked to share their memories about a person who was viewed almost universally as a notorious outlaw, someone who was often described as the incarnation of evil. On the other hand, if they were interviewed in the 1930s, they were sharing their memories of a person who had become a heroic champion of the downtrodden.

Even so, we can be relatively certain about a few facts from the Kid's time in Silver City. He moved to Silver City in the spring of 1873 with his mother, stepfather, and brother when he was about twelve years old. His family lived on the corner of Broadway and Main, which is now known as the "Big Ditch." He and his brother, Joseph, attended school in Silver City. His mother died of what the local newspaper called "an affection of the lungs" (most likely tuberculosis) on September 16, 1874. One year later, on September 25, 1875, fourteen-year-old Henry escaped from the Silver City jail after being arrested for being an accomplice in the theft of some goods from a Chinese laundry. Within the time frame of those known events, historians, artists, and entertainers must fill in the blanks to construct a story about the Kid's time in Silver City.

A few recurring motifs about the Kid's time in Silver City have been debunked by historians. Henry McCarty, for example, never beheaded a

323

neighbor's kitten with a knife. He never killed a Chinese immigrant living in Silver City. He was also never arrested for parading down Main Street in women's clothing. The biggest myth, a myth that just won't go away, has the Kid killing a man in Silver City for insulting his mother.

According to those who knew Henry McCarty in Silver City, he was a relatively well-behaved boy raised by a spirited and devoted mother. As his teacher said, "He was no more of a problem than any other boy growing up in a mining camp."[549] He held many jobs including working at a butcher shop, a blacksmith shop, and a hotel waiting tables and washing dishes. He enjoyed music, reading, marbles, pirates, and running races up Market Street. He performed in musical theater and helped his teacher with errands around the schoolhouse.

On his more mischievous side, he enlisted a younger boy to help burglarize a Silver City business, a plan that was never carried out. He also stole a keg of butter from a rancher's wagon, and during a fight with the Silver City sheriff's son, he pushed a boy's face into a stream of water running down Main Street. Most famously, he helped an older boy known as Sombrero Jack hide some stolen goods from a Chinese laundry. A local newspaper reported that Henry was "simply a tool of 'Sombrero Jack' who done the stealing whilst Henry done the hiding."[550] Henry was arrested for the crime, an arrest that led to him crawling up a chimney in the Silver City jail and escaping to Arizona where he learned to survive as a horse thief and cattle rustler.

For biographers and mythmakers, these tales provide information to construct a narrative of Billy the Kid's life and the origin story for an American legend. For Silver City historians, however, these tales also provide a portal into understanding a town at a fascinating time in its history. What began as a mining camp in 1870 would blossom into a town "built to last" in the late 1870s and 1880s, a town that, unlike many other mining camps of the time, would survive and thrive into the twenty-first

---

549   Jerry Weddle, *Antrim is My Stepfather's Name: The Boyhood of Billy the Kid*, p.19.

550   *Grant County Herald*, September 26, 1875.

century.

When the Kid left Silver City, the town was populated by about 1,000 people (two-thirds Hispanic) sitting on the cusp of a surge in population, a territorial charter, and the construction of many new buildings. Other than the buildings that today hold the Sierra House at 116 S. Bullard Street and Millie's Assisted Living at 600 N. Hudson Street, little remains of the town as the Kid knew it.[551] Main Street, where the Kid lived, is now the Big Ditch, and the home where he lived is long gone, the ground washed out from under it during a flood in 1895.

Although the buildings might be gone, some of what the Kid knew in Silver City remains. He was a witness to the establishment of public education in Silver City, and he was probably still in town when work began on the St. Vincent de Paul Catholic Church.[552] However, many questions about Silver City in its early years can help construct a more complete understanding of the town Henry McCarty knew.

We might, for example, create an architectural map of Main Street from the period 1873-1875. We might also ask ourselves questions about the town's society and culture. How, for instance, did the town survive in such an isolated area of the United States? How did people obtain supplies and how reliable was the supply chain? What did people wear? What did they eat and drink? What did they do for entertainment? What did the town smell like? What did it sound like? Was a doctor available to care not only for the Kid's mother when she was suffering from tuberculosis but also provide medical care for other residents of the town?

In economic terms, we might ask ourselves questions about the profitability of the town. How well did the town survive the so-called Crime of '73 when the US government demonetized silver? To what extent, if any, did the government's "crime" cause economic hardship in Silver City? How was Silver City different from other mining camps, and why did Silver

---

551   Susan Berry and Sharman Apt Russell, *Built to Last: An Architectural History of Silver City, New Mexico*, p. 85

552   Ibid.

City survive when so many other mining towns failed? To what extent, if any, was it a "progressive" town with an eye on permanency, a town that would not only survive but also thrive?

In social, cultural, and political terms, we might ask ourselves about the relationship between Hispanics and non-Hispanics. To what extent, if any, did Silver City show signs of the social segregation that would characterize the town in later years? What role, if any, did Hispanics play as leaders in politics and business?

As for the Kid himself, many questions remain about his time in Silver City. Where, for example, was the exact location of his mother's burial in 1874, and does the current location of her headstone accurately mark where her remains are located? Where was the exact location of the Kid's home on the corner of Broadway and Main, and what happened to the jail that he escaped from in 1875? Did the Kid, who was fluent in Spanish, learn to speak the language while he was in Silver City, and is Silver City the place where he developed his seemingly sympathetic relationship with the Hispanic culture?

In the end, Billy the Kid presents an ever-changing legend that reveals much about American society and culture, and due to the chameleon-like nature of the Kid's legend, his life will remain fertile ground for storytellers, artists, and mythmakers for years to come. In the process of shining a spotlight on the Kid's life, those who tell his story will also be shining a spotlight on Silver City. Billy the Kid and Silver City are forever linked to each other, and an attempt to know more about the town during the time the Kid lived in it can help us form a complete story of a unique community that has survived for over 150 years. Like the Kid's legend itself, Silver City should survive long after everyone reading this paper has passed away.

ADDENDUM

A Sample of the Variety of Media about Billy the Kid

Phase One (1880-1925)
"A Low-Down Vulgar Cutthroat"

1. *The Authentic Life of Billy the Kid* - **biography/memoir by Pat Garrett and Ash Upson (1882)** Published only a few months after the Kid's death. Portrays the Kid as a charming but short-tempered and violent outlaw.

2. **Dime novels of the late 1800s** Sensationalized adventure stories that portray the Kid as evil, anarchist, and foreign; an outlaw who represents everything threatening the American way of life.

3. *Billy the* **Kid - staged melodrama by Walter Wood (1903)** A play that toured the nation for twelve years. Portrays the Kid as a good boy gone bad.

4. **"The Caballero's Way" - short story by 0. Henry (1904)** Uses Billy the Kid as a model for an outlaw named Cisco Kid who kills for fun.

5. *The Death of Billy the Kid - memoir* **by John Poe (1919)** A first-hand account of the Kid's death written by one of Pat Garrett's deputies. Published in London because it could not find a publisher in the United States.

6. **"Who Remembers Billy the Kid?" - article by Harvey Fergusson published in** *The American Mercury* **(1925)** Describes the Kid as "the key figure of an epoch" who had been "forgotten and overlooked by history."

Phase Two (1926-1954)
"Robin Hood of the West"

1. *The Saga of Billy the Kid* - **biography by Walter Noble Burns (1926)** Portrays the Kid as a champion of the oppressed who was fighting a corrupt political machine. Views the Kid as the personification of a type of individualism that had become extinct by the 1920s.

2. *Billy the Kid* - **film directed by King Vidor, starring Johnny Mack Brown as the Kid and Wallace Beery as Pat Garrett (1930)** Portrays the Kid as a warrior against villainous bankers and landowners.

3. *The Real Billy the Kid* - **biography by Miguel Antonio Otero (1936)** Portrays the Kid in a positive light as a sympathetic figure, a boy who was courageous, gentlemanly, and fair-minded. Based on interviews with many Hispanics who had known and loved the Kid. Written by a former New Mexico Territorial Governor {1897-1906) who had met the Kid in 1880.

4. *Billy the Kid* - **orchestral score composed by Aaron Copland (1938)** A ballet that portrays the Kid as a tragic figure, a boy who is isolated and alone after the death of his mother. Romanticizes the Kid's death as an event marking the end of the Old West.

5. *Billy the Kid* – **motion picture directed by David Miller, starring Robert Taylor as the Kid (1941)** Portrays the Kid as an individual fighting corruption at a time when people needed to pull together. The Kid's death brings an end to the individualism of the Old West.

6. **Fifty-Two Motion Pictures from the Producers Releasing Corporation (1940-1946)** Portrays the Kid as a peacemaker standing up for powerless people against evil bankers and landholders.

7. *The Outlaw* – **motion picture directed by Howard Hughes, starring Jack Buetel as the Kid and Jane Russell as Rio (1943)** Portrays the Kid as a troublemaking hero feuding with Doc Holliday over a horse and a woman named Rio.

8. **Billy the Kid Comic Books - published in the US, Great Britain, France, and Italy (1950s)** Portrays the Kid as a hero fighting for widows, orphans, and the American way. Several editions portray the Kid wearing a mask (á la the Lone Ranger).

Phase Three (1955-1980)
"Rebel without a Cause"

1. *The Death of Billy the Kid* - **teleplay by Gore Vidal, starring Paul Newman as the Kid (1955)** Portrays the Kid as a social outcast and victim of the media.

2. *The Tragic Days of Billy the Kid* - **biography by Frazier Hunt (1956)** Portrays the Kid as a romantic idealist, a charming young man who only wants to be free and left alone.

3. *The Left-Handed Gun* - **film directed by Arthur Penn, starring Paul Newman as the Kid (1957)** Portrays the Kid as an individualist in conflict with the laws of society, unable to live up to how he is portrayed in the media.

4. *The Collected Works of Billy the Kid* - **literary fiction by Michael Ondaatje (1970)** A series of poems and short writings that portray the Kid as a sensitive soul who is also a thief and killer.

5. *Chisum* - **motion picture starring John Wayne as John Chisum and Geoffrey Deuel as the Kid (1970)** Places the Kid, a representative of vigilante justice, in conflict with John Chisum, a representative of justice achieved within the law.

6. *Dirty Little Billy* - **motion picture starring Michael J. Pollard as the Kid (1973** Portrays the Kid as a cowardly punk who lives in a world of filth and corruption.

7. *Pat Garrett and Billy the Kid* - **motion picture directed by Sam Peckinpah, starring Kris Kristofferson as the Kid and James Coburn as Pat Garrett (1973)** Portrays the Kid as a rebel fighting a corrupt system that is trying to take away his freedom. Portrays Pat Garrett as the Kid's friend, a man who sells out to the system and kills the Kid.

Phase Four (1981 to the Present)
"The More Versions There Are, the Truer It Is"

1. *Young Guns* - **motion picture directed by Christopher Cain, starring Emilio Estevez as the Kid (1987)** Portrays the Kid as an unreasonable, ill-mannered, and unlikable young man who is the hero of the story only because he is killing bad people.

2. *Billy the Kid: A Short and Violent Life* - **biography/history by Robert Utley (1989)** A well-documented book written by the chief historian of the National Park Service. Portrays the Kid as a jovial, friendly, and often cheerful young man who was also a criminal, an outlaw who was a product of his time and place.

3. *The Ancient Child* - **novel by N. Scott Momaday (1989)** Portrays the Kid in a medicine woman's dream as handsome, daring, articulate, and good-humored. Written by a Kiowa author who won the Pulitzer Prize for Fiction in 1969.

4. *Young Guns II* - **film directed by Geoff Murphy, starring Emilio Estevez as the Kid (1990)** Perpetuates the myth that Pat Garrett did not kill the Kid, letting him escape to Mexico.

5. **"Sallie Chisum Remembers Billy the Kid" - music for orchestra and soprano composed by Andre Previn (1995)** Describes the Kid through the eyes of a woman who loved him.

6. *Billy the Kid: The Legend of El Chivato* - **novel by Elizabeth Fackler (1995)** Portrays the Kid as a young hero trying to survive in a treacherous and violent society. Focuses on the women in the Kid's life, including Susan McSweenn, Sallie Chisum, and Paulita Maxwell.

7. *The West of Billy the Kid* - **biography/history by Frederick Nolan (1999)** A well-documented book that portrays the Kid as a young man whose violence was understandable in the context of the violent world in which he lived.

8. *Anything for Billy* - **novel by Larry McMurtry {2001)** Portrays the Kid as an illiterate, ugly, filthy, murderous half-wit who kills people

without remorse. Written by the Pulitzer Prize-winning author of *Lonesome Dove.*

9. *Requiem for Billy the Kid* - **documentary French film directed by Anne Feinsilber and narrated by Kris Kristofferson (2007)** Portrays the Kid as a sympathetic young rebel, comparing him favorably to Arthur Rimbaud, a nineteenth century French poet.

10. *Joy of the Birds* - **novel by Gale Cooper (2008)** Provides a psychological study of the Kid as a freedom fighter confronting his fears and his love for Paulita Maxwell. Written by a Harvard-educated MD specializing in forensic psychiatry and murder case consultations.

11. *Lucky Billy* - **novel by John Vernon (2008)** Portrays the Kid as a wild teenager with no adult supervision. Written by an English professor affiliated with the Center of the American West at the University of Colorado.

12. **"Jesus Christ and Billy the Kid as Archetypes of the Self in American Cinema" -academic paper published by Michelangelo Paganopoulos (June 2010)** Compares depictions of the Kid and Jesus in film, showing how those depictions are expressed in the "collective consciousness" of American culture. Written by a professor at the University of London and published in the *Journal of Religion and Popular Culture.*

13. *The Kid* - **motion picture directed by Vincent D'Onofrio, starring Dane DeHaan as the Kid and Ethan Hawke as Pat Garrett (2019)** Portrays the Kid as a likable and self-aware young man who does not want to hurt people, a young man who kills only so he can stay alive.

14. *The Gospel According to Billy the Kid* - **novel by Dennis McCarthy (2021)** Portrays he Kid as a middle-aged man who did not die in July 1881 and was given a second chance at life.

JAMES L. SMITH, taught U.S. history for thirty years and gained recognition as the New Mexico Teacher of the Year. Jim is the author of an American history textbook titled Ideas That Shape a Nation. Jim has published articles and book reviews in The Journal of Southern History, Phi Delta Kappan, AP Central, Historical Times, and Healthy U. He has been a recipient of the James Madison Fellowship, the Christa McAuliffe Fellowship, and a two-time recipient of the William Robertson Coe Fellowship. The Gilder-Lehrman Institute of American History has recognized Jim as the U.S. History Teacher of the Year.

CHAPTER 9:

People, Places, and Politics: Government's Role in Grant County 1868-1912

By Douglas M. Dinwiddie, PhD

Archaeologists have determined that the region we now call New Mexico has hosted human groups for at least twelve thousand years. The earliest of these, designated the "Clovis Culture" by modern science, were migratory hunter-gatherers whose small numbers left very little impact on the delicate ecology of the Southwest. Anthropologists theorize that these groups were of Asiatic ancestry, and for perhaps as long as twenty thousand years had been gradually drifting southward from Alaska and Canada via a Siberian Land Bridge that had formed during the Ice Ages, permitting intercontinental travel by foot. These people were succeeded by later but similar cultures such as the Folsom people. There is evidence of little change in their way of life for several millennia. (Marquez, 1)

By roughly three thousand years ago, change was finally underway. Probably utilizing knowledge and technology developed far to the south in Mexico and Central America, the scattered groups of people in the Southwest began the first hesitant steps toward cultivation of maize. By about 500 CE, the transformation had fully taken hold, with the cultures now heavily dependent upon agriculture, growing not only maize (corn) but also beans, squash, chile, and even cotton. The changeover from migratory hunting and gathering to farming transformed the way of life to one that required the construction of semi-permanent homes and villages to allow for continuous care of the fields. (Marquez, 2)

The Gila, San Francisco, and Mimbres River Valleys offered sufficient water and fertile soils for the establishment of some of these villages. Archaeologists have determined that by 900 CE a culture they designated as Mogollon-Mimbres had established a number of permanent settlements, mostly but not exclusively clustered in the drainages of those streams. While populations are difficult to determine, it is estimated that there were probably a few thousand individuals scattered in the region, living the lives of farmers. This included the development and reliance upon ceramic pottery for food storage and preparation. Some of that pottery was beautifully made and decorated, particularly in the Mimbres Valley, and its elegant but striking design continues to awe even today.

The lives of these people were upended by climate change and the social transformations that it almost certainly brought with it, beginning near 1200 CE. Scientific evidence indicates that a severe and persistent drought struck in the late 1100s, forcing the abandonment of many villages and the dislocation of the people who lived in them. Scholars continue to debate the details of this social disruption, but it is clear that much of the region was depopulated. It would be several centuries before some of the village sites would be re-occupied by later peoples such as those called the Salado culture, whose differing pottery styles hint at a different ancestry than the Mogollon. (Handbook, 2-3)

By the 1500s CE, peoples belonging to the language group anthropologists call the Athapascans had made their way into the Southwest. These people included the cultures that would become known as the Navajo and the Apache. Practicing a far different lifestyle than the farmers who they found occupying the fertile valleys, these migrating peoples gradually adapted to the harsh conditions of the Southwest. By the time the first Spaniards arrived in the mid sixteenth century, the Athapascans were present in increasing numbers, and had begun raiding the settlements the Spaniards called "pueblos." The stage was set for centuries of conflict as these competing cultures scrambled for control of the region's resources.

Far to the south, fair-skinned Europeans burst upon the scene with the arrival of a conquering force of Spaniards on the coast of Mexico in 1519. Within two years, these aggressive and well-armed newcomers crushed the native Aztec empire and established themselves as the rulers of the central valley of Mexico. The Spaniards' restless search for wealth beckoned them northward, and between 1539 and 1598 they penetrated the Southwest with powerful scouting expeditions that paved the way for the establishment of a permanent colony by the end of the sixteenth century. Claiming a vast region of what is today the western and southwestern United States, the Spaniards referred to it as the northern provinces of New Spain. By 1600, the region drained by the Rio Grande and its tributaries was being called "Nuevo Mexico," although its boundaries were poorly defined.

Settling first in the river valley they would christen "Rio Grande," the Spanish established an uneasy dominance over the agrarian Native peoples they encountered in the valleys. Their attempts at similar conquest over the mobile Athapascan speakers met with little success. Even the names the Spanish and Pueblo peoples used to describe the Athapascans reflected their inability to subdue them: both "Apache" and "Navajo" generally derived from borrowed Puebloan words meaning "enemies." In 1680, the Pueblo peoples, with some help from Athapascans, rose in a unified revolt that drove the Spanish out of New Mexico for over a decade. Returning in force in the 1690s, the Spanish re-established control over the Pueblos, but again were unable to defeat the Apache and Navajo. As the nineteenth century dawned, Spanish maps showed little detail of the region of the Gila, Mimbres, and San Francisco river drainages, often displaying a single word spread over a vast region: "Apaches." (Beck, 39)

In 1821, following a decade long struggle, the new nation of Mexico emerged, overthrowing Spanish rule that had lasted for three hundred years. Meanwhile, the former English colonies along the east coast of North America had broken away from their mother country nearly a half century earlier. This had resulted in the establishment of a new, vigorous nation that was bent on rapid expansion toward the west. During the

1820s, English-speaking fur trappers and traders from the United States began entering the New Mexico region, risking imprisonment in order to make a profit. Some of them found their way to the upper Gila River, including such adventurers as Sylvester and James Ohio Pattie, and a young frontiersman recently arrived from Missouri, Kit Carson.

These hardy mountain men were the first Anglo-Americans to visit the famed Santa Rita del Cobre mines, where Spaniards and then Mexicans had been extracting copper since 1803. Impressed by the opportunity to prosper, the Patties even arranged a short-lived lease on the property. The reports that these newcomers shared about both the copper and other potential mineral deposits were the first to reach Anglo-American ears about the potential for profitable mining in the region. New Mexico in general was gradually inspiring the imagination of entrepreneurs interested in establishing trade between the United States and Mexico as the fateful decade of the 1840s reached its midpoint. (Huggard and Humble, 19)

The Americans Take Over

The year 1846 marked a decisive turning point in New Mexico history. In May of that year, the United States declared war on Mexico, following years of tension between the two nations. The dispute mainly stemmed from the desire of the U.S. to acquire territory that had been claimed by Spain and its successor, Mexico. When Mexico proved unwilling to sell off its northern territory, U.S. President James K. Polk decided to provoke a war that would allow the U.S. to seize it by force. As part of the American strategy to defeat its rival, an American army invaded New Mexico along the Santa Fe Trail during the summer of 1846.

Marching west then south along the famed route of commerce, the Army of the West was commanded by Stephen Watts Kearny. Sweeping aside halfhearted Mexican resistance, the Army occupied Santa Fe without firing a shot in August. Kearny issued a proclamation to the people of New Mexico assuring them that the conquering army would respect their religion and their private property, but also making it clear that they were now the subjects of the government of the United States. Once Kearny was satisfied that northern New Mexico was firmly under American control, he moved southward along the Rio Grande with part of his army, seeking to find a suitable route to turn westward toward California, his next major objective. He soon encountered Kit Carson, who happened to be on his way back to Washington, D.C. carrying important news from California.

Kearny ordered Carson to instead accompany the Army of the West, showing them the best route to California. Reluctantly agreeing, Carson led Kearny's force out of the Rio Grande Valley, and over the mountains later called the Black Range. In October, they arrived at the abandoned mining village of Santa Rita del Cobre. Anxious to secure peaceful passage for his force through Apacheria, Kearny sought an audience with local Apache leader Mangas Coloradas. Through emissaries this was arranged, and near a water source later known as Mangas Springs, the two leaders conferred. On the way from the copper mines to the meeting place, Kearny's force passed through a small valley at the southern end of which was a marshy area known as San Vicente de la Cienega by Spanish-speaking people. Twenty-four years later, the discovery of silver nearby would lead to the development in that valley of a community that would be named Silver City. (Beck, 133)

Among those accompanying Kearny's army was Lieutenant William H. Emory, who was an officer in the Army's Corps of Topographical Engineers. Emory's mission was to "collect data and render his opinions in order to 'give the government some idea of the regions traversed.'" He understood that his work would be relied upon to provide an assessment of the "strategic and economic worth of this vast region." When published a few years later, Emory's work became an important reference work that not only captured a moment in time, but also served as a scientific preview of the potential for economic development of the region, especially in terms of mineral wealth. (Norris)

American military power proved too great for the young Mexican nation to resist, and in February of 1848, with American forces in control of the national capital in Mexico City, representatives for the warring countries signed an agreement ending the hostilities. Subsequently called the

Treaty of Guadalupe-Hidalgo, when it was finally ratified by the U.S. Senate in 1850, it confirmed the cession of about half of the original Mexican nation to the United States, in return for a payment of fifteen million dollars. The two nations also agreed that a joint Boundary Commission would be given the task of determining the final border between the countries.

That commission commenced its work in December of 1850 and immediately made a major mistake in accepting an erroneous map that ended up granting Mexico 6,000 square miles of territory that it should not have had, according to the terms of the Treaty. Importantly, the agriculturally rich Mesilla Valley remained on the Mexican side of the originally drawn boundary. Although this mistake was eventually rectified, it required delicate negotiations, and eventually the purchase of additional territory from Mexico in 1853, in order to provide a suitable route for a transcontinental railroad. Known as the Gadsden Purchase, it resulted in the current recognizable boundary between Mexico and the United States. (Norris, 141)

The area today occupied by Silver City (and most of Grant County) lay north of the originally agreed upon boundary, and, therefore, was not part of the Gadsden Purchase. Recognition of the importance of the mineral deposits such as those at Santa Rita had impressed the American Boundary Commissioners on the need to be certain the boundary safely put those resources inside the American zone.

Following a long and difficult debate, largely driven by the question of whether slavery would be allowed in the newly acquired territory, Congress had passed the highly significant Compromise of 1850 prior to the Boundary Commission embarking on its work. Among the many provisions of that agreement, New Mexico Territory was officially created in 1851. This dashed the hopes of some who hoped that New Mexico would be granted immediate statehood, like California. Those overly optimistic hopes would not become reality for more than six decades.

One of the first priorities for the United States was to establish a permanent military presence in the newly created territory to provide general protection for the citizens and to help enforce American laws.

338

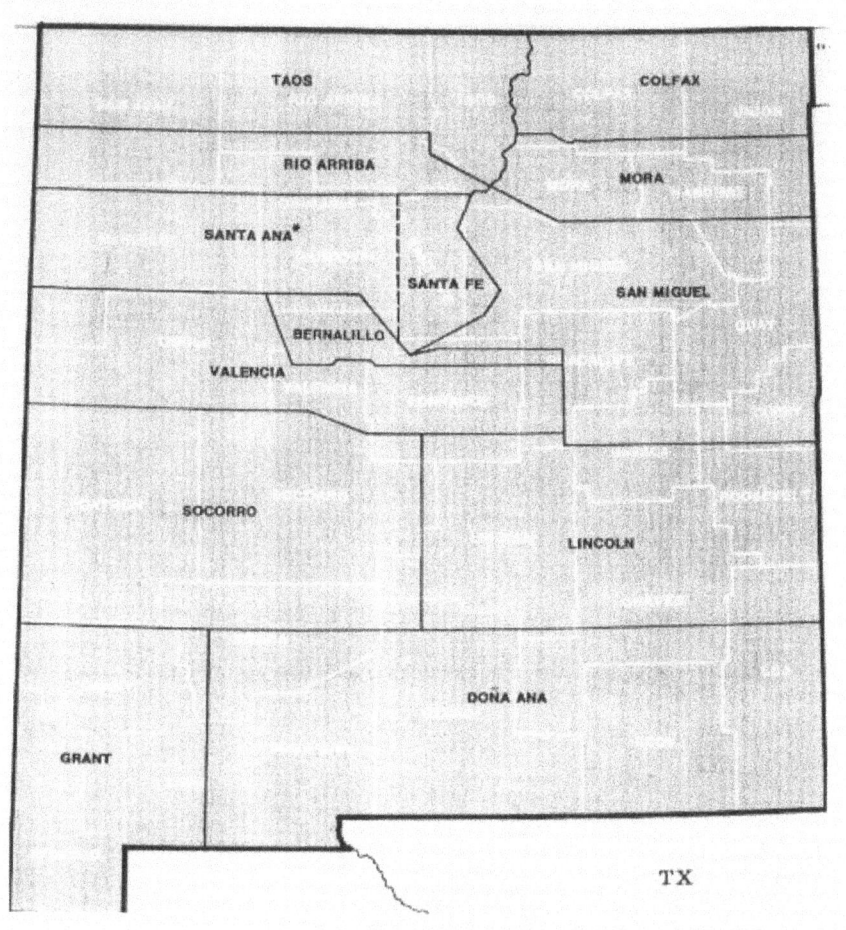

New Mexico Territory's County boundaries of the 1870s. County boundaries shifted frequently in territorial days as population increased, economic factors changed, and political winds blew. Source: Author's collection.

This was considered especially important in regard to Native Indian populations, as well as to discourage any latent Mexican nationalism among the citizenry. The Army began establishing military posts throughout the territory, and the first of them in southwestern New Mexico was placed at the Santa Rita copper mines in 1851. It was

339

designated Fort Webster. Over the next 15 years, several more forts would come and go: Fort Webster No. 2, along the Mimbres River near the village of San Lorenzo; Fort Floyd, a.k.a. Fort McLane, a few miles south of the current town of Hurley; Fort West near the present-day village of Cliff; and finally, Fort Bayard, between the Santa Rita copper mine and the future site of Silver City. (Giese, 15)

Fort Bayard, established in 1866, would become one of the enduring symbols of the presence of the federal government in the region. From 1866 to 1899, it served as an active military post, hosting companies of both cavalry and infantry and providing a base of operations to battle against Apache resistance to white settlement and coercion. From 1899 to 1920, the facility served as the Army's tuberculosis hospital. Following two years of operation by the United States Health Service, the property was operated as Veterans Administration Hospital No. 55. Federal operation ceased there in 1964 when the property was sold to the State of New Mexico, which continues to own it today. For over 154 years, Fort Bayard has served as a visible, important, and influential governmental installation in the lives of the residents of southwestern New Mexico. It was designated as a National Historic Landmark by Congress in 2004.

In 1852, the first Territorial Legislature of New Mexico established nine counties, seven of which stretched from the Texas boundary on the east to the California border on the west. Dona Ana County included the area that would later be known as Grant County, then was expanded two years later to include the area of the Gadsden Purchase. (Beck, Atlas)

With the coming of the Civil War in 1861, New Mexico Territory found itself bounded by the Confederate state of Texas on the east and south, and the Union state of California on the west. Colorado Territory to the north remained loyal to the Union. There were considerable numbers of Confederate supporters in southern New Mexico, particularly in the Mesilla Valley. Many of the miners who had flocked to the booming camp of Pinos Altos in 1860 supported the Confederate cause. When Mesilla was seized by secessionist militia in the summer of 1861, their leader John Baylor declared the "Confederate Territory of Arizona," headquartered there. The Pinos Altos men then formed the "Arizona Volunteers" and promised their support to the Confederates.

A full-scale Confederate invasion of New Mexico was launched in January 1862 under the command of former Union officer Henry Hopkins Sibley. His 3,000-man army scored a victory over pro-Union forces near Fort Craig at the Battle of Valverde in February of that year and went on to occupy the territorial capital of Santa Fe, forcing the government to flee. Within weeks, however, the Sibley force was outmaneuvered in the Battle of Glorieta Pass, between Santa Fe and Las Vegas, and the invasion collapsed. Sibley withdrew his army from New Mexico, and the territory was not threatened again by Confederates.

In response to the Confederate invasion, the Union had dispatched reinforcements from southern California, but this California Column failed to arrive in time to assist in the defeat of Sibley's brigade. They did, however, rescue besieged miners at Pinos Altos who were under attack from the Chiricahua Apaches. The Column's commander, Brigadier General James Carleton, established himself as the military governor of the territory and organized a punitive campaign to quell resistance from Apaches and Navajos throughout the territory. Part of the California force lured local Apache leader Mangas Coloradas into a trap at Pinos Altos, took him prisoner, then killed him under treacherous circumstances soon afterward at the ruins of nearby Fort McLane. This act of brutality further inflamed the ongoing war with the Apaches, and guaranteed violence between the groups for years to come. (Sweeney, 460)

In 1863, with the Confederate threat to New Mexico ended, the federal government divided New Mexico into two territories, creating Arizona Territory from roughly the western half. With the end of the Civil War in 1865, settlers and prospectors gradually returned to their pursuits in New Mexico. The establishment of Fort Bayard in 1866 encouraged the repopulation of Pinos Altos and other mining camps that were beginning to spring up in the region. The village of Santa Clara prospered from nearby Fort Bayard and positioned it to become the first county seat when the reconvened Territorial Legislature created Grant County from western

Dona Ana County in 1868. By this time, Santa Clara had been renamed "Central City" by the Army. Soon, Pinos Altos managed to pry the honor of county seat away from Central City, but the birth of a new settlement only seven miles to the south guaranteed another move for the seat of county government.

The Birth of Silver City

As the decade of the 1860s drew to a close, a few bold settlers had risked the wrath of the Apaches by locating their homesteads near the San Vicente Spring, a traditional watering and resting place for that culture. Although they suffered from Apache attacks and lost family members to the violence, these settlers persisted, and in 1870 discovered rich silver ore in the hills to the west of the spring. News of the discovery spread rapidly, and soon scores of prospectors and speculators were swarming into the once peaceful valley. At first, there were only shanties and tents, but soon more substantial houses were also under construction. A meeting was held, and the name was changed to Silver City, in spite of the observation by prominent early citizen Richard Hudson that the name was "One hell of a thing to call a town on a mud flat!" (Naegle)

As the community grew, the Territorial Legislature was petitioned to move the county seat to the new town, and that was accomplished at the end of 1871. Departing from the common practice in boomtowns, the citizens of Silver City pressed for clear titles to land within the community, and by the mid-1870s, surveys had been completed and clear title was established. The first attempt at incorporation had been made in 1872, but it failed due to turmoil in the Territorial Legislature. At the time, only one other community, Elizabethtown, had been incorporated in the territory. In spite of a strong desire on the part of Silver City's inhabitants, they would have to wait another six years before incorporation would succeed.

The Santa Fe Troubles

The ambitions of the citizens of Silver City soon collided with those of politicians jockeying for power in the territorial capital of Santa Fe. A group of lawyers had arrived in the territory soon after the Civil War and had quickly seized upon what they saw as an unlimited opportunity to acquire power and wealth. Regardless of political party, they often cooperated in business, social, and government arrangements, and soon had established themselves as the most influential body of men in the territory. Their critics soon dubbed them the "Santa Fe Ring." Headed by Thomas B. Catron and Stephen B. Elkins, their influence was largely based in their ability to manipulate land ownership and acquire vast acreages for themselves. They were especially adept at feasting upon the Spanish and Mexican land grants found in much of northern New Mexico. Although Grant County had no such grants, so much time was devoted to the politics of the ring in Santa Fe, the needs of the southern counties seemed to be routinely neglected. This was especially true in regard to the dysfunction of the Territorial Legislature.

Since at least 1872, a massive power struggle between the pro-ring faction and its opponents had paralyzed the ability of the legislature and territorial governors to enact much needed reforms and to deal with issues ranging from public safety to education. While the situation in the territory was by no means unique in America at that time, it exacerbated the growing calls for drastic action by the leading citizens of Silver City. •

The County Secession Movement
Ever since the developing mineral wealth of the southwestern section of New Mexico had become evident, there had been murmurings of seeking union with the Territory of Arizona, where, it was perceived, mining was given more respect by the political powers. These murmurings became a roar in the autumn of 1876, with the publication of an editorial in the Grant County Herald. That paper called for a meeting to discuss formal measures to separate Grant County from New Mexico Territory and ask for annexation by Arizona. Organizers based their idea on three factors: 1) Lack of redress of grievances; 2) Grant County was considered simply an "appendage of the body politic" by the Legislative Assembly; and 3) a racially charged observation that legislation by "Americans" would be

better suited to the progress of the county, an obvious slap at the number of Hispanic legislators sitting in Santa Fe. This third point certainly strikes a nerve in twenty-first century discourse, but it illustrates the fact that New Mexico, more than any other territory, had a unique challenge with democratic inclusion of all of its citizens.

On October 4, 62 of the "most prominent citizens" of Grant County met and signed the proposal asking for annexation to Arizona. The proposal listed the familiar set of grievances with the status quo, including the lack of action to quell Apache raids and expressed no confidence in hope of relief in the near future, owing to the "peculiar temper and habits of the native New Mexicans," who seemed to have undue influence in the territorial government and, in any event, were under the control of the ring. Contemplating these rationales with the perspective of a century and a half of hindsight, it is difficult to overlook the racist elements of the arguments, but the frustration with the lack of cooperation from the territorial government· is understandable. (Naegle, 39)

Thomas Benton Catron,
Attorney General of the Territory of New Mexico, 1869–72.

New Mexico Territory's County boundaries of the 1870s. County boundaries shifted frequently in territorial days as population increased, economic factors changed, and political winds blew. Source: Author's collection.

So why did the secession movement not bear fruit? The answer is that although the separation never occurred, the mere threat of it had an effect. In general, the Arizona government was not

344

opposed to annexation of their dissatisfied neighbors, as it would have brought a great deal more wealth into the Arizona orbit. In fact, Arizona's representative to Congress introduced the resolution in the House, and it was referred to the Committee on Territories where it languished, then died. (Every student of government knows that committees are where most proposals go to die.) However, in 1878, Silver City was to have its greatest demand fulfilled.

Silver City Gets Its Charter

Two years earlier, in 1876, New Mexico's Territorial Legislature had rejected Silver City's petition for incorporation on the grounds that it failed to specify provisions for electing and inaugurating the town's officers. On January 31, 1878, Silver City Representative Richard Hudson introduced a new bill calling for incorporation, with the needed provision for election added. Perhaps anxious to put the secession issue to rest for good, this time the Legislature passed the bill unanimously, and on February 15, 1878, Governor Samuel Axtell signed it into law. With the approval of this legislation, Silver City became the "only municipality in New Mexico to operate under a special charter granted by the Territorial Legislature." (Naegle, 50) The town continues to operate today under this charter.

Among the most significant elements of the charter was the provision that allowed the town to levy and collect taxes, and to seize and sell property in order to collect delinquent taxes. That provision was upheld in court cases in the 1930s, when the town won out over legal objections from the Atchison, Topeka, and Santa Fe Railroad, among others. Importantly, the town was able to move forward with civic improvements, including the funding of a public school. Perhaps one of the most interesting provisions of the charter are to be found in Section 11, where the following is stated: "The council shall have the power to . . . "to prevent and punish for the firing of firearms, the galloping or furious driving of horses and mules, fighting, quarreling, Sabbath breaking, drunkenness, indecent and profane language, and all offenses against public decency and good order, within the corporate limits of the town . . ." (Charter) [Council members today are challenged by the flying of certain politically motivated flags that would seem to be in violation of this section of the charter].

Silver City holds this charter in such high esteem, that beginning in the twenty-first century, the town officially celebrates Territorial Charter Day each February. The town, on occasion, must find ways to reconcile the charter with modern situations and changing laws at the state and national levels. One example is the decree from the state government to unify local elections with state election dates, contrary to the provisions granted in the Charter.

The Federal Government. Its Influence in Grant County Before 1912
The Constitution of the United States establishes a unique relationship between the national, state, and local governments. Political scientists refer to this concept as "federalism," and every community in the United States lives with its effects on a daily basis. Grant County and Silver City are no exceptions. From the moment that the national army of the United States set foot on the soil of southwestern New Mexico in 1846, the federal government has played a role in the area. The first visible presence of the federal government was the military. The establishment of Fort Bayard in 1866 made that presence long term. The Federal Hospital facility that succeeded the active military post at Fort Bayard extended that federal presence into the mid-1960s.

The creation of the National Forest system in the late nineteenth and early twentieth centuries brought another facet of the federal government into the life of Grant County. The Gila Forest Reserve was established on March 2, 1899, by the General Land Office and was renamed the Gila Forest Reserve on July 21, 1905. The next year it was transferred to the newly created U.S. Forest Service, and officially became the Gila National Forest on March 7, 1907. (Gila National Forest Website)

The growing conservation movement that produced the federal management programs such as the National Forest System also led to national legislation that had effects in Grant County. For example, the Antiquities Act of 1906 helped to protect historic and archaeological sites

346

such as the nearby Gila Cliff Dwellings. While the massive presence of the national government in peoples' lives was not yet evident, the pre-statehood years nevertheless were impacted by laws made at the national level.

THE NEXT CANDIDATE FOR STATEHOOD.

Political Cartoon regarding New Mexico's quest for statehood. This cartoon appeared on the cover of the satire magazine "Puck" during one of New Mexico's failed attempts at statehood, in 1901. Stereotypes of the Territory's population are easy to spot in the artwork. Source: Library of Congress, artist Rose Cecil O'Neill.

Both Native and non-Native American groups were greatly impacted by the policies of the Indian Bureau. The Native Apache peoples of the Grant County region were forced into the relocation program established as part of the Grant Peace Policy, which came into being in the early 1870s. That policy was based on the establishment of reservations, where Native people would be treated as wards of the national government. Rejecting earlier plans, the Indian Bureau decided against any reservations in southwestern New Mexico. Instead, the Apaches were to be concentrated at sites in San Carlos, Arizona, and Mescalero, New Mexico. Those who resisted resettlement to these places were to be treated as hostiles and became subject to military force. Ultimately, following much bloodshed, the last of the Apache holdouts were made Prisoners of War (POWs), and transferred to penal facilities in Florida. Later moved to Oklahoma, they would remain POWs until their release in 1913, after 27 years of captivity. This outcome was, of course, viewed in very different ways, depending on the individual's perspective and ethnicity at the time.

Government Brings Higher Education to Silver City

In 1893, the Territorial Legislature of New Mexico designated Silver City as the home for New Mexico Normal School. Filling the need for an institution devoted to the training and education of teachers, classes began in the First Presbyterian Church building in Silver City, while construction progressed on a facility to house the new school. Local leader, John W. Fleming, donated land on high ground northwest of the town center for the school. On September 4, 1894, a ceremony was held to lay the cornerstone of "Old Main," the first building on the campus. In 1895, Miss Isabelle Eckles received the first diploma granted by the school. Over the years, the institution has progressed through several name changes to accompany its expanding mission: New Mexico State Normal School, New Mexico State Teachers College, New Mexico Western College, and finally Western New Mexico University. (Bell) The university remains one of the greatest accomplishments by government for the community of Silver City.

The Long Wait for Statehood

Citizens of New Mexico had hoped for immediate admission to statehood after the approval of the Treaty of Guadalupe-Hidalgo in 1850. Since California had been quickly admitted, there was reason for optimism, it was believed. This proved not to be the case, and, in fact, New Mexico would have to wait for over six decades for the dream to become reality. There were multiple factors that contributed to the long delay. One of the most vexing and persistent was the belief in the Congress, as well as the nation in general, that New Mexico's large Native Hispanic and Indian populations were not "suited" for the responsibilities of self-government. In the charged atmosphere of the debate over non-whites and their civil rights, which played out against the background of the slavery issue, New Mexico faced a steep climb to achieve any semblance of equality with other states and territories.

The ferocity of the Indian Wars in New Mexico and Arizona, the lack of effective law enforcement in many parts of the territory (including Grant County at times), and the slow extension of railroads into the region all contributed to the notion that the territorial style of government was still the better option. Under the territorial system, the federal government maintained a tighter hold over the organs of political power, including the appointment, rather than the election, of governors. Appointed officials were responsible only to their patrons and not to the people at large. To use a family analogy, the territorial system provided a stern parent who could impose discipline and set the rules, while statehood would allow for the people of the state to have the greatest say in how they were to be governed, much like an adult living with his parent.

While the benefits of statehood were clear, there was far from unanimous support among New Mexico's population for the idea. Some entrepreneurs feared federal regulation and taxation and preferred the "every man for himself" attitude that had become a feature of the western frontier. Some also worried that statehood would empower groups in ways that would threaten the status quo among the power structure, whether it be women, racial minorities, or outside economic interests.

Grant County's contingent of Rough Riders preparing to board the train at the Santa Fe depot in Silver City, May 1898. Recruited and mostly led by Theodore Roosevelt, the Rough Riders gained fame along with their exuberant commander in the Spanish-American War, fighting in Cuba for a few months. More members of the Rough Riders came from New Mexico than any other place, and their fame and notoriety helped pave the way for statehood, with Roosevelt's help. Source: Silver City Museum Collections

New Mexico also fell victim to national politics, as the Republican, Democratic, Populist, and Progressive parties vied for majorities in the U.S. Senate. Groups of Republican senators formed coalitions to block statehood for New Mexico, Arizona, and Oklahoma in the early 1900s, fearing that rival parties, especially the Democrats, would be able to elect party members to the Senate, thereby wresting control of that body out of the hands of the Republicans.

One of the factors that eventually ended the stalemate over statehood was the ascension to power of Theodore Roosevelt. Before being brought into the presidency by an assassin's bullet in 1901, Roosevelt had gained national fame for his role in the Spanish-American War. In 1898, he had formed the First Volunteer Cavalry, popularly known as the "Rough Riders" and led them into battle in Cuba. His famed regiment had more men from New Mexico Territory than from any other place, including a contingent recruited in Grant County. (His memoir about the Rough Riders particularly praised Grant County cowboy Thomas Darnell for his skills as a breaker of wild horses.) Roosevelt never forgot his New Mexico connection and became a powerful advocate for admission of the territory to statehood.

President William Howard Taft signing the New Mexico Statehood Bill, January 6, 1912. New Mexico finally achieved statehood, 66 years after being seized from Mexico by force, entering the union as the 47th state. Source: Library of Congress

It fell to William Howard Taft, Roosevelt's hand-picked successor, to finally bring statehood to reality for New Mexico. Roosevelt, in spite of his national popularity, decided not to seek another full term in 1908.

Although they would split over differences regarding conservation and other issues in subsequent years, Taft shared Roosevelt's commitment to ending the long wait for statehood in New Mexico and Arizona. Both territories were obliged to call conventions for the purpose of writing state constitutions, which then had to be approved by Congress. This was accomplished, but not without great debate and political maneuvering of a partisan nature. After much political wrangling, Taft signed the hard-won congressional resolution for New Mexico statehood on August 21, 1911, and New Mexico's voters (all of them male) elected the first state governor, two U.S. senators, and a congressman three months later. On January 6, 1912, Taft signed the official admission document at 1:35 p.m., in front of a New Mexico delegation, at the White House. New Mexico's long wait for statehood was over. [We citizens of New Mexico all have stories of our experiences indicating that many of our fellow Americans haven't gotten the message that we did indeed achieve statehood!]

Conclusion

While certainly earning a reputation as a unique community, Silver City is also the embodiment of the American dream, and in that sense is a perfect example of the Great American Experiment. Born on a rough and tumble frontier, the community grew into a mature town, prevailing through economic, social, and political challenges that had resulted in disaster for many of its contemporaries. As the town entered the second half of its second century, it could point with pride to its perseverance in the face of many forms of adversity. Inspired by the ideals set forth in the founding documents of the nation, generations of citizens from a wide variety of backgrounds and cultures have succeeded best when working together. That sets an example for the future that presents both a model and a challenge for future citizens of the community.

DOUGLAS M. DINWIDDIE received his Ph.D. in US History from Northern Arizona University and became Adjunct Professor of History, Colorado State University, 2010-2015; Professor of Social Science, New Mexico State University-Carlsbad, 1987-2009; History Faculty, Front Range Community College, 2009-2013; Curator/Director, Western New Mexico University Museum, 1974-1987

CHAPTER 10:

The Evolution of the Hospitals in Grant County, 1883-1937

by Heather Moorland

In the latter part of the nineteenth century, Silver City in Grant County played its part in the development of the Territory of New Mexico, particularly in the area of mining. Adventurers flocked to the district after the American Civil War in hopes of sharing in these riches, whether directly from mining or the more lucrative and reliable occupation of merchandising.

One of the families that arrived in Silver City to help build the growing community was that of the Warrens, who came in 1882. While O.S. Warren tended to his insurance business, his wife, Elizabeth, became acquainted with other local women. One of their diversions came in the form of a sewing club.

While stitching, the dozen or so club members discussed ways to improve their growing town. Through their efforts, a public school was already being built in 1883, and they next identified that Silver City needed a charity hospital.

Health care at the time had few of the elements of the modern aid we know today. Hospitals were used to care for the poor, while well-to-do people were treated sometimes in doctors' private offices, and usually in their own homes where family members could nurse their relatives. (Charles E. Rosenberg. *The Care of Strangers: The Rise of the American Hospital System.* Baltimore: Johns Hopkins University Press, 1995, 116.) Grant County was replete with indigent miners and transients who had neither the means nor family to help with any medical emergencies or illnesses. In fact, the nascent town initially housed destitute patients in the county jail. Falls, explosions, accidents, infections, and disease plagued all residents, but the needy were at a severe disadvantage. The members of the sewing circle felt the remedy for this situation was to start a hospital to "provide some sort of shelter, care, and treatment for the aged and sick prospectors and miners". (*Elizabeth Warren, speech given at Silver City's Woman's Club, December 1937.*)

Silver City's first hospital was originally a small cabin used to house workers at a planing mill in the northeast part of town. John Miller owned the plant, and his wife, leader of the sewing club, requested of him its use. Miller was then the area's representative to the Territorial legislature. While in Santa Fe, he wrote his wife, Martha, suggesting that if the ladies incorporated their board, he may be able to acquire funds from the legislature to help defray the expenses of the hospital, a necessity because the mundane cost of running the facility was not being met by local donors. On March 18, 1884, the Grant County Charitable Hospital Society was created and soon received monthly funding from Santa Fe. (*The Southwest Sentinel, March 12, 1895.*) Run by a cadre of determined women, it became known as the Ladies Hospital.

The Grant County Commissioners presently supplemented the Territory's $250, based on the number of indigent patients at the hospital. Soon the Commissioners realized a stipulated amount would be less costly to them and provided $125 per month to pay for the indigent patients' medical attention and medicines. (*Grant county Commissioners Meeting Minutes*, February 3, 1886. *The Southwest Sentinel*, June 27, 1885.) The son of the murdered New Mexico Chief Justice, Dr. William McLean Slough, occasionally provided medical services *gratis*, and later received a regular stipend from the county. The founders themselves donated much of the furnishings, linens, and lamps as needs arose. (*Elizabeth Warren, speech given at the opening ceremony of Grant County General Hospital at Silver City's Woman's Club, December 1937.*)

Soon it became apparent that the cottage hospital would not be adequate for the needs of the growing town. Providentially, in early 1884, county officials were moving from their offices on Hudson Street to a newly built courthouse at the head of Broadway. It was agreed that the County would furnish the hospital managers, rent-free, the office recently occupied by the probate clerk. Over time, the Hospital Society took over all of the four-room building, (*Southwest Sentinel March 5, 1884*), the detached jail, and some of the surrounding grounds. (*Silver City Enterprise* 19 November 1886.) Two of the offices were made into wards, while another was converted into a kitchen, and the fourth into the matron-housekeeper's living quarters.

Throughout New Mexico, villages and towns sent their patients away, so as not to have to pay for indigent care. (Jake Spidel *"'An Army of Tubercular Invalids': New Mexico and the Birth of a Tuberculosis Industry" New Mexico Historical Review* July 1986.199.) In this vein, patients were sent to Silver City from around the vast county, adding to the expense of running the facility and necessitating further expansion. *(Southwest Sentinel July 18, 1885.)* The county helped by providing out-buildings for storage and a morgue, and foundations were laid for additional rooms. *(Southwest Sentinel and Enterprise November 19, 1886).* To supplement the income, the hospital began taking in paying patients. Eventually eight more rooms were added, and the exterior remodeled. *(Southwest Sentinel September 22 1885 and Southwest Sentinel October 20, 1885)*

Sufficiently funding the hospital proved difficult. The promise of a monthly award from Grant County was rescinded in 1888, deciding instead only to reimburse expenses, not maintenance or upkeep. The directors continually planned dances and theatrical evenings in hopes of raising enough money to keep the hospital solvent.

The Sisters of Mercy arrived in Silver City in 1883 to provide education at their newly built Our Lady of Lourdes Academy, located at Kelly and Cooper Streets. Four years later, they obtained a two-story house nearer downtown to start a hospital. The Sisters entered into an agreement with the Pacific and the Key mines to "care for the sick and wounded of their camps." *(The Silver City Enterprise, 17 May 1889.)* As with the Ladies Hospital, the nuns soon realized they needed a larger facility, and through the parish priest obtained land on the western edge of town. *(The Silver City Sun News and Enterprise August 21 1891.)* This property had on it a house with an L-shaped veranda that became the base for what would become known as St. Joseph's Hospital. The Sisters, too, requested funding from the territorial legislature, and *(Susan Berry and Sharmann Apt Russell. Built to Last, Silver City: Silver City Museum Society, 1995, 38)* also received money from a local mill levy.

While St. Joseph's and the Ladies hospitals were supported over the years through donations and various fundraisers, not all the citizens of Silver City appreciated their work. In 1891, a petition was filed by a number of taxpayers who alleged that the Territory provided a sufficient allowance "for the maintenance of the pauper patients at the Grant County Hospital," and, therefore, the county commissioners should cease adding to the coffers. *(Enterprise January 15, 1886.)* These citizens also alleged mismanagement of the territorial appropriations made to both the Grant County Charity and St. Joseph's Hospitals, stating that the sums were "ample to defray all expense of pauper sick within the district." The citizens suggested the county see to it that a single territorial appropriation be distributed between both hospitals in proportion to the number of patients cared for. Because of the alleged fiscal mismanagement, the Commissioners appointed a committee to investigate the accusations.

Routinely, a grand jury audited the hospitals' finances. Interestingly, the accusations of mismanagement occurred soon after the release of the report of 1890, in which the Ladies Hospital had been given a "clean bill of health," *(The Enterprise September 5, 1890)* as was St. Joseph's. *(The Silver City Enterprise 30 Aug 1889.)* Certainly, this accusation must have felt a betrayal to those working intently to keep the hospitals afloat. After a two months' investigation, it was found that the books were "in excellent condition, the accounts carefully and correctly kept, and vouchers on hand for all bills paid." *(The Silver City Enterprise, 29 May 1891.)*

Two women sitting on the porch of the Grant County Hospital, also known as the "Ladies Hospital" it was founded and operated by the Grant County Charity Hospital Society. The women are identified as Mrs. Lula Kirkpatrick & Mrs. Anna Howell Black. Source: Silver City Museum

Late nineteenth century views on hospital management dictated that they be run as efficient Victorian households, with the expectation that the facility be kept clean, and expenses kept down. *(Rosenberg 119.)* The Charity Hospital Board agreed and saw to it that their facility was run this way. Not only were they careful with the monies allocated to them, but they also saw to it that nothing was wasted and that patients were 'deserving' *(Rosenberg 105)* of staying at their hospital. For example, in 1895, Matron Mary G. Foote strongly relied on her housekeeping abilities to see that the hospital survived financially. Further, she expected those in her domain to obey her as would servants, but various Board Minutes reveal tensions with some male nurses under her command. After feeling disrespected over the next year, Matron Foote tendered her resignation to the board. *(GCCHBMM February 14, 1896)*

As the century closed, houses of ill-repute located near the Ladies Hospital, and caused the Board concern enough that they felt it necessary to pass a regulation that no "lewd women" would be allowed to visit sick men at the hospital. *(GCCHBNM September 2, 1895.)*

Although two enterprising prostitutes dressed up as nuns to falsely collect funds for a hospital, the Sisters at the St. Joseph's Hospital did not have to deal with the presence of "fallen women." (*Enterprise May 23, 1884*) Extensive improvements were made on their property in 1891, to make it "a cozy, cheerful home." (*Enterprise October 18, 1891*)

The financial difficulties that had led the Grant County Commissioners to curtail their monthly support to the Ladies Hospital worsened in the last decade of the nineteenth century. The national economic depression of 1893, coupled with the establishment of the Gold Standard where the value of silver fell, compounded the troubled economy of southwestern New Mexico Territory. It was an unexpected source that allowed Silver City to regain its financial footing. Ironically, the world's great killer, tuberculosis, gave renewed life to the town.

Consumption was the leading cause of death in the nineteenth century, particularly between the productive ages of 15 and 45. (*Jake Spidle "An Army of Tubercular Invalids': New Mexico and the Birth of a Tuberculosis Industry" New Mexico Historical Review July 1986.190.*) It had been known in the ancient world, and soon was endemic in Europe and beyond. The etiology of tuberculosis then was unclear. Many thought it was hereditary. By the beginning of the nineteenth century, TB had killed one in seven of all people who had ever lived. (*The Forgotten Plague American Experience PBS accessed 29 April 2014.*)

Since germ theory was a concept that would not take root until the latter nineteenth century and after Robert Koch's demonstration of the tubercle bacillus, treatments were a mixture of remedies and folk-lore. Creosote, laudanum, whiskey, bleeding, cod liver oil, turpentine, or quinine might be called upon to effect a cure, or at best provide some relief from symptoms.

In the 1870s, physicians in Europe noticed improvement in tuber-culosis cases of those who spent time at high altitude. With no curative medications on the horizon for decades to come, any therapy that might meliorate this often fatal disease became coveted. The idea caught on in the United States by the following decade. Branching out from upstate New York, rural sections around the country that could claim high elevations vied for "lungers" who were seeking the cure, although the relatively flat state of Florida had its own successes. Colorado, California, and New Mexico Territory advertised for patients to come West.

Throughout New Mexico, sanatoria sprang up, particularly if near the newly constructed railways. Las Vegas, Santa Fe, Albuquerque, Socorro, Las Cruces, Roswell, and Silver City became well-known locations for treating tuberculosis. The three leading enterprises in New Mexico became cattle ranching, mining, and the TB business. *(Spidle "'An Army of Tubercular Invalids': New Mexico and the Birth of a Tuberculosis Industry" New Mexico Historical Review July 1986. 190.)* By 1913, an estimated 20%-60% of households had at least one family member diagnosed with tuberculosis. *(Spidle "'An Army of Tubercular Invalids': New Mexico and the Birth of a Tuberculosis Industry" New Mexico Historical Review July 1986. 190.)*

In 1899, the military reserve known as Fort Bayard, located eight miles outside of Silver City, changed from its original purpose of fighting Apaches and protecting settlers to a hospital for tubercular soldiers and sailors. One military physician in particular, Earl S. Bullock, himself a sufferer of the infection, made studying the White Plague his life's ambition. After much observation and trial and error, Bullock determined the U.S. Army was not going to follow the treatment paths he saw as most promising. He resigned his commission and approached the Sisters of Mercy at their St. Joseph's Hospital to see if they would be interested in developing a TB sanitorium that followed the lines of treatment Dr. Bullock recommended. Mother Paul made a bargain with the doctor, saying, "You can take those seven rooms and start your hospital and if by the first of January you shall have made good, we shall see what can be done." *(The New Mexico Cottage Sanatorium" Santa Fe Trail Magazine, vol. 2, no. 5. May 1914. p7.)*

The plan was that, once the hospital had been prepared, Dr. Bullock would solicit patients in need of what he and Silver City could offer.

Bullock also solidified the popularity of the sanatorium by creating a medical advisory board made up of doctors from the eastern part of the country who specialized in tuberculosis, and who could refer their well-to-do patients to Silver City for care. *(The Silver City Enterprise, 27 Sept 1901.)*

St. Joseph's Hospital remodeled, incorporating designs specific to TB patients' needs, and was renamed St. Joseph's Sanatorium. The conceptual focus was on ventilation, having no interior hallways or dead-air spaces where the tubercle could hide. *(Susan Berry and Sharmann Apt Russell. Built to Last, Silver City: Silver City Museum Society, 1995. 46.)* The tree-filled central courtyard with its greenery was designed for "those who come from a distance and are not accustomed to the monotony of a barren country." *(The Silver City Independent, 15 July 1902.)*

Despite plenty of patients, good work and care, Dr. Bullock longed for freedom of self-employment. After four years, he left St. Joseph's, and started his own treatment center known as the New Mexico Cottage Sanatorium.

Not to be outdone, the Grant County Charity Hospital initiated its own improvements through paint and other repairs and being fitted throughout with electric lights. But the concern continued that the presence of the ladies of the evening so close to the Ladies Hospital decreased the value of the facility and negated any improvements made.

When Mrs. Abbie Potter of Georgetown and her husband heard of this predicament in 1912, they donated $5,000 with the stipulation that the money be applied towards the relocation of the structure to the west side of town, far from the soiled doves. *(Silver City Independent, 22 October 1912.)* The $5,000 could be used as a down payment, but the trustees knew the balance of the funds needed to build another hospital would be hard won. But the writing was on the wall; a structure built in the early years of Silver City's founding was past its prime; scientific improvements in health care required a different type of building. At the request of the directors in October 1912, the county authorized the

St. Josephs Sanatorium, long hallway with nuns standing in doorway.
Source: Silver City Museum

buildings on Hudson Street be sold, with the hope that the proceeds "be turned into the fund for the new hospital. *(GCCHBMM October 15, 1912.)* To move things along, the commissioners offered land south of the courthouse on Cooper Street for the next location. Newspapers deemed the site "ideal." *(The Silver City Independent, 22 October 1912.)* But no buyers came forward to purchase an old building that admittedly was in such a condition that it was "no longer safe or feasible" to be used. Furthermore, it was revealed that the land on Cooper was not owned by the county and could not be used. *(Independent October 22, 1912)*

In 1918, the now-widowed Mrs. Potter made it known that she planned to reclaim her unused $5,000. Mrs. Warren immediately negotiated a deal with the Sisters of St. Joseph, new owners of Our Lady of Lourdes Academy who were selling the large building in order to open another Catholic school, St. Mary Magdalene Academy, on Alabama Street. The agreed-upon price for the property was $15,000, which was paid in full, four years later. *(The Silver City Enterprise, 24 November 1922.)*

For all their good intentions, the managers of the Ladies Hospital, however, were not trained in any medical field, and had always operated on the Victorian housekeeping premises they established forty-five years earlier. The women now were confronted with the specter of modern medicine. By 1900, developing sciences and technology had changed not only the practice of health care, but that of the public attitude to being treated in hospitals instead of at home. Besides changes in standards of care, there existed specialized equipment such as Finsen lamps, X-ray machines, autoclaves, and laboratories—items that would not be kept at home or charity cottage hospitals. Medicine turned the corner into modern practice at the turn of the twentieth century. *(Rosenberg 99)*

In 1929, local physicians such as county health officer Dr. N. D. Frazin and town councilman Dr. Randolph Watts complained that the condition of the Ladies Hospital was not keeping pace with the "rapid advancement made by the community" or present standards of health care. *(The Silver City Enterprise, 8 November 1929.)* Frazin observed that people were traveling to El Paso and other large cities for their hospitalizations, occasioning a totally new hospital be built in Silver City. But as the country dealt with the stock market crash, little could be done to erect a modern building.

As the Great Depression worsened, Roosevelt's New Deal administration compensated with various programs to build up local economies. The Federal Emergency Administration of Public Works (PWA), funded through a combination of loan and grant monies, saw the construction of thousands of projects such as airports, warships, bridges, dams, schools, and one-third of the hospitals built between 1933 and 1939. Pushed by the local doctors and the need to provide modern health care, in January 1934, the Silver City Town Council

Elizabeth Warren Source: Silver City Museum

declared it would press for a government loan of "at least $50,000" to erect a new hospital. The Town put forth a bond issue, asking for the $55,000 "necessary for the purpose of securing funds for the construction of a hospital to be owned by the Town." *(Silver City Town Council Meeting Minutes, 2 March 1935.)* The bond issue passed. *(Silver City Town Council Meeting Minutes, 3 April 1935.)* By spring of that year, an architect from El Paso, Guy W. Fraser, was asked to draw up sample plans for a modern hospital that would include separate obstetrical, isolation, and tuberculosis wards. *(The Silver City Independent, 2 July 1934.)*

Although the directors offered to the Town the land on which the Ladies Hospital stood, the general feeling was a totally new placement would be expeditious. Various locations around Silver City were considered. A hill on the north side of town seemed suitable. The land was owned by John S. Swift Real Estate and Investment Company of

St. Louis, but negotiations for purchase failed. When the Town began discussing the right of eminent domain, the Swift company decided to donate the property. *(The Silver City Enterprise, 20 November 1936.)* To look more impressive, it was decided to increase the size of the hospital from three stories to four. *(The Silver City Enterprise, 23 October 1936.)* Now there would be ramps, ambulance driveway, emergency room and X-ray departments. A "hospital-size elevator" would allow access to the upper floors where one would find general wards, private and semi-private rooms, a tuberculosis wing, nurses' stations, a surgical unit, a solarium, and even a telephone booth. *(The Silver City Enterprise, 22 March 1935.)*

Application was made in 1935 through the Public Works Administration, based on a 45% grant and a 55% loan. On advice from the state's PWA director, the request was amended to 35% grant and 65% loan. The following year, the government agreed to the original 45% grant, with a view to moving construction along. El Paso contractors, J. E. Morgan and Son, won the bid, and construction started in December 1936. To balance increasing costs, certain plans were changed or put on hold. Now the exterior would be stucco, not cut stone. The items omitted until more funding became available were tile wainscoting, floor coverings and baseboards, heating, a spectator's gallery in the operating room, dark room equipment, and fixtures in six of the bathrooms. A less expensive model of water heater was purchased. Early in 1937, further funds were found, allowing some of the finishing touches to be completed that had previously been set aside.

"Local civic-minded clubs and organizations" offered to furnish items for each room. While the new facility would have modern equipment, such plans were reminiscent of the cottage hospital started by the ladies' sewing club over a half century earlier, when townsfolk supplied furniture and other items needed to run it. Just as in the previous century, supplemental funding was raised through dances and other entertainments. The newspaper declared, "When our sparkling new hospital, with its comfortable and well-furnished rooms has been completed, everyone who has contributed towards it...will be proud...." *(The Silver City Enterprise, May 7, 1937.)*

Construction was completed before the government deadline, and the Grant County Hospital (later called Swift Memorial, and finally Hillcrest General Hospital) opened at a cost of $110,000. *(SCTCMM September 20, 1937)* Sunday, November 19, 1937, was the grand opening. Patients were set up in the hospital on Monday. Locals donated items of varying expense, such as a fern and pedestal and operating room lamps. In December, a special dedication was arranged at the Silver City Woman's Club. To recall the early hospital started fifty-four years before was Mrs. Warren. *(Daily Press December 17, 1937)*

Over the years, the hospital was put to good use. The increasing population, World War II, and the development of sulfa drugs expanded the need for the facility and trained staff. As with the earlier locations, the staff was just as dedicated, but had a different type of struggle than did the founders of the Ladies Hospital. Yet both generations did their "duty to meet this crying need." *(Warren speech 1937)*

REFERENCES

Berry, Susan, and Sharman Apt Russell, Built to Last. Silver City: Silver City Museum Society, 1986.

Grant County Charity Hospital Board Meeting Minutes.

Lisetor-Lane, Clara A., "The New Mexico Cottage Sanatorium" *Santa Fe Trail Magazine*, May 1914, 2(5), 1-13.

Lewis, Nancy Owen, *Chasing the Cure in NM and the Quest for Health*. Santa Fe: Museum of New Mexico Press, 2016.

Rosenberg, Charles, *In the Care of Strangers: The Rise of America's Hospital System*. Baltimore: Johns Hopkins University Press, 1995.

Sanborn Fire Insurance Map from Silver City, Grant County, New Mexico. Sanborn Map Company, Oct, 1883. Map. Retrieved from the Library of Congress, <HYPERLINK "http://www.loc.gov/item/sanborn05713_001/"www.loc.gov/item/sanborn05713_001/>.

The Silver City Enterprise

The Silver City Sun-News

Silver City Town Council Meeting Minutes

The Southwest Sentinel

Jake Spidle. "'An Army of Tubercular Invalids' : New Mexico and the Birth of a Tuberculosis Industry" *NM Hist Review* 1 January 1986, 61(3), 179-201.

Spidle, Jake, *Doctors of Medicine in New Mexico*. Albuquerque: University of New Mexico Press, 1986.

Warren, Elizabeth. Speech given at the Silver City Woman's Club, 17 December 1937, np.

HEATHER MOORLAND, Ph.D., holds bachelor's and master's degrees from Western New Mexico University, and a doctorate in the History of Medicine from the University of New Mexico (1996). Dr. Moorland has published articles on New Mexico's nurses, and British health care givers Mary Seacole, and Ethel Gordon Fenwick, and presented papers in other countries. She has a particular interest in local history and how the town dealt with issues of health care and disease.